LA SERENISSIMA

LA SERENISSIMA

The Story of Venice

JONATHAN KEATES

An Apollo Book

First published in the UK in 2022 by Head of Zeus Ltd,
part of Bloomsbury Publishing Plc

9 7 5 3 1 2 4 6 8

A catalogue record for this book is available from the British Library.

ISBN [HB]:   9781789545050
ISBN [E]:   9781789545074

Design, typesetting and cartography
by Isambard Thomas at Corvo

Colour separation by DawkinsColour
Printed and bound in Wales by Gomer

Head of Zeus Ltd
First Floor East
5–8 Hardwick Street
London EC1R 4RG

WWW.HEADOFZEUS.COM

previous pages
A view on the Cannaregio Canal, 1775–80, by Francesco Guardi.

Remembering Alex Burnett

Esto perpetua!
(May she live for ever!)

The last words of Fra Paolo Sarpi,
addressed to Venice on his deathbed in 1623.

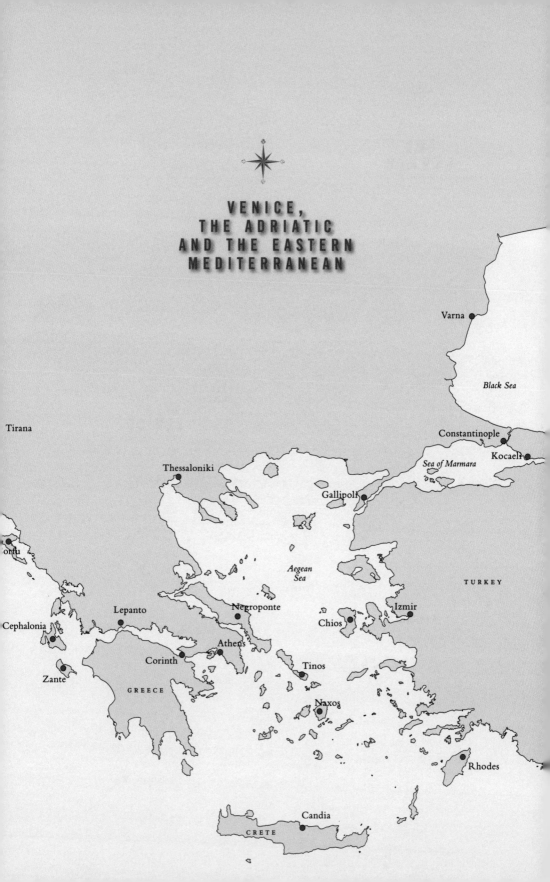

VENICE,
THE ADRIATIC
AND THE EASTERN
MEDITERRANEAN

Varna

Black Sea

Tirana

Constantinople
Kocaeli

Thessaloniki

Sea of Marmara

Gallipoli

*Aegean
Sea*

TURKEY

orfu

Izmir

Lepanto

Negroponte

Chios

Cephalonia

Athens

Corinth

Tinos

Zante

GREECE

Naxos

Rhodes

Candia

CRETE

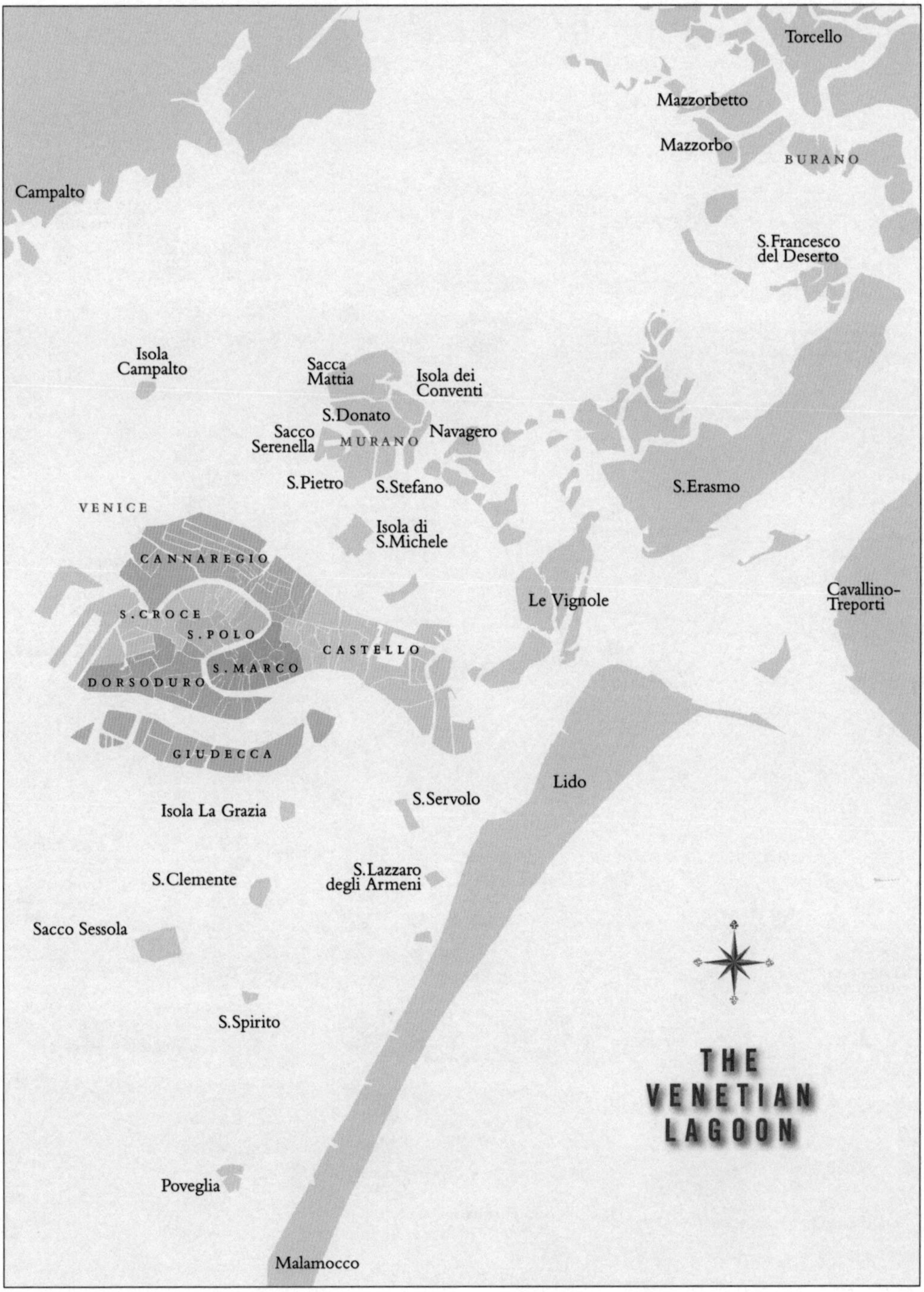

Torcello

Mazzorbetto

Mazzorbo

BURANO

Campalto

S. Francesco
del Deserto

Isola
Campalto

Sacca
Mattia

Isola dei
Conventi

S. Donato

Sacco
Serenella

MURANO

Navagero

S. Pietro

S. Stefano

S. Erasmo

VENICE

Isola di
S. Michele

CANNAREGIO

Le Vignole

Cavallino-
Treporti

S. CROCE

S. POLO

S. MARCO

CASTELLO

DORSODURO

GIUDECCA

Isola La Grazia

S. Servolo

Lido

S. Clemente

S. Lazzaro
degli Armeni

Sacco Sessola

S. Spirito

THE
VENETIAN
LAGOON

Poveglia

Malamocco

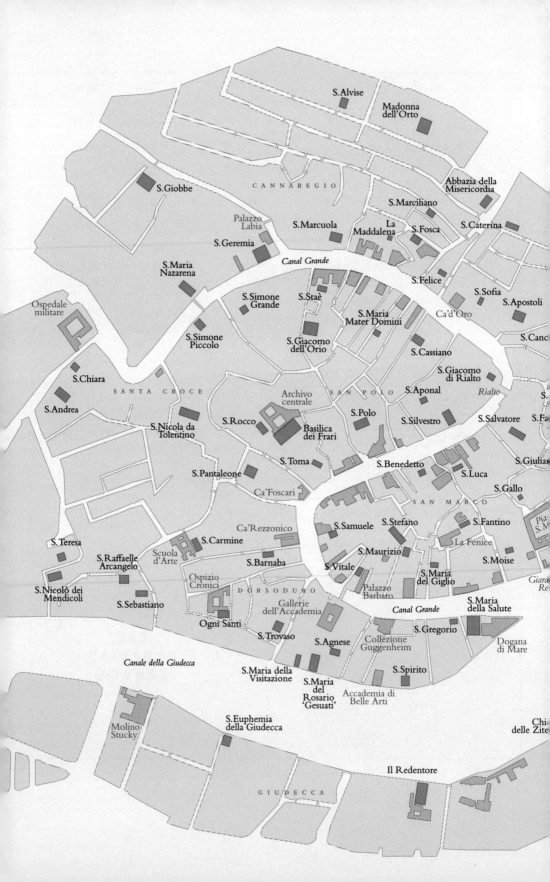

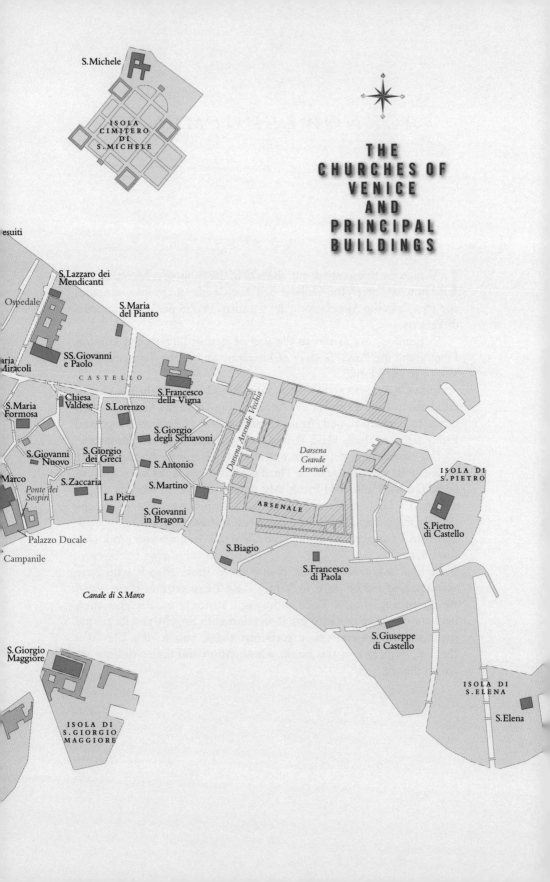

ACKNOWLEDGEMENTS

In Venice my thanks are due to the staff of the Biblioteca Marciana, the Biblioteca Correr, the Gallerie dell'Accademia and to my colleagues and friends in the Associazione dei Comitati Privati per la Salvaguardia di Venezia.

In London, my thanks to the staff of British Library, the London Library and the Royal Society of Literature and to the Trustees of the Venice in Peril Fund.

Individual thanks go to the late John Julius Norwich, the late Gianni Guidetti, to Emma Bassett and Annabel Randall of the Venice in Peril office, to Richard Bassett, Anne Chisholm, Mrs G. Fallows, Hugh and Fanny Gibson, Sheila Hale, Robin Lane Fox and Jonathan Sumption.

I'm especially grateful to my agent Peter Straus for overseeing the project at its various stages. At Head of Zeus I was lucky once again to be edited by Richard Milbank. My thanks to him, to Matilda Singer and Aphra Le Levier-Bennett. Elodie Olson-Coons was an exceptionally shrewd and thoughtful copy-editor. I would also like to thank Isambard Thomas for his layout, and Clémence Jacquinet for producing this book.

A final acknowledgement is due to all those friends who have accompanied me on visits to Venice since I first set foot there on an April morning in 1966. Their enthusiasm, curiosity and perceptiveness have continued to enhance my absorption with the city and its unique narrative. In this context, a particular thank you to the late Alex Burnett, dedicatee of this book, whose vision and understanding are always missed.

INTRODUCTION

In accepting a commission to write this book, I was aware of what Goethe, as long ago as 1786, resignedly acknowledged, that 'about Venice everything that can be said has been said and printed'. The present work is not a detailed historical account: for anything like that you need to turn to Frederic C. Lane, Alvise Zorzi or John Julius Norwich. Instead I have sought to focus on key moments in the evolution of this amazing city, as a unique community and built environment, over the course of its 1,600-year existence. I have included little or nothing, I realize, about Venice's shifting relationship with mainland Italy across the centuries, about the changing ecology of its lagoon, about Murano glass, Burano lace and the role of Torcello in the early centuries of the Serene Republic. I hope, nevertheless, that some idea of my lifelong engagement with Venice, a work in progress, during which I go on learning, can transcend these limitations and omissions. We all have a share in her ongoing narrative, whether as an inspiration, an inheritance, a warning or a responsibility.

AEQVORA TVENS
PORTVS LIBERO
HIC NEPTVNVS

PROLOGUE

It is the evening of 17 March 1846, and we have been invited to the first performance of a new opera at Venice's Gran Teatro La Fenice. The theatre is not the original building by the architect Antonio Selva, opened in 1792. That unfortunately burned down some forty years later, leaving only the portico and the delightful Sale Apollinee assembly rooms immediately behind it intact. An immediate reconstruction by the brothers Giambattista and Tommaso Meduna and their team of expert craftsmen, aided by the stage designer Giuseppe Borsato, has resulted in one of the most elegant and lavishly adorned theatres in Italy, challenged only by Milan's La Scala and the Teatro San Carlo in Naples as a temple of the musical arts.

There are five rows of gilded and curtained boxes, converging on the massive central *Palco Imperiale*, with its pink velvet swags topped by the crown of the Habsburgs. For Venice, since 1814, has been part of the Austrian empire, whose representative, Governor Count Lajos Pálffy zu Erdödy, will be present tonight, along with his staff, for whom Borsato has designed three smaller boxes below. In the area between this and the orchestra there is a scatter of chairs but most of the audience are happy to stroll about and sit down only if they fancy it. In this particular section of the horseshoe auditorium there are no women present and most of the men are wearing their black top hats. The orchestra remains fully on display, as in other opera houses at this period, and the conductor will direct the performance from an armchair. A good number of those present down here have come principally to see the ballet, a key feature of this evening's entertainment, since the star ballerina in *La Jolie Fille de Gand* is none other than Fanny Elssler, the Viennese dancer who has captivated Europe and America with her virtuoso footwork.

overleaf   Teatro La Fenice:
the interior of the auditorium.

The *clou* of the occasion, however, is to be the premiere of a new lyric drama by the most sought-after young composer of the age, the thirty-three-year-old Giuseppe Verdi. His *Nabucco* took La Fenice by storm in 1843, fresh from its triumphant premiere in Milan, and Venetians remember the thrilling experience of *Ernani* at its first performance here the following year. This evening we shall see *Attila*, an opera based on a German play about the King of the Huns and his downfall. In the course of working on the project, Verdi, they say, has been wracked with gastric fever and rheumatism and its completion has been further delayed by the hurried departure of his librettist Temistocle Solera for Spain, leaving the composer's Venetian friend and collaborator Francesco Maria Piave to complete the text.

Luckily the maestro has recovered enough to direct tonight's first hearing of *Attila* in person. The cast is an excellent one, with German soprano Sophia Loewe as the warrior heroine Odabella, bass Ignazio Marini in the title role and baritone Natale Costantini as the astute and pitiless Roman general Ezio. 'Give me plenty of passion and pathos,' Verdi has instructed Piave, 'and as much brevity as you can manage.' Though the actual premiere is not quite what opera-lovers call '*un successo strepitoso*', 'a clamorous success', the next few nights will see Venice clutching *Attila* to its bosom as the piece becomes one of the most popular works given at Teatro La Fenice so far.

What do we Venetians love so much about *Attila*? If our politics are anti-Austrian and favourable to a free and united homeland, then we shall appreciate Ezio's suggestion to the Hunnish conqueror that if the pair of them are to divide the Roman empire, then 'You are welcome to take the entire universe, just so long as you leave Italy to me.' We may enjoy the delicacy and refinement of Odabella's opening *scena*, '*Liberamente or piangi*' and the deftly crafted final trio '*Te so, te sol, quest'anima*'. But there is one moment that as true Venetians we shall take as the most gratifying of compliments to our city, to its absolute singularity, its indomitable spirit of survival, its power to enrich the whole of humanity. This occurs at the end of the opera's prologue, in a scene which Solera indicates as taking place in 'Rio Alto in the Adriatic lagoons'.

He is specific as to the stage picture. Visible are a few huts raised on wooden piles. A stone altar stands in front of a cabin next to a timber structure which will become the bell tower of the church of San Giacomo. The darkness is fading amid stormy clouds: by degrees a rosy light increases until, at the scene's close, the rays of the sun, suddenly flooding everything, gild a sky of the most serene and limpid blue. The slow tolling of a bell greets the morning. A group of hermits sings praises to God for the passing of the storm and watches people arriving in boats from the direction of Aquileia on the mainland. Led by the Roman warrior Foresto, these are fugitives from Attila and his invading Huns. Foresto urges his followers to seek refuge here and build their huts. Though their Italian homeland, 'mother and queen of generous sons', is now made a desert, yet 'from the seaweed of these waves you will rise again, a new phoenix, prouder and more beautiful, the wonder of both land and sea'.

He is singing of us, of our city, of its foundation and its marvels, a place without paragon across the wide world. How can we not applaud as this phoenix spreads its wings for the first time?

overleaf *The Meeting of Pope Leo I and Attila*, by Raphael. According to legend, refugees from the Hunnish king's assault on the Roman cities of northern Italy were among the original inhabitants of the Venetian lagoon.

A PLACE
OF REFUGE

Cities all over the world begin with myths. Their foundation stories scoop together the epiphany of gods, the divine intervention of saints, the auguries occasioned by a flight of birds, a wandering animal or a suddenly blossoming tree. Such legends freely borrow from ancient sagas or heroic poems so as to invoke the concept of a prestigious and venerable descent, rooting the place, before any foundations were dug or structures raised, in the continuity of enduring ideals.

Venice, by its very nature always a trifle implausible, begins within this mythic dimension, but to grasp its particularity we need to start with the very element out of which the city sprang, the sea. A long, narrow marine lake within the wider Mediterranean, named perhaps for the ancient Etruscan port of Atria, in the delta of the River Po, or from the word 'adur' meaning water in the language of the Illyrians, who lived in modern Slovenia and Croatia, the Adriatic acquired its own myth-history at a very early date. Ithaca, for example, one of the seven Ionian islands, was the kingdom of Odysseus, doomed to wander for the ten years following the siege of Troy before returning to his devoted and resourceful wife Penelope. On Kithira, remotest outlier of the same archipelago, the goddess Aphrodite had chosen to dwell, at least according to Greek merchants who brought her cult there from Cyprus and the Levant during the second millennium BCE. Refugees on the losing side in the Trojan War, meanwhile, were honoured as the legendary founders of towns and cities all along the east and west coasts of the Adriatic, each eager to be reputed a nursery of doughty warriors and brave women.

Centuries later, by the time Rome had brought all of Greece beneath its sway, these ports had grown rich with a trade extending overland into Asia Minor and north across the mountains into central Europe. Towns like Pula, Split, Durrës and Butrint formed confident links with merchant communities in Ancona, Brindisi and Bari on the Italian shore, making the entire Adriatic littoral one of the Roman empire's busiest and most prosperous areas. Development under Emperor Augustus Caesar of the harbour at Trieste enhanced the seaway's commercial importance and the affluence of its ancient cities is still apparent today in the sheer substance and grandeur of such ruined structures as the amphitheatre at Pola, Ancona's arch of Trajan or the massive imperial palace at Split raised by Diocletian that encloses the entirety of its old town.

As emblems of a triumphant administrative template extending from the Atlantic Ocean to the River Euphrates or from Scotland to the edge of the Sahara Desert, enduring for almost five hundred years, such cities enshrined a permanence within the homogeneity of their built environment which local populations found essentially reassuring. When at length the entire Roman imperial initiative started to fragment, with new powers and peoples seizing the different territories formerly under Roman rule, some vestige of a communal civic inheritance from the days of empire managed here and there to hang on. What Rome had represented in terms of law, government or hierarchy remained an ideal, if only as a folk memory or the stuff of certain traditions. Nowhere in Western Europe clung more tenaciously to this concept of a virtual Rome, made real through a reverence for its governmental structures and political echelons as a sacred inheritance, than the city state which grew out of the empire's imminent dissolution to become the Republic of Venice.

Names matter at this point. Before the rise of Rome, Italic tribes living in the Adriatic's north-western corner, where the Po and lesser rivers joined the sea, collectively called themselves Heneti, Eneti or Veneti, from an Indo-European root word meaning 'lovely' or 'striking' (in the broadest sense of this term). They spoke a language akin to Latin, they built the strongholds which grew into towns like Padua, Verona and Vicenza and they bred a race of horses swift and strong enough for Greek kings to seek them for their armies. As the Roman Republic grew more powerful, the Veneti became its firm allies, earning privileged status once its hold on northern Italy became consolidated. Their legendary origins were similar, after all. Just as the Romans, according to myth, descended from followers of the fugitive Trojan prince Aeneas, so the Veneti claimed a heroic ancestor in the wise counsellor of his father King Priam, Antenor, traditional founder of the city of Patavium, modern Padua. Thus the two peoples could look one another confidently in the face and something of this pride underlay the prosperity and good government of north-eastern Italy during the centuries of empire.

By the same token Venetia formed a vulnerable frontier for barbarian invasion, hence the significance of its major fortress city at Aquileia. The place had originally sprung up as a market for amber, brought south across Germany from the shores of the Baltic. Its wealth and consequence enormously increased during the imperial age, making it a rival to other northern Italian cities like Verona and Milan, a metropolis favoured by the emperor Constantine, who settled a provincial governor there and raised its diocese to an archbishopric. Trade depended heavily on the town's river link with the port of Grado, major export hub of the northern Adriatic.

Both Aquileia and Grado were buffeted, over several centuries, by attempted alien incursions into their territory. Illyrian pirates from Istria offered a sporadic menace, Celtic tribes had harassed the earliest Roman colonists, Emperor Augustus drove off an attack by the Slovenian Iapydes, while Marcus Aurelius only narrowly prevented a Germanic confederation from invading Aquileia's immediate surroundings. During the late fourth century CE the city assumed an ever-greater strategic significance as Roman imperial frontiers contracted, with Italy lying open to hostile migration on a more resistless scale than any it had yet experienced. Individual communities, anxious to sustain some sort of civil order, looked to their bishops and senior clergy for leadership and an equivalent authority to that of the old imperial secular governing class represented by prefects, magistrates, 'correctors' and 'censors'. What these had symbolized in terms of stability and continuity was too valuable to be rejected altogether. It could be revived, in spirit at least, wherever opportune, even if the built environment of towns in Venetia began swiftly to decay.

Around 400 CE the Goths, under their king Alaric, invaded northern Italy. Originating in southern Sweden, this Germanic people had moved south and east over several centuries in search of richer grazing grounds, trading with the Romans but never wholly absorbed within the empire. Their push across weakly garrisoned frontiers was due in part to migration into their territory by another people, the Huns from central Asia, soon destined to play their own part in the fragmentation of Roman rule and the Western empire's ultimate collapse. Led by Attila, a monarch so formidable as to exist ever afterwards in legend as much as reality, they fell upon Aquileia, besieged and set fire to it before moving on to devastate Roman cities further south. From both these barbarian invasions by Goths and Huns a headlong flight from settlements across the mainland began, with refugees retreating either westwards towards the relative safety of places like Milan, Como and Pavia, south to Rimini and Ravenna or else, securest of all, into the marshy, very lightly inhabited lands bordering the broad lagoon in the north-west reach of the Adriatic.

Shaped like a crescent moon, this watery world was protected from the open sea by a long line of sandbanks, the Lidi − from 'litus', the Latin word for beach or shore − inside which lay a scatter of muddy islands known as *barene*. Amid these, several mainland rivers, Brenta, Piave, Sile and others, emptied their waters. Such communities as already existed here were small or seasonal, either based on fishing or else on the collection of salt in pans for sale inland. As a place in which, temporarily at least, to hide from the sweep of barbarian raids, this lagoon, a marine wilderness amid its channels and mudbanks, offered an ideal refuge. Those escaping could gather on the more extensive islands and re-establish some kind of settled order, safe in the knowledge that the invaders had as yet no skill in the sailing or boatbuilding needed to carry them from the mainland with their weapons, armour and horses.

From this earliest incarnation, as a huddle of refugees in simple wooden, reed-thatched huts made from whatever could be gathered or salvaged from the larger islands, there arose the legend of Venice's foundation. By the sixteenth century, at the zenith of the city's prosperity and significance, this essential myth had coalesced sufficiently to have a precise date assigned to it, not to speak of an exact date and time − the hour of twelve noon on Friday, 25 March 421. Given that Friday is traditionally the day of the week linked to misfortune, this looks a shade paradoxical, yet at the same time it is *dies Veneris*, assigned to the goddess of Love, born, according to classical myth, from the sea. Surely the symbolism, in either case, can be made to seem appropriate to a city whose very existence, arising literally out of the waves, seems self-contradictory, a defiance of accepted possibilities. There is, it need hardly be said, not the slightest documentary evidence for any of these details being correct. This has not stopped the modern Venetians, at the time this book is in preparation, from celebrating a 1,600th anniversary, as good an excuse as any for a party.

The lagoon areas most heavily settled from the outset were the lido of Malamocco, the network of mudbanks and streams that formed Torcello (nowadays an archetype of vanished splendour and romantic remoteness) and, closest of all to the Italian mainland, the group of close-packed islets known as *rivus altus*, 'high bank', from which Rialto, Venice's central zone, derives its name. It would be the last of these, in the early Middle Ages, that came to dominate the others and from which most of what we now accept as a connected historical narrative for Venice, the state, the city and its people, began to develop. Of a once-magnificent and commanding Malamocco almost nothing nowadays remains. On Torcello the two churches of Santa Maria and Santa Fosca, together with a scatter of worked stones in the little archaeological museum next door, are all that survives of a thriving medieval town. It was on the banks and shoals of the Rialto, more specifically on the island called Luprio, that a firmly established urban community started planting itself over the course of the fifth and sixth centuries CE.

Building at first with wood, wattle and plaster, the earliest Venetians would move eventually towards construction in brick and stone, while always retaining the foundational technique needed to raise any kind of substantial edifice on a basis so inherently weak and unstable as the impacted lagoonal mud of the *barene*. All around these settlers, both on the mainland and on the banks of the Lidi, grew thick forests of pine, trees which were already used to make the masts and spars of seagoing vessels. Now whole trunks, stripped of their branches, bark and roots, were harnessed to the business of creating piles for driving deep into the mud. Over these a platform of larch boards could be stretched and on top of that a similar flat surface made of elm and alder wood, all of which would harden satisfactorily within the surrounding soil. This identical method went on being used over the next thousand years, when Venice was building in brick and marble. Thus the wonder increases when we think of such lavishly conceived projects as the great Gothic basilicas of the Frari and Santi Giovanni e Paolo, the doge's palace or Santa Maria della Salute being designed, all of them, to rest upon this timber infrastructure. In 1902, when the tallest building in Venice, the Campanile of San Marco, collapsed, its wooden foundations were discovered to be wholly intact. Fresh piles, using the same system, were driven into the site when the existing replacement was erected ten years later.

Who were the pioneers of this unique initiative? The fifteenth-century diarist Marin Sanudo describes them as 'a lowly people who esteemed mercy and innocence and preferred religion to riches. They scorned to wear ornaments or jostle for honours, but answered to the summons of virtue when needed.' This is a classic appeal to ancestral values, implying that Sanudo's contemporaries are falling far short of such standards. The reality is somewhat more nuanced. What developed in this earliest Venetian epoch was a resourceful, keen-

overleaf An aerial view of the *barene*, the muddy islands of the Venetian lagoon.

eyed, commercially motivated refugee community, whose collective loyalty to the project of a safe haven from chaos and implosion that had engulfed the cities they left behind was strengthened by an awareness of mercantile opportunities to be had for the asking around the coasts beyond their precious lagoon.

The shrewdness of their calculations comes across in a famous letter written by Cassiodorus, praetorian prefect of Ravenna, to Venice's leaders, the so-called maritime tribunes, in 523 CE. He is asking, in the name of the Gothic king Theodoric, for wine and oil from Istria to be conveyed safely to his city. 'Bring them hither with all speed, since you have many ships which sail this sea. You live, after all, like sea birds, your homes scattered on islands across the water's surface. The firm ground on which these dwellings stand is secured only by wattle and osier [referring to the lengths of paling used to hold outer mudbanks in place]. Your people have a single great resource – enough fish for them all.' Cassiodorus goes on to extol the same intrinsic qualities which Sanudo, writing a millennium later and doubtless drawing on this very same letter, would be happy to praise. 'Among you no distinction is made between rich and poor. You eat the same food, your houses are alike. Envy, rife everywhere else, is unknown to you.' Finally, before recommending the repair of 'those boats which, like horses, you keep tied up at your very doors', he identifies the earliest source of Venetian wealth. 'All your energies are concentrated on your salt-pans, in these lie your riches and your ability to acquire what you do not possess. For while there may be those who have scant need for gold, nobody alive does not crave for salt.'

Quoted by everyone writing about the origins of Venice, this letter is valuable not just by virtue of providing the first glimpse of a community very much in being, taken seriously by its neighbours and evidently prosperous. It also emphasizes those qualities of distinctiveness and permanence in the way of life among this already remarkable people, possessed of its own ideals, priorities and aspirations. From certain aspects we might say that nothing has changed in the fifteen hundred years since Cassiodorus wrote his letter. The essential egalitarianism is still strong among ordinary Venetians, boats are still moored outside their doors and fish still form a key element in their cuisine. Yet more significantly, there is a sense, to which the tone of the prefect's letter bears witness, that these people are different from ordinary mainland Italians and require treating with a certain cautious respect. Such exceptionalism has remained constant within Venice until the present time. Italian whenever it should suit them, Venetians have nevertheless made much of their separateness, autonomy and independence across the centuries. Italy, whether as a collection of sovereign states or, since 1870, as a united country, has maintained an answering wariness in its attitude to Venice, as though never quite certain what to make of such a place or its inhabitants or how to accommodate them in a shared national culture and inheritance.

The whole question of whom Venice belonged to and who was fit to govern the island communities stood at issue from the very outset of its history. Cassiodorus was addressing a group of maritime tribunes, elected representatives of the new settlement, ready at this stage to defer to King Theodoric and later to the Byzantine emperor Justinian, whose successful reconquest of Italy from the former's Ostrogoth successors was part of an ongoing attempt at fashioning the former Roman empire anew. Byzantium now became, at least nominally, overlord of Venice and set its visual seal upon the built environment across the lagoon islands. Though Christianity here was always Western and Roman Catholic, the visual imagery and artistic media employed by those who raised its first churches was memorably that of Constantinople and Greek Orthodoxy. Features such as the gorgeous mosaics of Torcello and San Marco, the placing of a pictorial screen in the manner of an iconostasis to divide priests in the sanctuary from the body of the congregation in the nave, the use of variegated marble panels and decorated plaques on exterior walls, these are all witnesses to the impact, over several centuries, of Venice's inclusion, however peripheral geographically, within the eastern empire.

Yet it was this very same distance from the centre of power in Constantinople itself which encouraged the lagoon communities to take more control of their own affairs. As yet there was no single entity known as 'Venice'. The tribunes mentioned earlier acted on behalf of several different towns, Grado, Altino and Heraclea, Torcello and Malamocco and the fast-growing island settlement known as Rialto, nearest the mainland. A sense of collective purpose and shared resources among them all grew strong enough, by the late seventh century CE, for a name, 'Venetici', to be attached, taken from the area's ancient tribe, the Veneti, and its region, Venetia. Given the continuing instability of northern Italy, invaded now by another Germanic people, the Longobards, in search of fertile farmlands and a place to settle, the need grew still stronger for some sort of unified leadership among the lagoon cities. Further impetus towards this came in the year 726, when the charismatic Byzantine emperor Leo III started issuing a series of edicts banning the worship of pictorial and sculpted images in the

overleaf   Mosaic of the Madonna and Child with the
Twelve Apostles, in the church of Santa Maria Assunta
on the island of Torcello.

churches of his realm. Doubtless such iconoclasm was in some sense meant as a challenge to the rise, at this time, of Islam, signalled by Arab assaults on his southern frontiers which Leo had successfully beaten back. To many in Byzantine domains, however, such new puritanism was unwelcome and the Western church, led by a strong-willed pope in the person of Gregory II, was determined to resist it. Soon the whole of the north-western Adriatic coastal territory, known as the Exarchate of Ravenna, rose up against imperial authority, a revolt bringing with it the earliest stirrings, among the Venetians, of a move towards complete independence from Byzantium.

It used to be thought that the first leader to emerge as *Dux Veneto-rum* was Paoluccio Anafesto, whose portrait, along with those of other doges, adorns the walls of the Sala del Maggior Consiglio in Venice's Palazzo Ducale, but this is simply an example of those blurred edges in early medieval historiography between myth and actuality. The years 723 to 727 during which Paoluccio or Paulicius is said to have reigned coincide with the rule of the contemporary Exarch of Ravenna named Paulus, murdered by anti-iconoclasts, an event later garbled by the chroniclers. Modern historians tend instead to agree on the earliest doge as Ursus, or Orso, of Heraclea, who assumed the official Byzantine title of *ypathos*, consul, that became his family's surname, Ipato.

Orso turned out to be not much safer than Paulus the Exarch, given the violence and instability surrounding both men in northern Italy during the eighth century. After ruling for just over a decade, he was murdered in 737, probably at the instigation of a new Exarch in Ravenna, and it was another five years before his son Diodato was chosen to succeed him as doge. By now, despite a continuing Byzantine presence along the Adriatic, the imperial hold on the Venetians was beginning to loosen, even if cultural and commercial links between the lagoon and the Bosphorus stayed strong. 'Many a Byzantine maiden was to be shipped off to the West, into the arms of a Venetian bridegroom; many a Venetian was to send his son eastward to finish his education in Constantinople,' says a modern historian. This much is true, but the sense of a unique communal identity and the relish of a new autonomy, strengthened by existing geographical conditions, were both too strong for Venetians to want to knuckle under completely to an empire visibly losing a grip on its frontiers. Doge Diodato's decision, in 742, to shift his centre of power from Heraclea, vulnerable from the mainland, to Malamocco, at that time the dominant port on the Lidi, was as much a political gesture as a practical expedient.

The nature of Diodato's ducal office, together with that of his immediate successors, would be a hotly contested issue over later centuries, never wholly resolved until the fatal hubris of Doge Marin Falier in 1354 prompted the republican government to ensure that the *Dux Venetorum* should henceforth be nothing but a constitutional figurehead. Was the new state arising in Malamocco and on the neighbouring islands to become a dynastic fiefdom, passed from one family member to another like a hereditary monarchy, or did it lie in the gift of electors confident of choosing the most capable and competent figure to place at the apex of government? The earliest sequence of doges reveals an unruly series of power grabs, palace revolutions, assassinations and factional struggles, setting at naught any subsequent efforts by Venetian propagandists to project their mode of governance as a child of quiet, calm deliberation or justifying its self-assigned title of 'La Serenissima', 'The Most Serene'. How Venice ultimately devised an administrative system which, generally speaking, worked efficiently for almost a thousand years was in essence a prolonged exercise in damage limitation. Serene, at least initially, it was not.

External forces and the movement of events beyond the lagoon played an important part in the process. The eighth century's closing decade witnessed the rise, with astounding success, of the Frankish kingdom, first under Charles Martel, who drove Muslim invaders out of southern France, then in the person of his son Charlemagne, one of European history's most dynamic figures, whose conquest of the Longobard kingdom in Italy had seen him rewarded by being crowned as the first Holy Roman Emperor in Rome itself on Christmas Day, 800. The Venetians were quick to see the potential advantages in cultivating this new western empire while maintaining their strong commercial ties with Byzantium, though the nuanced diplomacy required here made their Frankish allies suspicious. The Byzantines, meanwhile, resentful of the challenge presented by Charlemagne and the Western church to their imperium, resolved to pull Venice back into line, sending a fleet into the Adriatic as a warning gesture. At that moment, 810 CE, the Republic was headed by no fewer than three doges, the brothers Obelerio, Beato and Valentino Antenori, all eager for help from Charlemagne's son Pepin, whom the emperor had made King of Italy. Their aim was to guarantee Venice's safety through the permanent armed presence of Frankish garrisons in towns and strongholds around the lagoon.

The brother doges had seriously misjudged their fellow Venetians. When Pepin gathered his army and began landing an expeditionary force at the southern end of the Lidi, he was met with open resistance, as if to a hostile invader. Though the towns of Chioggia and Pellestrina were taken easily enough, the Franks had a far harder time of it when trying to seize hold of Malamocco. By now the Venetians had rallied around the resourceful figure of Agnello Participazio, tribune of the westernmost Rialto islands. It was he who organized a line of defences, had key channels blocked up and rallied boats of all kinds to carry men and supplies across the lagoon. Women and children were carefully moved from the more exposed sectors to the safety of Rialto before Pepin could start besieging Malamocco in earnest.

What he brought about was an inevitable by-product of such situations, the triumph of a collective loyalty and common cause among those who up till this moment had been mired in petty disputes. During the siege this sense of a general voice among Venetians found utterance when Pepin, following ancient custom, attempted what was known as 'summoning' the town, the protocol of addressing its chief citizens and urging them to open their gates on fair terms of surrender. 'You are my subjects,' he called up to them, 'since you are under my lordship and belong to my land.' With typically Venetian opportunism, given their recent defiance of Byzantium, the answer came back: 'We are servants of the emperor at Constantinople and never shall we be yours.' As it happened, the same Greek fleet that had earlier been sent to awe them into submission had now been mobilized to come to their rescue. Even if Pepin's troops were successful in other areas of the lagoon, Malamocco maintained its sturdy resistance, the inhabitants at one point pelting the besiegers with loaves of bread to prove they could not be starved into surrender. By the end of summer in 810 the Frankish enterprise had failed and Pepin himself was dead. Even if the peace terms entailed Venetian payment to the Franks of a substantial indemnity in the form of an annual tribute, victory belonged to Venice, whose independence was now demonstrated to a wider world.

Such defiance shown to an ostensibly stronger and better equipped power became part of an essential folk memory, of the sort from which the myth-history narrative of states and peoples is formed. What surely consolidated the episode's significance in the early story of Venice was the aftermath of the Franks' defeat and withdrawal from the lagoon. Revealed to the Venetians was the vulnerability and overexposure of Malamocco and its neighbouring settlements along the Lidi. Some sturdier refuge was needed forthwith and the obvious place to establish this was on the two large island clusters centred on Rivus Altus, Rialto. It was here that Agnello Participazio, a Rialtine himself and a force to be reckoned with following his triumphant defence measures, now ordered his fellow Venetians to migrate and put down roots. At this moment, in the ninth century's opening decades, Venice as we now know it began arising in earnest.

By swift stages a population gathered from towns around the lagoon, Heraclea, Grado and what was left of once-dominant Aquileia, as well as from battered Malamocco, settling on the islands along the big central waterway we now call the Grand Canal and on either side of the broader expanse between Dorsoduro and Giudecca (then called Spinale). The earliest community of Luprio spread eastwards, while other groups of incomers raised dwellings on Canaleclo (modern Cannaregio) and the northerly Olivolo island. Streams in between were made navigable for small, narrow kinds of craft rowed or poled through a growing town whose thoroughfares were principally across water rather than paved land. There was an abundance of gardens and orchards and the open spaces around which houses clustered retain to this day their generic name of *campo*, 'field'. Venice has only one piazza in the accepted Italian sense, at San Marco, and even this was once a low-lying stretch of marshland. In a wide range of interpretations the historic urban environment remains what it was at the outset, a green city, in which wild nature somehow still hangs on amid the most showy and grandiose manifestations of human artifice.

Besides their plants and saplings, the early medieval settlers brought with them many of the portable decorative features that had adorned their former houses – a column or two, a fragment of antique sculpture, a relief panel or, most favoured of all, a carved patera showing doves, peacocks or animals within a circular frame. These latter held obvious spiritual significance and the presence of a pivotal religious element within the newly established communities was crucial to their sense of bonding and endurance. Nobody is wholly certain as to the age and seniority of Venice's oldest churches, though we know that at the city's extreme northern edge a cathedral was founded close to a castle which gave the area its name Castello. A church dedicated to the Greek soldier saints Sergius and Bacchus was rebuilt as San Pietro in Castello and assigned to a bishop under the authority of the Patriarch of Grado. While Grado itself quickly declined in importance, the patriarchate somehow remained established until 1451, when Pope Nicholas V amalgamated the two dioceses, making the saintly Lorenzo Giustiniani, then Castello's bishop, the first Patriarch of Venice.

Elsewhere in a city which eventually boasted 200 churches, some of its oldest are found in the western San Polo district. San Polo itself

San Giacomo di Rialto – by tradition the oldest church in Venice
but likely to be rather younger – in a pen-and-wash drawing
(1720s) by Canaletto.

features work from the ninth century, as does San Giacomo dell'Orio – the '*orio*' is probably '*lauro*', from a big bay tree that stood beside it – a building whose very appearance is that of some remote rural hermitage rather than a city temple. More basic still is nearby San Simeone Profeta, known in Venetian dialect as San Simon Grando, a basilica making use, like many of these earliest churches, of columns brought from ruined Roman structures on the mainland. Closer to the Rialto area, San Giovanni Elemosinario, though rebuilt in 1527, retains its Greek-cross pattern, while the dedication to Saint John the Almsgiver, seventh-century Patriarch of Alexandria, suggests a Byzantine connexion, adding to the sense of an early foundation. Most venerable of all, through sheer force of tradition, is San Giacomo di Rialto, 'San Giacometto', 'Little Saint James', not much bigger than a chapel and perhaps built as such to serve the traders and shoppers at the Rialto market. Venetian legend likes to maintain that this is the oldest church in Venice, built by a carpenter from Crete, its foundation laid at the very hour of the day on which the city was begun. Actually, sober evidence suggests, San Giacometto is somewhat younger than the others mentioned above, though its plan and its fabric are still very much in keeping with that Veneto-Byzantine style which writes the first chapter in La Serenissima's architectural chronicle.

The importance of Venice as a Christian metropolis cannot be too highly emphasized. Whatever its continued struggles with papal authority, the protection, at various moments, shown towards free-thinkers and heretics, and the ambivalent attitude it maintained over the centuries towards a flourishing Jewish community, the city was from the outset a place of fervent and elaborate Roman Catholic devotion, its civic calendar marked with a sequence of feast days and commemorative events involving solemn acts of prayer, worship and ceremonial. Saints of all kinds thus played a major role in the lives of dwellers in the various parishes and their individual cults were vigorously sustained. When the Venetian republic took an active part in the Crusades during the twelfth and early thirteenth centuries, the importation of looted relics from churches and shrines in the Holy Land, Egypt and Asia Minor served to enrich Venice's own religious establishments, adding further status and significance to the city. Holiness in this form was as serious a commercial enterprise as silks or spices for what was, at the time, Europe's most prosperous community.

Venice herself, however, must also have a patron and to begin with she was content with Saint Theodore, one of a host of military martyrs who had perished during Roman imperial persecutions of the third century CE. Little was known of his life save that he wrought an abundance of miracles, refused to worship idols and set fire to a pagan temple before being subjected to an exquisite series of tortures that ended with his death. A small church dedicated to Theodore was built on a site now occupied by the north side of the Basilica of San Marco and he continued to be venerated by the Venetians even after this was taken down and replaced by the far larger church raised in honour of the Evangelist. 'Todaro', the local form of 'Teodoro', went on being a favourite baptismal name in Venice well into the nineteenth century and a statue of the saint, accompanied by an oddly placid-looking dragon (not part of his associated hagiology) occupies one of the two columns in the Piazzetta. Like the winged lion on its companion pillar, it is a composite work, the head taken from an ancient Greek figure of King Mithridates of Pontus, the body having formed part of a second-century Roman statue and the dragon probably added during the Renaissance.

By the mid-ninth century, with Venice starting to thrive as a port whose venturesome traders voyaged beyond the Adriatic into the wider Mediterranean, a feeling of the city's consequence and potential independence made its citizens more aspirational. Mercantile links with Egypt were already well established and Alexandria was a haven for Venetian vessels whose captains brought home cargoes of pepper, nutmeg, mace, cinnamon, ginger and cloves carried from southeast Asia to Yemen, thence across the Red Sea and overland by camel caravan. For the next seven centuries this spice trade was to form one of the principal pillars of Venetian prosperity, handled by a cosmopolitan merchant echelon at ease in the Islamic world, speaking fluent Arabic and maintaining its own warehouses, brokers and factors within the famously multicultural atmosphere prevailing in Alexandria from its Hellenistic foundation right down to the mid-twentieth century, when the Suez crisis of 1956 effectively snuffed this out for good.

Appropriately enough, it was a pair of Venetian merchants in Alexandria whose enterprise, courage and chutzpah brought their city what became a key factor in its identity as a state and a civic community, generating ideals of devotion, service and loyalty not just in Venice itself but across its mainland Italian domains and throughout its Mediterranean empire. In the year 828 the two traders, Buono da Malamocco and Rustico da Torcello, were informed, while in Egypt, of a decision made by the Abbasid Caliph al-Mamun to order the splendid Alexandrian church dedicated to the Evangelist Saint Mark to be converted into a mosque. The Coptic Christian guardians of the saint's shrine were anxious that his body be rescued and preserved as an object of devotion and readily accepted the merchants' offer of help. Money may indeed have changed hands, since it seems unlikely that otherwise the Copts would have consented to the removal of such a precious relic from Egypt altogether.

The problem of how the body was to be moved from church to ship through the crowded streets of Alexandria appeared considerable. After opening the tomb and the coffin inside it, the Coptic priests cut open the shroud surrounding the corpse and providently substituted that of another martyr, Saint Claudian of Hierapolis. Before putting their prized relic into a basket, Buono and Rustico took the precaution of wrapping it in pieces of pork, knowing that nobody among Muslims or Jews inspecting potential cargo would want anything to do with such uncleanness. According to the Venetian chronicler Martino da Canal, writing his *Les Estoires de Venise* as a French *chanson de geste* in the thirteenth century, the saint's body now started to give off the odour of sanctity traditionally supposed to arise from the remains of those who would later be presented as candidates for canonization. 'Were all the world's spices gathered together in Alexandria,' says Martino, aware of the port's international role in this respect, 'they could not have filled the city with such a perfume.' Desperate not to attract attention with this, Buono and Rustico freely displayed what looked like a basketful of bacon to the investigating customs authorities, who recoiled in horror, crying '*Kanzir! Kanzir!*', the Arabic word for 'pig'. This particular episode can be found displayed in the mosaics in the Basilica of San Marco portraying the saint's translation by the wily merchants, but surely the most dramatic of all treatments of this moment was created by the painter Jacopo Tintoretto in 1562. In an extraordinary proto-Romantic vision assembled from a tempestuous sky, a resonantly empty classical townscape, a scatter of spooky white figures in the distant background and the brilliant anchoring of realism created by the presence of a camel to remind us that we are in Egypt, the corpse, seemingly incorrupt and given the youthful, toned appearance of a dead Christ, is borne away hugger-mugger towards its new and totemic destiny in Venice.

Raising their valuable cargo, wrapped in a tarpaulin, to the mast-head of their ship, Buono and Rustico swiftly set sail. The voyage itself was not without incident. At one point a storm blew up that seemed likely to dash the boat onto the rocks until Saint Mark himself miraculously intervened to awaken the sleeping captain, who ordered the sail lowered so that they could ride free. When the ship reached

Venice, the reigning doge, Giustiniano Participazio (son of Agnello who had recently died), commanded the saint's body to be placed in a specially built chapel in the garden between his palace and the church of San Teodoro. The relic, that of nobody less significant than one of the four holy Evangelists, conferred instant importance on the city at a time when it demanded respect from neighbouring powers and from the emperor in distant Constantinople.

Yet the fact that the doge had ordered it to be kept within the purlieus of his own residence, rather than being given to the cathedral church of San Pietro in Castello, adds a further dimension to the story. For what would soon evolve around the cult of the saint would be the creation of a splendid basilica, combining the radiant sumptuousness of a Byzantine church interior with the dignity of a palatine chapel. So often taken for a cathedral by visitors to Venice, San Marco – 'Saint Mark's' – is nothing of the kind. It was built within the precincts of the doge's palace and remained, in its various incarnations across almost a millennium, something always other than a metropolitan church, whatever its magnificence. Only in the nineteenth century did it officially assume the role of a diocesan cathedral, though even now it is never referred to as *il duomo*, unlike similar grand ecclesiastical buildings elsewhere in Italy.

The first basilica lasted just over a hundred years until, in 976, during a rebellion in Venice against vain, dictatorial and overweening Doge Pietro Candiano, it was burned down along with St Theodore's church and the entire Palazzo Ducale. Candiano was assaulted and killed by a throng of angry nobles and his successor Pietro Orseolo seems to have been chosen on the basis of being as unlike him as possible. Austere and deeply pious – he was ultimately canonized – this new doge busied himself with restoring both the chapel and the palace from his personal funds. It was in 1063, towards the end of Doge Domenico Contarini's long reign, that the building now familiar to us took shape. Shaky foundations under the earlier structure prompted Contarini to undertake a thoroughgoing programme of repairs, including the addition of a narthex – the church's outer portico – and the major mosaic adornments. Besides all this, he appointed special officers of state, the Procuratori di San Marco, to supervise the basilica's finances and the overall conduct of affairs such as charitable provision for widows and orphans.

But where, amid such reconstruction, had the saint's body actually ended up? It was not until the reign of Doge Vitale Falier (1084–1096) that its location was rediscovered. A devout worshipper in the church,

Falier instituted a series of prayers and fasts, culminating in a solemn procession to the basilica. There the collective power of a huge crowd imploring divine guidance seemingly caused the faithful to witness 'with as much amazement as joy, a slight shaking in the marbles of a pillar near the altar of the Cross, which presently falling to earth exposed to the view of the rejoicing people the chest of bronze in which the body of the Evangelist is laid.' According to the Renaissance diarist Marin Sanudo, one of our key sources for so many aspects of Venetian lore, culture and history, 'a great light shone from the pillar and a hand was thrust forth, its middle finger bearing a golden ring, and the whole space was suffused with a marvellous fragrance'.

Consecration of the rebuilt church took place on 8 October 1094. The subsequent history of San Marco as a religious edifice is one of ceaseless embellishment over the course of the next four centuries. Nowadays we marvel at the polychrome richness of the exterior, its brick core so lavishly faced with marble, porphyry and alabaster, its arches decorated with typical Romanesque carved sequences representing the months of the year and with plaques illustrating Venice's different trades and 'mysteries' – boatbuilding, masonry, woodworking, fishing, the cobbler, the butcher and the baker. Above the central doorway prance the four famous copper horses brought back as loot from the shameful sack of Byzantium during the Fourth Crusade in 1204, which saw so many spoils of conquest carried home to deck the churches of Venice. Are these splendid beasts Greek or Roman in origin? Scholars can only agree on the fact that they adorned a large public building – perhaps a hippodrome – in Constantinople. As symbols of Venetian glory they swiftly became emblematic of Venice for its citizens, so that it amounted to a deliberate insult by Napoleon Bonaparte when in 1797 he carried them off to Paris to crown his Arc de Triomphe. Their return, following his defeat at Waterloo, was an emotional moment, even if the whole operation of putting them once more in place was supervised by the Austrian imperial government to whom Venice had been unceremoniously handed through the terms of the Congress of Vienna.

The sumptuousness initiated by Doge Contarini in his palatine chapel blazes unrestrained in the mosaic sequences decorating San Marco's interior. The term 'an orderly transgression of sacred illusions' has been well used in connexion with the worshipper's first encounter here, since it is always some time before our visual sense can adequately engage with the various narratives set before us, whether in Old and New Testament scenes, in the retelling of Buono and Rustico's discovery and smuggling of Saint Mark's body (the '*Kanzir! Kanzir!*' is here too) or in the fine hagiology of Saint Isidore adorning the chapel decorated to him on the north side of the church. The same calculated impact is made by the Pala d'Oro, that stupendous altarpiece originally fashioned by Byzantine goldsmiths in 1105 for Doge Ordelafo Falier and further remodelled a century later. Thirty pounds of gold and three hundred pounds of silver, set with precious stones and cloisonné enamel, frame figures of Christ and the Blessed Virgin and scenes from the life of Saint Mark.

What is this whole gorgeous manifestation of the beauty of holiness, through its various occupational layers of spirituality, intended to prove? The tendency of so many commentators on the church has been towards a tame acceptance of the idea that early medieval Venice simply wished to be seen as a Western lookalike of the Byzantium under whose shadow it grew to prominence as a city state. Since so much of our modern engagement with Byzantine culture is clouded over by nostalgia and sentimentality, we are sometimes too eager to embrace a notion of San Marco as Greek Orthodoxy's westernmost outlier, with the Latin liturgy and rubric substituted for a world of icons and archimandrites. There was always more, however, to the basilica than this.

From its inception under Domenico Contarini to the miraculous recovery of Saint Mark's body and the moment the building stood ready for consecration, the work was a Venetian enterprise, designed to proclaim Venice as a bulwark of the Roman church, a stout defender of Catholic doctrine and practice, ready, by the same token, to challenge the Eastern empire's hegemonic presumption by annexing its most significant discourses in architecture and decorative art. The place creates, what is more, its own cosmopolitan language, not just in terms of Greek-style mosaics, columns and carving, but in the way it absorbs essential features from Romanesque building elsewhere across northern Italy and in its obvious allusions to the mosques, shrines and palaces of that Islamic world where Venetian merchants went to trade. What the makers of San Marco achieved during those crucial last decades of the eleventh century was something equivalent to their distant ancestors' exploit in hammering the earliest larch piles into the mud of the *barene*. This building, more than any other, anchored Venice in its own peculiarity, that singular arc of history and human experience spanning 1,600 years.

The Abduction of the Body of Saint Mark (1562),
Tintoretto's portrayal of the secret translation of the evangelist's
remains from Alexandria to Venice.

overleaf The Pala d'Oro, the enamelled and bejewelled
retable on the high altar of the Basilica of San Marco.

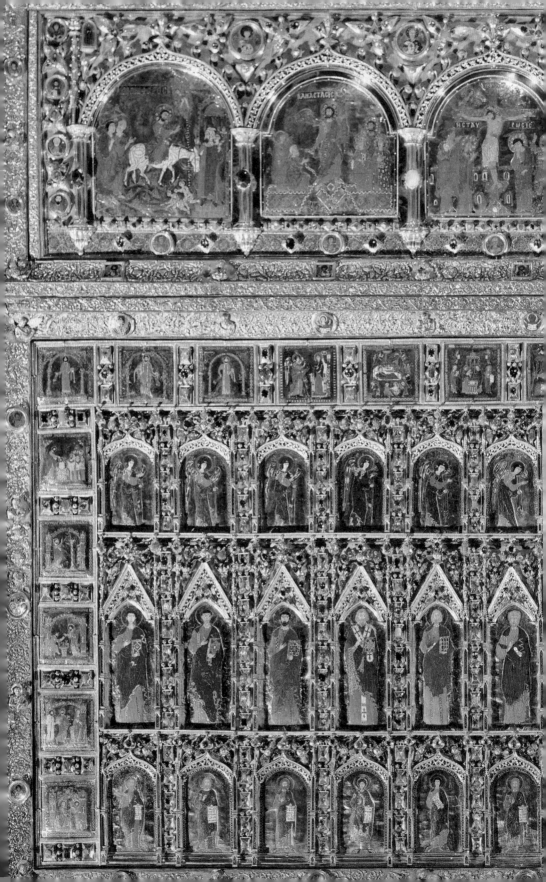

MAKING
VENETIANS

Travellers in the eastern Mediterranean – the Adriatic and Aegean seas – will become familiar with a particular badge or sign, encountered again and again, especially on islands or in mainland coastal regions. You will find it above the gateway of a half-ruined fortress in the Cyclades, on the harbour wall of a Croatian port, fixed to the base of a church tower in the fiords of Kotor or, faint and crumbling, on some windswept bastion in a remote spur of the Peloponnese. It is the Venetian winged lion of Saint Mark, holding an open volume between its forepaws, its pages bearing the Latin inscription '*Pax tibi, Marce, Evangelista meus*'. Legend tells how, as the saint was journeying from Aquileia on a ship that eventually took him to Ostia, the port of ancient Rome, he had occasion to land on an island in the Venetian lagoon. Here he was visited by an angel, who greeted him with the words 'Peace be unto you, Mark, my Evangelist. Here your body will find rest.'

In northern Italy itself the badge of St Mark's winged lion is seen everywhere across the fertile plains of the Veneto, down the lower valley of the great River Po, along the foothills of the Dolomites – the eastern Alps – and westwards into Lombardy, almost to the gates of Milan. Cities like Padua, Verona, Vicenza and Bergamo carry this image, a seal set on their gates, defensive walls and civic buildings, with conscious pride. The memory of all it embodies in terms of belonging to La Serenissima is not darkened by the least shame or resentment. In the last days of the Venetian Republic, during Napoleon Bonaparte's campaign of 1797, it was these towns which most strenuously resisted his French armies. Fifty years later, in a struggle for Italian unification in 1848, doomed to failure though this was at that moment, a recollection in such places of that earlier upheaval and a sense, however fragmentary, of what Venice had once meant to them inspired a still more passionate fightback, this time against the military might of Habsburg Austria.

When those two merchants Buono and Rustico brought Saint Mark's body from Alexandria to Venice in 828, it is doubtful that either saw the whole enterprise in broader terms than a successful attempt at bestowing credit on their city through the trophy of a highly prestigious saintly relic, at a period when such things held talismanic significance for the Catholic faithful and their spiritual world. Successive stages in the building and enrichment of the Basilica of San Marco, whether as a palatine chapel for the doge or as an ideal setting for those elaborate ceremonies of state through which the Serene Republic validated its importance to Venetian citizens and the outside world in the possession of a major saint. Within his gorgeous shrine, the numinous presence of the Evangelist was a focus of faith, of a belief not just in the truths underlying Christian doctrine as formulated by Jesus in Mark's gospel, but also in Venice itself as an abstract concept, an ideal city enshrining an ideal state and thus demanding and receiving its subjects' passionate dedication.

Hence the badge of the winged lion, with his open book and '*Pax tibi, Marce, Evangelista*', became what nowadays we call a brand image. Venetians shared in the brand loyalty, and this concept of themselves as sons and daughters of St Mark was embraced in turn by the peoples they made subject to them as their empire spread across the eastern Adriatic, into Slovenia, Croatia and the Greek-speaking domains beyond, the realm known to its rulers as the *Stato da Mar.* Many who never actually made the journey to Venice itself felt drawn to it in spirit and imagination. The administrative machinery of La Serenissima may not always have worked to the benefit of those under its sway – Cyprus during the sixteenth century bears abundant witness to this, as does the Peloponnese a hundred years later – but for the most part, in Istria, for example, or the Ionian islands, the Evangelist and his lion were a valued guarantee of continuity.

Like other empires, the *Stato da Mar* sprang from a rapid pursuit of commercial opportunity. Trade, and nothing more to begin with, was the driving force, but markets require security to function adequately and it was an assurance of safety for the passage of precious cargo up and down the Adriatic which Venice most needed for her economic survival. By the early eleventh century Venetian merchants had established certain basic principles, hammered as firm as the pine trunks on which their warehouses rested, for the conduct of business enterprise. Chief among these was a calculated refusal to let political alliances, difference in religion or even an ongoing war stand in the way of profit and increased sales. Modern visitors to Venice need reminding, on occasion, that the beauty they see around them, in the marbles and mosaics of the Basilica, the altarpieces in the Frari or the opulent immensity of Santa Maria della Salute, all arose, essentially, from whatever was carried in the holds of merchant ships or the strings of barges bringing goods down the rivers of northern Italy. God and money in Venice worked together as business partners.

Perhaps the most potent example of the way in which we voluntarily blind ourselves to such a prosaic truth is offered by Vittore Carpaccio's much-loved sequence of paintings in the Scuola Dalmata di San Giorgio degli Schiavoni, prized as one of the perfect jewels of Venetian Renaissance painting. We adore the detail in these scenes from the hagiology of Saints George, Tryphon, Augustine and Jerome – the little dog, the lion frightening the monks, that sleepy-looking dragon, those exotic Turkish musicians. Hardly any of us, it is fair to say, takes into account what paid for all this, embodied by the building itself, in the side chapel with its sober memorials to worthy Croat merchants, adoptively Venetian but with names ending in 'ić' or 'čić', in the pictures on the staircase of traders with their ships (one of them sporting the kind of neckwear which gave us the word 'cravat', meaning a Croatian-style tie) or the fine upper assembly hall, whose decoration, while not to Carpaccio's standard, celebrates exactly the combination referred to earlier of religious faith with the counting house.

It was indeed among the ancestors of these devout Dalmatians that Venice first started planting an empire. Notorious for its storms and the tricks played with shipping by its various winds at different times of year, the Adriatic carried additional dangers for Venetian merchants in the form of pirates, whether on single vessels or in small, compact fleets lurking amid the scattered archipelago along the coasts of Slovenia and Croatia. There had always been a menace from these shores. In antiquity the people known as the Illyrians

Vittore Carpaccio's *The Lion of Saint Mark*, commissioned in 1516.

presented a continual threat to Greek and Roman traders and at various times they had come raiding ports along the lagoon as big as Aquileia or Heraclea. With the end of the Roman empire and an increasingly slackened grip on the northern Balkans by Byzantium, the Croats, Slavic incomers, had settled here in large numbers, operating pirate enterprises from the islands and mainland harbours, challenging Venice's efforts to guarantee safe passage for its merchant fleets. The problem of what to do about Dalmatia increased exponentially with Venice's rapid expansion of its markets across the eastern Mediterranean, either within the Byzantine empire or else in the Islamic ports of Egypt and Palestine. Whatever Constantinople might expect was due to it in terms of deference and submission from Venice, its emperors during the tenth century had been forced to confront the reality of a Venetian commercial presence, not just in their capital city but around the Black Sea coast and among the islands of the Aegean. From around 950 onwards relations between Byzantium and its erstwhile satellite had undergone a marked decline, until the advent of a new doge in the year 991 brought a dramatic change of direction.

Pietro Orseolo II was the son of an earlier Pietro Orseolo, the doge who had turned his back on the ducal office to become a monk, leaving his wife and child in the process, a wholesale renunciation of worldly concerns for which he was subsequently made a saint. Via the resulting family trauma this younger Pietro Orseolo may well have been inspired, as often happens, to take precisely the opposite path to his parent. The dogeship, in his hands, turned out to be one of Venetian history's most game-changing, at a time when occupying the role of the Republic's head of state meant more than simply acting as a ceremonial president, wearing an ermine-trimmed robe and sporting the *corno dogale*, that distinctive horn-shaped headdress which completed the official regalia.

An obvious influence on the younger Orseolo was Basil II, then ruling the Byzantine empire, a dynamic figure whose charisma, vision and energy saw his domain rising to a moment of unparalleled influence across the medieval world. The doge had grasped the need, if Venice were to prosper, for putting the Republic on as advantageous a footing as possible with Constantinople, so a prolonged and painstaking sequence of negotiations began which ended in a commercial treaty decidedly advantageous to La Serenissima. In the spring of 992 Emperor Basil granted what was known as a chrysobull, literally a document bearing a gold seal, that allowed Venetian merchants to pay greatly reduced tariffs on goods carried directly from their city to Constantinople and gave them swift access, whenever needed, to senior court officials and ultimately to the imperial presence chamber. The hugely elaborate nature of the Byzantine palace establishment, imitated, in however modified a form, by other royal courts (with an inevitable influence on Venetian protocol), meant that this was a genuine coup for Orseolo's diplomats, who were briefed to offer in return the provision of Venice's ships as troop transports whenever the emperor should require them.

Orseolo's success in clinching the deal, represented by Basil's chrysobull, was nuanced by his awareness of Venice's unique political and economic opportunities as a bridge between Byzantium and the Holy Roman Empire. The whole issue of this double glance, turned simultaneously eastward and westward, has become something of a historical cliché in writing about Venice, but it seems to have been this immensely resourceful figure who first saw the Republic's immediate destiny in terms of such a balanced solution. Having squared Constantinople to Venetian advantage, the doge now turned his attention to the Western empire as represented by Otto III. Much younger than Pietro Orseolo and just a small child when he became King of Germany, Otto was crowned in Rome at the age of sixteen by his cousin Bruno of Carinthia, whom he had helped to install as Pope Gregory V. On his way there he met up with Orseolo in Verona and granted similar privileges to Venice in northern Italy to those enjoyed by its merchants in Byzantium. The beginnings of a more emphatic presence on the part of La Serenissima in the commercial and political affairs of the Veneto, Friuli and eastern Lombardy were now detectable, once again owing to the doge's wise diplomacy and in this case to a shared respect between the two rulers.

The major alliances thus forged would allow Orseolo to focus on the most pressing problem of all for Venice at this juncture, that running sore created by Dalmatia's pirates and their depredations. Unless these salt-water bandits were summarily dealt with, he realized, the Republic's entire credibility as a trading nation would remain in continual danger. Now the Croat corsairs threatened cities like Pula and Trieste on the Adriatic's northern curve. With such ports under their control they could easily sweep across into the lagoon itself and attack Venice as Pepin and his Franks had sought to do a century earlier. Former doges Giovanni Participazio and Pietro Tradonico had tried in vain to quash the pirates with punitive expeditions and ended up needing to buy them off with yearly tribute money. Orseolo, deciding that the time had come for a major operation, decreed an end to all further payments and gathered his fleet together.

Following mass at San Pietro in Castello, where the patriarch gave a solemn benediction to the banner of Saint Mark, the navy sailed down the Dalmatian coast, easily securing the loyalty of various towns, until they reached the channel lying between the islands of Brač, Lesina and Korčula and the mainland. Orseolo's target was the estuary of the River Neretva, called the Narenta by Venetians, forming a delta among scattered islands and shoals, a perfect hiding place for pirate vessels. By now the freebooters' fighting spirit had begun to ebb away as the naval strength deployed by La Serenissima, hardly seen in action before, became a fearsome reality. Envoys were hurriedly sent to Doge Orseolo with the idea of bribing him to turn round, which he had no intention of doing. When an entire shipload of pirates fell into his hands, he dispatched them into the estuary to warn those dwelling there to submit or face destruction. Against the larger islands the fleet now launched ferocious assaults, dislodging the pirates and crushing any last resistance. 'The enemy,' says the chronicler known as John the Deacon, a personal friend of the victorious doge, 'now dejected in spirit, surrendered their weapons and knelt down, suing for their lives. The doge was a merciful man and agreed to spare them, on condition their towns were destroyed. Journeying homeward, visiting those cities at which he anchored earlier, he returned at last to Venice triumphant.'

Pietro Orseolo's expedition sealed La Serenissima's overlordship of the Adriatic for another five hundred years. There would be further troubles, other mercantile competitors, more corsair raids and individual outrages against Venetian shipping, but essentially the Republic was now the regional power most feared and respected up and down either coast, 'la Bella Dominante' as she was later styled. Quickly grasping the nature of their victory, the Venetians determined to mark it in high style, not with a one-off celebration but through a commemorative yearly event which became part of that extraordinary calendar of rituals designed to identify the city and its state as things unique in the world, singular in the eyes of both humankind and God himself.

Regarding this particular jubilee, the idea from the outset was that it should coincide with one of the Christian year's most joyous occasions, the summer Feast of the Ascension, that day when, by a sanctified tradition, Jesus Christ, having been crucified and then risen from the dead, was received into heaven by his Almighty Father. To loyal Venetians any analogy between this and Venice's triumph over Adriatic pirates would not have seemed in any sense blasphemous. The

Venetian Dalmatia depicted on an eighteenth-century map.
Dalmatia became the earliest acquisition of Venice's seaborne
empire in 998, when Doge Pietro Orseolo suppressed the pirates
of the Narenta estuary.

Saviour's ultimate triumph over death and hell was a divine harbinger of that victory La Serenissima had achieved over those who sought to overwhelm her. Survival, endurance and an ultimate pledge of eternity beneath God's favouring watchfulness was what this key moment each year signified to passing generations in the lagoon.

Venetian dialect turned the Italian word *ascensione* into the more plain-sounding *sensa*, and 'La Festa della Sensa' was how the whole occasion became known. What happened on this special day often seemed, to those present who were not Venetian or to those in other places who read or heard accounts of it, to be a gesture of quite breath-taking arrogance. Yet its symbolic import for everyone in Venice, from the patricians in their palaces to the gondoliers, fishwives and beggars, was never questioned or denied, and from certain aspects, even nowadays, we can feel the spirit underlying this festival still vivid in the consciousness of that small number of resident Venetians keeping the city alive at the present time.

As centuries went by, so the Festa della Sensa grew ever more grand and elaborate. What happened is evoked for us with due wonder and excitement by a host of travellers to the city who counted themselves lucky to be present on the occasion. Englishman Richard Lassels, visiting in 1654, described it as 'the stately Sea triumph which they yearly celebrate... when the Duke is commonly said to marry the Sea'. This symbolic act of marrying the Adriatic on Venice's behalf lay at the centre of the whole ritual sequence. The doge and senators, accompanied by the papal nuncio and the patriarch, boarded the Bucintoro, the immense ceremonial galley with its carved and gilded transom and life-size allegorical sculptures. 'The anker is furthwith weighed and the Bucentauro beginns to move gravely and slowly to the tune of trumpets and the musick of the voices which sing chearfull Hymeneal tunes.' Lassels admired the gondolas surrounding the vessel, 'richly covered overhead with the richest canopies they can make of velvets, silks, satins and broad gold laces', rowed by liveried gondoliers. Several carried 'Embassadours of fforein Princes' who 'waite upon the Duke's Galley for the space of a good English mile, where the Duke, stopping and throwing a ring into the Sea, is said to marry the Sea'. Lassels was truly overwhelmed by the splendour of the spectacle. 'I confesse, of all the sights that ever I saw, nothing ever appeared to me more majestical... as if Neptune himself had been going to be marryed; and all echoing with the fanfarres of trumpets.'

Almost a century later the German traveller Johann Georg Keyssler wrote a still more detailed account of this remarkable ceremony, which contemporary painters like Antonio Canaletto, Michele Marieschi and Luca Carlevarijs show us must have been genuinely dazzling in its visual impact, regardless of the fact that by then – the year was 1730 – the state of Venice was in political and economic decline and its importance had irretrievably diminished. Keyssler marvelled at the thousands of boats following 'this pompous procession', at the continual music and 'discharge of great guns' as the Bucintoro moved slowly towards the Lido and the island of Sant'Erasmo. 'Here the patriarch pours into the sea some water that has been consecrated with particular prayers and is said to have the virtue of allaying storms… After this the doge drops a gold ring into the sea through a hole near his seat, at the same time repeating these words: "*Desponsamus te, mare, in signum veri perpetuique dominii*" – "We espouse thee, O sea, in sign of our real and perpetual dominion over thee."' After this the doge and the patriarch visited the church of San Nicolo on the Lido, where a solemn mass was sung. In the evening, at Palazzo Ducale, a banquet was served 'where the dessert, which represents gondolas, forts &c, is exposed the whole day to the imagination of the populace'.

During the whole triumphant festivity the name of Doge Pietro Orseolo II was probably not once mentioned, yet it was he whose achievement had been to secure Venice's mastery of the Adriatic, with which, in the fullness of time, there came the acquisition of a maritime empire. The story of nations building empires can so often be compressed into a one-size-fits-all narrative of looting, land-grabbing and racial oppression. Little of such bitter experience was true for those in the Mediterranean who came under the domination of La Serenissima. That being said, resentment of her greed and high-handedness there undoubtedly was, as well as a deep suspicion, on various occasions, of her ulterior motives. During Venice's occupation of the Peloponnese from 1687 to 1718, for example, a genuine fear seized Greek Orthodox communities as to the possible imposition of Roman Catholicism by the government through promoting missionary activity and a grant of special privileges to alien clergy and religious orders. Otherwise subject populations were content enough to become, by adoption, sons and daughters of Saint Mark, living in relative safety and public order under the badge of the winged lion.

There was no specious imperial ideology. Venice never produced a Rudyard Kipling, a Henry Rider Haggard or a John Buchan, never evolved the equivalent of France's '*mission civilisatrice*' or the USA's Project for the New American Century. Like all other empires, that of La Serenissima began as an affair of trade and the consequent need for

overleaf The Return of the Bucentaur to the Molo on Ascension Day (1730), by Canaletto.

safeguarding and control of key geographical positions to guarantee the passage of essential commodities to and from her markets. Individual populations, in the island of Crete especially, grew fractious and staged rebellions, while other powers, especially Genoa, Venice's great trading rival, attempted to seize her outposts in the Aegean or along the coastline of mainland Greece. In the Balkans the kings of Hungary periodically cast an envious eye on Dalmatian port cities like Zadar, Trogir and Split which Venetians controlled. At the same time in this context the Byzantine empire, once an authority to be reverenced and obeyed, developed a nuisance value which would need, in due course, to be dealt with. To Venice what mattered beyond everything else was keeping the trade routes open and seeing off commercial competitors or local despots with territorial ambitions.

The high Middle Ages – the tenth to the thirteenth centuries – saw Venetian power expand via a series of clashes between the Republic and a scatter of neighbouring states and dynasties. First of all, following Orseolo's defeat of the Neretva pirates, several cities on the Istrian and Dalmatian littoral either voluntarily accepted Venetian rule or else found themselves annexed by Venice as being useful within a broader strategy of Adriatic dominance. Pula took its first oath of fealty in 1145 and was finally absorbed in 1331. Šibenik – 'Sebenico' – founded by a twelfth-century Croat king, was tussled over by Hungarians and Byzantines before submitting to Venice in 1412 and Trogir followed suit soon afterwards, after a bruising from either side during the prolonged conflict with Genoa. Relations with the city of Zadar – 'Zara' – were stormiest of all. It had been given special privileges by the Byzantine emperors and though its citizens and clergy were grateful enough for Orseolo's expedition, this was no guarantee of meek acceptance where direct Venetian rule was involved. Between 1000 and 1409 there occurred a whole series of attempts by its people to shake off the overweening Republic, which at one point, as we shall see, deployed an army of international Crusaders, en route to the Holy Land, to sack this refractory town. In 1409, however, Venice was able to buy Zadar from King Ladislas of Hungary, to whom it then belonged, and make it one of the Adriatic's most heavily defended ports.

Further south within the same stretch of sea, Venice had always coveted the island of Corfu and its surrounding Ionian archipelago. When, in the eleventh century's closing decades, the Normans under Robert Guiscard invaded Puglia and Calabria, the Venetians were called to help the island's Byzantine rulers in driving them out of the area and were granted trading rights in a new chrysobull from the Greek emperor. Venice's merchants then embarked on a stealthy infiltration of the islands, whose oil, wine and salt were all valued commodities. To these they later added a trade in currants and raisins that was to become a mainstay of the Ionian economy when La Serenissima at length assumed full command of the so-called Heptanesioi, the Seven Islands, which for centuries she had regarded as essentially her own.

As Venice's reach expanded into the broader Mediterranean, so she began at the same time to survey the Italian mainland at her back, with an eye to protecting supply routes of goods and materials needed for her growing navy and for the city's survival. With increasing prosperity came inevitable changes in the built environment of what had become, by the year 1100, Italy's busiest trading port. The merchant oligarchy from among whom the doge was chosen built itself canal-side mansions which combined the space, at water level, for unloading and storage of trade goods and, on the upper floors, ample quarters for family residence. Design features in such houses derived mostly from Byzantium, visually as much as politically a presence in the world of medieval Venice, though the Venetians themselves were evolving a vernacular architecture which proclaimed its own idiom in features such as the double-arched window and those turret-like chimneypots familiar to us from Renaissance urban panoramas.

Grander in dimensions though these palaces became, the city was still markedly rural, a town of gardens and orchards among which horses were ridden and where the canals were often little more than large ditches or streamlets. Boats were being built and repaired everywhere in the timber-framed yards known as *squeri*, derived from the Byzantine Greek word *eskharion*, a workshop, in which specialist carpenters and joiners could fit up everything from a large fishing boat, the *bragozzo*, to a small two-oared *sandalo*. The craft most often seen was of the kind that has become the symbolic archetype of all things Venetian, the gondola, unique in form, technology and the particular nuances of its propulsion through the water.

Nobody has yet determined, for good and all, the etymological origins of the name itself. Is it from another Greek word, *kontilion*, meaning an oblong glass bowl? Does it derive from a species of boat known as a *condura*? What about the Latin word *cymbula*, applied to a small vessel like a dinghy or a cutter? There is even, it seems, a school of thought that favours a link between the gondola's basic shape and the shell of a clam, *vongola*, eaten with spaghetti in Venetian restaurants. All

overleaf A view of the Dalmatian town of Zara (Zadar in modern Croatia), from the travel journal of the medieval pilgrim Konrad von Grünenberg. Zara was a Venetian vassal from 998.

Darnach hetten wier gegen wind, also dz wier fliehen
müsten, das ist mit vmb gefaren, vnd ware von
Parentz, c.xxxj mil, vnd liessen wider hindersich loffen
dz wier gen Parentz nit me denn xxxx mil hetten
vnd komen zu ainer stat Polo genant, ligt og in Histeria
vn ist der Venediger, Aber wier mochten aber nit hin ze
port komen, vnd wurfen v. mil vor Polo anker, vnd
lagen stil die nacht,

ores des vij tag junij lagen wier vm iiij gegen
nacht denacht ain anker, Kun ain klainer wind
do machten wier segel, vnd furend die nacht, vn ward
ain frischer wind, also dz wier morndes vm viij
wol c. mil komen, do ward aber kemazen, vff
den abend kam aber ain guter windt

Sara in windischen landen

Alß dz wier den abend komen gen Sara ligt
8 8 mil von pareng / vnd ist die hobtstat zu
dem land Sclaffonia / vnd ist gar ain gross schöne
lustige stat / furbindig zu der wer / vnd ist och ain
Ertzbistum / vnd ligend apttigen vnd sint meng frawen vnd
mang clöster hin der stat Sara habent kofft die venedig
von kunig wentzelauß von vngern vnd bechem
tem ze Sara ligent sier hailgen / der lieb sant Simeon / der
vnsern hern empsieng in tempel / dem hat ain kunig von
vnger als lang der corpel ist / ain segaine gulding sarch
lawsen machen / Aber der hailig sant Simeon / hat nit dar in
welen ligen / vnd ligt dar vnder in ainem stain in grab gar
wol verschlossen / do ligt och da santa Donata vn santa
Anastassia / me santa Grisogonij /
¶ Item die insel zara ist funfzig mil lang / vnd ligt ain castelen
macht vor der stat Sara haist sant michels berg / ist der
lantschafft zu dienst gebawen / darauff zu flehignen fier den grossen
turken

we can be certain of is that the name was standard parlance throughout the Venetian lagoon by the end of the eleventh century, when a document issued by Doge Vitale Falier allowed the fishing community at Loreo, on the lagoon's southern fringe, a dispensation from having to supply a 'gondula' for his special use.

To rally ships from harbours and boatyards for naval expeditions presented a problem to successive doges as Venice established its imperial sway. Clearly needed was some kind of central workspace, where the fleet could undergo essential maintenance, ships could be docked or moored for victualling and refitting and where tackle of all kinds was fashioned and stored. Thus there came into being what many later generations of visitors to Venice reckoned to be one of the principal wonders of the city, the Arsenale, that massive complex of yards, rope-walks, docks and boathouses behind a girdle of lofty walls, employing a team of expert technicians in everything from caulking a hull, raising a mast or fitting out a galley with its benches of oars to making the spars and deck timbers or testing the various strengths of the cordage and 'sheets' needed for different shipboard operations like raising sail and dropping anchor.

The name Arsenale passed into English as 'arsenal', meaning a store for weapons and ammunition. Probably introduced by Venetian merchants trading with Alexandria and towns in North Africa, it comes from the Arabic *dar as-sina'a*, a boatyard. The Muslim world had already begun making a strong impact on Venice by the time Pope Urban II preached the First Crusade in 1095, an expedition in which the Republic was at first reluctant to take part, given the Middle Eastern markets' crucial contribution to its economy. It was to be another four years before a Venetian squadron set out from the lagoon in support of the papal initiative and even then its commanders were more interested in securing the best trade terms and opportunities than in saving the Holy Land for Western Christendom. A strong foothold was established in the Crusader kingdom founded after the capture of Jerusalem. After a Venetian fleet under Doge Domenico Michiel was instrumental in overcoming the key port city of Tyre in 1123, La Serenissima's trading rights were guaranteed and a lively export–import business began, lasting for another hundred years.

It was Doge Michiel's immediate predecessor, Ordelafo Falier, who had grasped a real need for concentrating the state's shipbuilding activities in Venice itself, rather than having to summon a navy from here and there among the lagoon islands. On the northern edge of the city lay two sparsely populated islands, the Gemelle, or *Zemelle*, as

Venetian dialect called them – 'the Twins', from which the inhabitants were ordered to move as the first stages of planning, excavation and building of this truly spectacular complex now began. The Arsenale's first sector, linking, at its broadest extent, the two Venetian parishes of San Martino and San Pietro in Castello, opened for work in 1104, as a nineteenth-century memorial tablet on one of its former naval barracks reminds us. In that year, 'when Venetian arms, avid for glory and conquest, occupied Syria, this Arsenal had its beginning'. Doge Ordelafo Falier was proud enough of his achievement to have a coin struck, bearing the inscription 'Ordelaph Dux Arxsenatus S.Martini transferre fecit' and the Roman numerals 'MCIV' on the reverse side. This was indeed a major stride in consolidating Venice's maritime supremacy and understood by other nations as such. Today, when the place is no longer a going concern, when the modern Italian navy has relinquished most of its control and much of the space, including the vast Corderia or rope-walk, is given over to the international art exhibitions of the Biennale, it is still possible to grasp something of the Arsenale's importance as a nerve centre of Venice's historic energy, creativity and resilience.

Qualities such as these remain vivid in the language spoken by ordinary Venetians, with their proverbially loud voices and sing-song intonation, a dialect that has nurtured its own poets and playwrights down the ages and one which in past times blurred the class barriers between all-powerful patricians, their household servants and gondo-liers, each of whom discoursed in a similar tongue and accent. This vigorous local idiom is a variant on the standard Italian nowadays taught in schools. Yet just how Italian was Venice in the Middle Ages? Or, put another way, how Italian did the rest of Italy consider Venice? Since Pietro Orseolo's decisive strike against the pirates, La Serenissima had consulted her own interests, being careful to avoid making any kind of alliance which might bind it too closely to one particular sphere of interest among several. She was always ready, besides, to challenge any attempt at empire-building by other powers in the region, the Normans in Puglia and their descendants the kings of Sicily, or the Hungarian monarchs and their client princes in Croatia. Venice was unconcerned with trying to ingratiate itself with neighbouring states and happily ran any risks created by envy and unpopularity. What mattered above all to Venetians in these early centuries of the new millennium was the preservation of their autonomy, bringing its own visceral awareness of freedom as a birthright, and the safeguarding of that wealth which kept their city in being.

They could scarcely stand back for ever from the theatres of conflict developing beyond the lagoon, in that Italy from which geography and natural forces could not detach them completely. The Italian peninsula has always been a focus for covetousness and desire in one form or another. 'Italy' as a name derives from an ancient word meaning 'the land of cattle', suggesting a place whose fertility and pastoral wealth make it ripe for raiding and possession (the modern Italian word *vitello*, 'calf' – from the Latin *vitulus* – has the same root). In the twelfth century, at the start of the crusading era, when Venice had its first experience of international power and importance, a struggle developed for the mastery of Italy between the pope and the Holy Roman Emperor. This had begun in 1075 when Pope Gregory VII, Hildebrand of Sovana, at a synod in Rome, had issued the so-called *Dictatus papae*, a document setting out the absolute power of the papacy over earthly sovereigns and vaunting unchallenged supremacy as regarded matters of privilege and authority. Two years later Gregory, at the Apennine castle of Canossa, gave a practical demonstration of his doctrine, having excommunicated Emperor Henry IV for defying it, calling him 'a rebel against the Holy Church' and absolving all imperial subjects from their allegiance. The emperor, having lost the support of his nobles, was now forced into abject submission after being kept waiting for an interview for three days on the snow-covered slopes outside the castle.

As it happened, Henry had not finished his struggle with Gregory, though the meeting at Canossa represented a major victory for the church. Over the coming decades this reverberated across the whole of Italy, as both men's successors in office faced up to one another over the major issue of a right to appoint senior clergy. Fierce as the confrontation was, Italian princes and bishops, let alone the civic leaders of its powerful urban communes, were unprepared for the violence unleashed by the election, in 1152, of Frederick, Duke of Swabia, as Holy Roman Emperor. Known as Barbarossa for his red beard, Frederick, perceptive and ruthless in quest of his goals, first of all settled affairs in his German realms before descending on Italy, determined, as he told Pope Adrian IV (the Englishman Nicholas Breakspear), 'to restore to the Roman Empire its greatness and glory'. Since many Italian towns and cities had by now endured quite enough of feudal subjection to foreign rulers, this declared resolve was met with cold suspicion, soon turning into open hostility. Led by the Milanese, several of the northern communes joined, with Pope Adrian's blessing, to form the Lombard League, an alliance against the emperor that swiftly mushroomed so that by the year 1167 it had drawn in almost twenty towns.

Among them was Venice, despite the fact that Frederick's uncle Conrad of Swabia had granted privileges to its merchants which Barbarossa himself confirmed. Clear-sighted as so often in reviewing the likely outcome of a crisis such as this one, the Republic grasped the benefits of linking itself more closely to its own mainland region. From Frederick's egregiously brutal conduct of hostilities, what is more, there may have come an atavistic warning rooted in memories of those barbarian invasions by Goths and Huns that brought about Venice's very foundation. She was happy therefore to lend the League both money and ships if these meant Barbarossa's ultimate defeat. When he tried to punish the Venetians by sending the German patriarch of Aquileia – these were the days of warrior bishops – to attack the lagoon town of Grado, their fleet neatly foiled the attempt, rounding up the patriarch and twelve of his senior clergy. The priests were set free after agreeing to an annual tribute, consisting of a bull, a dozen pigs, twelve loaves of bread and several casks of wine, all to be presented to the doge in Piazza San Marco on Ash Wednesday.

Following a series of wasteful and blood-soaked campaigns, Emperor Frederick was decisively vanquished by the Lombard League at Legnano in 1176. This historic defeat became a red-letter day in the calendar of the allied communes, most of whom had followed Venice's example in embracing republican forms of civic government. Centuries later, during the widespread revolutions of 1848 in Italy, the battle would take on a totemic significance for those who fought for unification and independence from Habsburg Austria, the dominant power in the peninsula at that time. When the composer Giuseppe Verdi was commissioned to write an opera for performance in Rome, then governed by the revolutionary leaders Garibaldi and Mazzini, it seemed entirely appropriate that its title and theme should be *La battaglia di Legnano.*

Bruised and exhausted, Barbarossa realized that his only option, if he was to maintain any kind of credibility as Holy Roman Emperor, was to submit to the pope. His earlier attempts at meddling with candidacy for the Roman church's highest office had ended in failure. Though the Sienese cardinal Rolando Bandinelli, as Alexander III, had been forced into exile, he was able to return to Rome with support from a host of northern European rulers (including King Henry II of England) having pronounced a thunderous excommunication of the emperor. Reinstalled on St Peter's throne, Alexander was now in a position to dictate terms and these were as sharply defined as possible. Frederick was confirmed as emperor, but he must make peace with the Lombard League, restore all church property he had annexed or confiscated and acknowledge the legitimacy of the pope. Any reconciliation between the two men must be staged in public, with as much fanfare and ceremony as possible and this solemn act should take place in a city with sufficient resources to provide a suitably prestigious reception for the parties concerned.

From every aspect Venice seemed the perfect choice. Its role in the Lombard League had been a secondary one in comparison with cities like Milan or Brescia and the wealth of its citizens made it particularly attractive from the practical aspect of lodgings and hospitality. Its newly elected doge Sebastiano Ziani was a canny and highly competent administrator, capable both as a diplomat and as a manager of state funds. Well off financially, he was ideally selected as La Serenissima's public face, a benign chairman of negotiations and a serene master of ceremonies when it came to the central proceedings which at length brought the two adversaries together.

The course of actual peacemaking was not always smooth – at one point the various plenipotentiaries from the League, the Kingdom of Sicily (a peripheral player in the conflict) and the Holy Roman Empire were on the point of quitting altogether. Barbarossa himself, staying first of all at Ravenna and then at Chioggia, grew predictably impatient and angry but gave in at last, after two months of bargaining and stalling. One nineteenth-century historian notes that 'the Emperor complained much of the mosquitoes and other less volatile vermin while at Chioggia. Dare we assume that these irritants were not without effect in hastening the conclusion?' At last, on 23 July 1177, Frederick was brought to the Lido and undertook, in the presence of four cardinals, to recognize Alexander's rightful claim to the papacy. Early the following morning at San Marco the pope formally lifted the excommunication and pronounced absolution of the emperor. Doge Ziani then set off in his barge to bring the contrite sovereign to the city, where he was led into the Piazza by a procession of the clergy. An eyewitness describes the specially erected stage in front of the Basilica – 'thither were brought timber, deal planks and steps' – and the 'lofty and magnificent throne' upon which His Holiness was due to sit.

Before Pope Alexander could take his place, an embarrassing dispute over precedence broke out between the archbishops of Milan and Ravenna which threatened to wreck the proceedings before they had even begun. The pope, aware of the whole moment's political

The Submission of the Emperor Frederick Barbarossa to Pope Alexander III,
as depicted (*c.*1585) by Federico Zuccaro (*c.*1541–1609).

resonance, at once stepped in to rescue the situation by diplomatically offering to seat himself on a platform below them both, so that neither should gain the coveted position at his right hand. Soon afterwards the doge led Emperor Frederick to the dais. There Barbarossa cast off the scarlet cloak he wore and prostrated himself in His Holiness's presence, kissing first his feet and then his knees. Triumphantly magnanimous, Alexander stood up to embrace and kiss the emperor before asking him to sit in the vacant right-hand chair, saying 'Welcome to you, son of Holy Church.' Descending together to the Piazza, the pair then entered San Marco to hear a Te Deum sung. That evening Alexander sent Barbarossa a quantity of gold and silver canisters full of provisions. Together with these came overtly symbolic provender in the form of a fatted calf. Most of those present would have grasped the implications of this gift in its reference to Jesus Christ's Parable of the Prodigal Son, which the pope was now pleased to quote. 'It is fitting that we should rejoice together,' he said to Barbarossa, 'since my son whom I thought was dead is alive again and he who was lost is found.'

For Venice this whole episode, bringing pope and emperor together, represented an invaluable propaganda coup. Something in its essential theatricality, in the fact that the protagonists, including Doge Ziani and the two squabbling archbishops, were performers on a stage before a numerous audience, seems quintessentially Venetian. The credit and kudos achieved through this single event gave it an enduring importance in that story which La Serenissima had begun to write about herself and would embellish over succeeding ages. Myths evolved accordingly. It is not true, for example, that the ring given to the doge by His Holiness, staying over to celebrate the Festa della Sensa, initiated the custom of marrying the sea. Neither is the tale of Barbarossa resentfully muttering, while at Alexander's feet, 'Not to you but to Saint Peter', to which the pope is said to have rejoined, 'To me *and* Saint Peter.' Undeniable, on the other hand, was the message conveyed to the rest of Italy and the world in general that Venice was now a power to be reckoned with, a player, a broker, an arbiter, to be taken seriously for contriving to reconcile two such mighty opposites. The diplomacy involved in the process would become a speciality of Venetian statecraft over future ages.

Surely the real hero of this hour, in a last analysis, was Sebastiano Ziani, thoroughly deserving of the gifts showered on him by Pope Alexander. Known officially as the Alexandrine Donation, these included the six silver trumpets blown before the doge at every *andata* – grand procession – taking place throughout the Venetian state calendar.

It was Ziani's discretion, sensitivity and foresight that had brought the whole occasion to its gratifying climax, adding dignity, in the process, to his ducal persona. His achievement looks the more impressive in the context of everything else he managed to do for Venice in the course of a mere six years in office. It was Ziani who instigated a wholesale review of different government institutions, bringing home to his fellow patricians the vital importance of being seen to match their exalted rank with a serious sense of duty towards the citizenry they dominated. It was Ziani too whose reform of the electoral system for choosing his successor ensured that among a hierarchy never wholly free from corruption and nepotism, whatever it liked to claim otherwise, this aspect of state administration at least should meet the highest standards of probity.

All who love Venice owe a profound debt to this particular doge for what he created for us in opening up Piazza San Marco and the adjacent piazzetta so that both of them might form a space of suitable magnificence in which to frame the Basilica. A canal originally running in front of the church was filled in and lines of houses with shops on their lower floors were erected along the northern and southern sides of a brick-paved square, at whose western end the church of San Geminiano was rebuilt after Ziani had pulled down the original structure, shifting it here for the sake of greater amplitude in his original design. The piazzetta in the meantime was cleared of an unsightly defensive wall across it and the two antique columns lying beside this were raised to their present position, with Saint Theodore and his dragon atop one of them and Saint Mark's lion on the other. Since the main entrance to San Marco at this period was via the graceful south portico, nowadays blocked in, this new open space held out an ideal welcome to the waterborne visitor.

A year after the momentous encounter of Alexander and Barbarossa, Sebastiano Ziani stepped down from his role and retired to the monastery of San Giorgio Maggiore as a humble lay brother among its Benedictine monks. This transition, as so often happens, proved far too abrupt – he died almost at once and was buried in the church. A portrait bust of him adorns Andrea Palladio's beautiful façade but Doge Ziani really deserves a statue to himself as one of the essential makers of Venice.

ANOTHER
BYZANTIUM

That elaborately choreographed ceremonial of July 1177 which saw Venice playing the role of diplomat and peacemaker between the pope and the emperor set a seal on the Republic's standing among the great powers of medieval Italy. They might not ultimately trust its motives and intentions – nobody ever trusted Venice where such things counted, we might say – but its influence, its money and its ships were always needed and a certain grudging respect for Venetian grit, toughness and cunning had developed among other cities and states in those turbulent years leading up to Barbarossa's encounter with Pope Alexander in Piazza San Marco as Doge Ziani looked benignly on.

This age of the Crusades was an era when La Serenissima could expect to profit as never before. The word 'crusade' has gained a resonance almost wholly unjustified by its etymology. We identify the concept nowadays with idealism, piety, struggles on behalf of a good cause and triumph over adverse circumstances so as to arrive at a result which will be beneficial not just to certain individuals, but to society as a whole. Some of these aspects, it is true, fired the impulses of the original Crusaders and most of them would surely have claimed that their exploits were carried out in the name of all those sacred principles enshrined in the teachings of the Redeemer of humankind. Yet a glance at the two and a half centuries when the Crusades were a driving force in the affairs of Europe, the Middle East and North Africa evokes a very different picture. Violence on a scale undreamt of, commercial exploitation, untrammelled greed, dynastic conflict, pillage and treachery were the signature values of this extraordinary impetus in the name of a loving and compassionate God – and Venice was not slow to perceive what advantages might be reaped from it all.

The earliest crusading ventures had been stirred by an appeal to the pope and other powers in western Europe from Byzantium, troubled

overleaf The nave and aisles of the basilica of San Marco.
The basilica is dedicated to Saint Mark the Evangelist,
patron saint of the city.

at the loss of those Christian Holy Places in Palestine of which the Greek emperor was traditional guardian. Islam, for whom these sites held comparable importance, had been carried by Muslim conquerors, Umayyad, Mamluk and Seljuk, deep into former Byzantine territories in Syria, Egypt and eastern Anatolia. The Greeks seemed powerless to resist the surge of a rival faith in arms. In 1095 Pope Urban II, Odo de Lagery, a Frenchman, first preached a crusade among the knightly aristocracy of his homeland, then proclaimed it officially at a church council in Clermont-Ferrand, assuring those who took up the cross in the name of recovering hallowed shrines for Christendom that they would be granted forgiveness of all past sins they might have committed. By the following year an international army, almost 70,000 strong, had gathered in Constantinople ready to march against the Turkish hosts – 'the infidel' or 'the pagan', as Christians chose to call their devoutly Muslim enemies.

Venice did not at first join in. For a century and more its merchants had been profitably trading with Islamic powers around the eastern Mediterranean littoral, as the story, albeit semi-legendary, of the seizure of Saint Mark's body from Alexandria illustrates. What mattered, and would always matter, to Venetians was the security of the various routes into the East, by sea and overland by camel caravan, that brought the spices, fabrics, precious stones, foodstuffs and medicaments from as far off as India and China at length to the markets of Rialto. Only in 1099 did Doge Vitale Michiel judge it prudent to send a fleet of 200 ships towards Constantinople. Even if, by then, the dynamic between the Greeks and their western allies had radically shifted, so that it now looked as if the latter were poised to establish their own outposts of Latin Christendom in territory the Orthodox eastern empire regarded as its own by right, the Venetian Republic was not too scrupulous as to forging steadfast alliances with one side or the other. There was, after all, a whole new theatre of mercantile opportunity developing among the coastal cities of Syria and Palestine which Venice resolved to exploit, spurred on in any case by the presence of its three Italian commercial rivals, the maritime republics of Pisa, Amalfi and Genoa.

In the years immediately following, and indeed through the whole of the twelfth century, Venetian involvement in the affairs of the different Crusader states establishing themselves in the Levant was a distinctly selective business, conditioned by the Republic's enduringly ambivalent and uneasy relationship with Byzantium and by a need to place its financial interests first and foremost in whatever dealings it might have with other powers, Christian or Muslim. Successive naval strikes against Sidon, Haifa and Tyre gained Venice a strong foothold in each of these ports. Though the crusading ideal might not have been her most important motive for undertaking or assisting in any of these enterprises, their propaganda value was considerable. She could demonstrate her strength as a maritime power, adding an effective backup to what was principally a land campaign led by armoured and mounted knights, showing how necessary such a contribution was through her transport of supplies, munitions and reinforcements, and she could lend a whole range of technical skills to those prolonged siege operations that formed such a vital element in Crusader warfare.

The fundamental difference between Venice and her allies during these two centuries of strife in the Middle East was due, as historians have pointed out, to the nature of Venetian society as opposed to those of its mainland counterparts. In Venice itself a visual epitome of this distinction is to be found in the presence of a particular effigy, dating from the fourteenth century, in the north transept of the Dominican church of Santi Giovanni e Paolo. The whole building is celebrated as a pantheon of medieval Venetian doges, their tomb sculptures showing almost all of them in their robes of office, complete with the *corno dogale* and their respective family coats of arms. Thus it comes as a total surprise to find, amid such company, the recumbent figure of a warrior in full armour, helmet, sword, gauntlets and greaves included. We are used to seeing this kind of memorial in northern Europe, in English parish churches especially. In Venice, on the other hand, the temptation is to ask what exactly this steel-clad paladin is doing here and, by extension, what the effigy's presence signified, either to the family who installed it or to others in their patrician class.

For the crucial difference was that the Venetian oligarchy had no armoured knights. This was not, by its very nature and composition, a chivalric, feudal nobility, imbued with the sort of values we traditionally associate with such an echelon or presenting similar challenges to a despotic ruler. The office of doge was elective, shorn by its nature of the personal powers enjoyed by a monarch, whose privileges would include that of being 'the fountain of honour', capable of bestowing titles of nobility on his followers and the lands to go with them. The success of the Venetian political system and the reason it lasted, relatively unaltered, for nearly a thousand years were each due, in part, to the fact that its nobility had nobody to rebel against. These oligarchs might give themselves family trees that stemmed from ancient Roman senators or even from those Trojan heroes honoured as the legendary founders of cities in the Veneto region. They might bear coats of arms, live in spacious, marble-fronted palaces and deem themselves worthy only to marry within their own aristocratic class. Yet, as noted earlier, they had begun, in order to survive, as a race of waterborne vendors, peddlers and hagglers, as far from the traditional world of crusading warriors as it was possible to imagine – and as such, in this medieval context, they would remain. Only in later centuries, with their empire diminished, their commercial reach drastically reduced and La Serenissima clinging to memories of erstwhile magnificence, would they turn to being a landed nobility living off their estates like others of their kind in Europe. Even then the splendid country villas designed for them by Andrea Palladio and others retained the practical function of farmhouses, just as their palazzi on the Grand Canal enshrined something of the spaciousness of those storerooms and warehouses from which their wealth had first derived.

Much of this money was gathered during the most energetic crusading decades, those of the second half of the twelfth century, when Venice busied itself with consolidating its advantages in the Levant and capitalizing on the political instability of the imperial government in Constantinople so as to extort concessions and privileges from Byzantium. Following attempts by Emperor Manuel Komnenos in 1171 to cut out Venetian traders entirely from the city by fomenting tensions between them and the Genoese as a pretext for mass arrests and seizure of property, the Republic determined on retaliation but a projected naval assault never got further than the Aegean island of Chios, where a plague epidemic decimated the ships' crews. Biding their time after the emperor rebuffed their ambassadors, the Venetians saturninely looked on as a succession crisis following his death in 1180 brought anarchy to the empire. When, after four years of chaos, Isaac Angelos II, a distant relative of Manuel, seized the throne, he could see a practical wisdom in enlisting Venetian support and swiftly made a treaty with the Republic. Its key clauses proved abundantly favourable to Venice, as if Isaac were only too anxious to compensate for the injuries sustained in Manuel's purge sixteen years previously. Though Venetian shipyards undertook to supply the emperor with nearly a hundred galleys, these were all to be paid for with Byzantine money. Extra funds from the imperial coffers would offer redress for the damages and confiscations of 1171. In addition, Isaac agreed to assist Venice if either the city or its territories were attacked by a foreign power.

For several leading figures in La Serenissima's Grand Council, however, the implications of Emperor Manuel's violence against the Venetian merchant community were too ominous and sinister to be

The Venetian doge Enrico Dandolo preaching the Fourth Crusade, in a painting by the seventeenth-century artist Jean LeClerc.

brushed aside. One of these was Enrico Dandolo, who had earlier acted as envoy to the Italian city of Ferrara and was one of the diplomats sent by Doge Vitale Michiel to engineer some kind of compromise with Manuel that might lift the embargo against Venice's commercial activity in Constantinople. Dandolo was now an old man, extremely old by his era's standards, and completely blind besides. What caused his loss of sight was never determined. Though he himself ascribed it to a blow on the head, this was all he ever said on the subject. Evidence suggests that it might have been the result of an attack on him during his visit to the imperial court, but the gradual degradation of his signature on documents after this period suggests that the impact of whatever took place was not immediate. Wilder theories attributed Dandolo's blindness to a dastardly order from Emperor Manuel to have broken glass thrust into his eyes, and some supposed that the disability was little more than an elaborate pretence on the part of a shrewd, cunning and extremely ruthless operator in Venice's cause.

From a patrician family with a distinguished record of public service, model Venetians as it were, Enrico Dandolo was universally respected for his sound judgment and unquenchably restless energy. A single heretical voice from among his contemporaries is that of Byzantine historian Niketas Choniates, who calls him 'faithless and an inveterate enemy to the Greeks, a devious and arrogant man, driven by a thirst for fame beyond anything or anybody else'. Which may all have been true, but Dandolo is certainly an archetype of that hoary old trope (probably deriving from a novel by Walter Scott) 'Cometh the hour, cometh the man'. The Republic certainly believed this and he was to gain an imperishable niche in the folk myth of its past constructed by Venice over subsequent centuries. When the city became part of the Austrian empire after Napoleon's defeat at Waterloo in 1815, Venetians summoned up Dandolo's memory as an inspiration in their efforts to regain independence, mirrored in Byron's lines

> Oh for one hour of blind old Dandolo,
> The octogenarian chief, Byzantium's conquering foe.

He was certainly well into his seventies when elected doge on New Year's Day, 1193. Advancing age seems to have sharpened rather than blurred his faculties and he moved swiftly to deal with what looked like two of the most looming problems standing in Venice's way. One of them was the endlessly troublesome Dalmatian city of Zara, whose prosperous burghers had never knocked under to La Serenissima with what she deemed a suitable deference and humility.

Instead they preferred to place themselves under Balkan sovereigns such as the Prince of Croatia or the King of Hungary. With the latter, in 1181, they had signed a treaty and it was further suspected that they were negotiating trade agreements with Pisa and Genoa.

Dandolo's resolve to bring Zara to heel was gratified by the wider turn of political events across Italy. When Pope Alexander III died, after bringing Emperor Frederick to heel in Venice, he had been followed by a series of inept or sickly holders of the pontificate, each of them reigning too briefly to make much impact either on the church they ruled or on that secular world over which the papacy claimed ultimate dominion. This would all change when, in 1198, Cardinal Lotario di Segni, a learned canon lawyer whose studies in Paris and Bologna had hardened his sense of spiritual mission, was elected pope at the age of thirty-eight, as Innocent III. His strength of purpose was clear from the outset in a determination to unite the church by crushing heretics and bringing the Eastern Orthodox faithful back into the fold, by asserting his power as Holy Father over all Christian rulers and by securing his rights as a territorial sovereign within Italy itself. He would do this with the aid of the so-called 'Donation of Constantine', a forged imperial diploma first circulated in the eighth century, seeming to guarantee papal control over the city of Rome and its surrounding region.

All good Christians, Pope Innocent maintained, must be prepared to take up arms in an ongoing holy war fought not only in Palestine but against the Moors in Spain and the Cathar heretics in southern France. In addition a campaign was being launched against recalcitrant monarchs like England's King John, who refused to obey the pontifical will in appointing senior clergy. One of Innocent's first acts was to proclaim a new eastern crusade, identifying the recovery of Jerusalem, recently lost to the great Muslim warlord Saladin, as the central initiative in a movement to protect the integrity of the church and restore its primacy in the very land where Christ was born.

The pope's combination of idealism and spiritual dictatorship had the desired effect, reinforced by his offer of a special indulgence for would-be Crusaders, declaring that 'all who take the Cross and remain for one year in the service of God in the army shall obtain remission of any sins they have committed, provided these have been confessed.' A group of influential senior nobles from northern France and Flanders was galvanized into action by the renowned preacher Foulques de Neuilly, acting under papal direction, and chose six of its number as envoys to Venice to arrange transport for the expedition. Innocent was in fact already negotiating this with the Venetians but

remained wary of their nuanced relationship, as traders, with the world he was hoping to overwhelm with his Christian onslaught. Hence he demanded guarantees from the Republic that nothing in the way of warlike matériel – ships, tackle, timber or weapons – should be sold to Muslim buyers, bidding the Venetians to remember that 'There can be no doubt whatever that he who tries, through deceit and against the dictates of his conscience, to evade these decrees, will undergo the penalties ordained by God.'

Despite an iron conviction in the rectitude of his words and deeds as God's vicar on earth, the pope was aware of exactly how much or how little Venice was prepared to respect him where its own settled policies were involved. Accordingly he kept a close eye from Rome on what now began unfolding as the French Crusaders made a first contact with the Venetian Senate in the spring of 1201. 'The Doge of Venice, a very wise and able man whose name was Enrico Dandolo,' says Geoffroy de Villehardouin, Marshal of Champagne, one of the six ambassadors, 'paid the French great honour and gave them a very cordial welcome, both he and his household.' Dandolo, though professing complete unawareness of why the Crusaders had come to Venice, clearly guessed what they wanted yet knew how long to keep them waiting. They in their turn were conscious of the immensity of the enterprise in which they were asking him to share. Even given the superiority of the Republic's naval resources, an operation on the scale demanded had never before been proposed to it.

Reading between the lines of Villehardouin's chronicle, however, and knowing what we do of Enrico Dandolo, there arises a sense of the whole venture of this Fourth Crusade as an irresistible challenge both to him personally and to Venice in general. After a week or more of talks, the doge announced his conclusion, 'provided of course that we can persuade our Grand Council and the commons of this state to give their assent'. What he offered was enough transports for 4,500 horses and their 'squires', further ships to accommodate 4,500 knights and what Villehardouin calls '20,000 foot sergeants'. Nine months' rationing and fodder were added to the bill and the period of engagement was for 'one year from the day on which we set sail from the port of Venice, to act in the service of God and Christendom, wherever this may be'. In addition, the Republic was ready to add fifty armed galleys 'for the love of God', on condition that whatever might be won on land or sea should be divided equally between either party to the agreement. If the envoys assented to all this, the necessary work was estimated to take just

Pope Innocent III recognizes Saint Francis of Assisi's rule of the Franciscan order; fresco by Giotto di Bondone, c.1295/1300.

over a year, so that the full crusading contingent would board its ships on the feast of Saint John, 24 June 1202.

Confident of raising the 94,000 marks stipulated, Villehardouin and his ambassadors accepted the terms. Dandolo, 'this very wise and able statesman', then summoned the Grand Council and 'through his good sense and his keen intelligence, qualities that he possessed to the highest degree, brought them to approve the proposed covenant'. What now remained was to win the consent of ordinary Venetians. For this the doge arranged a grand public event – another piece of political theatre, essentially – in the form of a mass in the Basilica of San Marco, 'the most beautiful church in the world', where the congregation, 'ten thousand of the common people', prayed for God's guidance as to whether or not to accept the envoys' request. Once the service itself was over, the Frenchmen were invited into the building and Geoffroy de Villehardouin addressed the assembled Venetians (in what language we are not told) saying that he and his fellow knights acted on behalf of 'the noblest and most powerful barons of France', who asked them 'to take pity on Jerusalem, now in bondage to the Turks, imploring you in God's name to join with them in avenging the insult now offered to Our Lord'. The pitch of emotion now rose so high that everybody, including the doge and his counsellors, burst into tears and the crowd cried with one voice 'We consent! We consent!' Next morning Dandolo wept again as the formal treaty was signed and the envoys set out on their long journey home, having sent a copy of the document to Pope Innocent for ratification.

What would nowadays be called spin or news management was an important feature of the agreement between Venice and the Crusaders. The treaty's signatories did not go into detail publicly as to where the great expedition was intending to land: the words 'Christendom, wherever this may be' on the document are noteworthy. Most of those weeping for joy in San Marco were content to be assured that it would be heading for the Levant and the Crusader kingdom of Outremer. As far as the French envoys knew, however, the destined landfall was in Egypt, 'because from there the Turks could be more easily crushed than from any other part of their territory'. They did not suspect that Dandolo and his closest advisers had other plans altogether. Even while the last details of this holy alliance were being discussed, the Venetians knew that their own embassy to the sultan in Cairo was giving him precise guarantees that Egypt would not be attacked, in return for the continuing safety of La Serenissima's commercial interests among the *fondouks* (warehouses – this Arabic word passed into Venetian as *fondaco*) which held its precious goods in Alexandria. The doge had a different use for the Crusaders entirely. They were to be the instruments of his long-meditated project for dealing once and for all with the nuisance of Byzantium.

An initial enthusiasm among the French barons for the proposed crusade began nevertheless to falter as the months drew on. While the Venetians pushed forward with the task of building and fitting out the galleys and the transports, it was a more difficult matter for the envoys, returning home, to convince those whose zeal had sent them to Venice in the first place. Many Crusaders had decided to leave from the ports of southern France instead of making the journey through Italy, so that at one point Villehardouin found himself in the embarrassing situation of trying to intercept groups of knights and their followers so as to reroute them towards the Venetian lagoon. A looming problem, unless an army could be gathered in sufficient numbers by the appointed feast of St John, was that of fulfilling the original financial pledges delivered to the Republic during the emotion-packed days leading to the mass in San Marco. Even when the forces rallied, together with a large number of unarmed pilgrims, in designated encampments on the Lido, it became obvious that its cohorts numbered only about a third of what had been promised. A massive fleet stood ready, meanwhile, with too little money to pay for it.

Justifiably angry, Enrico Dandolo faced the French barons with their bad faith. 'My people, having lost much, require you, as I do, to pay the debt you owe,' he said. 'If you cannot do this, then you will not leave the island until we are satisfied, neither shall anyone be allowed to supply you with meat and drink.' As the army on the Lido grew increasingly bored and fractious, with sickness predictably sweeping through its ranks, Venice, haunted by a serious financial crisis threatened by its commitment to the whole project, was becoming rebellious towards both the doge and his council. It was up to Dandolo to provide a compromise which could fill the state's empty coffers, pacify the citizens and move all available Crusaders in the direction of the Holy Land. His solution came in the typically Venetian form of a grand public gesture accompanied by some carefully concealed hard bargaining.

First of all came Dandolo's own declaration, made in San Marco before the assembled council and citizens, together with the leading Crusaders, that he himself, age notwithstanding, was ready to join the expedition. 'I myself am old and infirm, needing repose, but since nobody knows better than I, your doge, how to lead you, then if you

overleaf Mosaic of Christ Pantocrator in the south dome of the inner narthex of the Church of the Holy Saviour in Chora, Istanbul. Most of the fabric of the building dates from the second half of the eleventh century.

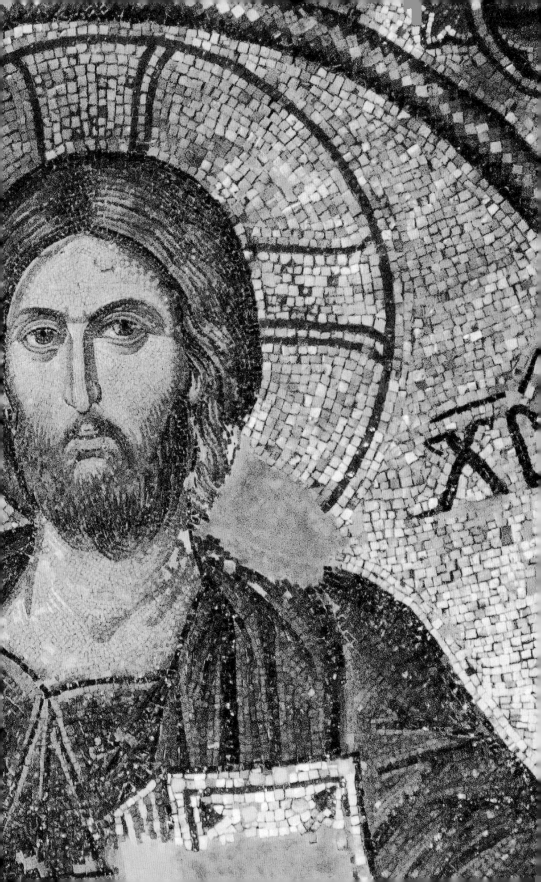

let me take the sign of the cross while my son assumes my duties as the city's guardian, I shall accompany the pilgrims to live or to die.' Instead of trying to persuade him otherwise, the crowd called out 'For God's sake, agree to do this and go with them!' Villehardouin tells us that 'many tears were shed because this excellent man, had he wished, might indeed have stayed behind with good reason'. What moved them all still more was that at the high altar Dandolo knelt down so that the red cross of the Crusaders could be sewn on to his ducal headdress.

With as much of the money gathered as possible (several donations coming from individual barons digging still further into their own coffers) the fleet was finally ready to sail. On 8 November 1202 the Venetian armada of 480 ships set forth into the Adriatic, led by the aged and blind Dandolo himself on a flagship painted red, with trumpets playing and everyone aboard singing the canticle *Veni Creator Spiritus.* After all the frustration and postponement, the zigzagging between hope and despair, it must have seemed to many as if the holy errand on which they were bound had victory inevitably written into its contract with the Almighty.

Over whom or what remained another matter entirely. The doge and his council had kept one important bargaining counter almost until the very last. Zara, that most unwilling and rebellious of cities in Venice's Dalmatian domains, required teaching a lesson and who better to do this than the force now surging with such wrathful enthusiasm down the Adriatic? At present the town was now occupied by the army of King Emerich of Hungary. Taking it back for Venice would, if not absolutely settle the debt still due to La Serenissima, at any rate allow it to be deferred for the time being. Thus quickly the Fourth Crusade, instead of reserving its energy and fighting spirit for recovery of the Holy Places from Islam, was to be deflected towards the seizure of a Christian city. The fact that Emerich himself was preparing to take the cross appeared immaterial. Zara was duly threatened, but before a siege could begin in earnest the citizens surrendered and Dandolo took possession of the town. Triumph for the Venetians was nonetheless clouded by the arrival of an emissary from Rome with a furious letter from Pope Innocent, excoriating the whole expedition for having violated the essential spirit of the Crusade and threatening excommunication for anybody prepared to take a further part in it.

While opinion of how to respond to the papal ban was divided within Crusader ranks, the Venetians settled down to overwinter in Zara. At this critical juncture there came messengers from the Byzantine prince Alexius, exiled son of the recently deposed Emperor

Isaac Angelos, whom a usurping brother had blinded and imprisoned. They brought with them a letter from Frederick Barbarossa's son Philip, married to Isaac's daughter, outlining a bold and enticing plan for restoring Prince Alexius to his rightful inheritance in Constantinople while offering to fund the invasion of Egypt and supply troops for the purpose. Besides this, as if to answer Pope Innocent's prayers for a universal Roman Catholic church, Alexius undertook to bring the whole Greek empire back into the fold of Western Christendom. 'If God lets you restore all this to him,' said the messengers, 'then His Highness will place the whole of Romania [the name by which the Byzantine realm was officially known] beneath the sway of the church of Rome from which it has been divided.'

Innocent had in truth already got wind of Alexius's scheme and rejected it, once again through a horror of Christians being mobilized to attack one another. Knowing heads among Venetians and Crusaders had probably guessed in any case that such a promise to wrench several million Greek Orthodox worshippers away from their traditional rites and tenets and seek to deliver them to the Holy Father must be utterly worthless. Meanwhile numerous knights, disillusioned by the unfolding realities of what had suddenly become a punitive exercise in freebooting among rival dynasties, started falling away, ready to head for the Holy Land on their own initiative.

Enrico Dandolo, on the other hand, saw powerful advantages in embracing Alexius's offer. His plan to use the Crusade as a means to punish Byzantium could now be consolidated. Those slights and injuries offered to Venetians in Constantinople thirty years earlier by Manuel Comnenos were not forgotten. There was enough in that great city, one of the richest and most thriving in the world at that time, to distract the Crusaders from their stated object of invading Egypt. The outstanding debts could be amply serviced and Venice herself, as ultimate facilitator of the whole venture, could not fail to regain her lost trading privileges and reaffirm her competitiveness against the other Italian maritime republics. All of a sudden papal excommunication, however dreadful a weapon in Innocent's hands, looked far less threatening when set against the opportunities held out by this latest project. When young Alexius arrived in person he was given an elaborate welcome and the expedition moved onwards to Corfu, the Venetians having taken care to humiliate Zara by razing all its chief buildings except churches to the ground so it would never again dare to challenge La Serenissima's authority.

After some sharp words in Corfu between Crusaders keen to move on at once towards Palestine and those who, like Villehardouin, accepted Alexius's proposal at face value or joined Dandolo in supporting it for other reasons, the fleet sailed once more, with fair winds and fine weather assisting, until in the last week of June 1203 they reached the Bosphorus. For the Crusaders a first sighting of the great city was an overwhelming experience. 'Nobody', says Villehardouin, 'would have believed it to be true if he had not glimpsed it with his own eyes… There was no man so brave and daring that his flesh did not tremble at the sight.' For the plan was that a full-scale siege of Constantinople would start as soon as a successful landing from the transports was accomplished. What Pope Innocent had most dreaded in seeking to rouse the Crusaders to action in the first place, an outright attack by Christians against one another, was about to become a reality, in a spot, what is more, where the churches preserved countless holy relics of saints and martyrs and the foundations had been laid by an emperor converted from paganism to the true faith.

On 5 July 1203 the Crusaders' attack began on Galata, most vulnerable spot on the Golden Horn, where many Venetian, Genoese and other traders lived. Though it proved easy enough for the besiegers to raise the immense chain blocking the strait and let in their fleet, the rest of the city held out for almost two weeks longer, until Enrico Dandolo, with his uncanny shrewdness, located the weakest area of the fortifications and urged his galley towards it. He stood, according to Villehardouin, 'fully armed on the prow, an old man and totally blind, with St Mark's banner waving before him, ordering his crew to drive the ship on shore'. There they planted the flag, while the doge, evidently relishing his role in the forefront of the battle, remained on board directing operations. By the evening the combined Venetian and crusading forces had seized control of the entire area within the walls, the usurping Alexius had fled the city and, to all intents and purposes, the mission was accomplished. The sightless prisoner Isaac Angelos was restored to his imperial throne and his son raised to the purple as co-emperor Alexius IV. The Crusaders, it now appeared, were free to travel on towards Palestine or Egypt.

Matters, as Dandolo and his Venetian entourage soon realized, were not altogether this simple. For one thing Alexius had no money with which to honour his pledge to the crusading army, while many of the latter in any case were disgruntled by Venetian efforts to persuade them to stay as a police force until Constantinople was in a more receptive mood towards its new regime. The long tradition of Byzantine contempt for these gross, ignorant Westerners, 'the Franks' (this is notably audible in the *Alexiad*, the history written a century earlier by the new emperor's collateral ancestor Anna Komnena) now gained fresh energy from the detestation swiftly aroused in the Greeks by the occupying foreign force. The citizens were reluctant besides to accept Isaac and Alexius as their lawful sovereigns. In January 1204 a member of the noble Ducas family nicknamed Murzuphlos – 'shaggy brows' – rallied fellow malcontents to seize and murder Alexius, following which he had himself crowned as Emperor Alexius V. This new state of affairs would hardly suit Dandolo's plans for a puppet empire in which Venice pulled the strings, added to which Murzuphlos began displaying an alarming level of military competence and resourcefulness by instigating a wholesale repair of the city's battered towers and ramparts. Clearly it was time to act.

Early on the morning of 9 April 1204 the Venetians and Crusaders launched a fresh assault on the walls but were beaten back by the pitiless accuracy of Byzantine bowmen and by an avalanche of massive rocks aimed at shattering their siege engines. A contrary wind, what was more, buffeted the Venetian ships to seaward so that despite repeated efforts it proved impossible to land enough men in support of the earliest attacking force. A second day's impetus was no more effective and the Crusaders were losing heart, when all of a sudden the wind shifted so that the besiegers began crowding up beneath the walls. A single weak spot in the masonry was located and battered down by Aleaumes de Clari, a former monk who had taken the cross with his brother Robert and who now clambered inside, terrifying the defenders while his comrades crawled across the breach after him, leaving 'so many dead and wounded that their number might not be reckoned' in the ensuing slaughter. For Murzuphlos the game was all too quickly up. As an orgy of murder and looting began, he slipped away to Thessalonica aboard a local fishing boat, 'fearing lest he be served up to the Franks as a tasty morsel for their table' and careful to take with him Emperor Alexius's wife Euphrosyne and her daughter Eudoxia, with both of whom he had been carnally involved.

To get some notion of scale regarding the sack of Constantinople we need to turn to the most moving and detailed of contemporary Byzantine sources, the *Annals* of Niketas Choniates, a nobleman and court functionary whose anguished account of those April days of 1204 can still move its readers to an almost tearful pitch of indignation. What happened was what so often occurs on such occasions throughout history – a culturally inferior, uncomprehending army, victorious by brute force over an enemy altogether more refined and sophisticated,

overleaf The Four Horses of St Mark were taken to Venice from Constantinople in 1204, and placed on San Marco's façade. The horses there today are replicas; the originals (shown here) reside in the interior for their protection.

grows fearful of the assault on its senses made by the sheer lavishness of the beauty and creativity on which it chances and can only desecrate or destroy these accumulated wonders. The numerous fires that burned across the city as the combined Franco-Venetian force roamed its streets, squares and public buildings constituted the most elemental manifestation of that terror which a superior civilization, like some sort of malign magic, is capable of inducing at a first encounter. To ravage and despoil the whole achievement was thus, for the Franks at least, a species of apotropaic exercise.

Choniates can hardly begin to report what he and others witnessed of all this. 'I do not know how to give any order to my account,' he acknowledges. 'These forerunners of the Anti-Christ smashed the sacred images, used consecrated vessels as drinking cups, destroyed the high altar of Hagia Sophia and set a common prostitute on the throne of its Patriarch to sing bawdy songs and dance obscenely.' The wealthiest mansions were ransacked, 'nor was any mercy shown to virtuous matrons, innocent young girls or the virgin nuns dedicated to Almighty God'. The Franks had no scruple as to raping their victims inside churches and chapels, 'fearless of divine wrath or human vengeance'. Choniates saw the entire three-day carnival of vandalism, carnage and sexual excess as being, in whatever sense, a punishment from heaven. 'Oh city, city!' he exclaims, 'You eye of all cities in the world, have you drunk, at God's hand, from the cup of his anger?'

For the Venetians, on the other hand, the sack represented the most heaven-sent of opportunities. Many of those present knew their way around Constantinople, with an excellent notion of what was where, so that now they could freely help themselves to whatever proved portable in the way of gold, silver, jewellery and precious stones. Back to Venice went shiploads of church ornaments, icons, monstrances, crosses, altar frontals, panels adorned with gemstones and cameos, items of marble sculpture and carved relief. Back too went the four gilt bronze horses that became San Marco's own, arrogated to Venice for an essential badge of identity, as potent in their way as the winged lion with his open book. The ultimate trophy of conquest was a profusion of holy relics, many of them to be sold on to eager buyers across Europe, others, including a vial of the Holy Blood, a fragment of the True Cross and several incorrupt bodies of saints, to be reverently deposed within the churches of Venice.

On the orders of Enrico Dandolo and the Crusader barons, such treasure as had not already been abstracted as personal booty was to be brought to one or other of three named churches, where it was heaped up with estimates taken. The barons' bill from the Crusaders was then settled and the remaining spoils could be divided equally among the two forces. Just as important for Venice as closing this account was determining the share La Serenissima would receive of the former Greek empire once a puppet emperor had been chosen in the shape of Count Baldwin of Flanders. By the terms of Dandolo's final agreement with the crusading leader Boniface of Montferrat, the Republic could now claim possession of most of mainland Greece, including the Peloponnese in its entirety, the Ionian islands and a scatter of the Cyclades, the large almost-island of Euboea (known to Venetians as Negroponte) and, biggest prize of all, Crete in its entirety, an ideal staging post for that precious trade with Egypt that the doge had so cunningly protected by steering the Crusaders in the direction of Constantinople.

Dandolo stayed on in the city he had plundered, burned and de-populated, occupying himself with the inevitable regrouping of Greek forces seeking to recover Byzantium in the name of the different dynastic claimants. In May 1205, aged ninety-eight, he died in the agonies of an untreated inguinal hernia and was buried with due honours in the gallery of Hagia Sophia, where a marble slab still bears his name. As the most skilful and resolute among the Fourth Crusade's movers and shakers he had given the Venetians, in the words of a modern historian, 'much more than they bargained for, indeed much more than they wanted'. Trading with Byzantium was one thing: owning and administering three-eighths of it was quite another. The *damnosa hereditas* of the whole despicable enterprise represented by the Crusade, and by Venice's part in it, would condition her destiny until La Serenissima's downfall six hundred years later.

TRADERS
AND
TRAVELLERS

From its very foundation Venice has been a cosmopolitan city. True, it possesses a robust local culture and a wonderfully idiosyncratic spoken and written dialect of Italian. The powerful sense, what's more, of exceptionalism created by its unique urban layout and corresponding relationship with the lagoon and the wider Adriatic beyond might have helped to keep alien influences at a distance. Yet the whole essence of its survival has been based, from the outset, on a gift for absorbing and transmuting whatever is foreign, exotic and distant, so that these elements come to form part of a singular discourse bringing vigour, sophistication and singularity to the place itself and the experience of those who live there.

There are times indeed when, looking about us at the Venetian scene, we end up with an impression that almost everything in front of our eyes belongs somewhere else than to an actual Venice. The Piazzetta's two tall columns, the four bronze horses on the façade of San Marco, the carved ensemble of the Diadochi on the south side of the basilica nearest Palazzo Ducale were all of them brought here from Byzantium. The decoration surrounding medieval doors and windows – and often the very shape of these – has an obvious ancestry in the architectural language of the Islamic world, while the great marble lions outside the main gateway of the Arsenale were looted from Greek sites boasting remains of classical cities and shrines. Tuscan artists created the graceful loggetta of the Campanile in Piazza San Marco, designed the staircase and reading room of the Biblioteca Marciana next to it and sculpted the thunderously imposing equestrian statue of Bartolomeo Colleoni outside Santi Giovanni e Paolo. The cast-iron lamp standards came from Austria-Hungary, the railway was built using technology and materials from England and a Spanish architect devised the most recent of the Grand Canal's four bridges. Even Saint

Mark, that numinous figure whose presence sealed Venetian identity for ever more, is an incomer, his body brought from far-off Alexandria by Arabic-speaking merchants.

We catch this Venetian delight in otherness from paintings by its Renaissance artists. Jacopo Tintoretto's image of Buono and Rustico spiriting away the saint's remains conveys this sensation vividly in its juxtaposition of a phantasmal architecture in the background with a strikingly authentic camel at the centre of the canvas, signifying Egypt for the viewer. At the Scuola di San Giorgio, meanwhile, Vittore Carpaccio shapes for us some of the best-loved of all eastward glances through western eyes in his scenes from the life of Saint George which include a fully equipped band of Turkish musicians and the exotic backdrop of an Oriental court full of parrots and giraffes. Elsewhere, at more or less the same period – the earliest decades of the sixteenth century – Gentile Bellini and Giovanni Mansueti were recording still more accurate glimpses of Mamluk Damascus and Alexandria, with kufic inscriptions, domed mosques and carefully differentiated turbans so as to render the spectacle suitably genuine for the curious onlooker.

By the time we reach the *vedutisti* – view painters – of Venice's last great burst of painterly exuberance during the late Baroque and Rococo eras, it is taken for granted that the crowds along the waterfront beyond the Piazzetta will feature a scatter of exotic figures, patently non-European from the hang of their robes and the shape of their headgear. Venice in the age of Canaletto, Carlevarijs and Guardi was enjoying its latest incarnation as the resort of foreign travellers, having lost its primacy as a commercial port though a cosmopolite spirit still charged the overall atmosphere. One of the most enchanting musical works from this period, *Le Carnaval de Venise* (1696), an opera-ballet by the French composer André Campra to a libretto by the dramatist Jean-François Regnard, puts this on stage to striking effect in its light-hearted story of amorous intrigues among a youthful quartet of Parisian tourists. They visit an opera house, try their luck at the Ridotto, Venice's most frequented gambling hall, and become swept up in the seasonal round of masking and festivity. While the two heroines Léonore and Isabelle are plotting in Piazza San Marco to deceive their lovers Léandre and Rodolphe, 'a company of Bohemians, Armenians and Sclavonians with guitars enters to enjoy the carnival', cue for a song-and-dance episode in 'this peaceful abode within the bosom of the sea'. When, at the very end of the work, the genius of Carnival appears in person, sung by a bass soloist, he leads 'a troop of maskers of different nationalities'. While nowadays we might sombrely see Campra's opera as a harbinger of twenty-first-century Venice's surrender to saturation tourism, it can also be taken as reflecting that mixture of outlandish influences, modes and idioms which formed such an essential component of La Serenissima's *raison d'être* from the very beginning.

So much of her trade depended, after all, on the market for Oriental spices to which, for almost six centuries, she held the key in Europe. Egypt, more especially Alexandria, provided the crucial entry point from the Indian Ocean for this kind of trade and, as noted in the previous chapter, it played an indirect but highly important role in directing the agenda of the Fourth Crusade. So too did ports and major inland cities of the Levant like Acre, Beirut and Damascus, where the Republic maintained extensive warehouses and ensured that its commercial interests were substantially represented. Gaining a foothold on the island of Crete, following the discreditable venture of 1204, the Venetians could turn this to advantage (despite sporadic revolts by the Cretans themselves against colonial dominance), making the major cities of Heraklion, Rethymnon and Canea into valuable staging posts along the sea route to and from the East. At the same time a growing trade war with Genoa during the thirteenth century saw Venetian merchants seeking a large share of the market along the coast of the Black Sea, where many of the overland spice caravans reached their terminus.

Spice was not simply a luxury add-on for the kitchens of medieval Europe but regarded as a key necessity in the preservation of food, whether to enhance a quickly vanishing flavour or, in frequent instances, for concealing biological decay. During the so-called Islamic Golden Age – the five centuries from 750 to 1250 – many of the recipes and techniques for using these precious commodities in the household had arrived in the West either from Moorish Spain or via the merchants, many of them Venetian, who brought them to market from the eastern Mediterranean. As for the spices themselves, these had already made some amazing journeys before being traded in the shops and warehouses of the Rialto, Venice's fast-expanding commercial heart. Though cumin, for example, is mentioned in the Bible and began to be used amid the ancient civilizations of the Middle Eastern fertile crescent and though the culture of coriander is probably even older, dating back to the Hittite cities of Anatolia in the third millennium BCE, others like ginger, cinnamon and cloves travelled far further to the holds of Venetian ships. The ginger plant's knobbly rhizomes, originally growing wild in the forests of western China, had been carried along the Silk Roads into India and Persia, where it was cultivated for sale to Western merchants. Cinnamon, which the ancient Egyptians had used for embalming the dead as mummies, came from the bark of trees grown around the Indian Ocean in Bengal, Sri Lanka and Myanmar, while cloves had an even more exotic provenance in the south-east Asian islands of the Moluccas, Banda, Ternate and Tidore.

The value of these, together with cardamom, nutmeg, mace and the universally prized varieties of pepper, was enhanced by their portability and the simple fact that none of them degraded easily during a long voyage. They could be bagged and stored with confidence since the usual vermin in ships' holds or merchant godowns had no special love for their flavours or scents. What mattered to the Venetians most of all was to ensure that the trade routes to the Mediterranean and the Black Sea ports were kept open, while at the same time safeguarding the secrecy in that chain of mercantile interchanges reaching, in some cases, halfway across the globe. As in so many other areas of Venetian life, confidentiality, keeping precious information secure and operating away from the inquisitive scrutiny of a public sphere, was vital to the success of La Serenissima as an independent going concern. While a veritable army of clerks, accountants and civil servants recorded details of everything from a tax demand to a government corruption enquiry, the written material itself, sedulously labelled, dated and classified, remained inaccessible except to privileged eyes within specific departments of the state. This amalgam of clerical meticulousness and a universal habit of privacy across all official channels of administration built up, over the centuries, what constitutes one of the richest historical archives surviving until the present time.

Trade in spices, like that in other commodities, had its own rhythms and seasons. A Venetian merchant gifted with any sort of professional expertise needed to know not just what his ship could carry in terms of volume and quality, but when exactly it could set out and how long the voyage ought to take. Alexandria and Constantinople required a basic twenty days, Beirut perhaps a week longer and a Black Sea destination like Trebizond more time still. The system, for such indeed it became, depended on the arrival of trading fleets from across the Indian Ocean in the ports of the Persian Gulf and along the Red Sea. Thence the precious cargoes could be loaded onto camel caravans and taken overland, so that buyers from Venice could meet them in the crucial autumn months when purchasing mostly took place. The importance of this seasonal timing (the Indian merchants inevitably depended on monsoon winds to carry them westwards to Arabia) was matched by a need, once arrived in harbour, for the Venetians to feel safe beneath the umbrella of whatever rights and privileges might have been granted them by local rulers. In this context we should look at a painting dated 1511, by a follower of Gentile Bellini, now in the Louvre gallery in Paris, showing the visit to Damascus of a Venetian embassy to the Mamluk sultan's viceroy. The anonymous artist plainly has some first-hand experience of the city and is eager to convey the scene as accurately as possible, but this image is more than just a colourful essay in Renaissance Orientalism. Commemorated here is the peaceful resolution of a potentially harmful episode, in which the Shah of Persia had sought to enlist the two Venetian consuls in Damascus, Pietro Zen and Tommaso Contarini, in a plot against the sultan. When the viceroy discovered this, he had them imprisoned, revoked the merchant community's privileges and confiscated its goods. Only the dexterity of diplomatic intercession by a special envoy, Domenico Trevisan, sent from Venice to Cairo, managed to settle the situation, with Zen and Contarini released and the resident Venetians in Damascus restored to the most-favoured-nation status they formerly enjoyed.

Diplomacy of this kind became a specialized technique within the Venetian state machine, with the Republic's ambassadors developing an extreme sophistication in the field. Their extensive reports on foreign affairs are some of the most valuable historical sources available, especially during the Middle Ages and the Renaissance. Even when La Serenissima underwent a notable decline in power and political significance, it was Venetian diplomatic finesse that helped to broker international peace treaties such as those of Westphalia in 1648 and Utrecht in 1712, though Venice herself had not been an active participant in the wars each of these brought to a close. At the root of this ambassadorial enterprise lay the priorities of the merchant class from which these accomplished envoys sprang. Negotiation, the art of give and take, the skills required to bargain, make offers, feign indifference, hold back concessions until the crucial moment and sustain an atmosphere of harmony and encouragement whatever the circumstances, these were all acquired in the marketplace and never forgotten, even when the patrician class to which an ambassador belonged had renounced its direct involvement in trade several generations previously.

This opportune blurring of lines between merchant and diplomat plays a part in the story of one of the best known of all Venetians, a man whose name is so resoundingly synonymous with travelling and crossing continents that it has been proudly bestowed on Venice's own

overleaf The reception of the Venetian ambassadors in Damascus, 1511, as depicted by a follower of Gentile Bellini. The Venetian state possessed diplomatic skills of a high order.

airport. He was someone whom at first few people believed when, returning to the city after more than twenty years' absence, he told his tales of eastern kingdoms and unknown seas, of an island full of gold, others rich in spices, sandalwood, ambergris and frankincense, of an emperor who hunted cranes on the back of an elephant, lined his tents with sable fur and kept ten thousand concubines, of a unicorn with hair like a buffalo and feet like an elephant's, of people who drank fermented mare's milk and wine made from rice, of sledges pulled by dogs, bats as big as goshawks and of a little deer in the province of Tangut, beyond the desert of Lop, from which a tiny sac of blood beneath the belly produces the finest musk in the world. That he was not, indeed, lying or fantasizing became more obvious when later on he was taken prisoner by the Genoese and recounted his travels to a fellow captive, who helped him to turn the material into a coherent literary narrative. The ghostwriter's name was Rustichello of Pisa. The man whose stories and memories he collated and worked up was Marco Polo.

Rustichello appears to have been well versed in the French courtly culture of his era, the late thirteenth century. His book, called in the earliest surviving manuscript *Le Divisament dou Monde*, is indeed written in French and cast in the form of a prose romance, using the tropes and conventions – 'Let it be known', 'What can I say?' etcetera – familiar to readers of the genre. In addition the writer has no scruples as to framing particular events from Marco's narrative within passages adapted from earlier retellings of Arthurian chivalric legends, let alone as to inserting various fables regarding the Far East which could be found in European and Islamic sources. To confuse the issue of authenticity still further, the sixteenth-century geographer Giambattista Ramusio, including the work in his *Navigationi e Viaggi* of 1550, printed a version apparently based on a Latin manuscript derived from a much more substantial first text by Rustichello that has since disappeared.

What shines through, despite Rustichello's embellishments, is the distinctive voice of someone who was clearly the real Marco Polo, practical, resourceful, intensely observant and always alert to potential opportunities for trade wherever he should find himself. It is this perspective above all which tells us why Polo deserves to be believed. Objections such as the fact that he failed to mention the Chinese custom, introduced during the tenth century, of binding women's feet so as to enhance their grace and social status are not valid when we bear in mind that he spent long enough in China for him to take such an aspect of daily life for granted. In recalling his eastern travels, Polo

Medieval Venice in a fourteenth-century manuscript illustration for Marco Polo's *Travels*. Marco, his father and his uncle are portrayed on the brink of their departure from Venice (1271) on an epic journey to Asia.

focused on what he felt would most interest his own community, in a city whose economic survival depended on its inhabitants' willingness to undertake long journeys in search of profit and financial advantage.

Maybe he and his companions, members of his own family, had never quite intended to go as far as they eventually succeeded in doing or to cover such a wide range of terrains and microclimates. It is hard not to feel, as we read what are nowadays known as *The Travels of Marco Polo*, that the peculiar doggedness and grit characteristic of the Venetian spirit played a major part in the whole venture. Some time around the year 1260 two brothers, Niccolo and Maffio Polo, based in Constantinople, set out across the Black Sea towards the Crimean port city of Sudak, a place of exchange for beaver and squirrel furs from Russia and for textiles brought from Western Europe by the Venetians and the Genoese. The town had lately fallen under control of the Tartars, a Turkic people who had joined the victorious westward onslaught of the Mongols which convulsed the whole of Christendom at this time. Though both the Roman Catholic and Orthodox churches blasted the Mongol hordes as 'the scourge of God's wrath, bursting, as it were, from Hell's most secret regions' (the words are those of Pope Alexander IV, writing in that same year of 1260), Italian merchants beadily identified potential new markets among a people whose rulers might grant them useful privileges.

The Polo brothers had a sibling, also called Marco, already based in Sudak and the three of them set off northwards into Russia to visit Barka Khan, leader of the Tartar horde, taking precious gemstones with them, and met with an encouraging reception. We are not told what the 'goods of fully twice the value' were which they received in return, but Rustichello notes that they were able to sell them very profitably. Heading home to Sudak, on the other hand, proved less easy because of a war breaking out between Barka and the Mongol Khan Hulagu. Moving eastwards the Venetians reached the great city of Bukhara (in modern Turkmenistan) where a Mongol envoy persuaded them to accompany him all the way to the court of Hulagu's brother Kubilai, 'the Great Khan', effectively emperor of China, in Beijing. Here, according to the ambassador, they would be received with honour, though being what Rustichello calls 'Latins' they would also be objects of serious curiosity, not least to Kubilai himself. With nothing to lose by the journey, the Polo brothers set off with their guide, having taken due care, while in Bukhara, 'to gain a good understanding of the Tartar language'. So gratifying was their treatment along the route and the welcome offered them by Kubilai that they happily stayed several years in China before being sent as his ambassadors to the pope. Their task was to beg His Holiness for missionaries to be sent who could explain the truths of Christianity to the Great Khan and bring him consecrated oil from the Holy Sepulchre in Jerusalem.

Once again the return trip had its frustrations. When at length they arrived in the Crusader port of Acre, it was to discover that Pope Clement IV had recently died and that a conclave which had been in session for many months was still not ready to choose his successor. Determined to keep their word, the Polo brothers left Kubilai's messages with Teobaldo Visconti, papal legate in the Holy Land, before heading back to Venice to await the outcome in Rome. It was to be another two years before Visconti himself, a rare example of a secular candidate for St Peter's throne, was named pope, as Gregory X, and the Polo brothers could make the voyage back to Acre with at least two of the invited missionaries accompanying them. A much more significant member of this expedition, it would turn out, was Niccolo Polo's seventeen-year-old son, christened Marco like the good Venetian he was.

The two missionary friars, soon daunted by the rigours of the impending journey, headed homewards, leaving the Polos to continue along more or less the same route they had followed earlier from Bukhara. This time the weather was against them, so that it took almost four years before they arrived in China. Showing them every condescension, the Great Khan was particularly struck by the presence of young Marco. 'If this youth lives to manhood,' declared Kubilai, 'then he cannot fail to prove himself a person of good judgment and true worthiness.'

As indeed he did. That Venetian diplomatic know-how, an adaptability to circumstance, an instinct for the main chance and an evident readiness to make himself agreeable to those around him all seemed to work in Marco's favour. Kubilai perhaps saw the young man's alienness as a particular asset when he needed somebody to send on missions beyond the frontiers of his empire. As a foreigner Polo would attract attention and respect, representing a species of living trophy for the Great Khan, powerful enough, it must seem, to employ a man from the other side of the world as his emissary. What the Khan valued most of all – and what posterity has prized ever since – was Marco's retentiveness in memorializing and archiving whatever he felt would be of value while travelling through Asia. 'He continued', says Rustichello, 'to bring back reports of many new and curious things, and observed more of the characteristics of this part of the world than anybody else, since he travelled more extensively than anybody ever born, and also since he applied himself more closely to observing such things.'

Understandably, however, the three Polos – Marco, father Niccolo and uncle Maffio – grew impatient to see Venice again or just to get as far along the homeward route as those Levantine cities where so much of their adult life as merchants had been spent. The one major problem lay in that very same princely favour and proud possessiveness through which Kubilai had enabled them to flourish as ornaments in his vast entourage. 'Time and again they asked for the Khan's permission to depart, but so attached to them and delighted by their company had he become that nothing could persuade him to yield on this point.' It was only when Kubilai's great-nephew Arghun sent envoys to ask him for a suitably exalted Mongol princess in marriage that a chance finally presented itself for the Venetians to leave. Arghun's messengers took it into their heads to ask the Polos to go with them. The bride, named Kokachin, having been selected and a sea voyage rather than an overland journey having been decided on for security reasons, the Khan reluctantly gave his leave.

Somewhere in the Persian Gulf the voyage ended but by the time Princess Kokachin was delivered to the court of her prospective husband he had died, so she was married off to his son instead. Like everyone else she had grown attached to the Polos and 'you must know', says Rustichello in his prologue to the *Travels*, 'that when they left her to return to their own land, she wept for sadness at their departure'. Go nevertheless they did, eventually arriving at Trebizond and journeying home via Constantinople and Venice's Greek colony of Negroponte (modern Evvia) to reach Venice at last in the year 1295. According to Giambattista Ramusio, who may either be embroidering plain facts or relying on two centuries of oral tradition, their families at first failed to recognize them, more especially because of the travel-stained clothes they wore. When a homecoming banquet was hastily arranged, the three Polos still insisted on wearing these ragged old robes until, at an agreed moment, they all stood up and tore open the linings to scatter pearls, emeralds and rubies across the table. True or false, this story has a satisfying arc to it, since it was as traders in gemstones that they had first moved eastwards all those years before.

Does Marco Polo deserve the acclaim and respect he has received ever since? He was not the first Western visitor to a Mongol court: in 1245 Pope Innocent IV had dispatched Father Giovanni de Pian de Carpini on a mission to Kubilai's cousin Kuyuk Khan and eight years later King Louis IX of France sent the Franciscan Guillaume de Rubruquis to 'the lands of the Tartars', both European rulers in hopes of gaining Christian converts to aid them on crusade. The *Travels* are not strictly Polo's own work, having been transcribed and collated by his fellow prisoner, the courtly, French-speaking Rustichello of Pisa. Nor is the resulting book anything like a travel narrative in our modern understanding of the term. Occasionally Marco himself obtrudes in the first person, 'I, Marco', but this is purely so as to authenticate, from his own experience, something he fancies the reader may be inclined to doubt. Today's readers may get impatient, by the same token, with his particular absorptions, more especially with the paganism of those, Mongols, Chinese, Indians, Malays, among whom his wanderings led him. Phrases like 'the inhabitants are idolaters' occur frequently enough, while Marco's attitude to ethnic religions is less that of the curious anthropologist than that of a detached or else frankly nauseated spectator.

The fact is, nevertheless, that whatever Rustichello may have added by way of narrative grace notes to his material as retailed by Marco Polo, the book remains a highly individual and absorbing achievement and a major document in the context of East–West relations during the Middle Ages. There's a sense, what is more, that Marco felt that it all needed to be written down before the details faded altogether. What strikes us at once, on beginning the account itself, following Rustichello's introduction, is the singular precision of Marco's memory. Doubtless the tedium of imprisonment in a Genoese gaol had allowed him time to gather his recollections and focus adequately on a variety of different topics. The sheer clarity with which he summons up details of circumstances, location, lifestyle and atmosphere is extraordinary, even if we reflect that he and his contemporaries relied far more than we do now on powers of memorizing.

First and foremost, the work is conceived from the point of view of an experienced traveller offering practical wisdom to those coming after him. Take, for instance, the fourth chapter, describing a journey from Beijing southwards across China, through the province of Yunnan and eventually into the Indian region of Bengal. We are not told why Marco was sent on this mission by Kubilai Khan or to whom in particular, but as with every other trip recorded in these pages, the Venetian was on reconnaissance, eyes wide open for whatever his master might need to hear but equally alert to anything useful for merchant venturers following in his footsteps. The city of Cho-chan, for example, produces gold, silk and the kind of fine fabric known as sendal, and has good inns for travellers. Tai-yuan-fu is surrounded by mulberry orchards for silk production and has vineyards nearby for making wine. The country on either side of the River Kara-moran is famous for its ginger plantations, its stout bamboo canes and an amazing profusion of birds – 'three pheasants can be bought for a single Venetian groat'.

Now and then on this expedition Marco pauses to retail an incident from past history or a glimpse of local customs. At the castle of Kaichu he elaborates on the figure of the Golden King, who was 'only attended by beautiful young damsels, of which he kept many around him' and was drawn around his palace grounds in a chariot pulled by several of these handmaids, 'ministers in every way to solace and please him'. In Tibet Polo makes a detailed note of the inhabitants' curious preparations for marriage. 'No man will ever take a virgin for his wife, since a woman is held to be worthless unless she has a thorough knowledge of men.' Thus when travellers are approaching, mothers from surrounding villages bring their daughters to wherever the camp is pitched and call upon the strangers to take them and have intercourse, which they do, choosing the girls who best please them, while the rest go home disconsolate. The young women remain with the travellers, who may not take them away when they leave but will give them some kind of token to show, when at length they marry, that they are sufficiently experienced. 'In this way custom will demand each girl to wear over a score of such adornments around her neck, showing she has had many lovers. When a wife is taken thus she is most highly esteemed.' To this arresting account Marco – or maybe it was Rustichello – cannot resist adding the comment 'Obviously this country is a fine place to visit for a young lad of sixteen to twenty-four.'

Effectively Marco Polo's book bucks our modern stereotype of the medieval traveller, of the kind represented by Sir John Mandeville or the creator of the Hereford Cathedral Mappa Mundi, with its sciapods, Blemmyes and troglodytes and its cosmological focus on elements from the Bible such as Noah's Ark or the Garden of Eden. Polo has been and seen: the prevailing emphasis throughout his narrative is on his first-hand experience or, failing this, on as accurate and detailed a report as he can gather. Its unique value is enhanced for us when we look at the context of travel records being produced on a similar scale during this period, the era of the Crusades from the twelfth to the fourteenth centuries. Apart from the interesting accounts of their Mongol missions by the Franciscan friars mentioned earlier, most of these are by Muslim or Jewish writers such as Ibn Battuta, Ibn Jubayr or Benjamin of Tudela. *The Travels of Marco Polo* is notable for its substance, the quality of its detail and the real sense of a personal, selective view at the heart of the story it unfolds.

To anyone looking closely at the history of Venice at this time the *Travels* are significant from a purely Venetian aspect. Though Polo hardly mentions his native city during the course of the book, save when assessing the weight or price of a given commodity, he connects the modern reader significantly with the priorities, attitudes and aspirations of a medieval Venetian engaged in the principal activity which kept his city alive, the buying and selling of goods across the globe. Hence Marco is not primarily a teller of tales, a dispenser of wonders and marvels, bent on harrowing our imaginations with the amazing or the bizarre, even if elements of all this enter his discourse. What he seeks to recount first and foremost is the wealth of practical details as to natural resources, saleable commodities, climate, local customs and the lie of the land along particular routes, all of which will prove useful for a profitable merchant venture by those who come after him. Thus the *Travels* assume even greater importance as we encounter the mentality and world view of a medieval Venetian at the moment when his fast-expanding city was seeking to establish her absolute primacy in the Mediterranean commercial sphere, competing or eventually in direct conflict with similarly ambitious Italian republics.

When the Polos returned to Venice after twenty-odd years and scattered their jewels across that banquet table, they were still only half believed. Marco's travel talk, with its emphasis on immense sums and vast quantities of this or that, in proportion, as it were, to the huge distances he had covered, was listened to with a certain cynicism, whence arose his nickname of 'El Milion' from the seemingly continuous pitch of exaggeration that littered his anecdotes. This sobriquet later figured in an official document and occurs in the title of the first Italian version of his book. The Piedmontese friar Jacopo di Acqui, in his *Chronica sive imago mundi* (1330), which incorporates lost sections of the *Travels*, says that Marco, while lying on his deathbed, affirmed the truth of all his claims, declaring that there was much more he might have added.

Released from the Genoese prison in which he had beguiled a year's confinement by telling his story to Rustichello, Marco came home again to Venice, where his family had bought a palace close to the little church of San Giovanni Grisostomo. In 1300, aged forty-six, he married Donata Badoer, daughter of a fellow merchant, and the pair had three daughters. Content with managing his share of the family

CORTE SECONDA
DEL MILION

business, he was not prompted to begin travelling again. From the evidence of his will, made just before he died in 1324, he seems to have lived prosperously and generously, able to leave bequests to various guilds and religious houses, including the convent of San Lorenzo, where he was buried. Among these legacies was one to the Tartar slave, christened Pietro, whom he probably brought back from his sojourn in China and now formally set free.

Marco's journey and his book about it were his most enduring gifts to Venice, an inspiration to other travellers (including, at one stage, Christopher Columbus) as also to astronomers, geographers and map-makers. Little trace of him survives, on the other hand, within the city's built environment. San Lorenzo was reconstructed in 1592, with Polo's sarcophagus removed in the process. The church, an enormous brick barn, was closed after damage during the Great War and remains inaccessible. A slightly battered marble plaque beside San Giovanni Grisostomo reminds us of his original achievement. Nearby, close to Teatro Malibran, is all that survives, in the shape of Byzantine arches, Gothic windows and ancient beams, of the Polo family palace. This gloomy, dank, rather squalid little courtyard, connecting the *campo* outside the theatre to a bridge bearing Marco Polo's name that spans a small canal, is still called Corte Seconda del Milion. If there was a Corte Prima it has long since disappeared.

The claim made by Marco Polo as he lay dying that he had so much more to tell was a spur in itself to Venetians across later centuries. Any history of the ways in which the globe opened itself up to Western exploration, adventure and curiosity will reveal a host of such wanderers beyond the confines of the lagoon, driven as much by the stir-craziness and cabin fever engendered by its limited spaces as by a hard nose for business opportunity. We find Venetians sailing with the Spanish conquistadors Pizarro, Balboa and Cortez to South America, voyaging with Portuguese merchants to India or with Catholic missionaries to Japan, China and the Far East. They are not in any of these places as the Serene Republic's official representatives, neither do they seek, when awarded special trading privileges, to make these a basis for territorial empire-building. The values they carry with them are those shared by their fellow citizens, those of resilience, inquisitiveness and an ability to make the best out of the most limited and unpromising resources.

Armed with all these, it was a young patrician from fifteenth-century Venice, Alvise da Mosto, known to history as 'Cadamosto', who showed the Portuguese that route down West Africa's coastline that ultimately encouraged them to round the Cape of Good Hope

All that remains of Marco Polo's Venetian palace – located in a little square, the Corte Seconda del Milion, not far from the Church of San Giovanni Grisostomo.

and sail on towards India and the Spice Islands. A member of the Da Mosto clan, with its palace on the Grand Canal, close to the Rialto, Alvise was barely into his teens before he joined *colleganza* voyages to Crete and Alexandria, even journeying as far as the ports of Flanders to bring home the fine textiles being woven in Bruges, Mechlin and Courtrai. Family disgrace involving a bribery scandal which drove his father into exile in Istria saw the young man looking to set up on his own account as a merchant and it was while sheltering from bad weather on Portugal's Algarve shore that he met Prince Henry, known to history as 'the Navigator', whose obsession was with exploring Africa beyond the Equator and the Sahara. In 1455, aged twenty-three, Cadamosto set off on a momentous voyage to Senegal and the estuary of the River Gambia.

He had Marco Polo's gifts of alertness to detail, a mind uncluttered by dogma or presumption and singular powers of memory and observation. Everything grabbed his interest, from the geopolitics and strategic manoeuvres of western Africa's kingdoms and statelets to the ways in which precious commodities such as gold and salt were moved hundreds of miles along caravan routes through the Sahara Desert and the great empire of Mali. He caught the essential rhythms of life in villages along the Senegal and Gambia rivers, noting differences in tribal custom, trading habits, the music he heard and the dances he watched. Cadamosto was equally fascinated by the wildlife and flora of the forests, savannahs and semi-desert regions around him, writing one of the first European descriptions of a hippopotamus and going so far as to taste the flesh of a recently slaughtered elephant, whose foot he later brought home and presented to the Duchess of Burgundy.

The two voyages of Alvise Cadamosto – he began preparations for his second trip almost as soon as he got back to Portugal – proved crucial in expanding a Portuguese commercial reach into Africa and added substantially to the contemporary European awareness of the whole area's geography and navigational features. Somewhere around 1460 he was able to return to Venice to recover both his family's lost credit and its financial standing, enough to acquire various key appointments as a diplomat and administrator for the Republic in Dalmatia and northern Italy. After his death in 1483, his travel narratives, known to historians as the *Navigazioni*, were published as part of a collection of voyages whose title translates as 'Countries Newly Discovered, Along with the New-World, So-Called by Amerigo Vespucci', containing the earliest account of mainland America. Despite attempts by Portuguese nationalist historians, during the Salazar dictatorship of the mid-twentieth century, to claim that the itinerant Venetian had cribbed his information from sources in their own language, it now looks as if Cadamosto was indeed writing about what he knew at first hand and that the *Navigazioni* make him a worthy heir of Marco Polo.

The anthology in which they first appeared was printed in 1507 in Vicenza, by then a flourishing centre of Venetian rule over the *terraferma*. One of those who surely read them, as he had read Marco Polo, was young Antonio Pigafetta, born here in 1485 but receiving his education in Venice. At some stage, as a member of a Vicentine noble family, he had become a Knight of Malta and gained his baptism of fire during one of that order's battles against the Turks. In 1519 he was sent to Barcelona as part of an embassy from Pope Leo X to Emperor Charles V, who gave him permission to join a voyage setting forth from Seville for the Spice Islands, the Moluccas, on the other side of the globe. The expedition's leader was a Portuguese nobleman, Fernao Magalhaes, who had already gained wide experience of the East in Sumatra and Ceylon. Disgruntled at the lack of interest shown by King Manoel of Portugal in his proposal for an argosy sailing westwards rather than east to the islands, Magalhaes – Magellan as history knows him – left for Spain, where Emperor Charles eagerly backed the project in hopes of challenging Portuguese domination over the precious spice trade.

Antonio Pigafetta joined the flotilla as its chronicler and secretary. At first he and Magellan reacted warily to one another but eventually developed a mutual respect, with Pigafetta coming genuinely to admire the indomitable strength of character with which his 'captain general' confronted hostile natives, saw off an attempted mutiny and piloted his little fleet through the hazards of Cape Horn into the vast, hitherto uncharted ocean he named 'the Pacific'. Magellan in his turn appreciated and encouraged Pigafetta's curiosity as to the cultures and traditions of the different peoples they encountered, which led to his habit of compiling an extensive glossary for each local language heard along coasts and islands from Patagonia to the Philippines.

In this latter archipelago catastrophe befell the expedition, during what its members all now knew to be a pioneering journey, conducted as it was without any kind of map or much in the way of navigational aids. Magellan, like most of his crew, was devoutly Catholic and got to work, while in the Philippines, on trying to bring the islanders to Christianity. A number of local rulers willingly accepted his missionary activity, but Rajah Data Lapulapu of Mactan held out, to a point at which Magellan decided that some show of force might be necessary,

overleaf The Cantino Planisphere, a world map smuggled from
Portugal to Italy by Alberto Cantino, agent of Duke Ercole
of Ferrara, in 1502, and showing the latest Portuguese discoveries.

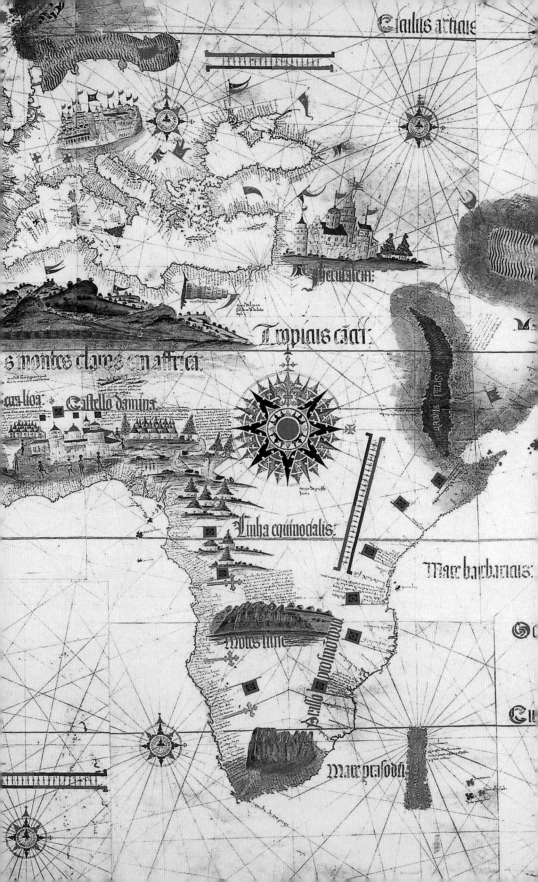

though not until he had tried a little more argument and persuasion. Landing on Mactan with fifty men, some armed with muskets and crossbows, he was met by a force Pigafetta calculates at 'over fifteen hundred persons, charging at us with furious cries'. Trying to calm the situation, Magellan told his followers not to shoot, until the hostile islanders began hurling their spears, when he gave orders to burn the huts nearest the beach. A cutlass knocked his helmet off, a spear disabled his sword arm and before he could retrieve the lance needed to ward off another attacker he was stabbed in the leg, brought down and hacked to death. Rajah Lapulapu gave orders that what remained of the man Pigafetta calls 'our mirror, our light, our comfort and true guide' was to be kept as a trophy of war.

Regrouping, the expedition headed southwards towards the Moluccas, where its two ships were expecting to load a cargo of spices. When one of them, the *Trinidad*, began taking on water, its crew joined the *Victoria*, whose hold was later stuffed with a precious freight of cloves, and the solitary vessel limped homewards across the Indian Ocean and around the Cape of Good Hope, arriving in Seville's harbour of Sanlúcar de Barrameda on 6 September 1522. Of the original 270 men on the voyage 'there were left only eighteen of us, mostly sick', says Pigafetta, before adding proudly, 'From the time we left this place until our return, we had sailed 14,460 leagues and more, completing the entire circle of the world from sunrise to sunset.' The next day such of the little crew as could manage it walked barefoot, wearing only their shirts and carrying torches, to offer thanks and prayers at shrines to the Blessed Virgin. Afterwards Pigafetta hastened to Emperor Charles's court at Valladolid, 'to present him, neither with gold nor with silver, but with the things that such a worthy gentleman knew how to appreciate', including a copy of the unique record left to us of this amazing journey, the earliest such ever known. Three years later Pigafetta published, in Venice, his *Relazione del primo viaggio intorno al mondo*, offering its dedicatee, Philippe Villiers de L'Isle Adam, Grand Master of the Knights of Malta, 'my little book describing all the watches, fatigues and wanderings of my voyage'. In its fusion of reportage, travel diary, humanist speculation, natural history and anthropology, Pigafetta's *Relazione* would have made Marco Polo, a spiritual ancestor of his, extremely proud.

THE CRISIS OF
CONTROL

From that very same China to which Marco Polo, his father and uncle journeyed in the thirteenth century there derived a distinctive feature of the Venetian hierarchical system, a visual signifier which would endure until La Serenissima's extinction in 1797 and one which set its governing echelons apart from those of other Italian states. This was the adoption of particular kinds of official robe – a toga as it was often called, in reference to the Republic's notional roots in Roman antiquity – which identified the wearer's rank and status. These garments, with their differing sleeve lengths, colours and trimmings, reflected the influence both of the Byzantine court in Constantinople and, more indirectly, that of Chinese and Mongol emperors further east, at the end of the Silk Roads. In Venetian art we see them resplendent in the paintings of Titian and Veronese and in the many senatorial images created for grand Venetian families during the seventeenth century, when the plethora of such full-length canvases seems to swell in inverse proportion to the Republic's importance on the international political scene.

The arts of luxury textile weaving, especially those involved in the making of velvet and brocade, developed in Venice through its contacts with the Greek empire in mercantile centres like Patras, Thebes and Corinth, the Aegean island of Andros and the peninsula of Euboea, acquired by the Republic after the sack of Constantinople in 1204 and known to Venetians as Negroponte. In such places mulberry trees were grown for the silk thread brought to Venice to be woven into fine fabric for the splendid official togas of *procuratori, provveditori* and members of the several councils carrying on the business of state. From much further afield, along the shores of the Caspian Sea, from Azerbaijan and Georgia, there came a whole range of other silks, the *mercadascia*, the *inrea*, the *colusmia de Soldania*, while from China itself there arrived that prized variety known as *cattuia* or *captovia*, derived from the name 'Cathay' given to that region.

A major boost to the industry in Venice was contributed by the growth, during the thirteenth century, of a community of merchants and artificers from the little Tuscan republic of Lucca, itself rich from trading fine textiles with France. Establishing their warehouses in the Cannaregio district of the city, the Lucchesi introduced the specialist techniques centred on the making of so-called *panni tartarici*, 'Tartar cloths', interweaving the silk with gold thread and making use of traditional Chinese patterns incorporating floral designs, broad leaves and sprays and sometimes dragons, animals and birds. In the same part of Venice, along Fondamenta Contarini, close to the church of Madonna del Orto, we can find a sculpted tribute, in the form of a marble relief on the medieval Palazzo Mastelli, to the prosperity brought through this same precious material. It shows a turbaned man leading a camel, bearing one of the typical oblong corded bales in which the silk began its journey across land and sea to the looms of Venetian weavers.

The gorgeous brocade from these workshops became a key socio-political signifier for its wearers, more especially since Venice, like other medieval states, operated a strict series of sumptuary laws decreeing what garments, colours and materials were appropriate for the different classes of society. By the close of the thirteenth century the Serene Republic had succeeded in evolving the hierarchical structure in which, more or less unaltered, it would go forward for the next few centuries until its Napoleonic dissolution. Questions not merely of class, power and influence were involved here but issues of governance within the city and throughout the empire, as well as principles as to what those holding office owed to the state in terms of duty and responsibility. Whether the latter were actually honoured was another matter: part of Venice's mythical construct of itself required a belief that such ideals would be taken for granted among its governors.

To achieve this process of executive consolidation entailed power struggles sometimes so bitter and traumatic that the memory of them would never be allowed to fade, enshrined as it became within the historical traditions through which La Serenissima nurtured a sense of cohesion among her subjects. While this was all in progress, we should note, Venice was plunged into a desperate fight for survival against her biggest commercial competitor, the maritime republic of Genoa, and suffered a visitation, in 1348–9, of the Black Death that killed two thirds of the city's population.

At the apex of Venetian government, since Orso Ipato in 726 became the first to assume the title, sat the doge, officially the dux, the duke, leader of the state in peace and war. Though the office was elective, it could not be resigned except under circumstances of ill health or, as happened in one case, of extreme piety. The chosen wearer of the *corno dogale* and ermine-trimmed robe was expected to die while still *en poste*. Such a title was not supposed to be hereditary, though, as we have seen, some of the earliest doges had clearly aimed at achieving this for their families. By virtue of his oath on taking office, what is more, the holder of this supreme title had become increasingly restricted from personal initiatives of any sort through a series of sanctions applied over the years by senior counsellors to ensure that nothing in the way of corruption, peculation or bribery should be allowed to taint the integrity his role embodied. A doge was forbidden to make contact with alien rulers unless authorized by the Senate, he was bound to keep all the deepest confidences regarding government manoeuvres and negotiations to himself, and he was strictly enjoined to refuse any sort of gift except the token presents offered in the course

A fragment of the fine brocade in whose production medieval
Venice excelled.

of that multitude of processions and celebratory church services which his function required that he attend. Most important article of all in this contract of service to the state – for that was what, in the end, his oath and its terms amounted to – was a clause expressly barring the doge, whether in sound health or on his deathbed, from naming relatives or friends as his successors. His wife, styled the dogaressa (or earlier the *ducissa*), had to make several similar undertakings.

Effectively the pair of them became prisoners of the official machinery of state. Their apartments in Palazzo Ducale were furnished out of their private coffers and their gondola was to be the same plain black vessel in which the sumptuary laws required all Venetians to travel regardless of rank or wealth. Their official chapel was the Basilica of San Marco and the doge assumed the guardianship of the relics of the Evangelist. In a city full of sacred bodies, this ranked as the holiest and most potently thaumaturgical of them all. That he was felt to have a right to intervene in the nomination of senior clergy added to a continuously problematic relationship with the Vatican. Not for nothing was Venice at several moments in its history placed beneath a papal interdict, with the whole matter of the doge's powers being tabled for discussion during the Council of Trent (1545–63), though this did not result in any clearer demarcation of authority between La Serenissima and Holy Church.

How was a doge to be chosen in the first place? Following the death of Doge Renier Zen in 1268, the Grand Council resolved that further steps were needed towards purging the entire electoral process, let alone the exercise of power once a candidate was appointed. Zen had discharged his office impressively enough, given the problems presented by ongoing tussles with the Genoese in the Adriatic and the Aegean, but the Council now felt it was time to test its strength against potential bids for power from certain ambitious individuals within the city. The *Maggior Consiglio* had been brought into being almost a century earlier by Doge Sebastiano Ziani, that same wondrously assertive and capable figure who later presided over the crucial confrontation between Pope Alexander and Emperor Frederick Barbarossa in the shadow of the Basilica. Numbering 480 members, nominated from each of Venice's six districts, the *sestieri*, and holding office for a year, this Great Council chose from within its own ranks all the principal officers of state. Ziani further expanded the hierarchy by adding four more special counsellors to the original pair advising the doge, a body becoming known as the Signoria, and gave extra powers to the senatorial group called the Pregadi which oversaw finances and foreign affairs. His successor Orio

Mastropiero went still further in creating a so-called 'Consilium Minus' among these ducal advisers, with increased executive authority.

Over successive decades there developed, under the Grand Council's supervision, an astonishingly elaborate process for selecting, from among its ranks, the ideal candidate for doge. What happened was customarily as follows. On the morning of the agreed day, the youngest member of the Signoria, after praying in San Marco, would go into the Piazza and engage the first boy he met there to accompany him to Palazzo Ducale. The young lad's task was to take thirty slips of paper, each of them bearing the name of a Grand Council member aged over thirty, from out of an urn. From these he would select a further nine, who then chose from forty names which had each received seven nominations. A third drawing of lots now took place, with twelve names taken from the forty and these dozen voters were required to produce twenty-five candidates with nine nominations each. Nine was once again a key number in choosing forty-five names with seven votes, from among whom the boy drew eleven names. These picked a further forty-one and it was this final group which went into a closed meeting to select a doge, having taken a solemn oath to serve the needs of the state. Their assembly took place in Palazzo Ducale behind locked doors, with a guard of sailors outside.

The boy playing so essential a role in the voting process was called *il ballottino*, from the *ballotte*, little balls to which the names were attached, whence we derive our English word 'ballot'. This whole singularly meticulous electoral system, a process equivalent to the phases involved in the programme of a washing machine, was both puzzling to non-Venetians but also seen as an inherently impressive aspect of a political system unique in contemporary Europe. Over the centuries the term 'Venetian', used in a political context, would come to embody certain concepts of state which enshrined its transcendency over personal or dynastic interests and its essence as a collective enterprise representing all its citizens. For seventeenth-century England, in the age of Thomas Hobbes and John Locke when such ideas were hotly debated, and for its runaway children the United States of America a hundred years later, the governance of the Republic of Venice held a major resonance.

Pressure to refine the working of checks and balances in different areas undoubtedly grew among Venice's 'most potent, grave and reverend signors' (a phrase aptly borrowed from one of Shakespeare's two Venetian plays) when they looked at what was happening in other Italian states as the thirteenth century drew to a close. Factional strife among Guelphs and Ghibellines, deriving from the power struggle in Italy between the pope and the Holy Roman Emperor, had torn Florence and its surrounding towns apart and looked set to encourage the rise of individual families wealthy and influential enough to seize overall control from citizen governments. The French Angevin princes had established their grip on Naples and, for the time being, on Sicily as well, while in Milan the Visconti clan was busy strengthening its credible leadership and in Verona the Ghibelline warlord Mastino della Scala had managed to unite an entire urban community behind him.

This kind of rule, thrusting bosses, opportunists and 'godfathers' to the forefront and laying a heavy emphasis on clientelism and dynastic loyalties, anticipates our clichéd notions as to the ways in which the mechanisms of administration and public life have always operated in Italy. That things were not like this in Venice is due to the speed with which its already established governing class saw off the challenges at a moment when the order of affairs might so easily have been reconfigured, with the Serene Republic's entire polity tilted beyond recovery towards clan feuding and despotism. Zeal to preserve the essential fabric of La Serenissima was unquestionable but the interests fuelling it were scarcely altruistic. The key advantages were reserved for one clearly defined sector alone within the Venetian community, the merchant oligarchs who filled most, though not yet all, of the seats on the Grand Council and the principal executive roles in the various branches of government.

By swift degrees, during the thirteenth century's closing decades, authority over the city's affairs and those of its satellite territories in Crete, Euboea and Dalmatia crystallized within the hands of some thirty well-established Venetian families. A proposal to limit admission to the *Maggior Consiglio* on a hereditary basis had initially been cast aside but when Pietro Gradenigo was elected doge in 1289 he saw every reason for reviving the idea. He was only thirty-eight years of age, dynamic, impatient and conscious of the need, at this instant, for a focus on internal efficiency so that Venice might more easily deal with ongoing maritime threats from Genoa. In 1297 Gradenigo oversaw what is traditionally reckoned the turning point in Venetian administrative history, the so-called *Serrata del Maggior Consiglio*, the closure of the Grand Council, whereby an already assertive patrician grouping was guaranteed its position as La Serenissima's governing caste. A new decree limited membership of the assembly to those who had acted as counsellors during the past four years or were related, through the male line of descent, to former counsellors. Appointments would be supervised by the Quarantia, the council of forty members originally

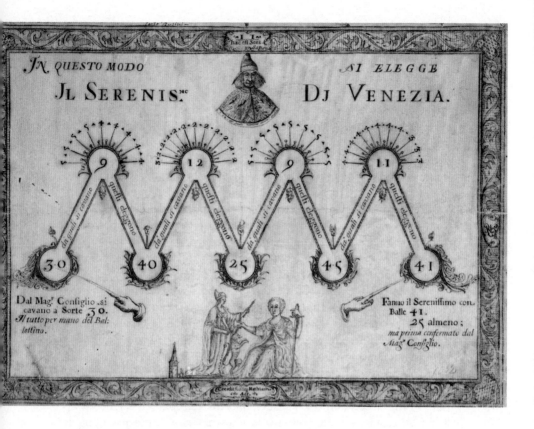

set up to approve candidates for the dogeship and nominations to the judiciary.

This *Serrata* – effectively, as the meaning of the Italian word suggests, a locking-out of citizens and plebeians from the Republic's executive – naturally triggered a broad resentment among those who felt that their wealth and enterprise entitled them to some say in civic affairs. What then ensued was the most violent and unstable period in Venetian politics, when any kind of smug assumption on the part of patricians that the necessary finishing stroke had been given to their ascendancy was challenged from sources they had least expected or felt they had cause to fear. In 1300, three years after Pietro Gradenigo presided over the crucial reform, the merchant Marin Bocconio, whose ventures had recently taken a severe knock during the conflict with Genoa, arrived outside the Council Chamber with a party of nine supporters, demanding admission and a share in the government. Doge Gradenigo cunningly seemed to agree with them but said he preferred to listen

A diagram of 1730, explaining the complex voting system for the office of Doge of Venice.

to each of them individually rather than as a body of protestors. One by one they were promptly seized, flung in gaol, then hanged upside down outside the Porta della Carta, main gateway to the palace from Piazza San Marco.

Anger at the new oligarchy nevertheless continued to simmer, fuelled by Gradenigo's wildly overconfident attempt, in 1308, to extend Venice's grip on the *terraferma* by challenging Pope Clement V over the vacant lordship of the city of Ferrara. The Holy Father promptly excommunicated the doge and his council, seized Venetian goods and property in Ferrara, nullified all existing treaties with the Republic and ordered the clergy to quit its territories forthwith. Though the young doge remained defiant, sending a force to garrison the disputed town, this army was soon decimated by plague, so that papal troops easily stormed the gates and Venice was compelled to sign a humiliating treaty, acknowledging the pontifical fiefdom and agreeing on a heavy indemnity in return for its trading rights.

As several members of the Council had feared, factionalism was starting to develop within its ranks, along what seemed like Guelph and Ghibelline lines. Those who had opposed the Ferrara enterprise included members of the Querini, Tiepolo and Badoer clans, all of whom nurtured private grievances against the doge and felt justifiably angry at its wastefulness and the consequent loss of face Venice had been made to suffer. Scuffles broke out between supporters of either side in the streets and open spaces, and the tension was ratcheted up still further when arrests were made across the city by the armed night watch known as the *Signori di Notte*. The Querini sought to gather support in favour of a coup d'état aimed at unseating Pietro Gradenigo as doge by the use of armed force. To lead the rebellion they fixed on a kinsman, Bajamonte Tiepolo, grandson of a former doge, who had quit Venice for an estate on the mainland after being accused of financial irregularities as governor of the key fortresses of Methoni and Koroni in the Peloponnese.

Bajamonte – his first name derived from a Norman ancestor Boemond de Brienne – was a glamorous figure known as *il Gran Cavaliere*, whom many felt to have been unjustly slandered by Gradenigo's partisans and to deserve a fair hearing. His own ambitions, however, embraced more than merely rewriting a record of tainted honour. Current unrest offered an ideal opportunity for completely overturning the established order in Venice so as to install the house of Tiepolo, himself at its head, as the state's ruling dynasty. On Sunday, 14 June 1310, the eve of Saint Vitus's day – 'San Vio' in Venetian – the conspirators would strike in a three-pronged operation, two armed groups marching on Palazzo Ducale from different ends of Piazza San Marco while a third platoon gathered on the mainland, awaiting a signal to cross the water and sweep through the Cannaregio district's gardens and orchards towards the heart of the city.

As often happens, the intended takeover was betrayed from within. One of the plotters, Marco Donato, alerted the doge in enough time for him to rally the different authorities and their loyal squadrons, including a gang of workers from the Arsenale. For the conspiracy's scheme to succeed, timing was crucial, but the dawn raid planned from the mainland had been thwarted by a sudden storm so that there was no armed backup available for the men now advancing on the Piazza. Heavy rain began falling as a group led by two of the Querini now burst into the square only to find it bristling with ducal guards, who either killed or arrested the rebels. Bajamonte himself rallied his forces by the church of San Giuliano, then moved swiftly down the narrow lane beyond it towards San Marco, where he might have rescued the whole operation had it not been for a singular accident, one which would find a permanent place in the folklore of Venice.

Closing in on the Piazza, the rebels became increasingly aware, as they moved on through the city, of the coldness and hostility shown by ordinary citizens of Venice. Like so many others in a similar situation, they had counted on a wave of popular reaction, which, given the doge's reputation and the failure of his Ferrara expedition, should have been instantly forthcoming. In fact it was replaced either by curses or by an ominous silence. The ultimate gesture of rejection arrived as Bajamonte's force prepared to enter the square, shouting 'Freedom! Death to Doge Gradenigo!' Leaning out of a high window, an elderly woman named Lucia Rossi flung a stone mortar, of the kind used for pounding spices or meal, into the street below. She had aimed it at Bajamonte Tiepolo himself but it hit the head of a standard bearer just in front of him, knocking the man dead. Whereupon the whole troop panicked and fled back to the Rialto, where they crossed the bridge and barricaded themselves within the narrow lanes of the market on the other side.

It took some time before the doge's men could dislodge them and in any case the area around the Rialto market and the church of San Polo was more partisan of Bajamonte and his cause than anywhere else in the city. Wanting to avoid further street battles, Gradenigo offered a sentence of exile in exchange for Tiepolo's surrender. The rebel leader left for Dalmatia, where he spent the next two decades planning new

uprisings until he was murdered by a government agent. His house in Campo Sant'Agostin, close to the basilica of the Frari, was pulled down and what, as elsewhere in Italy, was called 'a column of infamy' recorded the confiscation of Bajamonte's property 'for his wicked treachery and to inspire terror in others'. In this, as in other gestures such as the seizure of a Querini palace so as to turn it into a municipal slaughterhouse, Venice clearly wished to be seen remembering its mythic Roman origins in the exercise of a *damnatio memoriae* of the kind posthumously given to certain emperors.

By the same token honours and rewards were bestowed on anybody who had assisted in thwarting the intended coup. Marco Donato, for having denounced the conspirators to the Senate, was given membership of the Grand Council, which would be handed down to his descendants, three of whom were destined to become doges. The parishioners of San Luca, who had bravely attacked Querini's rebel squadron, were awarded one of the Republic's official red flagpoles from which to fly their banners. Ornamental masonry from Bajamonte's demolished palace was added to the church of San Vio, on Dorsoduro, where the doges thereafter attended a solemn annual mass to mark Venice's rescue from the uprising. As for Lucia Rossi, whose tumbling mortar had so effectively turned the tables, the state freely granted her the two favours she asked. One was to be allowed to hang out the ceremonial flag of St Mark on special feast days and the other was that the fifteen-ducat rent she currently paid should remain fixed for as long as she or her descendants lived there. Her house, known to Venetians as *Casa e bottega della Grazia del Morter*, has long since been rebuilt, but if you look up at its replacement you will see a nineteenth-century stone bas-relief of Lucia and her kitchen weapon of destruction set into the façade.

Reaction to Bajamonte Tiepolo's revolt took the form of a nervous precautionary strengthening of the government's already sweeping powers over ordinary citizens with the establishment of a special body of ten members whose task was to guarantee security throughout Venice, using every means available for gathering and sifting information that might lead to the arrest, detention and trial of those deemed a danger to the state. The Council of Ten, as it was known, became a byword in later ages for the Republic's ruthless efficiency in dealing with the slightest hints of sedition or dissent and it undoubtedly furnished a model – or at least a hint or two – for security committees in times closer to our own. Though the doge and his half-dozen counsellors of the Signoria sat in on its meetings, overseen by a special lawyer, and

A high-ranking Venetian senator in his robes of office, with St Mark's Square and the campanile visible in the background.

though the members were supposed to defer to these dignitaries, the core activity was undertaken by its ten constituent members. Each was elected for a year, no two representatives from the same family could sit at the same time and though this was one of the hardest-working, most intensely focused branches of government, no extra payment for such a vital service could be expected.

The Council of Ten harvested information from everywhere in the city, through a wide network of spies, through written depositions and through the use of the letterboxes sometimes referred to as *Bocche di Leoni* – 'Lions' Mouths' – in which anonymous tip-offs or denunciations could be posted. Arrests related to any of these would be made at night and suspects were meticulously examined in darkened rooms, following which it required a series of five initial ballots, followed by four stages of confirmatory voting, before the Ten proceeded to sentence the criminal. Punishments involved everything from fines,

Lucia Rossi with her death-dealing mortar, which put paid
to Bajamonte Tiepolo's plot of 14 June 1310 to depose
Doge Pietro Gradenigo.

opposite   A 'lion's mouth' postbox for secret
denunciations of malefactors to the Council of Ten.

whipping and prison sentences to a spell on the rowing benches of a galley and, very occasionally, various forms of mutilation. The death penalty was handed down sparingly – La Serenissima's government may have been ruthless but it was not, whatever the fantasy and exaggeration rife among historians, playwrights and novelists of the Romantic era, a cruel or barbarous one by the standards of its time. The so-called 'Black Legend' of Venice, created after the fall of the Republic, is something we shall glance at later in this book.

Instituting the Council of Ten was not the only measure felt to be necessary following the shockwaves of the Tiepolo revolt. Exactly who might be eligible for entry to the Grand Council following the *Serrata* became a highly controversial issue and in 1315 an official index was introduced, overseen by officers called *Avvogadori*, whose task was to scrutinize the candidates' background and suitability as fully as possible. Another register under their supervision was what eventually became

known as the *Libro d'Oro*, the Golden Book, in which the marriages and children of every patrician were sedulously recorded in volume after volume over succeeding centuries. This work was the godmother of all subsequent aristocratic directories, from the *Almanach de Gotha* to *Burke's Peerage, Baronetage & Knightage*, and inclusion within its pages would become a vital issue for the Venetian nobility and, as will be seen, for several families not born into this privileged class.

However tightly sealed the patricians might have imagined their ascendancy through measures such as these, an audible simmer of discontent at the *Serrata* and its impact on society endured through the decades following Doge Pietro Gradenigo's death in 1311. Those joining the annual summer procession to mass at San Vio in commemoration of the Republic's avoidance of catastrophe at Bajamonte Tiepolo's hands might well have pondered the likelihood of something similar happening again, whatever the constitutional safety measures introduced or the bulwark created by the Council of Ten. What few people could have suspected was where such subversion, in its newest form, might spring from. The coup had, after all, been effectively suppressed through the energy and determination of a strong doge. Forty years later it would be just such a figure whose profile threatened La Serenissima's downfall.

Marin Falier – or Marino Faliero as he became known to non-Venetian writers – was not cut out, in theory at least, to be the leader of a revolution. What heroism or panache attach themselves to him derive largely from the makeover contrived by writers, artists and composers during the Romantic era at the beginning of the nineteenth century. In 1821 Lord Byron led the way with his tragedy *Marino Faliero*, presenting the doomed doge as someone whose altruism in striking back at the arrogance and entitlement of his patrician caste is compromised by the bitterness of his private motives. Like everything else Byron wrote, the play is, to a significant extent, about the poet himself, in this particular case about his experience of alienation and exclusion from society following an unfortunate marriage and its scandal-ridden aftermath. Four years later, inspired by Byron's play, the young Eugène Delacroix devised a masterly reconstruction of the doge's last moments in his painting *The Execution of Marino Faliero*, while in 1835 Gaetano Donizetti's opera *Marin Falier* made bold use both of the original drama and a French adaptation of its material by Casimir Delavigne to explore the genuine nobility of soul within the title character, his failure of ambition notwithstanding.

The real-life Marin Falier could count two distinguished holders of the ducal office among his ancestors and had an outstanding record of service to the Republic by the time he was elected as doge in 1354. At seventy-six years old he could look back on membership of the Council of Ten, on a spell as governor of the cities of Padua and Treviso, on the command of a naval expedition to the Black Sea and valuable work as a diplomat in Austria and at the pope's court in Avignon. Summoned home from France to take up his new role, Falier no doubt had time en route to consider his options. The moment seemed to offer an ideal opportunity for the kind of decisive leadership that his forebear Ordelafo Falier had shown two centuries earlier in reorganizing the Venetian navy and strengthening the resources of the Arsenale. The position of doge must have seemed like the ultimate reward for his conscientiousness and breadth of experience but the implication carried by such an honour was that La Serenissima should expect, in return, to benefit from her choice.

A doge was customarily addressed with a range of different titles – 'Most Illustrious', 'Most Glorious', 'Magnificent Sir', 'Most Eminent' or 'Your Serenity', in allusion to the state's concept of itself as 'the Most Serene Republic of Venice'. Serenity was a word, however, which few would have chosen to connect with Marin Falier. A major flaw in his character was a tendency to overreact if he felt in any sense let down or ill-served by those on whose punctiliousness and efficiency he depended. Surly and unforgiving, he invariably let them know where they fell short. Council electors with long memories might think twice about voting for him when recalling an embarrassing scene outside Treviso Cathedral in 1339, when Falier boxed the ears of the elderly diocesan bishop Pietro Paoli for being late in joining a church procession.

A far better reason for his anger was provided at the inaugural banquet in Palazzo Ducale which celebrated the new doge's investiture. When a young patrician got drunk and made advances to one of the ladies-in-waiting attending the dogaressa, Falier had him thrown out, but the offender contrived, before leaving the feast, to attach an insulting scrawl to the ducal throne in the Council Chamber declaring the doge to be a cuckold to a wanton wife. There was no proof of this whatever but harm had been done to Falier's honour and the damage, as far as he was concerned, needed repaying in full. Reporting the slander to the Quarantia, the Council's legal committee, he had every reason to expect that the wrongdoer would be suitably punished and was furious when it chose instead to administer a mere slap of the wrist on the grounds of youth and a hitherto unblemished character.

Falier's rage quickly blossomed into a positive detestation of that same oligarchy from which he and his traducer both sprang. During his absence from Venice the younger nobility seemed especially to have gone to the bad, as a collection of wastrels and bullies presuming on their status to protect them. From here it was an easy step to believing that an entire echelon needed the proverbial smack of firm government which he himself was admirably placed to lay on. Soon enough further ammunition was supplied by the conduct of the nobleman Marco Barbaro towards the foreman of works at the Arsenale, Stefano Ghiazza, known as Gisello. By now the Arsenale, where the great merchant galleys and war vessels were made, had become the nerve centre of Venetian power. Its workers, everyone from teams of shipwrights to the makers of ropes and sails, the boilers of tar and bakers of ship's biscuit, enjoyed a special importance well beyond the big walled enclave in which they laboured. Thus when Barbaro, while arguing with Gisello over various matters, struck him across the face, this contemptuous gesture was like a challenge to combat, the more so because a ring on the offending aristocratic hand was big enough to inflict an actual wound. Gisello is said to have gone directly to the doge in search of redress, his face still bloody, muttering dark imprecations as to killing savage beasts and encouraging Falier to exterminate the patricians and make himself master of Venice.

The doge, assured of Gisello's backing, had found other allies, both in his own family circle and among the citizens. Plans for an armed assault on his enemies broadened into a full-scale conspiracy against the oligarchs, culminating in their massacre, to be carried out in the Piazza on 15 April. It has been convincingly suggested that Gisello was simply manipulating the hot-tempered Falier in order to stage a popular uprising. The latter was calculating enough, on the other hand, to see where his advantage lay and it must have been appealing to imagine himself as Venice's duke in more than name, a despot like those currently governing Milan and Verona. To antagonize Venetians against the nobles still further, the plotters hired troublemakers to pose as just such young bloods as the one who had slandered the dogaressa and to commit offensive acts under cover of the privileges guaranteed by patrician rank.

Once again a knot of conspirators was betrayed by one of their own. Privy to the intrigue was a certain furrier, Beltrame of Bergamo, who, for reasons either of conscience, personal regard or fear of losing a rich customer, warned the patrician Niccolo Lioni under no circumstances to set foot outside his palace door on 15 April. Lioni promptly ordered his servants to seize Beltrame and keep him safely locked up while he himself consulted with two of his fellow nobles on the safest procedure to adopt. They alerted the Council of Ten, who gathered in the sacristy of San Salvador near the Rialto, ascertained as much as they could as to details of the plot and those involved, then returned to Palazzo Ducale, where members from all the different government committees were hastily assembled and extreme security measures put in place. On the day itself arrests were made across the city, the bell-ringer charged with sounding the tocsin meant to signal the start of the revolt was ordered to stand idle and ten of the ringleaders were summarily hanged from the palace's south-facing windows, opposite the two columns of the Piazzetta, their mouths stuffed with iron gags.

How to proceed against Marin Falier himself was somewhat more problematic. There could be no doubt as regarded his private ambitions in staging the coup. He had fully intended to make himself master of Venice by destroying its republican system and establishing himself at the head of a ruling dynasty. To his fellow patricians it seemed both bizarre and thoroughly outrageous that one of their own, elected with such scrupulousness at each stage of the process, should have plotted to ruin the state and exterminate them all into the bargain. A public example thus needed to be made and so a special council, the *Zonta* (from the word *giunta* or *aggiunta*, meaning 'added'), made up of twenty among the wisest and most experienced senators, was summoned by the Ten to deliver its verdict. The assembled thirty unanimously pronounced the doge guilty and on 17 April sentenced him to be beheaded within the palace precincts.

Falier's conduct was a textbook illustration of Shakespeare's 'Nothing in his life became him like the leaving of it.' Fully acknowledging his guilt and the fitness of his punishment, he surrendered his ducal headdress and robes of office. Dressed in black, he was taken to the head of the staircase in the courtyard, where an executioner stood ready beside the block. A single blow severed the head, which was then carried to the palace balcony and shown to a waiting crowd with the words 'The supreme judgment has been carried out upon the traitor.' The decapitated body was then displayed to the people in gruesome confirmation.

Not enough has been made of the implication behind some of the circumstances surrounding the execution and its aftermath. The fact that it was carried out as a kind of 'ticketed event', solely for members of Marin Falier's own social class, is not without significance. His treachery and punishment were matters for the Senate alone, not for the mass of citizens excluded from the business of government, and his betrayal of his caste was to be dealt with in a way that symbolically shut out those who were not members of it. Displaying the doge's head to the commonalty was a gesture of pure tokenism, as was the exhibition of his corpse. None of those who crowded around it had, after all, been privileged to hear his final speech, in which he asked pardon of the state and declared himself rightfully sentenced.

What followed smacks as much of the nobles' shame and embarrassment that their trusted fellow oligarch had disgraced his office as of a genuine wish to heap opprobrium on him for doing so. Falier's body was hurried by night to an unmarked grave in his family chapel next to the Dominican church of Santi Giovanni e Paolo and his estates and possessions were confiscated. An exception was made here for the 2,000 ducats left to Dogaressa Alvica, victim of the slander which stung him to act. Within the Grand Council a deliberate process of *damnatio memoriae* was carried out. The minutes of the Ten which ought solemnly to have recorded the sentence on the doge were left silent, with only the words '*Non scribatur*' – 'May it not be written' – across the relevant page, as if the whole episode were too dreadful to be recalled. When, twelve years later, as part of a frieze made up of portraits of past doges decorating the Council Chamber, Falier's image looked set to be included, the Senate decreed instead that it be replaced with a black veil carrying the words '*Hic est locus Marini Faletro decapitati pro criminibus*' – 'Here is the place for Marin Falier, beheaded for his crimes'. And there indeed, in a late sixteenth-century repainting, it survives. The white damask cloth spattered with blood from his execution was carried in procession to high mass on Saint Isidore's day, 16 April, which became an annual public holiday. Venetians were expected to celebrate a deliverance, but who had been delivered from what exactly – well, that was another matter.

AEQVORA TVENS
PORTV·RESI·DEO
HIC·NEPTV·NVS

SAINT MARK
VICTORIOUS

The triumph of the oligarchs, sealed by the swift suppression of Marin Falier's bid for power, was not simply a matter of social ascendancy or seizure of the initiative by a carefully restricted political caucus. Its basis was also economic, with the Venetian nobility taking control of the essential motors of trade that had turned the Republic into one of medieval Europe's most successful states, universally envied for its wealth and prosperity. At the heart of the whole mechanism lay what is known as the *colleganza* system, a forerunner of the modern concept of joint-stock companies, that had developed from practical issues created by trading voyages across the Mediterranean. So as to thrive, Venice needed to rely on a sequence of fundamental rhythms evolving around certain prescribed routes and the timing of seasonal weather events, such as the Indian Ocean monsoon which dominated operations in the spice trade. Merchant galleys sailed to Alexandria and Beirut, for example, in late summer to pick up the richest yields of pepper, nutmeg and cloves brought by Arab traders to the Red Sea ports or by camel caravans through Syria. Others in search of different commodities set off in March for Constantinople, the Black Sea and the northern European markets of Flanders and England.

Called the *muda*, a word whose origin remains obscure, these annual expeditions each carried heavy risks. Shipwreck was an obvious danger, piracy another, while sickness of all kinds could swiftly decimate the crew. There was always a likelihood that for one reason or another a galley would arrive too late to pick up sufficiently saleable cargo or to make a profitable venture from its own freight. As part of the solution to such problems there arose a system of risk-sharing referred to as *colleganza*, literally 'joining together' or 'connexion', from the same root as the English words 'colleague' and 'college'. The two

overleaf A medieval galley in full sail, from Konrad von Grünenberg's diary of his pilgrimage to the Holy Land, which took him from Venice to Jaffa in the summer of 1486.

Vetlicher etwas besunders sehen Als das die frowen und Junkfrowen des ge war
lachten und wie wol es yegund mittag was Vnd doch keiner zum essen der
herberg gedenken Vetlicher sagt besunders gesehen haben Ach ward da zu
worten bracht den hass ze Santhestor des kings Artus wissen wichti
Von schaume vnd cost der frowen vnd Junkfrowen

Unfer galleig

Item hernach stond die ämpter vnd gewon
haiten des schiffs ovh die namen aller segel
vnd anders des man sich gebrucht vf
der galleigen

elements of this scheme are a voyage by the trader in his galley and the funding for it offered by an investor, who does not himself move out of Venice. If and when the merchant returns successfully, the moneyed partner receives 75 per cent of the profit, while the venturer takes the remaining 25 per cent. Any losses will be covered by the partner's original capital. When the enterprise is completed, the contract, drawn up in proper form by a notary, comes to an end and the two parties concerned are free to enter upon similar agreements elsewhere.

Reconfigured and spurred on by a sense of its unlimited power, the Grand Council turned its attention to the *colleganza* system as a key source of wealth which needed keeping in the right hands. Whereas formerly the merchant galley had sailed as part of a private enterprise, such vessels now became the property of the Republic, annually auctioned to individual speculators or syndicates who had to respect a particular calendar set out by the state regarding the destination of each voyage and the day of its embarkation. The auction was confined to the nobility alone and assessments of wealth were made according to a new law, the *Capitulare Navigantium*, passed in 1324, which decreed that no galley could load merchandise to a value beyond the assets of its owner for that year. This put paid, effectively, to the aspirational aspect of Venetian commerce that had given social and political mobility to its traders in past centuries. The *colleganza* now belonged, in essence, to the aristocracy of the Golden Book, whose shareholding in its chartered galleys became increasingly linked to family interests and marriage connexions within this privileged echelon.

For several historians of Venice the roots of its prolonged decline lie here and not, as tradition has otherwise maintained, in the Portuguese mastery of the spice trade at the close of the fifteenth century, the rise of Ottoman Turkey at the same period or La Serenissima's failure to develop an adequate land army to maintain its empire. The late medieval evolution, following the *Serrata del Maggior Consiglio*, of a heavily stratified society, its three class brackets formed by patricians, bourgeoisie and populace, eventually created a sclerosis which rendered the Republic's very survival a thing of wonder. For now, however, to those visiting from other more obviously unstable regions of Italy, the whole phenomenon of Venetian success, the physical paradox of the seaborne city, the triumph of its pseudo-democracy, the sheer volume of its commercial resources, the global reach of its trade and the pride of its community in the singular construct their forebears had brought into being, all these things made La Serenissima marvellous in the eyes of a wider world.

What Venetians themselves, on the other hand, knew all too well was the inherent vulnerability of this in the face of greed, competitiveness and aggression from other powers active on a similar commercial basis. With Pope Urban II's proclamation of the First Crusade in 1095, the Italian maritime republics had scented mercantile opportunity in the establishment of a Christian realm in the Holy Land, with ports like Acre and Tyre as a growing source of wealth for those who knew how to traffic the trade goods of the East across the Mediterranean. To begin with there were three of these to rival the Venetians and their enterprise. Amalfi, the smallest of them, had been the earliest to prosper, partly from its geographical position on the west coast of the old Longobard duchies ruled from Salerno, Benevento and Naples. It had grown rich from trade in precious stones and textiles, striking its own coinage which circulated in the markets of north Africa and formulating a maritime code of laws, the *Tabula Amalfitana*, which became standard among the seafarers of the Mediterranean during the eleventh and twelfth centuries.

The biggest challenge to Amalfi arose from a city further north along the Italian coast, the Republic of Pisa. Nowadays, owing to the silting up of the River Arno on whose estuary it stands, the town is some distance from the sea, but in the early Middle Ages it boasted a busy harbour and by the end of the tenth century had become one of Italy's most flourishing states. There were Pisan quarters in cities of Puglia like Bari and Trani, Pisan ships helped the Byzantines drive Islamic invaders out of Calabria and later played their part in the Norman conquest of Sicily. So well, indeed, did the Pisans fare from the seizure of Palermo in 1062 that the treasure acquired on that occasion paid for the building of the city's original Romanesque *duomo* of Santa Maria Maggiore.

Some two decades later, without much difficulty, Pisa mounted a raid on Amalfi, though failing ultimately to crush the rival republic. More serious competition for them both arose from the seaborne merchant state of Genoa, crammed into narrow confines between the western spurs of the Alps and the Ligurian coast. Rich, ruthless and in constant search of fresh market opportunities, the Genoese had fallen eagerly on various trade concessions offered by the Crusader states of the Levant while at the same time pursuing their advantages in Byzantine domains, either in Constantinople itself, where they controlled an entire enclave within the city, or on Aegean islands like Chios and Samos and in the Black Sea, where their merchant colonies dominated ports such as Caffa and Trebizond.

Pisa's bitter and costly struggle with Genoa for mastery of the Mediterranean would last for over 150 years, beginning in a quarrel over mastery of Corsica in 1116 and fuelled by the fluctuating relationship of both states with Emperor Frederick Barbarossa and his successors, including Frederick II. When King Louis IX of France, eager in 1248 to launch a Sixth Crusade, looked around for ships to carry his soldiers to Egypt, his thoughts naturally turned to the Levantine fleets of Pisa and Genoa. He was sickened to discover that their crews preferred fighting each other to carrying a holy war into the lands of the infidel. For either side the ultimate reckoning arrived in 1284 when 83 galleys sailed from Porto Pisano, at the mouth of the Arno, to do battle with a Genoese squadron of 130 vessels off the rocky islet of Meloria. Forty of Pisa's ships were boarded and captured, 16,000 of their crewmen were killed, drowned or taken prisoner and the Republic never fully recovered from the catastrophe. To consolidate their triumph, the Genoese sailed into the harbour of Porto Pisano and filled it up so effectively with rubble of various kinds that no further expeditions could ever be launched from there.

Victory at Meloria meant that Genoa could now focus with total confidence on an effort to eliminate her single remaining competitor in Mediterranean trade and the transport of pilgrims to the Holy Land. Venice, as the Genoese saw it, had done far too well from the attack on Constantinople under Enrico Dandolo's sightless leadership almost a century earlier and this could never be forgiven. Rivalry between the two republics grew the sharper as, one by one, the last Crusader strongholds in Antioch and Tripoli fell to the Mamluk sultans of Egypt. When in 1291 the port of Acre was added to these, remaining markets for Christian merchants trading with the East were to be found either in Alexandria or else around the Black Sea. Here the Genoese purchased Kefe, the former Greek city of Theodosia in the Crimea, from the Tartars, turning it into a thriving port they called Caffa, dealing in Russian furs and grain as well as boasting a valuable market for slaves. Venice, not to be outdone, went in search of its own Black Sea trading hub and found it after sending an ambassador to Muhammad Uzbeg, ruler of the Tartar Golden Horde, at his capital Sarai, in modern Kazakhstan. Venetian diplomacy scored a triumph, as so often, and the Republic was granted a concession at Tana, at the mouth of the Don as it flows into the Sea of Azov.

Tana, though never more than an outpost and certainly not a rival to Caffa in terms of its amenities and built environment, meant that Venice, from 1333 onwards, had a stake in the varied merchandise flowing from Russia, from the lands around the Caspian Sea and, further afield, out of Afghanistan and China. Commodities like hemp for ropemaking, beeswax and corn could be purchased, along with different kinds of leather and rare wood, while links with the breakaway Byzantine state of Trebizond, ruled by a branch of the imperial Komnenos family, brought jewels and spices to market as well. In return the Venetians dealt in fine weaponry, metalwork, kitchen utensils and an increasing range of woven fabrics from the looms of Tuscany, Flanders and England.

For the Genoese a Venetian presence at Tana was the ultimate irritant in a series of tensions originating many years earlier. In 1255 Venice had gone to war with Genoa over Levantine markets, driving Genoese traders from Acre and seizing their naval squadron of twenty-five galleys. Festering strife between the two powers broke out again in the Greek islands on which each maintained strongholds and colonies, with continued jostling for the privileges to be granted by Emperor Michael Palaeologos, who in 1261 had reconquered Constantinople for the Greeks from the puppet Crusader 'Latin' regime established by the Venetians half a century earlier. Though it grew expedient, in the light of the Mamluk conquerors' successes in Palestine, for both republics to conclude a truce, this stand-down was grudging and uneasy, a classic example of either side making use of peacetime to ready itself for a major conflict with its hated competitor.

The fall of Acre to the Mamluks in 1291 galvanized Venetian merchants to seek out new markets and, where possible, to secure trading rights with these latest masters of Syria and Palestine. When Pope Nicholas IV, that same year, hit on the notion of reconciling Venice and Genoa by sending their combined fleets to defend the island of Cyprus from potential Muslim attack, fighting broke out between several ships from either side and the scheme was hastily abandoned. The real touchpaper was lit when news came that the Byzantine Emperor Andronicus, Michael Palaeologus's son and successor, had sought to bolster his fleet by hiring Genoese vessels. A Venetian navy speeding eastwards to deal once and for all with such opportunism met its match off the Syrian port of Alexandretta, where the enemy stood firm, seizing two dozen of Venice's newly launched galleys, then promptly swooped on Crete, looting and burning Canea, its chief city.

Venice bided her time until the following year, 1295, when brawling between the two merchant communities in Constantinople broke out in street wars and the Genoese sacked the entire Venetian quarter, massacring whoever they found. Emperor Andronicus blamed the Venetians for starting the trouble and arrested Marco Bembo, the *bailo*, chief consul, of the community, together with other leading merchants, flinging them all in gaol. A disingenuous attempt to calm the situation by sending Greek ambassadors to Venice merely made matters worse. No less a figure than Pietro Gradenigo happened to be doge at this time, who turned his rage on the envoys, demanding costly reparations. Byzantium was now to be regarded as a hostile power and in the summer of 1296 forty warships under the command of Ruggiero Morosini, known as '*Malabranca*', 'Evil Claw', sailed towards the Dardanelles, attacking the Genoese colony of Phocaea, under its hereditary governor Benedetto Zaccaria, en route. Once in the straits Morosini commanded that all Greek ships and those of Genoa should be set on fire. Reaching Constantinople, he ordered the burning of Genoese property in the Galata area, took a number of prisoners and then presented himself at the emperor's palace, refusing to leave without the indemnity demanded by the doge. A second Venetian squadron meanwhile burst through an attempted Genoese blockade of the entrance to the Black Sea and raided Caffa, only leaving when especially ferocious winter weather, approaching early, threatened to ice up the harbour.

Efforts by Pope Boniface VIII at yet another high-minded pontifical reconciliation, including an offer to pay half of Venice's claim for damages, failed utterly. The two sides resumed their vicious assaults here and there across the Mediterranean, leading to nothing in particular, wasting men and resources and undermining those valuable commercial initiatives that furnished the lifeblood of either community. A final reckoning came in 1298 among the scatter of islands off the coast of Dalmatia. Where Venice was concerned these waters were *mare nostrum*, 'our sea', and confidence was high among those who offered funds and ships to La Serenissima's naval strike force. Under the command of Andrea Dandolo, the ninety-five-strong fleet sailed south to meet the Genoese off the island of Korčula (Curzola to the Italians). Genoa's admiral was Lamba Doria, member of one of his city's foremost families, whose descendant Andrea would fight alongside the Venetians at a great sea fight of a later era [see chapter 11]. Doria quickly seized the advantage so as not to let the strong August sun dazzle his sailors. Dandolo's ships had bunched too early; fire broke out on one of them and spread across the fleet, a mere twelve galleys escaped and Doria took five thousand Venetian prisoners back to Genoa. Among them was Marco Polo, whose spell in captivity would result, as we know, in the travelogue that so beguiled Rustichello of Pisa. A more reluctant prisoner altogether was Andrea Dandolo. Agonized at the thought of being led in triumph through the streets of Genoa, he beat out his brains against a mast.

As Pope Boniface had doubtless predicted, neither side emerged as an outright winner from a war that had lasted the best part of a decade, yet the peace treaty between Venice and Genoa, signed in Milan in 1299 through the mediation of the city's new ruler Matteo Visconti, essentially settled nothing as to the lingering commercial rivalry. The Venetians now looked enviously towards those Black Sea markets and it would not be long before Nicolo Giustinian, the ambassador chosen to court the Tartar sultan's favour, would set off for central Asia to strengthen the foundations of La Serenissima's enterprise at Tana.

Ironically it was from this very same region that both warring states would bring home to their citizens something far more perilous and devastating than the mutual hostility of shipboard combat. It is not known for certain how *Yersinia pestis*, the Black Death, arrived in Europe, but it seems likely that either Genoese or Venetians or both were key transmitters in the earliest phase of a bubonic plague epidemic. The grim sequence is easily traced. In 1341 the Tartar khan Mohammed Uzbeg dies and his more volatile successor Zani Beg, following scuffles at Tana between members of the two Italian merchant colonies, descends upon the settlement, seizes Venetian merchandise and drives the traders away. Some of them flee for refuge to Caffa and are given shelter by the Genoese. Zani Beg, determined to oust the Italians from the Black Sea altogether, lays siege to the city in a campaign which, with one brief respite, he keeps up for the next two years. In 1346, however, the defenders note that a strange disease is starting to decimate the Tartar horde, 'the result of coagulating humours in their groins and armpits, followed by a putrid fever'. Crazed by the experience of so foul an epidemic, the Tartars tie the plague-stricken cadavers to their catapults and fling them over Caffa's walls. 'Huge piles of dead were hurled inside... the air became completely infected and the water supply was poisoned by rotting corpses.'

There is no reason to doubt this account, though the plague itself surely originated further east than at a Tartar encampment in the Crimea. What certainly occurred soon afterwards were major epidemics in nearby ports, including Constantinople, from which Genoese and Venetian ships carried the disease home to Italy. In Venice the Black Death struck with fullest force during the early summer of 1348. Walking the city nowadays, intrigued as the traveller may be by its ganglion of narrow streets, side alleys, courtyards and the dark connecting passages, known as *sottoporteghi*, under overhanging buildings, we can easily imagine, at the same time, just how quickly the infection could be transferred across a teeming population here. A contemporary writer, Lorenzo De Monacis, in his *Chronicon de Rebus Venetis*, describes these urban spaces as being literally crammed with corpses. Churches and chapels became dumping grounds for the dead, houses were abandoned with their moribund inmates left to perish and 'the whole city became a tomb'. Special plague pits were dug on the lagoon islands, where the heaped bodies were ferried on special rafts. According to De Monacis 'many of those on the rafts and in the pits were still breathing... most of the boatmen caught the plague and died'. Oddly there was no looting of the many houses left empty. 'An astounding sort of lethargy and fear seized hold of everyone in the city.'

There seems to have been little that the authorities could do in order to cope with the multitude of different emergencies arising from the epidemic's onset during a particularly torrid summer, encouraging the spread of the disease. Three special officers, the *Savi alla Sanita*, were appointed by the Grand Council '*pro conservatione sanitatis et ad evitandum corruptionem in terra*', but their public health measures were gestural, acts of desperation as the death toll mounted. Orders went out, for example, that all graves dug within the city should be at least five feet in depth and that each of its *sestieri* should nominate '*tres bonos homines*' to act in an official capacity, overseeing the movement of corpses and dealing with various kinds of antisocial behaviour which the sudden implosion of civic order might seem calculated to encourage. What people remembered afterwards was the sickening stench of decay in the air of every street and open space as the bodies were shuffled to and fro.

The habitual energy and restlessness of living Venice evaporated with sinister rapidity. Rialto markets came to an abrupt halt, canals were emptied of their gondolas, the Arsenale boatyards fell silent. Those who could leave town fled to the mainland, many of course unwitting plague-spreaders to other centres in the Veneto. In July 1348 the Senate, now reduced to a fraction of its membership, issued vain threats of punishment against public employees joining the mass exodus, more especially aimed at notaries involved in the drafting of wills and property transfers and at the multitude of doctors who had preferred safety in rural areas to carrying out their responsibilities in the foetid thoroughfares of pandemic-stricken Venice.

With the end of summer and a gradual fall in case numbers, the main question for the survivors was how to repopulate a city which had lost an estimated two-thirds of its resident community. The Grand Council, depleted as it was, had begun discussing ways of luring people back, 'since through the will of God the population is greatly diminished'. The idea was to bring in fresh inhabitants by means of tax breaks and special privileges, with a fast track to full citizenship, '*ad habitationem et reparationem civitatis nostrae*'. Once it became safer to enter Venice again, the scheme worked extremely well and by 1350 the place had started to recover something of its erstwhile vigour and vitality. The dismal trauma of the Black Death, however, could not easily be shaken off. Nowadays, as we enter the Accademia art gallery to marvel at the works of Bellini, Giorgione and Titian, it is worth pausing in its entrance hall, the former Scuola Grande della Carita, to seek out a marble lunette above one of the doorways. Below the kneeling figures of two angels holding the double-circled cross that represents the *scuola* itself is a lengthy inscription in medieval Venetian-inflected Italian, setting out the bare facts of the whole grim experience in remorseless detail. Symptoms of the plague are mentioned – 'Some spat blood from their mouths and developed swellings in their armpits and groin, others saw their flesh turn black as coal' – as is the psychic impact of sheer terror on the bonds of family life – 'people were so afraid that fathers dared not approach their sons nor sons go near their fathers'. This visitation of 1348 had been a baptism of fire for Venetians, as the first of several major epidemic outbreaks which would blast the city over the next three centuries. They had been warned.

For Genoa the sickness had been comparably devastating. A population of 60,000 was reduced in a mere few years to 24,000 and the plague was carried meanwhile into France, England, Germany and Scandinavia. Both the Genoese and the Venetians were all too aware of the fact that it was their own merchant crews, sailing home from the Black Sea, that had carried death with them in the holds of their galleys. As one chronicler from Liguria put it, 'Confess what you have done, oh Genoa! Venice, Tuscany, Italy, say what you did! We of Genoa and Venice are responsible for revealing this judgment of God. Voyaging home to our cities we brought with us the arrows of death. In the moment that our families kissed and embraced us, we spat poison from our mouths.'

Precisely none of this *arrière-pensée* spirit seems to have dampened the impulse on either side for the two republics to renew their struggle, with its rhythms of ancient grudge, advantage-seeking and naked aggression. Once more the Black Sea, the Aegean and the Adriatic became theatres of strife. The Genoese were soon back in Caffa and when in 1350 they seized Venetian ships at anchor in its port, this was signal enough to La Serenissima that any further truce was meaningless and it had become time to deal with the arrogant competitor. Fourteen Genoese vessels lay in the harbour at Negroponte (Khalki) on the island of Euboea, ten of which were promptly captured and set on fire by the Venetian admiral Marco Ruzzini. Reprisal was a foregone conclusion and in due season a fleet from Chios boldly descended on Negroponte, looted the town and planted the red cross of Saint George, Genoa's patron, on its battlements. The island enjoyed major significance among Venice's imperial possessions in the Aegean but the Senate now needed to look for allies so as to recover it. King Pedro of Aragon, nursing his own grievances against the Genoese in the Balearic islands and the ports of Catalonia, was ready to lend warships and so, apparently, was the Byzantine emperor John Palaeologos, irked by their bullying and presumption on his own doorstep in Constantinople. A sea fight in the Bosphorus resulted in a pyrrhic victory for Genoa. Though the combined Venetian and Aragonese fleets were scattered, so many of its ships were set on fire that, in the glum verdict of one chronicler, 'the triumph of that day is best forgotten'.

The truth was that in the wake of the Black Death and subsequent efforts to recover its commercial edge among the markets and trade routes of the East, Venice had begun to bounce back with surprising speed and resilience. A serious revolution in Crete in 1364 against La Serenissima's unreasonable tax demands to fund public works may have caused a brief alarm but was successfully quashed with the help of Luchino Dal Verme, first of those *condottieri* – hired military commanders – on whom the Signoria would increasingly rely as a new century drew near, so as to ensure its fiat was executed with a suitably mailed fist. Some in Venice believed, naturally enough, that Genoese agents had been busy fomenting the rebellion but there was no evidence for this. Though the Cretans accepted defeat sullenly enough, they never again sought to shake off the Venetian presence altogether and this would assume a symbolic importance many years later when the Ottoman Turks threatened to seize the island.

It was in another of the larger Mediterranean islands that Venice's final combat with Genoa was destined to begin. Cyprus was currently ruled by the Lusignan family, a French baronial clan who also laid claim to the Crusader kingdom of Jerusalem, now in possession of the Mamluks. At the coronation of the boy king Peter II in Famagusta fights broke out between Venetian and Genoese merchants over issues of precedence, with further squabbles taking place during a grand banquet that followed. When the Genoese started pelting their rivals with bread, the Cypriot guests, favouring the Venetians, angrily seized hold of Genoa's consul, threw him out of a palace window and later beat up and burned the Genoese quarter of the city. Since Cyprus was a key staging post for traders on the journey eastwards, Genoa needed to take immediate action, sending a fleet to take control of the island while allowing the fourteen-year-old Peter to remain its nominal king. Though the Venetians were not expelled altogether, their position grew ever more vulnerable, especially as tensions were once more rising between the two mercantile communities in nearby Constantinople.

Chiefly at stake here was the possession of Tenedos, a small but strategically crucial island lying at the entrance to the Dardanelles, which had proved its significance centuries earlier to the Greeks in the Trojan War and was to be a bone of contention between Greece and Turkey in later ages. Matters were not helped for either Venice or Genoa by the instability of a Byzantium in which a father and a son, John and Andronicus Palaeologos, were busy manoeuvring against one another for the imperial crown. While John favoured the Venetians enough to cede Tenedos to them, Andronicus, raised to the purple by Genoese who threw his father into prison, duly cancelled the gift and bestowed it on his benefactors. Though their attempt at snatching the island back from Venice failed, the expedition produced the necessary flashpoint for full-scale war, whose reverberations were felt across the entire Mediterranean.

Others besides Genoa, after all, were looking for opportunities just now to humiliate Venice and seize as much of its expanding empire as they could. The Habsburg duke Rudolf of Austria coveted the city of Treviso and its surrounding district, known as the Marca Trevigiana. A prospect of further advantages beckoned King Lajos of Hungary, who had earlier swooped on Friuli and the Veneto and gained control in Dalmatia, while Francesco da Carrara, lord of Padua, a thorn in Venice's side as he sought to push his mainland domains to the very edge of the lagoon, was clearly scenting blood. For the Doge of Venice, Andrea Contarini, the prospect of the Republic's survival as an independent entity, let alone as a territorial overlord, looked suitably bleak.

Contarini had never really wanted his supreme honour and twice sought to avoid it. His early life had been far from exemplary, that of a gambler and a libertine, until a curious episode took place while he was carrying on an affair with a beautiful young nun at the convent of Santa Maria della Celestia. As the pair prepared to consummate their liaison, Contarini noticed a ring on her finger and asked why she wore it. 'Because I am the bride of Christ,' answered the girl. Suddenly wracked with guilt, he took leave of her at once, feeling still more conscience-stricken when passing a crucifix which hung on the cloister wall. In the act of crossing himself, he thought he saw the figure of Christ nodding its head in a blessing on his current mood of remorse. That same night he had a dream in which the Saviour appeared and told him that he would become Doge of Venice at a moment when La Serenissima faced the greatest crisis in its existence.

He went on to marry, had several children and retired to his country estate. The two earlier offers of the dogeship were duly rejected but in 1368 the Signoria was not prepared to tolerate a third refusal. Back came Contarini to the city, donned the *corno dogale* and meekly prepared, in line with his dream, for living in interesting times. These duly arrived in 1372, first with the unpleasantness at King Peter's coronation in Cyprus, then with the gathering hostilities between the merchant colonies in Constantinople and the row with the two emperors over Tenedos. In 1378 Venice was ready to declare war, though at that critical moment she had almost no allies except for Ferrara and Milan, both of whose dukes in any case had their own internal problems to cope with. Otherwise the Republic's own resources, none of them infinite – those of her navy, of the Arsenale, of the funds she was ready to pay for hiring mercenaries on the mainland and the efficiency underpinning her governmental structures – were what she had left to rely on.

It was at this juncture that two outstanding maritime leaders stepped forward to meet the challenge. When the declaration of war against Genoa was issued, command of the Republic's fleet was entrusted to Admiral Vettor Pisani. From certain key aspects he was an ideal choice. Popular and charismatic, he was also adept at taking the long view of any strategic situation, even if, for a period, this might mean risking the confidence of the doge and the Grand Council. In the coming struggle around Italy's coasts Pisani was to be aided by the equally striking figure of Carlo Zeno, someone whose earlier career hardly prepared him to take a frontline role in a decisive naval war. His parents, designing him for the priesthood, sent the boy for ecclesiastical training to Rome, where he managed to acquire a bishopric from the pope before throwing all thoughts of a higher calling aside in exchange for a dissolute spell of university life at Padua, followed by several years of soldiering in Greece and Cyprus and a business career among the traders of Constantinople

Such a trajectory, an archetypal case of readiness to go with the flow, made Zeno a perfect counterpart to Pisani and their respective fleets now roamed in quest of the Genoese in the enemy's own waters off western Italy. While Zeno, whose earlier naval experience among the Greek islands always had a touch of piracy about it, sought his prey on the open sea, Pisani successfully engaged a Genoese squadron off the coast north of Anzio before returning to the Adriatic and a winter refuge in the harbour at Pola. Pursued by another hostile fleet, he was forced, against his better judgment, to give battle, but though he eventually beat off his opponents, only six battered Venetian galleys managed at length to escape to the relative safety of their home lagoon. Charged with dereliction of duty, Pisani was stripped of his command, impeached and given a six-month gaol sentence.

This would not be the last time that Venice abruptly misjudged one of her best men, for whose talent and courage she would later have cause to be thankful. The fate of Francesco Morosini, commander during the last phase, in 1654, of the long war with the Turks over Crete, has interesting echoes of Vettor Pisani's summary disgrace. As for Carlo Zeno, there was no immediate chance of recalling him, supposing anybody at that moment knew exactly where his fleet lay. All that seemed left for the Venetians was a reliance on a general will within their city to fight to the finish, even as enemy armies gathered on the mainland and Genoese ships lay comfortably at anchor outside the lagoon. Plans were already afoot in Genoa for the future of a Venice reduced to total subjection under the heel of its conquering rival. A fortress was to be built in the Cannaregio district, commanding a causeway linking this area to the mainland so that troops could easily be moved in to quell any potential insurrection. On 6 August 1379, meanwhile, Admiral Pietro Doria, at the head of some fifty galleys,

A bust of Admiral Carlo Zeno, a Venetian hero
of the War of Chioggia against Genoa (1378–81),
by the nineteenth-century sculptor Andrea Giordani.

ANDRE
QVI CL
IMPERAT
AT RO C
FELICIS
M.CCC.LX

entered the lagoon from the north and swept inexorably down towards the port of Chioggia at its southernmost entrance, burning and pillaging along the shores as he went. After ten days of frantic resistance by the Venetian garrison, the citadel yielded to a combined force of Genoese and their Hungarian allies, together with a Paduan army led by Francesco da Carrara. At the latter's prompting, ambassadors from Venice suing for peace were turned away, with Pietro Doria boasting that 'I have bridled the horses of Saint Mark'.

Not quite. That immemorial spirit of defiance that had seen their ancestors face off King Pepin and Byzantine emperors and which would later see them endure the long Austrian siege of 1849 now fired the Venetians, friendless and close to starvation as they were. In return for their steadfastness, Doge Contarini was now forced to grant the citizens' demand that Vettor Pisani be released from gaol at once and reinstated as admiral of the fleet. Waiting outside the prison was a huge crowd ready to carry him in triumph to San Marco. When they cried 'Viva Messer Vettor Pisani!' he protested, 'Be silent, or if you will, say "Viva Messer San Marco!"', to which of course the call came back 'Viva Vettor Pisani e San Marco!' After mass in the Basilica the admiral was chaired again to his own house and 'so great was the press of folk through the streets that a grain of millet seed might not have fallen on the ground where they trod'.

Pisani's release inspired fresh hope among those busy raising the various planned defences on the Lido and its islands and hastened the building of four new galleys in the Arsenale. A forced loan raised a massive sum, women gave their jewellery to the cause, foreigners were offered citizenship in return for donations and the Senate shrewdly dangled before thirty of the richest citizens a promise of noble rank and a seat on the Grand Council once the emergency was over. Pisani, back among his devoted crewmen, began watching for his moment against the Genoese, aware that they had grown sloppy and complacent in their winter quarters at Chioggia. Staging a diversion there with what looked like a landing force preparing for a siege enabled the admiral, on the night of 21 December, to place two large hulks filled with stones across the harbour entrance, leaving Pietro Doria and his fleet trapped and vulnerable to assault.

The struggle, known to history as the War of Chioggia, was not yet over. Only with Carlo Zeno's providential return to the lagoon with his eighteen ships, taking everyone by surprise on New Year's Day 1380, did Venice's fortunes start to turn. He had made good use of his time by harrying Genoese vessels in the eastern Aegean, including a

previous pages Paolo Veronese's (1528–88) portrayal of the triumphant return of Doge Andrea Contarini after the recapture of Chioggia in June 1380, which turned the tide of the Venetian–Genoese War in Venice's favour.

ship laden not just with a cargo worth 50,000 ducats but with several rich merchant passengers whose ransom money Zeno shared among his crew. Sailing now towards Brondolo, neighbouring Chioggia, he launched an attack on the town, a shot from the single cannon on his galley's forecastle bringing down its church campanile and burying Pietro Doria under the ruins. For a further six months, as Venice gradually regained control of the Lidi and the lagoon, Chioggia's defenders held on, clinging to a hope that either of the two Genoese fleets in the open Adriatic must eventually come to their rescue. It was Vettor Pisani who boldly grappled with one of these at Manfredonia, on the coast of Puglia, dying of wounds sustained in the fight. On 24 June the worn-out and disillusioned garrison at Chioggia surrendered and Doge Andrea Contarini, who had insisted on remaining with Zeno and his ships throughout the blockade, brought the Genoese prisoners back to Venice, many of them rowing the Bucintoro which carried him in triumph to the city.

The war on sea was over but the fight across the Veneto and Friuli continued for another year, until peace was concluded at Turin with the help of Count Amadeo VI of Savoy. Known as 'the Green Count', from a flamboyant emerald outfit he had sported at a tournament, Amadeo was a wily diplomat, with an eye on keeping the peace in northern Italy for the sake of his own interests in the region around Genoa. He persuaded the Venetians to accept a settlement that at first glance hardly looked advantageous. Dalmatia, for now at least, would remain in the King of Hungary's possession. Tenedos had its castle slighted and its Greek population dispatched to live in Crete, while the Genoese remained a dominant commercial presence around the Black Sea. Yet Genoa itself, demoralized by its sudden reversal of fortune in Chioggia, faced a period of serious political implosion and near anarchy, never recovering enough to challenge Venetian supremacy in the Mediterranean again.

It was Venice, brought to the edges of bankruptcy, starvation and ruin over the arc of prolonged warfare, which now began an astoundingly rapid economic revival. While those promised thirty new citizen names were added to the Golden Book, the Republic, through a careful husbanding of available resources and some skilful mending of fences with sovereign powers across the rest of Italy, could now embark upon what would soon reveal itself as a golden century of achievement and prosperity for the Venetian state.

overleaf The Battle of Chioggia, 1380, as imagined by the eighteenth-century artist Giovanni Grevembroch. Genoese flags can be seen flying on some of the buildings, while the Venetian ships display the Lion of St Mark.

'CONSISTING
OF ALL
NATIONS'

The mood of confidence and resolve with which Venice, after the victory at Chioggia, began the fifteenth century is nowhere better displayed than in its palaces, whether up and down the Grand Canal or overlooking the *campi* and quaysides in the city's six districts. Features of their design often reflected the Oriental world in which their owners – or the ancestors of their owners – had made the fortune that paid for the building itself. It has been pointed out, for instance, that the layout of several of these palaces resembles that of merchants' houses in Mamluk Egypt of the same period, constructed along an extended central spine, with an emphasis on depth and volume in their T-shaped halls. Their ogee arches, which we take for granted as the most characteristic feature of late medieval Venetian architecture, are another Oriental touch, originating in India, moving westwards to be adopted by builders of mosques in Alexandria and Cairo and finding their way to the lagoon during the decades following the Fourth Crusade. Beginning as warehouses, these mansions would gradually shift their function to residential spaces, each referred to not as *palazzo*, 'palace', but as *casa*, 'house', the latter shortened, in Venetian dialect, to '*ca*' – Ca' Foscari, Ca' Loredan, Ca' Morosini etcetera.

The city at the end of the Middle Ages was a place which, more than ever before, had evolved a passion for display, for a life in which performance, ceremony and decorum played a vital role and in which public observance of a whole roster of protocols formed part of the annual calendar. There was always something for ordinary Venetians to gape and marvel at. It was a place of unending processions to mark some feast or anniversary commemoration. Those brocade robes spoken of in a previous chapter added to the spectacle, together with the gold-embroidered copes, chasubles and dalmatics of a numerous clergy. Chief among these corteges were the *andate*, the solemn progresses made by

overleaf The Ca' d'Oro on the Grand Canal, built in Venetian Gothic style for the Contarini family, 1428–30, to designs by Giovanni and Bartolomeo Bon.

the doge to this or that place of worship, followed by an escort of patricians and selected representatives of the bourgeoisie, the *cittadini*, whose presence gave body and depth to the occasion as a symbol of Venice's uniquely communal government. The doge, wearing his horned headdress and ermine-trimmed robe, was accompanied by foreign diplomats, a number of important office-holders and the clergy of San Marco, in their capacity as ministrants to a palace chapel. To certain *andate* a musical component was added by the presence of a choir and instrumental performers, heightening the occasion's festive solemnity with canticles, anthems and motets.

Processional also, at various times and seasons, were the members of the different *scuole*, those charitable foundations which had become increasingly important in the life of Venice both for their valuable welfare initiatives and as a source of social cohesion among those who belonged to them. Chief among these lay confraternities, with their meeting halls and chapels, often close to churches dedicated to their patron saints, were the six Scuole Grandi, governed by the *cittadini*, each with a membership of around five hundred, drawn from very mixed backgrounds and with widely varying financial resources. The responsibility of richer members was to provide shelter and sustenance for the indigent inhabitants of the surrounding quarter, while brothers not so well off were expected to carry out spiritual exercises and say prayers for the souls of the *scuola*'s departed.

A favourite pretext for a Venetian procession was the parading of holy relics among the myriad such to be found in the city's churches and religious houses. The flavour of such occasions at the summit of Venice's splendour and prosperity is conveyed for us in a series of paintings dating from around 1500, commissioned for the hall of the Scuola Grande di San Giovanni Evangelista, not far from the Franciscan basilica of Santa Maria Gloriosa dei Frari. Most famous of all these works is Gentile Bellini's *Miracle of the True Cross at the Bridge of San Lorenzo*, now hanging alongside seven of the others in the Accademia gallery (a ninth painting, by no less a master than Pietro Perugino, no longer exists, alas). In 1369, while the newly crowned King Peter of Cyprus was trying to interest Venice in a crusade against the Turks and while the Republic itself was busy cultivating whatever alliance it could against Genoa, his chancellor Philippe de Mézières had presented the *scuola* with a precious fragment of the Holy Cross, traditionally considered to have been discovered by Saint Helen, mother of Emperor Constantine. Many years afterwards, during the annual procession of the relic through the streets of Venice, the reliquary containing it was accidentally dropped into the canal flowing beneath Ponte San Lorenzo, close to the church of that name. Attempts to rescue this treasured object were unavailing until Andrea Vendramin, Grand Guardian of the *scuola*, tucked up his robes and dived in to save it.

Gentile Bellini's canvas belongs to a distinctive genre of Venetian art which managed to renew itself across successive eras of the city's history, one where this dimension of public spectacle fuses with Venice's sense of its own exceptionalism to create a particular urban narrative found nowhere else in Italian painting. The scene is crowded, so busy indeed that the artist has had problems trying to cram the throng of onlookers into a canvas whose perspective depth he cannot master quite adequately. Some of the figures, such as the group of donors in the foreground, are plainly individualized portraits, including two heads in the throng on the left that appear to have been added later than the others, perhaps at the *scuola's* bidding. The white-robed Andrea Vendramin, rising from the canal with the relic's ornate monstrance brandished so triumphantly, is less clearly defined than the men in the gondolas behind him, but this is because Gentile seeks, not altogether successfully, to convey an idea of the water running off him and soaking his attire.

Truly engaging is the way in which the painter has sought both to render the excitement of the occasion itself – the recovery of the precious fragment was hailed as a miracle – and to capture the actuality of its Venetian setting. Here indeed are those grand palazzi with their ogival windows, their decorated exterior friezes and paterae, their green shutters, pantiled roofs and those typically Venetian chimney pots in the shape of inverted cones, of which a few can still be spotted today. Beneath them, on the bridge along the *fondamenta* – paved quayside – and on the blue-green water of the canal, the assembled spectators and participants in the procession mirror the huddled totality of Venice, whether at the time this event took place in 1420 or else when Gentile was at work on his version of it some eighty years later.

The physical nature of the medieval city, which it basically retains today, meant that with one notable exception it was largely impossible for its various social classes to distance themselves significantly from one another. There were no urban enclaves, fashionable districts or the equivalent of today's 'gated communities'. Hence the crowd on the *fondamenta* here gathers patricians and citizens together as well as priests, children and the ladies attending Caterina Cornaro, last Queen of Cyprus, whom we shall look at in more detail in a later chapter. Yet perhaps the most arresting presence, then as now, is neither that of

overleaf The *Miracle of the True Cross at the Bridge of San Lorenzo* (c.1500), by Gentile Bellini; one of a number of such works commissioned for the Grand Hall of the Scuola Grande di San Giovanni Evangelista.

Queen Caterina or of waterborne Andrea Vendramin in the foreground, but of the figure on the middle far right of the composition. He is a tall young African, naked except for his linen drawers, who stands perched on the edge of a wooden landing stage for boats at what is obviously a lane between a pair of dwelling houses, their window shutters folded back. Holding on to his outstretched arm is a young woman, perhaps a servant girl, who seems to have been encouraging him to jump into the canal and try, like the five other swimmers surrounding Vendramin, to retrieve the fallen monstrance.

This is not the only image of a black man in the Venetian art of this period. 'You have among you many a purchased slave', says Shakespeare's Shylock to the assembled court in the trial scene of *The Merchant of Venice*, and at least some of these slaves would have been black. In a painted treatment of a similar scene by Vittore Carpaccio, also for the Scuola di San Giovanni Evangelista but portraying another miracle, this time taking place close to the old wooden Rialto bridge, the most eye-catching of the gondoliers on a busy Grand Canal is a fashionably dressed young black man. He sports a jaunty feathered cap, a red doublet and chequered grey and white hose.

Both Gentile Bellini and Carpaccio are making use of these African men as tonal elements in their compositional scheme. The implication here is that a black presence among a predominantly white Venetian crowd is sufficiently unusual as to seize our attention as our eye travels across the canvas. We know almost nothing as to the lives and destinies of what would remain an extremely small black population in Venice until the present day. In Shakespeare's other Venetian play, *Othello*, the dramatist confuses the issue by using a source novella, Giraldi Cinthio's *The Moor of Venice*, in which the title character is North African, a Moor from the Maghreb, yet is portrayed in the tragedy as 'black', a 'thick-lips', namely sub-Saharan in appearance. Slaves there undoubtedly were, and markets for them in Venice itself could be found on the Rialto and elsewhere in the city but most of these came from the Black Sea regions, Armenia, Georgia and the Tartar domains, where Venetians competed with the Genoese in this particular trade. Occasionally Portuguese merchants visiting the city brought Africans for sale, and other such human traffic came from further afield.

Many of these slaves could be sold on to buyers from Italy and elsewhere in the Mediterranean. For those kept in Venice itself, life was better than they might expect, considered as they were in terms of household property and almost always granted an eventual freedom, either in a separate act of manumission or else through a clause of

Miracle of the Relic of the Cross at the Ponte di Rialto, by Vittore Carpaccio, *c*.1496. It is housed in the Accademia gallery, alongside seven other such canvases commissioned for the Scuola Grande di San Giovanni Evangelista.

their employer's will which, as far as can be known, was properly honoured. Freed male slaves often ended up working on the gondola ferries – *traghetti* – at various spots around the city, while women might find employment as textile workers, nurses or kitchen maids. The important difference between this species of servitude and the slave system operated in later ages in the West Indies and colonial America was that the former was never envisaged as perpetual. A slave in Venice was looked after, protected and given the wherewithal to thrive in the outside world once set free.

Black faces in a Venetian crowd added to a prevailing sense of exotic otherness, to the concept of a city whose air of transience and difference became an essential part of its attraction, drawing comment from all who visited it. A multitude of people here either came from somewhere far off or were on their way to somewhere else. Pilgrims, for example, provided a major source of income for those involved in *colleganza* ventures and the chartering of galleys. Setting off for the Levant, a ship transporting travellers to the Holy Land (which of course still welcomed the custom such people might bring, despite the fact that Muslim rulers now controlled the entire littoral of Syria and Palestine) was ritually sent on its way with a mass in the church of San Niccolo del Lido, blessings from priests as it made ready to leave, a fanfare of trumpets and the singing of sacred canticles by the pilgrims themselves. Less adventurous souls with equally devout intentions would visit shrines and relics in the churches of Venice itself, on which the enterprise of generations, including the pillagers of Constantinople in 1204, had bestowed entire incorrupt bodies of saints such as Athanasius, Lucy and Christina, as well as a mass of precious corporeal fragments like those preserved in the amazing Capella Molin in the church of Santa Maria Zobenigo.

Other travellers, visiting Venice for purely secular or practical purposes, shared in the feeling of singularity which the townscape invariably created. In 1494 the diplomat Philippe de Commines was sent by King Charles VIII of France on a mission, fruitless as this would turn out, to prevent La Serenissima from joining an alliance to force his royal master out of Italy with his invading army. Whatever the embassy's outcome, Commines was suitably impressed by the sheer novelty of the environment in which he found himself. 'I was extremely surprised at the situation of this city, to see so many churches, monasteries and houses, and all in the water', he writes, 'and the people having no other passage up and down the streets but in boats.' He counted at least seventy religious houses of different kinds scattered across the lagoon islands, 'very beautiful and magnificent both in building and furniture, with fair gardens belonging to them', and was frankly amazed by the number of sacred buildings within the city's confines – 'indeed it is most strange to behold so many churches in the sea'. To celebrate the so-called Holy League whose operations he had been unable to frustrate, there were 'extraordinary fireworks upon the turrets, steeples and tops of the ambassadors' houses, multitudes of bonfires were lit and the cannon all round the city were fired'. And of course there was the inevitable joyous procession, with 'the Signory and the ambassadors all very splendidly dressed, several of them in crimson gowns which the Signory had presented to them', followed by 'a great many pageants and mysteries exhibited to the people'.

What we see here, as in so many other accounts by distinguished foreigners visiting the city in an official or semi-official capacity, is the way in which Venice made use of form, ceremony and protocol as elements in a political rhetoric employed so as to compel respect for La Serenissima, to dictate the pace and rhythm of negotiations and to underline the Republic's uniqueness when contrasted with other states, as if to say, 'This is how we do it here and we know you will be impressed.' Sixty years before Philippe de Commines arrived, Emperor John VIII Palaeologos of Byzantium had come to Italy looking for support against the encroaching power of the Turks, both from Venice and from Pope Eugenius IV, himself Venetian, who was hoping, in the process, for a chance to reunite the Roman and Orthodox confessions. Greek historian Georgios Phrantzes, making use of a first-hand report by the emperor's brother, conveys the atmosphere perfectly in evoking the arrival of the imperial galleys at the Lido. 'A whole convoy of ships came out from the city of Venice to meet the Emperor, in such numbers that the sea was scarcely visible for the mass of vessels.' The doge, Francesco Foscari, 'with the great men of the city and all his Council', paid a ceremonial visit to the imperial galley and on the following day the Bucintoro was launched, 'beautifully decorated and adorned with scarlet hangings, at its prow golden lions and cloth of gold… one could see at a glance that it was the ship of a great chief of state'. On another vessel, a sort of maritime pageant-wagon, stood specially costumed actors representing angels, warriors and 'the princes of foreign lands', while trumpets played and a concourse of other ships gathered around it. 'Just as one cannot count the stars in the heavens or the leaves in the forest or the grains of sand in the sea or the drops of rain, so it was with these vessels.'

Even though recording all this at a distance, from somebody else's memories, the Byzantine chronicler is as dizzy with admiration as the Venetians intended, extolling 'the rich and lordly city of Venice, deserving of all praises', dazzled not only by the grandeur of San Marco and Palazzo Ducale but by the wisdom and intelligence of the citizens themselves. Of the Greek visitors Phrantzes writes that 'their souls were torn from their bodies at the sight of such glory; indeed they were quite beside themselves and could well say "Earth and sea are today become Heaven"'. For now, at any rate, the extreme ambiguity of Venice's relationship with Byzantium and the menacing Ottomans was carefully obscured in this subtlest of propaganda displays by the Signoria.

For other 'strangers' the place acted either as a refuge or perhaps as an ideal context in which to begin again in a life chronically disordered by political strife and personal fortune. One such was the Englishman Thomas Mowbray, Duke of Norfolk, part of a nexus of powerful noblemen surrounding King Richard II, who had come to the throne as a boy in 1377. Mowbray was ambitious and calculating, determined to make the most of his close connexions with the Plantagenet royal family but never fully able to master his impulsive nature, his exaggerated sense of entitlement and a consequent feeling that the world always owed him more than it seemed ready to provide in terms of influence, money and position. His involvement in the murder of the king's uncle Thomas of Woodstock, Earl of Gloucester, was the more problematic given Richard's own dubious wishes in the matter. When another member of the family, Henry Bolingbroke, challenged Mowbray to trial by battle, the king intervened, almost certainly to hide his own readiness to countenance Gloucester's death, and banished both men from the kingdom. Shakespeare makes this into the opening episode of his play *King Richard II*, with Mowbray leaving England never to return, though Bolingbroke almost immediately mounts a coup d'état with the aim of usurping the throne.

Soured by his experience at the centre of power in a society where the monarchs increasingly failed to maintain control over an aristocracy most of whose scions were royal blood relatives, Mowbray headed for Venice, to all intents and purposes a state in which noble oligarchs, ever since the days of Bajamonte Tiepolo and Marin Falier, were prevented from pursuing dynastic ambitions by virtue of checks and balances within the governmental system. Here he seems to have decided on making a pilgrimage to the Holy Land, leaving in one of the galley convoys and eventually fulfilling his vow. It was on the homeward voyage that he contracted a shipboard fever, vaguely referred to as 'plague', and died soon after landing in Venice where he was buried in the Benedictine monastery on the island of San Giorgio Maggiore. Would Mowbray otherwise have led a quiet life in exile on the lagoon? It seems doubtful, given the restlessness and discontent which had characterized his career in England.

A happier refugee altogether – at least for a while – was Francesco Petrarca, 'Petrarch', widely acknowledged throughout Italy as her greatest living poet. In 1341, aged thirty-seven, he was crowned laureate by his admirers in Rome and soon afterwards began a new phase of his career as a travelling sage, a peripatetic intellectual consulted by rulers not merely in his homeland but throughout the whole of Europe. Besides being a major influence on fellow poets, especially in their treatment of the sonnet form – he wrote several hundred to a beautiful but hitherto unidentified woman he named as Laura – Petrarch also produced works of philosophy, moral essays, biographies and verse epistles. His positive outlook and a belief in mankind's capacity for redemption and renewal through education and an understanding of what the past can teach us makes him one of the key figures in the foundational shift of consciousness we loosely call humanism, from which the Italian Renaissance began.

Petrarch's first visit to Venice had taken place in 1353, when he was living in Milan as an honoured guest of its ruling family, the Visconti. His earnest conviction as to a need for peace and co-operation between Italian states, in place of their habitual jostling and aggression, had found utterance in the anguished ode '*Italia mia, benché 'l parlar sia indarno*', exhorting the various warlords, factions and rival cities to stop fighting and seek instead 'something more worthy of you in body and mind, so that you gain praise and happiness here below, while the road to heaven lies open'. The last line of what would become one of Petrarch's most famous poems, '*I' vo gridando: Pace, pace, pace.*' – 'I go crying "Peace, peace, peace."' – had found its echo in a letter he wrote to Doge Andrea Dandolo, seeking an end to the ongoing war with Genoa. Now, during Dandolo's final year of office, the poet was sent by Archbishop Giovanni Visconti of Milan to broker a truce between the two republics. A heartfelt address to the Senate, however, induced no substantial change in Venice's generally hostile attitude to the Genoese.

Failure hardly discouraged the poet, who was in any case excited to make his acquaintance with the city, recovering now from its terrible visitation by the Black Death a few years previously. When a dangerous epidemic broke out in Milan in 1360, the lagoons seemed to offer an ideal retreat and the Venetians, deaf though they had been to his eloquent peacemaking, were happy to welcome so distinguished a figure among them as a resident. Petrarch was given a house, Casa Molin delle Due Torri, on the Riva degli Schiavoni (a memorial plaque to him can be seen there today), and settled down to enjoy life in a place he wonderingly referred to as '*mundus alter*', 'another world'. For him this 'most august city of Venice' was to be revered as 'the only home of liberty, peace and justice, the sole refuge of honourable men, haven for all those who, assailed on every side by the storms of tyranny and war, seek to live in quiet. Rich in gold but richer in fame, built upon solid marble but standing yet more firmly on a basis of civic concord, surrounded by the salt sea but the safer through the salt of good council.'

Even someone as footloose as Petrarch, having spent much of his life in France, visiting Ghent and Cologne and briefly contemplating a trip to England, could think of Venice as somewhere to linger and enjoy his status as a public intellectual. Understandably flattered by the Republic's concern for his well-being and its readiness to do him honour, he made plans to give his collection of books to the state as the nucleus of a public library, grateful towards what he once again referred to as 'the nest of liberty and only shelter for good men'. All he asked in exchange was that he should be given Casa Molin in perpetuity, so that his daughter Francesca and her husband could set up house there. The donation of about two hundred volumes, including a most precious edition of Virgil's *Aeneid*, illuminated by the great Sienese painter Simone Martini, was formally accepted by the Grand Council in 1362 and assigned for safekeeping to the Basilica of San Marco.

The arrangement, alas, got no further than this. After five happy years in Venice, busy with numerous projects, courted by influential friends and keeping up a vigorous international correspondence, much of it in his elegant Ciceronian Latin, Petrarch found himself drawn into a quarrel with a group of young Venetian intellectuals over the merits of Aristotelian philosophy as propounded and commented on by the Moorish writer Averroes of Cordoba. Rejecting their heretical beliefs, the poet was made a figure of ridicule, as he saw it, when they gave him a mock-trial for his doggedly orthodox opinions, the resulting verdict being that the poet was a good man but ignorant and illiterate. From being the seat of wonder and virtue, Venice suddenly grew odious to him and he quitted it in disillusion to spend his last days in the country village of Arquà, south of Padua, where he died in 1374.

For the Tuscan poet Francesco Petrarca (Petrarch; 1304–74)
– portrayed here by an anonymous sixteenth-century artist –
Venice was a refuge and a moral inspiration.

For outsiders like Petrarch, Mowbray and Commines it was Venice's essential difference and singularity, the paradox of its very existence in so flourishing a condition, that made them feel welcome and encouraged them to want to stay. Another kind of alien experience entirely was that shaped around a group of incomers whose contribution to the culture and prosperity of La Serenissima would prove vital to its survival but who in recompense would always be treated as second-class citizens, at times despised or hated yet, through pure Venetian opportunism, never suppressed altogether, given what the wider community could keep on taking from them.

Jews first figure in the life of medieval Venice during the late thirteenth century but the hoary old folk etymology regarding the name of Giudecca island, requiring it to mean 'where the Jews live', has been exploded in our own day as purely mythical. When a Jewish presence grows genuinely visible within the wider Venetian community is after the plague years of the 1340s and still more so following the defeat of the Genoese, when the Grand Council was seeking to restore the Republic's finances through a series of loans for which Jews would play a key role as brokers. The need was grudgingly acknowledged. According to Roman Catholic church dogma, moneylending at interest was forbidden among Christians. Since, on the other hand, most Christian states had legislation in place that prevented Jews from owning property or earning their living from the practice of individual trades or skills, this very same line of business was one of few that remained open to them. As one thirteenth-century rabbi, Jacob ben Elia of Provence, sardonically observed: 'Kings and princes have no thought other than stripping us of all our wealth. What is our life therefore, where are our powers? We must thank God who, by multiplying our riches, protects us against our persecutors.' The Jews would always be necessary to pious Christians and vilified, by the same token, for resources they alone could provide.

In 1381 therefore, Marco Correr, a senior member of the Quarantia, the doge's special council, proposed that Jewish moneylenders (referred to by the Latin term *foeneratores*) from Mestre, Padua and other mainland towns where they currently practised should be allowed to reside in Venice. Though the Senate initially rejected the suggestion it was brought back again the following year, this time to be accepted on certain conditions. The Jews were forbidden to stay for more than a few years, interest charged was limited to 10 per cent, their three banks had to operate on a regular timetable and each of these was assigned a colour, red, black or green. This last stipulation was due to the borrower's possible illiteracy, enabling him to take his coloured voucher to the appropriate lender. It was agreed, however, that the banks and pawn shops should be allowed to close on Jewish holy days and the Grand Council followed this up with injunctions to local authorities in the different *sestieri*, ordering them to protect the Jews and respect their religious scruples. In 1386 the growing community was given a burial ground next to the abbey of San Niccolò on the Lido, which remains a place of pilgrimage for Jewish visitors to Venice today.

To begin with, the relationship between La Serenissima and these newest aliens was not always comfortable. All the usual grievances against immigrants, agelessly familiar to us when we hear them now, were voiced to the Signoria. The Jews, it was said, were growing too truculent and encroaching, they were drawing overmuch wealth from the city into their own hands, they oppressed the poor and were only interested in acquiring gold and jewels for their pawn shops. At length the government, fearing that too much high-grade portable property was indeed passing into Jewish hands, revoked the original concession and expelled the community, with the proviso that individual members should be allowed to reside for periods of a fortnight before returning to the mainland.

An exception to this sudden reversal was made for Jewish doctors. The medical profession was the one area, throughout medieval Europe, in which Christians had to concede that the Jews possessed a special and indispensable skill, one that could hardly be ignored in a civil society. Here the privileged status of Jews in the Islamic world during this period played a major role, since so much of what Western doctors knew of their art had been transmitted through the science and research conducted and written up in the cities of the Muslim East or of Moorish Spain. Moving more freely than Christians between these two worlds, a Jewish physician had recourse to more sophisticated medical wisdom than his counterparts in Italy, France or England at that time and was respected accordingly. It comes as no surprise therefore to find that one of the very few people allowed to remain when the order went out in 1395 for the mass expulsion of Jews from Venice was a doctor named Salomone il Medico.

By its very nature the ban was bound to fail. It had been imposed, after all, by the government of a city which, more than any other in the Mediterranean at this time, was a staging post for everywhere else around 'the Great Sea', depending on its own porosity so as to prosper, enriched by global contacts and essentially welcoming to outsiders. Through whatever means and under whatever circumstances Jews were managing to get back into Venice, spurred on in various cases by pogroms in Switzerland and Germany and by the increasingly hostile environment created for them in Spain and Portugal as the old atmosphere of relative tolerance and *Convivencia* in the Iberian peninsula evaporated and it became opportune for its various monarchs to be seen as bulwarks of Holy Church and her most rigid orthodoxies. Accordingly the Signoria's steadfastness on the issue of Jewish residents started to waver as the new century began and in 1409 a new decree allowed them to return to Venice for more than fifteen days with a proviso that they should wear a yellow identity badge on their garments. Later on this signifier was to be enhanced by a cap of the same colour, though red was subsequently ordained, followed in due course by glazed black.

Such changes in colour somehow encapsulate the permanent ambivalence of La Serenissima towards its Jewish population. The official mind was never quite made up one way or the other, a situation that endured long after the fall of the Republic and the advent of Jewish emancipation in united Italy after 1870. The sense of this particular minority as being 'citizens of nowhere', a phrase rendered infamous by politicians in our own day, would make its own malign contribution to the fate of Venetian Jews under Mussolini's racial laws and in the two devastating years of Nazi occupation following Italy's surrender to the Allies in 1943.

Throughout the fifteenth century the issue of where exactly in Venice the Jews were to live remained controversial, as did their permitted level of interaction with the Christian community. In 1424 the Senate passed a law forbidding sexual relations between Jewish men and Christian women on pain of a six-month prison sentence if the female were a prostitute, together with a fine. If she were deemed respectable, then the sentence was increased to a year. Periodically the age-old blood libel accusation would surface, that of murdering Gentile children to provide a Passover supper, whether in the city or among the towns of La Serenissima's mainland empire. As elsewhere in Europe the supposed infant victims would often attract a local religious cult and find themselves added to the calendar of saints. In the case of little Lorenzino of Marostica, rumoured to have been crucified on a tree by a mob of enraged Jews on Good Friday in 1480, the canonization took place four centuries later, during a notionally more enlightened era, at the behest of Pope Pius IX, whose doctrinal antisemitism was part of his desperate struggle to preserve Catholic values amid a growing climate of secularism.

Venice, profoundly Catholic though its citizens liked to believe themselves, deeply committed to the rubrics and ceremonies of the church as so many of them were, never greatly cared for the papacy in its more dictatorial moods and invariably made it clear to successive pontiffs that where their ordinances were concerned La Serenissima had her own way of interpreting these and that it was up to her whether she accepted them in the form handed down from Rome. Thus in 1463, after prolonged debate as to revising the residence conditions for Jews, the Senate turned to Pope Pius II's emissary Cardinal Bessarion for his opinion, in full knowledge that he was unlikely, given his own cosmopolitan background as a Greek refugee from the Turks, someone who had embraced the Roman confession in place of his original Orthodoxy, simply to endorse an official Vatican view without significant comment or interpretation. To Doge Cristoforo Moro's enquiry on the point he responded with humanity and good sense, pointing out that while readmitting the Jews would be beneficial to Venice materially, it would also bring spiritual advantages, since kindness and generous treatment would surely encourage them at length to embrace Christianity.

The government was not quite persuaded. It took another fifteen years for the ban to be lifted at last and the exiled community to return. Even then concessions were grudging and it was only during the sixteenth century's early decades that legal strictures on where the Jews must settle were fully imposed. A statute of 1516 assigned to them the area in Cannaregio around the church of San Girolamo, a place that had formerly been the site of an iron foundry – *geto* in Venetian dialect – known as the Ghetto. There in the adjacent zones of Ghetto Vecchio and Ghetto Nuovo they would build their synagogues, known as *scuole*, and carry on their limited businesses of moneylending, pawnbroking and dealing in second-hand furniture and old clothes. Confined within this increasingly crowded quarter between two canals, both patrolled at night by special boats, and with the entrances to the Ghetto locked and guarded after curfew, the Jews of Venice created their own world, 'slighted but enduring', another of those wonders at which visitors to the lagoon's parallel universe would gaze with fascination and amazement.

overleaf The tall houses of the Venice Ghetto, moated by its canals.

AN ITALIAN
EMPIRE

The Franciscan church of Santa Maria Gloriosa dei Frari – the Frari for short – is one of the grandest and most venerable of Venice's sacred buildings, a big Gothic 'preaching barn' of the kind favoured by the friars, begun around 1340 and completed a hundred years later. Visitors flock to see its superb ensemble of artworks, dominated by Titian's thrillingly conceived *Assumption of the Virgin* above the high altar, but also including Donatello's austere wooden figure of John the Baptist, a stunning Bellini triptych showing the Virgin and Child with four saints and, for a *coup d'œil* as we enter the nave, that massive pyramidal monument to the sculptor Antonio Canova raised by six of his pupils following his death in 1822.

Amid this visual feast, few are likely to dwell for very long on a monument placed in the south transept, to the right of a doorway leading to the sacristy. Yet the ensemble, made up of two decorative panels, a lengthy inscription above them – between lion-head consoles bearing coats-of-arms, a sarcophagus of veined marble with figures of the Virgin and Child and an Annunciation, and on top of everything an imposing equestrian statue of carved wood – has its own totemic significance in the story of Venice. The horseman astride the prancing steed, with its dappled gold coat and martingale harness, is that of Paolo Savelli, who died in 1405 and was given the honour of a monument in the Frari because he had contributed money towards building the roof of this very same transept.

Born in 1350, Savelli came from a military family in Lazio which had switched its allegiance from Ghibelline to Guelph in the prolonged struggle for dominance in Italy between the papacy and the Holy Roman Emperors. Two of his collateral ancestors had become popes, as Honorius III and IV, the latter being instrumental in freeing Venice from an interdict administered by his immediate predecessor

Martin IV. Paolo Savelli himself was the first distinguished example in a line of those mercenary warriors who would enable La Serenissima to triumph over the territorial greed and ambition of her immediate neighbours and shape a mainland empire stretching from the Alps to the River Po and from the shores of the Adriatic almost to the gates of Milan. His is the earliest equestrian statue in Venice, but this caracoling presence within the Frari represents a new dimension in the Republic's political outlook, on which the Signoria would choose to build far more substantially as events changed the face of the *Stato da Mar* in the Mediterranean world mastered through the defeat of the Genoese.

Paolo Savelli was a *condottiero,* one of a whole generation of mercenary captains hired by different Italian states so as to manage and direct their wars against one another. The Italian word *condotta* means a contract – the Jews had settled in Venice on the basis of a *condotta* with the government – and the *condottieri* were warriors by contract, who could, if they chose, break the agreement at their own risk and go in search of a better deal with another regime. Though Savelli himself maintained ties with Venice beyond his period of service, there was normally no expectation of any particular attachment between the captain and those rulers acting as his current paymasters. Loyalty came at a price. What was not forgiven was any hint of a double game being played while the *condottiero* purported to be honouring the terms of his contract. Savelli was evidently a man of honour, from whose prudence and wisdom La Serenissima profited, and this is another reason why the compelling effigy of him as an armoured cavalier in scarlet bonnet and surcoat was allowed its place in the Frari.

The point made by its presence here, however, is that despite the ensemble's monumentality, with its fascinating blend of late Gothic with early Renaissance design features, this is not so much a private memorial to a departed individual as a proclamation of the victory achieved by those who engaged him and paid his salary. We know, from relatively recent conservation work on the wooden sculptures of rider and horse and of the tomb chest below it, that over subsequent centuries these were all repainted, presumably not at private expense, indicating an enduring significance in the ever-important context of Venice's official image-building. What Savelli thus represents is La Serenissima's ability to harness peerless talents in whatever field and deploy them in promoting her greatness. He is, by the same token, a harbinger of success in asserting her control over that very region of Italy from which the first Venetians had been forced to flee from barbarian invaders a thousand years earlier.

The monument to the *condottiero* Paolo Savelli in the Frari church. Venice's Captain-General during its conflict with the Lordship of Padua, Savelli succumbed to plague in October 1405.

Venice's Italian empire had started through pure practical expediency during the fourteenth century, when the *terraferma* towns (as in neighbouring Lombardy, Emilia and Romagna) had witnessed power struggles between local clans, threatening, in consequence, those supply lines for staple goods and construction materials on which the Republic depended. The city of Treviso, commanding the fertile Veneto region known as the Marca Trevigiana, was among the earliest to be annexed. In 1328 it had become clear to the Grand Council, headed by the popular Doge Giovanni Soranzo, that Verona's despot Cangrande della Scala was seeking to make himself lord of the entire region as he sent troops on expeditions to gain Vicenza and the subalpine strongholds of Feltre and Belluno. Admired as an illustrious patron of the arts who had welcomed Giotto and Dante to his court, Cangrande needed land and resources to give substance to his dreams of becoming a mighty Italian prince, a proconsul for the Holy Roman Emperor. When that same year he captured Padua, a mere few hours from the Venetian lagoon, there was genuine alarm among the Grand Council.

Doge Soranzo died, much lamented, on New Year's Eve and his successor Francesco Dandolo took up the task of bracing the Senate for war with the Veronese. An apparently unstoppable Cangrande della Scala moved onwards to Treviso, entering the town in July 1329, but fell victim that same month to what was described as 'eating apples when he was too hot'. His nephew Mastino, taking over the lordship of Verona and command of the army, had already attracted enough hostility across the region to draw allies to Venice's cause from as far off as Mantua, Ferrara and Florence. When Mastino aimed at placing a stranglehold on the Venetian salt trade along the River Brenta it became time to act. Once warfare opened in earnest, with a land army of 30,000 men mustering in Ravenna, retribution was swift. Its leader, Pietro de Rossi, whose family formerly ruled Parma, another of the Scaliger trophies, showed a masterly firmness of purpose in crushing Veronese forces and bringing the tyrant to his knees.

Mastino's desperation led him to a crucial error in trying to negotiate peace terms. As his envoy to Venice he chose, for some obscure reason, a man whose family had been grievously insulted by the Scaligers some years before. Marsilio da Carrara had formerly been lord of Padua and been maintained as its governor when the Veronese took over. A cousin of his had a pretty wife, who caught the eye of Mastino's libertine brother Alberto. An unspecified 'outrage' towards her took place and the Carrara awaited their hour of revenge. It arrived at a supper in Venice given to Marsilio by Doge Dandolo, at which the

A prospect of Treviso, a Venice in miniature amid its canals.
The town became part of the Venetian Republic in 1329,
La Serenissima's first possession on the Italian mainland.

pair discussed the terms on which Venice and its allies might accept surrender. There were other guests present as Marsilio whispered a request to the doge for a private word. Dandolo promptly let fall his napkin and as both men bent to the floor to pick it up, Marsilio asked: 'What would you give to me if I give you Padua?', to which Dandolo replied: 'Lordship of the city.'

Thus are significant bargains struck. Padua's gates were soon opened to Rossi and his army, Mastino della Scala 'made composition' in the old phrase, while Venice played the role of magnanimous victor. Into her lap fell the Marca Trevigiana, including the towns of Oderzo, Conegliano and Castelfranco, with Treviso at its centre. As for Padua, Marsilio Carrara found himself restored to its lordship, with Venetian rule, for the time being, a matter of light-touch supervision. The great Scaliger domain in northern Italy that Cangrande had fought so resolutely to establish was now reduced to the signory of four cities, Verona, Vicenza, Parma and Lucca. For this ultimate failure Mastino would compensate by ordering a fine Gothic tomb and overseeing its installation alongside those of other family members, the so-called *Arche Scaligeri*, 'Scaliger Arks', beside the church of Santa Maria Antica in Verona's Piazza dei Signori.

In Treviso we come across the first significant exemplar of a *terra-ferma* town governed with a prudent respect for citizens' rights and privileges. La Serenissima was not, by intention at least, tyrannical in its exercise of power. By now, in any case, lessons had been learnt from the experience of administering the *Stato da Mar* in Crete or the ports and islands of Dalmatia. Under a governor styled the *podestà* or *capitano*, essential issues of law and order, taxation, control of markets and street cleaning were addressed by a city council, supervised by its rector, whose task was to report on municipal affairs to the Signoria in Venice. This administrative template stayed in place, with various modifications, in all the larger towns which found themselves absorbed into the Venetian empire during the next hundred years and would not be substantially altered until the fall of the Serene Republic in 1797. Treviso itself felt the influence of Venice in other ways besides. The city's network of canals began playing a more emphatic role in its commercial life, while the architecture of its civic buildings and private palaces assumed a more noticeably metropolitan look as the ogee arch and the double-light window with its graceful Istrian marble columns became dominant features in their design.

If the Trevigiani were content enough to accept a Venetian mastery over their destinies, this was partly due to no less a figure than Marin

The Arche Scaligeri, elaborate Gothic monuments to the Scala family, Verona's fourteenth-century rulers, surround the church of Santa Maria Antica.

Falier, in a happier incarnation than his later role as overreaching and ultimately self-destructive doge. Maybe his appointment in 1339 as Treviso's first *podestà* planted the fatal seeds of the ambition which led to that fatal beheading in Palazzo Ducale, but at this stage Venice's newest subjects viewed him benignly enough. For their benefit as much as for that of the Signoria, Falier drew up a fresh set of laws for the town and the whole surrounding district, a code which laid emphasis on fair dealing and accessible justice, enjoining chief citizens everywhere that their main duty lay in imposing a light tax burden on their respective communities and in listening carefully to all accusations as to official malpractice.

With Padua Venice's relations were altogether less easy. The Republic had taken a part in the city's affairs since 1236 when a Venetian *podestà*, Pietro Tiepolo, had resisted the onslaught of the tyrannical Ezzelino da Romano, enforcer for Emperor Frederick II. Now, a hundred years later, the reinstatement of Marsilio da Carrara might well have seemed a short step towards annexing the ancient city, founded, according to legend, by the Trojan prince Antenor and birthplace of the Roman historian Livy. Padua was a desirable trophy not just as the metropolis of the eastern *terraferma*, a market for goods from all over the Veneto, but also as a notable place of pilgrimage for worshippers at the shrine of the miracle-working Portuguese saint Antonio.

Born in Lisbon in 1195 and originally intending to become a missionary in Muslim North Africa, he had been shipwrecked off the coast of Italy but was lucky enough, following his rescue, to be taken under the wing of the recently founded Franciscan order, which sent him on preaching journeys where he attracted a large following for his eloquence and holiness. Padua was his final destination and here he died in 1231. Canonized almost immediately, Antonio – 'Saint Anthony of Padua' – became one of the calendar's best-loved saints, patron of everybody from orphans, prisoners and army recruits to famine victims, postmen and the makers of majolica porcelain. His aid is traditionally sought in the recovery of lost objects and images of him are hung in cars, buses and railway engine-drivers' cabs as a guard against traffic accidents. Padua's Franciscan basilica dedicated to his cult, the building known simply as *Il Santo*, is still one of Italy's major pilgrimage centres.

Another compelling motive for seizing control of this city was its university. Just as, in medieval England, fugitive scholars from Oxford had founded a *studium* at Cambridge, so in 1222 a group of jurists from Bologna, Italy's most venerable university, moved north to Padua in search of greater academic freedom, successfully opening schools of law, medicine and theology which welcomed students from afar off as Bohemia, Hungary and Poland. During the second half of the fourteenth century, as the Veneto recovered from the ravages of the Black Death, the Paduan schools attracted academics from all over Italy, gaining a reputation for being 'ornamented with the flowers of every science'. Venice, we should note at this point, had no university of its own, so that La Serenissima's increasing desire to be seen as a patron of learning made the acquisition of Padua a necessity.

Prime movers in promoting and developing the Studium were members of the Carrara family, ruling the city since Marsilio's takeover. Their relationship with Venice, always uneasy, flared now and then into mutual hostility and their support for Genoa in the ongoing strife between the two maritime republics grew ever more open. In 1369, following a confrontation over the salt trade along the River Brenta, not unlike the earlier quarrel with Mastino della Scala and the Veronese, Francesco da Carrara prepared for an armed struggle with Venice by summoning aid from King Louis of Hungary, eager for any chance to humble La Serenissima in north-eastern Italy. Carrara had raised a series of forts on either bank of the Brenta which the Venetians now captured and demolished, the Hungarian commander Voyevode Stephen was taken prisoner and the Paduan army, having made too much of an early victory, when they carried off Saint Mark's banner to hang in the Santo, were reduced to submission once King Louis preferred to place his family's interest before that of his allies and abruptly withdrew from the war.

What alarmed the Signoria more than all the mainland fighting was the discovery that Francesco da Carrara had agents concealed within Venice itself. Among them was a friar from the Augustinian convent at Santo Stefano, who planned to bribe certain Grand Council members and murder several others. News of this had reached the Signoria from a party of pimps and prostitutes with whom the rogues had been carousing but who proved true-hearted Venetians in lodging the relevant information that led to the men's arrest. They were sentenced to being dragged by horses from the Rialto as far as San Marco, where their quarters were displayed between the twin columns of the Piazzetta.

In 1376, by now thoroughly humiliated, Carrara journeyed to Venice to kneel in homage before Doge Andrea Contarini. With him came Petrarch, that habitual would-be peacemaker. Following his bitter quarrel with the young Averroists, the poet had sought Francesco's protection in Padua but was happy enough on this occasion to make a brief return to the lagoon. A huge indemnity was wrung from Padua, making its citizens duly resentful of their overlords, yet this was not quite the last act in the drama. While in Venice, Francesco had taken note of its potential weaknesses when under pressure, as now, from the Genoese and realized how easily he might seize the initiative once again. Like many a ruler before or since, he needed a conflict with an alien power so as to reassert his ascendancy and distract his subjects from forming malcontent factions capable of unseating him. No sooner had Venice crushed Genoa at sea than in 1382, a year after the battle of Chioggia, she found herself threatened by another war with the Carrara as Francesco advanced into the Marca Trevigiana. For the past four years Treviso had been occupied by another of the Veneto's land-hungry chancers in the shape of Duke Leopold of Austria, whom La Serenissima had been unable to see off while fighting for its very existence in the lagoon. Now, packaging up the town with his other appropriations, Feltre, Belluno and Ceneda, Leopold sold them all on to Carrara.

For the time being Francesco seemed to be master of almost the entire Veneto with the exception of Verona and Vicenza, still in Scaliger hands. Yet again he miscalculated regarding his potential enemies, taking the indiscriminately ruthless and unprincipled Duke of Milan, Giangaleazzo Visconti, for an honourable partner before discovering too late that their alliance was worthless. Visconti, having grabbed Vicenza for himself, then sent an embassy to Venice to offer the recovery of Treviso and those other lost towns in return for the lordship of Padua. Shrewd statecraft and some sleight of hand in her diplomacy meant that La Serenissima would be content to await her moment. Cornered and desperate, Francesco da Carrara abdicated in favour of his son Francesco the younger, known as Novello, who at length surrendered to Visconti and was packed off to prison in the Piedmontese fortress of Asti.

After only a few months Novello managed to escape and began gathering powerful allies together to wrest Padua back into Carrara hands. Venice, having been zealous enough to bring his family down, now chose to throw in her lot with him, brought Milan to heel and regained influence over Padua. For the next decade a détente existed while Giangaleazzo Visconti rallied his strength before rampaging once more across northern Italy in quest of an empire. When in 1402 he was suddenly laid low with fever and died, Novello Carrara took this as a signal to pounce on the city of Vicenza, currently under Milanese control, which he believed was his family's fiefdom by right. The move was viewed by the Republic as a potential threat to its safety. If he went on to take possession of Verona, an entire network of valuable trade routes across the Veneto would be compromised. Vicenza's town council, meanwhile, probably taking into account the benign administration accorded to neighbouring Treviso, had readily offered their city to La Serenissima, which now sent a formal demand to Novello that he should quit the place and go home to Padua. Angrily he gave orders that the Venetian envoy should be 'turned into a lion of St Mark' by having his ears cut off and his nose slit open. This flagrant violation of one of the most sacred unwritten compacts of warfare, namely that messengers should be left unharmed in the preliminaries to any potential hostility, was the pretext Venice wanted. With *condottiero* Paolo Savelli at the forefront, its army drove Novello Carrara back into Padua, which fell during the autumn of 1405 after a prolonged siege.

The Venetians had already taken captive Novello's son Jacopo. Now his father and a brother named Francesco were dragged away to join him in the prison cells of Palazzo Ducale. On their way through Venice's narrow streets they were jostled, spat upon and cursed by an enraged mob, who believed them to be responsible for poisoning certain of the city's precious wells during the elder Francesco's attempt to bribe members of the Grand Council some thirty years previously. Venice has an infinitely long and extremely vivid communal memory and here was another example of it. The Doge Michele Steno and the Council of Ten saw absolutely no reason to delay passing sentence on the Carrara, for there could be little advantage in keeping them alive. Novello's petulant disfiguring of the envoy at Vicenza was a grave enough insult, but to this was now added all the evidence gathered by the Ten for his father's earlier plot against the government. Accordingly all three Carraras were ordered to be strangled in their cells, drawing from the citizens a laconic verdict '*Omo morto, vera finia*' – 'Man dead, war ended.'

The proceedings, however, were not quite over. Once more the long Venetian memory played its part. Wiping out the pestilential race of Carrara was suitably expedient but justice must be seen to take its course against those they had sought to suborn decades earlier. Among the names – thankfully not very many – emerging from Francesco Carrara's correspondence offering sweeteners to certain of the Maggior Consiglio was one that evoked a shudder of astonishment in the doge and his advisers. Carlo Zeno – Carlo Zen – we have already encountered and admired as one of the heroes of the War of Chioggia, a figure who should have been enjoying comfortable retirement as a saviour of the state. The Council of Ten had nevertheless unearthed him, while they worked inexorably through Carrara's damning catalogue, as the recipient of a bribe to the tune of 400 ducats, revealing this ideal Venetian as no better than a potential traitor to the very cause he had soon afterwards sprung to defend.

Though in view of such services rendered Zen was not sentenced to the same fate as his paymasters, the Ten (on this occasion numbering fourteen) acted with commendable firmness. First of all he was made to confess by being 'put to the question', a form of torture that involved attaching ropes and a pulley to the suspect before raising and dropping him with equal suddenness until repeated shock or injury prompted a confession. Acknowledging his crime he was then stripped of all his honours, forced to pay his ill-gotten gains into the public coffers and imprisoned for a year. The case was seen as exemplary in the best sense, since Zen, though belonging to the same patrician caste from which his judges were drawn, had not been let off lightly in consequence. A mild sentence might have been handed down in justice to his courage and patriotism at Chioggia, but the implicit shame it carried meant that he became a sort of 'former person' in the official prosopography of Venice. Worth noting all the same is that when he died in 1418 his funeral was attended by numerous crew members from the different ships under his command.

Padua, the bone of contention in all of this, now belonged inalienably to Venice and so, therefore, did its emblematic prestige as a spiritual centre and a university town. In return for the act of submission to the doge and Grand Council made on 3 January 1406 by its nobles, merchants, doctors and clergy, Venice awarded them a *Bollo d'Oro*, a Golden Bull – shades of the Byzantine 'chrysobull' from an earlier age – a document guaranteeing the privileges enjoyed by the civic guilds and the faculties composing the Studium. So keen to protect its new acquisition was La Serenissima that the Senate issued an order forbidding anyone in Venetian territory desirous of a university degree to study at schools other than that of Padua. Foreign undergraduates or postgraduates from other universities were welcomed, but for those where Saint Mark's banner flew, far away in the Cyclades, Negroponte or Crete, this was the only place from which a qualification would be acceptable for aspiring professionals throughout the Republic.

The positive effect of Venetian conquest on Padua can be gauged when we enter the basilica of *Il Santo*, containing Saint Anthony's shrine. Though the building itself was completed while the Carrara family still ruled the city, it is the presence of artists and architects working in the orbit of Venice which makes the most intense impact. The great Lombardo family of sculptors, Pietro and his son Tullio at their forefront, created tomb effigies and marble plaques here, Alessandro Vittoria and the young Andrea Palladio made works for the basilica and so did the versatile statuary Tiziano Aspetti, a native *Padovano* who completed his training in Venice. Besides talents like these, the Republic summoned figures from further afield, prominent among them one of the finest Renaissance artificers in the field of carving and bronze casting, the Tuscan sculptor Donatello.

'He made many things which look beautiful in the places where they are situated,' says Giorgio Vasari in his life of the artist. 'In his studio they did not appear half so remarkable as when they were set up in their designated positions.' If this was true of the bronze reliefs Donatello and his pupils fashioned for the altar in the choir of Il Santo, then it was even more striking in the case of the statue he designed in 1443 to commemorate the *condottiero* Erasmo da Narni, known by his nickname of 'Gattamelata', 'Spotted Cat', which dominates the piazza in front of the church. Vasari describes this as 'the bronze horse... displaying with great truth the chafing and foaming of the animal and the courage and pride of the figure who is riding him'. Donatello showed 'such skill in the size of the cast, in its proportions and general excellence, that it may be compared with any antique for movement, design, artistic qualities, proportion and diligence'. So indeed it may. Modelled on the well-known image of Emperor Marcus Aurelius on the Campidoglio in Rome, this was the first equestrian statue of any importance to be created for over a thousand years and it has rightly become one of Padua's proudest civic emblems.

But who exactly was Gattamelata and why should he have been honoured so momentously? 'Not only did it fill all men of that day with amazement,' says Vasari of Donatello's statue, 'but it astonishes everyone who sees it at the present time.' He came from the ancient hilltop town of Narni in southern Umbria, a poor boy named Erasmo who, as soon as he was old enough, joined the forces of the region's most powerful *condottiero*, Braccio da Montone, and grew battle-hardened in his service. When Braccio was killed at L'Aquila in 1424, Erasmo took command of the army and offered his prowess and leadership to the Florentines. The archetypal contract warrior of the period, he was looking for profitable deals and soon found himself working for Pope Martin V, who sought to recover the very lands in Umbria that Braccio had taken from his predecessors. When Martin failed to pay up on

time, Erasmo was happy to accept the terms proposed by the Republic of Venice in its struggle with Filippo Maria Visconti, Duke of Milan. Through the zigzags of war over the next six years, during which he lost as many battles as he won, La Serenissima was careful to remunerate him promptly and handsomely and when, in 1439, he recaptured the town of Brescia (a relatively recent acquisition of the Republic's) he was appointed Captain General of Venetian forces. From there he went on to win back the key stronghold of Verona, which had yielded itself to Venice thirty years earlier.

Where and why Erasmo got his nickname of Gattamelata has never been satisfactorily explained, but this, as Vasari's reference in his life of Donatello suggests, is how the seasoned and respected warlord became known. He had developed a particular fondness for Padua and a devotion to the cult of Saint Anthony, which is why his wife, Giacoma da Lionessa, asked for him to be buried here. The pair had five daughters, to whom Gattamelata was a careful father, leaving each of them marriage portions in his will, in which he also remembered his home town of Narni. Soon after recovering Verona, the Spotted Cat suffered a stroke and was taken back to Padua to die. Perhaps it was Giacoma, with a strong will to match her husband's, who prompted the Republic to commission Donatello's great work, though the traditional consensus is that the order came from the Senate. Its presence in Piazza del Santo would resonate across the years, more especially with the last *condottiero* to fight in Venice's cause, someone who had served his military apprenticeship with Gattamelata, the illustrious and unscrupulous Bartolomeo Colleoni.

From a gentry family in Bergamo, Colleoni had spent time in the traditional role assigned to boys of his rank as a page and squire to knights before seeking his fortune in the Kingdom of Naples, commanding armies for its queen Giovanna II. In 1424 he returned home to find better-paid employment with the Venetian state as it battled its way to supremacy over territory being claimed by the Dukes of Milan in the region around Lake Garda in north-eastern Lombardy. It was Colleoni who masterminded the capture of his native Bergamo and who in 1439 devised the operation which involved transporting six Venetian galleys from the upper reaches of the River Adige across the mountains to Lake Garda, where they could play their part in defending nearby Brescia from the Milanese.

La Serenissima had not always trusted Colleoni – he had briefly switched sides at one point over a pay dispute with the Senate and been sentenced to death *in absentia* – but she was happy enough, when peace

Donatello's groundbreaking equestrian statue of the *condottiero*
Gattamelata in Padua's Piazza del Santo.

was finally made between the warring states in 1454, to give him full command of her forces. The Venetians seemed to appreciate the way whereby their chosen warlord, during his professional career, had so often won his victories through guile and stratagem as opposed to direct military confrontation. For his part Colleoni enjoyed life in Venice but was equally pleased with spending part of each year at Malpaga, the country estate he bought near Bergamo. Here in 1475 he died, leaving a considerable fortune to be divided between his native city and the Signoria of Venice. In the former he had already established a permanent memorial through an order that its cathedral sacristy should be knocked down and replaced by the extravagantly decorated chapel which contains his effigy.

The *bergamaschi* duly obliged, but for Venice the *condottiero*'s bequest created far more of a problem. A sum of 216,000 gold ducats would have been irresistible if a condition had not been attached. Colleoni stipulated that a statue of him was to be raised in no less a place than Piazza San Marco. Of the Republic this was demanding too much. Shades of Bajamonte Tiepolo and Marin Falier doubtless rose in the collective memory of the Grand Council. The Venetian state's essential construct eschewed any glorification of individuals or personalities and the whole political implication of the Piazza lay in its deliberate shunning of such memorials. Hence, in 1479, an alternative solution was hit upon, whereby in a manner of speaking the terms of Colleoni's will might be honoured without scandal to the legatees. For in Venice there was an alternative open space which belonged to its patron saint, that broad green field stretching in front of the Scuola di San Marco and the plain brick façade of the Dominican basilica of Santi Giovanni e Paolo. It was here that the Senate decided the warrior's statue could be placed without offending either party.

The artist they commissioned for the task was the Tuscan sculptor and painter Andrea Verrocchio, one of the most able and influential figures in the world of Italian art at that time. As a painter he had taught Sandro Botticelli, Luca Signorelli and Pietro Perugino among others, while his sculpture in bronze, a medium in which, Vasari tells us, 'he delighted to work', was sought after both in Florence and Rome. The Colleoni statue represented Verrocchio's most ambitious project so far. Once arrived in Venice he set to work on creating a full-scale equestrian figure to rival Donatello's Gattamelata, that of an armoured knight on the type of heavy horse – *destrier* in Italian – which in itself was a feared element in any *condottiero*'s advance across the battlefield. Getting as far as making the model for this spectacular image, Verrocchio received

Bartolomeo Colleoni brooks no opponents in Andrea Verrocchio's bronze statue in Campo Santi Giovanni e Paolo.

news that a group of nobles in the Senate had settled on dividing the commission, giving him only the horse while the figure of Colleoni was to be executed by Vellano da Padova, whom he had beaten in the original competition for the project. A disgusted Verrocchio promptly smashed his own model and angrily returned to Florence. Compounding their error of judgment, the Signoria warned him that if he ever came back to Venice he would lose his head, 'to which', as Vasari says, 'he wrote in reply that he would take care not to, for though they could remove heads, they could not replace them and they would never be able to make one such as he had prepared for the horse and then broken'.

So defiant an answer apparently 'did not displease the Signoria', who duly backed down, restored the original commission and allowed Andrea Verrocchio to get on with the creation of what is, by common consent, the finest equestrian statue in the world. By a tragic irony the sculptor did not live to see his achievement take its place in Campo San Zanipolo. Catching cold while he supervised the casting, Verrocchio died in 1488 and the process was finished off by another of his competitors, Alessandro Leopardi, who designed the tall marble plinth on which the work stands and whose name is visible on the horse's harness. The whole compelling image, wondrous in its sense of fretful energy shared between animal and rider, has arrested visitors to Venice ever since.

It has been argued that Bartolomeo Colleoni hardly deserved quite so fine a tribute. He himself, having destroyed Bergamo's sacristy to raise his own funerary chapel, would certainly not have agreed. The essence of the man, and of *condottieri* as a breed, is summed up for us in his family coat-of-arms which Leopardi faithfully placed on the plinth below him. The shields flourish an example of what is called 'canting heraldry', the use of shapes or objects which play on the name of the armigerous possessor. On Colleoni's escutcheon we see three sac-shaped items, looking at first like ripe figs. They are in fact testicles, the one extra presumably intended either to forestall ribaldry or else to emphasize the exceptional manliness of the arms-bearer. 'Colleoni' sounds, after all, not unlike the Italian word *coglioni*, balls, so the canting here could hardly be bettered. Beneath the trampling hooves of his charger, the last of Venice's *condottieri* can be allowed a gonad in excess.

The role of Colleoni and his warrior predecessors in reshaping La Serenissima's destiny, following the end of its prolonged struggle with the Genoese, was vital and inevitable. Throughout the long fifteenth century, when the Republic was fully, often catastrophically, engaged with the formation and retention of a land empire in Italy, this whole process had its critics, doubters and detractors. It must have seemed to some as though the state, so singular in its essence and constitution, was busy vulgarizing itself by seeking to match and better the more banal aspirations of other Italian powers rather than continuing to bolster its unique position as holder of the precious *Stato da Mar*, its own imperial artefact in the shape of a network of ports, harbours, islands and markets embracing the entire eastern Mediterranean and the shores of the Black Sea. Others simply deplored the waste of energy, resources and manpower in pursuit of what they saw as a fundamentally unproductive and chimerical exercise carried out by egoists, self-seekers and profiteers.

Notable, however, is the fact that such points of view never succeeded in swaying the Grand Council as terrestrial Venice grew into a reality, with the Veneto's great towns falling one by one into the Signoria's lap and Saint Mark's lion taking his place above their gateways. In our three equestrian images, those of Savelli, Gattamelata and Colleoni, we can see a new kind of Venice becoming palpable, seeking predominance, deference and respect on the political stage of Renaissance Italy.

FRANCESCO FOSCARI

A DOGE IN PROFILE

The deathbed as a familiar social occasion has more or less vanished from contemporary life. For all sorts of reasons, mostly connected with health and safety or with advances in medical science, this prolonged ritual of farewell, with its potential for dramatic confessions, belated repentance, magnanimous gestures of forgiveness or moves towards reconciliation, no longer enjoys the central importance which it once held among families and communities. In the Middle Ages, on the other hand, the dying were accorded such a moment as a traditional privilege whose underlying paradox lay in the powers they themselves could exercise at the very instant when existence itself seemed to be fading away. Thus accounts are numerous of what sort of an ending had been made by the dead man or woman, of their final bequests and last words and of the behaviour, attitudes and aspirations of those gathered around the bed.

On 4 April 1423 Tommaso Mocenigo, sixty-fifth doge of Venice, lay dying in Palazzo Ducale. During his nine-year reign the Republic itself had pressed forward with its acquisition of an Italian mainland domain, taking control of a whole stretch of territory that included the Alpine region of Cadore and the north-eastern province of Friuli, where centuries earlier the Germanic Longobard invaders had first settled before pushing on into the heart of Italy. Mocenigo was shrewd, visionary and generous in approaching his great office. He had sought to initiate a rebuilding of the palace after a fire in 1419 by paying for the whole operation himself. He kept a careful eye, all the same, on the state of the treasury and the Republic's finances in relation to its spending across what was now the largest, most productive empire in the Mediterranean, well aware though he was of the growing threats to its security from the Ottoman Turks. He was anxious besides as to Venice's relations with her immediate neighbours, King Sigismund of

Hungary and Duke Filippo Maria Visconti of Milan. The former's bid for Dalmatia was seen off by admiral Pietro Loredan, who had earlier won fame in a battle with Ottoman galleys at Gallipoli. Visconti, on the other hand, could be better contained, so Mocenigo felt, through trade deals and mutual security arrangements than with overt hostility.

Eighty years old and feeling his age, the doge saw no profit in a league against the Milanese sought by ambassadors from Florence, though he knew enough of Duke Filippo's ambitions to see how fragile Venice's currently benign diplomacy might become. When, in the early spring of 1423, Mocenigo took to his bed, he had a point or two to make about all this to his senatorial advisers before death arrived to claim him and someone else donned the *corno dogale* and the ermine cape. Tommasone, 'Big Tom', as his friends called him, charged his fellow patricians to take particular care of the Republic's current prosperity, reminding them that the national debt from Venice's recent wars to recover Padua, Vicenza and Verona had been substantially reduced during his reign and enumerating the quantity of ships in the merchant fleet and the size of their crews. He went into considerable detail as to the achievements of the Arsenale, with its 3,000 carpenters and as many shipwrights, and dwelt on the superiority of Venice's textile industries, employing as many as 20,000 workers. 'If you go on like this,' Mocenigo enjoined his hearers, 'all the gold in Christendom will be yours... Only stand back, as if before a fire, from taking what rightly belongs to others or from making unjust wars, for God will never uphold leaders who commit such faults.' He praised 'your fights with the Turks, making you famous for valour and seamanship', he singled out the Venetian ambassadors and diplomats whose skill was admired throughout Europe and 'the doctors in various sciences, more especially the law, to whom foreigners appeal for counsel and judgment.'

This was a deathbed stocktaking worthy indeed of so prudent a holder of his great ducal office. Yet it must have been obvious to those around Doge Mocenigo that all of it was merely a prelude to a more important charge, one which came in the form of a sinister warning. 'You must pay heed to the choice of my successor,' he told them, 'remembering how much good or evil may arise from your decision,' and went on to list certain members of the Grand Council whom he could personally recommend. One name, on the other hand, was singled out for its consummate unworthiness. It was that of 'a vainglorious braggart, shallow and empty-headed, snatching at everything but gaining little in return'. If this man were to be elected doge, Venice

Francesco Foscari, the longest-serving doge in Venetian history (1423–57), in a portrait (1457) by Lazzaro Bastiani.

would be plunged into continual warfare. 'Along with your gold and silver, you will forfeit your honour and reputation. Where now you are masters of your *condottieri* and their officers, you will end up merely as their slaves.' The name of this man, thus closely identified with Venice's potential doom and destruction, was Francesco Foscari.

The Foscari were a relatively unimportant patrician clan, members of the Grand Council but not figuring prominently in the Republic's affairs until Nicolo Foscari was elected to the Council of Ten in 1390. His son Francesco was brought up in an atmosphere of entitlement, supported by considerable wealth, and gained early distinction as an ambassador. Elected one of the three presidents of the Quarantia (the Council of Forty) he could use this as an easy step towards membership of the Ten and an appointment to the prestigious office of Procurator of San Marco. His task here, along with his eight fellow dignitaries, was to administer the management of the basilica in its capacity as a palatine chapel, to superintend the Republic's charitable activities and to oversee the proper fulfilment of wills and testamentary depositions throughout the city's municipal districts, the *sestieri*. It undoubtedly helped Francesco Foscari's career that he was himself a generous man, a lavish spender, happy to share what he had with poorer citizens or needy members of his own class.

He was in any case an exceptionally able parliamentarian, all too plausible, thought Doge Mocenigo, in his oratory during sessions of the Grand Council, underpinning his rhetoric with hard fact in ways the Senate found irresistible and good at cementing alliances, although prone to making a few enemies along the way. He had married well, firstly to Maria Priuli, daughter of a leading banker, then, following her death, to the equally rich Maria Nani, from a family newly inscribed in the Golden Book. His popularity among his own echelon was boosted by a strenuous advocacy of the empire-building currently being pursued by La Serenissima across the Veneto. Foscari was emphatically not one of those who believed Venice's destiny to be grounded exclusively on seafaring, naval prowess and the dominant merchant presence of the *Stato da Mar*. There were new worlds to conquer and fresh markets to be opened in eastern Lombardy and the Po delta and Foscari was determined that the Serene Republic should profit from the spoils. In this context Tommaso Mocenigo on his deathbed had been right to worry. He must have known that the Senate would do precisely what he wanted them not to. Following his death on 14 April 1423 Mocenigo was barely cold in his grave at Santi Giovanni e Paolo, where a fine late medieval stone monument by Andrea Bregno commemorates him, when Francesco Foscari was named his successor. On this occasion the previously honoured formula of presenting the new-made head of state to the populace with the words 'This is your doge, if it please you' was set aside. The Senate's Grand Chancellor had earlier asked his fellow electors 'What if the choice should not be pleasing to the citizens?' to which the answer came back 'We shall simply inform them that a new doge has been appointed.' And that became protocol from then on.

An expensively-attired figurehead Venice's latest doge was definitely not prepared to be. There was work to be done and at a robust forty-nine years of age Francesco Foscari was the man to do it. By way of making his mark he launched a series of lavish celebrations throughout the city which are supposed to have gone on, in one form or another, for almost a year. The cult of a public image remained essential for him but his focus, from the outset of what was to prove the longest ducal reign in Venetian history, was already on the more pressing issue of the state's relationship with its Italian competitors or would-be allies, since the one, after all, could just as easily become the other. For now, friendly overtures were still coming from Filippo Maria Visconti in Milan, while ambassadors from Florence kept on trying to induce the Republic to join a projected league against him. Only in the spring and summer of 1424, when Visconti's armies successfully defeated Florentine forces in Romagna and seemed ready to push their conquests further north into Venetian territory, did Foscari judge this an appropriate moment to set his expansionary policies to work.

Into the foreground at this point steps the classic character of the malcontent *condottiero*. The risk of employing such figures lay in keeping them sufficiently humoured with money, honours and freedom of operation, something which Filippo Maria Visconti had signally failed to do with his chief warlord, Francesco Bussone, Conte di Carmagnola. The latter's title was earned rather than inherited, since he came from a peasant family living in a village near Turin and spent his earliest years as a swineherd. At the age of twelve he decided to enlist as a soldier in the Milanese army and quickly rose to earn the trust and respect of his commanding officers. Duke Filippo Maria saw how this young man might be useful to the dynasty as its strong right arm, awarding him a title of nobility from his native village and a wife, Antonia, from within the Visconti family. To boost such status indicators, the new-made Count of Carmagnola was given Lombard estates and allowed to build himself a palace. This, nevertheless, was as far as the duke was ready to go. Once he started to suspect that

Carmagnola held more questionable ambitions, the easiest solution was to sideline him with the governorship of Genoa, then in Milanese hands. It was at this point that the spirit of the *condottiero* triumphed over any more traditional values of honour and loyalty. Feeling unappreciated, Carmagnola sought an audience with the duke and was refused. It was time to take his generalship somewhere else, to those who knew how to value it. The Signoria of Venice looked, at this juncture, like the ideal paymasters.

He arrived at the perfect moment. The new doge, Francesco Foscari, had been exultant at the impact made on the Grand Council when a Florentine ambassador, rendered desperate by Venetian dithering over whether or not to commit the Republic to an alliance against Milan, had resorted to open threats. 'When we refused help to Genoa to fight Duke Filippo, they adopted him as their ruler. Thus, if we Florentines receive no help from you when we need it, we shall make the duke our king.' With Count Carmagnola's advent on the scene, the chance to launch a successful campaign against a dangerous territorial rival seemed too good to miss. The warlord was allowed to address the assembled council, railing against Milanese perfidy, disparaging Duke Filippo's military prowess, disparaging his resources and encouraging Venice to seize her hour. Foscari backed him at once, urging his appointment as commander in chief, 'for he is well-versed in war, nor can all Italy show his present equal in bravery and martial skill... Let us set on with this war, avenging our wrongs by trampling our common enemy in the dust and securing for Italy an everlasting peace.' The Republic now hastened to conclude a treaty with Florence and made Carmagnola 'Captain-General of San Marco' in a solemn ceremony at which, before the Basilica's high altar, Doge Foscari handed him the symbolic baton of command. In March 1426 hostilities between Venice and Milan opened in earnest.

Over the next four years the doge continued to back Carmagnola during successive phases of what turned out to be an increasingly dubious service record as generalissimo of the Venetian Republic in its Lombard campaigns. Filippo Maria Visconti had prepared saturninely for the fray, not specially dismayed by the treachery of his general, since it was precisely this quality on which the duke's slow-burning vengeance could get to work. Little by little he began what seemed superficially like an attempt to lure Carmagnola back to Milan, while making sure that Venetian intelligence was watching every step of his game. During the summer of 1431 a series of apparent tactical errors, misjudged orders and lost opportunities made it obvious to the Signoria that their captain-general might indeed be playing a double game with the Milanese. At length he was summoned to Venice, tortured and brought to trial. The Council of Ten, with twenty extra assessors, had amassed enough proof of his perfidy not to spend long on reviewing the case. A majority verdict meant the death penalty for 'injury wrought to our affairs and against the honour and prosperity of the state'. On 5 May 1432 the Count of Carmagnola, the proud *condottiero*, was led into Piazza San Marco, dressed in fine red velvet, to be beheaded with three blows of the axe.

Almost nobody appears to have intervened on Carmagnola's behalf, except for the man whose policy of territorial expansion he had been engaged to carry out. Francesco Foscari, the doge himself, together with three of his closest counsellors, had sought to have the sentence commuted to life imprisonment. The fact that this compromise was rejected made no difference to his overall policies of aggression and imperial enlargement and it was to be another twenty years before the wars with Milan were brought to an end. During those two decades there was no attempt by the various councils of state to undermine Foscari's position as a popular and charismatic figurehead, to whom no blame was to be attached for any of the problems that beset the economy as a result of the ongoing strife on the mainland or the damage to Venice's *Stato da Mar* occasioned by the rise of a Muslim superpower in the form of Ottoman Turkey.

Venetians in truth loved their generous doge, who knew how to welcome foreign guests in suitably extravagant style, thus burnishing the city's image, that of a handsome, well-ordered metropolis with sufficient resources enabling it to rise to any occasion. Its citizens worked hard for their living. What nowadays we so easily forget – and what to some extent we have been encouraged to forget by the nineteenth- and twentieth-century writers who helped to shape our appreciation of the city – is that Venice in the days of Doge Francesco Foscari was a busy and crowded industrial centre. The streets and canals were noisy and bustling, the place teemed with a big artisan population engaged in a wide variety of different crafts and trades and it was a major hub for shopping, especially in the Rialto area where the earliest settlements had sprung into life a thousand years before. Clustered around Campo San Bartolomeo, at the eastern foot of the bridge, were taverns and shops selling cooked food, while further towards the Piazza, in streets called Frezzaria and Spadaria, the makers of arrows, swords and other edged weapons could be found. On the other side of the bridge, in the *sestiere* of San Polo, precious cargoes of spices were on sale, fruit, vegetables, meat and fish could be bought in the markets beyond the little old church of San Giacomo and close by were the shops of jewellers and goldsmiths.

On the Grand Canal's opposite bank lies the Cannaregio district, which was still, in Foscari's time, something of a rustic outlier and has indeed preserved a hint or two of this in our own time. The quarter was much beloved of the different religious orders, with convents and monasteries springing up amid the market gardens, furnaces for making metalwork and ceramics, slaughterhouses for livestock carried from the mainland and what in contemporary England were called 'tentergrounds', open spaces for the drying of textiles. Its dominant church, almost like a small cathedral with its tall campanile, was the Madonna dell'Orto, originally dedicated to Saint Christopher but reassigned to the Virgin Mary after a miraculous image of her was found in a nearby orchard.

Beyond, in the northern lagoon, lay the islands of Burano and Murano, each of them a major centre for the specialized industries whose skills and techniques were jealously guarded by the Republic. Burano was a centre for lace-making, which began to assume a special importance as a feature of European fashionable attire during the late 1400s, becoming an essential status indicator for both women and men in the century which followed. The lace was worked individually on a pillow called a *tombola* by women sitting at their street doors. Its intricate styles, particularly the so-called 'Punto in Aria' and 'Punto Rosa', adorned the gowns of noblewomen in France, Spain and England and decorated the sleeves and collars of the doublets worn by their husbands.

On Murano the glass for which Venice became world-famous was made in furnaces whose artificers were expressly forbidden to leave the island, under legislation framed by the Signoria in the late thirteenth century. Ancient Roman glass-blowing techniques had been brought to the lagoon by the original refugees from Aquileia and applied to creating mosaics in the churches of Torcello and later to the resplendent decoration of San Marco. Glass objects such as goblets, jugs and bowls soon took on a captivating delicacy and translucence via the use of manganese oxide in the processes adopted among the island's furnaces. Fantasy was not confined to artefacts like these: mirrors, sconces and chandeliers grew ever more ornate in their abundance of leaves and panels, making Murano glass among the most prized of luxury items in households across the globe.

Everywhere between the islands there sped the boats, so varied in their forms and drafts, pulled up for unloading on the quayside by the *ganzer*, a man armed with a hook who was generally an elderly gondolier, retired from plying his oar on the canals. The oars themselves were fashioned in the Castello *sestiere*, adjacent to Cannaregio, in the long street to the north of Santi Giovanni e Paolo known as Barbaria delle Tole, full of the rasp and grating of carpentry tools and smells of resin and sawdust. Beyond the big Dominican church and its adjacent hospital is one of Venice's last remaining *squeri*, the boatyards which abounded in the fifteenth-century city, where every kind of craft was fitted or refitted, much of the outdoor work taking place on a slipway next to the big wooden boatshed.

The workers here and elsewhere in the city were pleased with their canny, big-spending doge and his ambitious plans for Venice. They saw nothing wrong with him being given a splendid palace, formerly assigned to the Marquis of Mantua but snatched back when he broke his alliance with Venice in support of Milan's new ruler Francesco Sforza. The building's Gothic façade looked out on the central bend of the Grand Canal and the doge was quick to extend the range behind it so as to create a mansion, Ca' Foscari, whose effect was one of ineluctable power and magnificence. Such an incarnation of late medieval *bella figura* found its echo in other aspects of Foscari's lifestyle and personality. The wedding of his beloved son Jacopo to Lucrezia Contarini on 29 January 1441 was a typical example, an occasion that mingled festivity with competitive ostentation and more than a touch or two of regal pomp. This latter was perhaps not altogether becoming to a doge, but the Venetians seemed to find it acceptable from the kind of man Francesco Foscari was known to be.

Thus the noble bridegroom and his groomsmen, clad in crimson velvet and 'silver brocade of Alexandria' rode their horses in procession through the city, with a band of musicians and a military escort. A special bridge of boats had been constructed across the Grand Canal to bring them from San Samuele to the bride's house at San Barnaba, where Lucrezia was escorted to church by no fewer than sixty bridesmaids. The nuptial mass was followed by orations in praise of the married couple and their families, delivered before the doge, foreign ambassadors and 'a multitude of nobles and people', followed by a grand banquet in Palazzo Ducale. To the feast Lucrezia and Jacopo were carried on the Bucintoro, with a suite of a hundred ladies 'amid the acclamations of the crowd and the sound of trumpets', while elsewhere across the city tournaments took place on Campo Santa Maria Formosa and Campo San Polo. There was an elaborate supper that evening in the palace and the following days saw jousting in the Piazza, a procession of boats on the Grand Canal and further junketings each night. Money, with Foscari, was no object and Jacopo was a sincerely beloved son and heir.

Too well beloved, it would later turn out. The younger Foscari had inherited much of his father's energy, courage and determination and already stood out as a likely candidate for high office, even if that of doge were a matter of election rather than dynastic succession. Glamorous and fashion-conscious, Jacopo was a member of one of the so-called 'stocking clubs', the *Compagnie delle Calze*, who sported the latest line in the coloured tights worn by young men at this period, particularly stylish and eye-catching when shown off by the various sprigs of the Venetian upper class. We can see these flashy hose in the work of contemporary painters like Carpaccio and Gentile Bellini, patterned, particoloured and sometimes embroidered with gold or silver thread, an indicator of the wearer's noble rank in a city whose sumptuary laws, governing who was allowed to put on which kinds of clothing, were extremely strict.

The stocking clubs came to greater prominence in the wake of Jacopo Foscari's wedding to Lucrezia Contarini and remained a feature of Venetian life for the next hundred years. Their focus was purely on pleasure, ostentation and expense. Needless to say, the Council of Ten saw it as a duty to issue proper licensing terms, periodically reviewing these and taking suitable action where needed, largely with the object of ensuring that only the right sort of privileged youngsters became members and that public order and decency were maintained so as not to damage patrician standing among the citizenry. The clubs themselves played up to the insatiable Venetian appetite for spectacle and performance by mounting impromptu shows in the streets and open spaces of the city and by various kinds of harmless fun, which included throwing eggshells filled with rose water at the windows of girls noted for their beauty, a kind of parody serenade. By the end of the fifteenth century there were at least forty *Compagnie delle Calze*, with names like *Floridi*, *Modesti*, *Concordi* or the one to which Jacopo Foscari belonged, *Pavoni*, 'Peacocks'. Visitors from elsewhere in Italy were dazzled by their elegance, the splendour of their festivities and their special entertainments known as *momarie*, to which the English word 'mummery' is related.

If only Jacopo Foscari had confined his activities to *momarie,* to parading in fancy hose set off by an embroidered codpiece, the short jacket known as a *zipon* (the French *jupon*) and the satin-lined cloak called a *zimarra*! Sadly, as it turned out, the stocking club of the Peacocks

Young Venetians sport the fashionable hose worn by the *Compagnie delle Calze* (the 'stocking clubs').

simply added fuel to his fretful, directionless ambition to become something more than the spoilt child of a popular and influential doge. His inherited rank as a patrician must naturally entitle him to consideration for membership of the Grand Council and eventual eligibility for one of the many posts within the government, whether at home or abroad. His wife Lucrezia Contarini, as well as being genuinely attached to him, had brought Jacopo a substantial dowry and his father's wealth was there to provide the necessary underpinning should he be summoned to high office.

Nevertheless, a mere four or five years after those lavish wedding festivities took place, Jacopo found himself seriously in debt. An obvious remedy was to exploit his extensive range of well-placed contacts within the government by letting it be known as discreetly as possible that he was ready to accept sweeteners in return for his influence in securing particularly well-paid jobs in different departments of state. The practice is a venerable one: ancient Greece and Rome were familiar with it and in one form or another it continues to flourish in our own day. Called *manzarie* by Venetians

JEVNE VÉNITIEN
XVᵉ SIÈCLE

(the Italian word *mancia* means a waiter's tip) such bribes were strictly forbidden by the government and an anonymous denunciation led to an immediate inquiry into Jacopo's conduct by the Council of Ten. As with Count Carmagnola, extra members were summoned to assist, though in this case the doge himself was obviously excluded. A charge was then issued which accused Jacopo Foscari of accepting 'without regard to God or man, gifts of money and jewels, contrary to the law'. When one of his servants was brought in for questioning Jacopo grew worried, gathered funds together and escaped to Trieste, in the Austrian emperor's domains, before his own arrest could be made. Tried in his absence, he was sentenced to banishment to the fortress of Modon (Methoni) in the Peloponnese and a galley was dispatched to bring him there. His mother, Marina Nani, the dogaressa, had earlier sued for clemency on his behalf and asked permission to visit him, which the Ten refused. When the Venetian vessel arrived in Trieste and its captain Marco Trevisan presented the warrant bearing the judges' sentence Jacopo angrily rejected it, a gesture that effectively made him an outlaw. Letters from his father urging compliance were set aside as Jacopo lingered in Trieste and Trevisan awaited further instructions.

After a year's stalemate Trevisan died and Jacopo fell dangerously ill, even as the Ten were busy uncovering yet more evidence of lobbying and bribery. Out of respect for their elderly doge, as much as through an anxiety to shield one of their own caste, the council offered a compromise whereby Jacopo, instead of being shipped to Greece, would be confined to house arrest at his villa in the Veneto countryside. On these terms the outlaw prepared to return and it seemed likely that a pardon might eventually be negotiated, thanks to pleading by the doge, whose deep love for his son transcended his duty to the state. In 1447 the Ten magnanimously declared that 'considering the necessity, in times such as these, for the Republic to have a prince with a free and serene understanding, at present denied him through knowing that his son is sick both in body and mind', Jacopo should at last be allowed home to Venice.

Several among the Ten nevertheless had lasting doubts fuelled by an earlier revelation that young Foscari had received a substantial present from Francesco Sforza, Duke of Milan, in the form of a set of silver plate and a bung of 2,000 ducats. One of those keeping a wary eye on Jacopo was Ermolao Donà, among the more prominent members of the Ten during the *in absentia* trial. On 5 November 1450, while walking home from a meeting of the Senate, he was set upon and stabbed to death. For a month or so Donà's attacker remained

Vittore Carpaccio's painting *Two Venetian Ladies* (*c*.1490–95) was originally part of a polyptych. Two bored-looking noblewomen, whose clothes and hairstyles proclaim their wealth, await their husbands' return from a hunting trip.

unidentified, but early in the New Year a signed note was found in one of the city's *bocche di leone*, the letterboxes where such denunciations could be placed, accusing Jacopo of instigating the assault, since one of his servants had been seen outside Palazzo Ducale as Donà left the building. Arrested and tortured, Foscari would confess nothing, merely muttering words his interrogators judged to be either a prayer or an incantation. They proceeded to sentence him all the same, on the basis, as it seems, of ridding the city of a tiresome malcontent for whom not even his own family could find a useful role. This time exile was fixed at a still farther distance, to Canea, chief town of Crete, where Jacopo was ordered to report every day to the governor.

Like everywhere else in La Serenissima's empire, Crete nurtured its own variant forms of Venetian culture and society. Once arrived there, Jacopo might have devoted himself to making the best of his surroundings and taking advantage of the enforced distance to review the nature of his life so far and reconfigure its not especially admirable priorities. As it was, he began brooding on the possibility of a return to Venice, so that after a few years government informers, naturally watchful of his movements and contacts, were starting to send confidential reports to the Ten that he was busy intriguing with foreign powers to contrive a rescue. A letter had been written to the Duke of Milan, asking him to intervene with the Senate. Worse still, Jacopo was found to be in correspondence with Sultan Mehmet of Turkey about the possibility of leaving the island on a galley sent from Constantinople. Such initiatives might be understandable in themselves but by their very nature they violated a fundamental principle of Venetian statecraft, so Foscari was arrested and brought home to face further questioning.

He confessed his guilt at once, perhaps prompted by a memory of his earlier tortures, and the Ten met to deliberate the penalty. For Francesco Foscari, now aged eighty-three and still in his ducal role, the situation had become more agonizing than before. The whole process of the Council's judgment was further clouded by the presence within it of Jacopo Loredan, member of a family with a simmering hostility towards the doge. Loredan's insistence that the miscreant now be sentenced to execution was set aside and a lighter doom imposed. Young Foscari would be returned to Crete, where he would be gaoled for a year before being given a conditional release with no likelihood of ever setting foot in Venice again.

A heart-wrenching last meeting between the two Foscari, father and son, took place in Palazzo Ducale before several witnesses. Scarred by his recent tortures, Jacopo cried out in despair, 'Oh my father, get

Ca' Foscari, Doge Francesco Foscari's family palace (1453), designed by Bartolomeo Bon, is now home to the University of Venice.

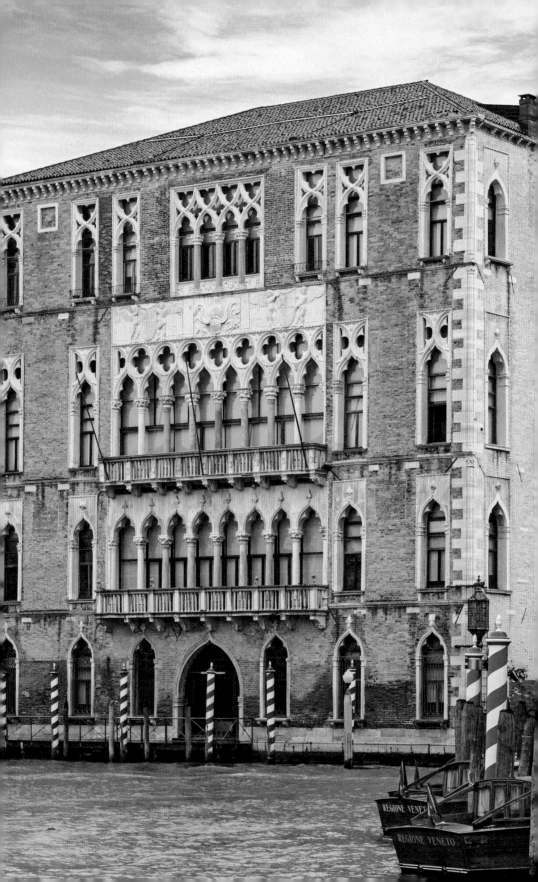

me leave, I beg you, to come home at last!' Francesco, however much he clung to his son, could still say 'You must submit to the state's decree and hope for nothing further.' When Jacopo was wrenched at last from his embrace and taken from the room, the doge shed bitter tears, exclaiming '*O pietà grande!*', 'Oh the great pity of it!' In less than a year news arrived from Canea that his beloved boy was dead.

For the doge the blow was mortal. On two previous occasions he had sought to resign his office and been forbidden to do so in the name of the Republic's greater good. Now the implacable Loredan, taking advantage of a moment when the distraught parent was unable to focus adequately on the cares of office, summoned a special committee whose decision was that Francesco Foscari should at last step down, 'taking pity on the state', in return for a pension of 1,500 ducats. To their surprise he now refused, declaring that proper legal formalities had not been followed and that the committee had, in any case, no genuinely established authority in the matter. They were not, however, to be gainsaid for much longer. A day later, after being fobbed off at a second attempt with the excuse that His Serenity had retired to bed, the committee delivered its ultimatum. He must resign within a week or else suffer forcible removal and confiscation of his property.

Worn out by the twin burdens of age and personal loss, Foscari offered no further resistance, letting them take the doge's ring off his finger and hammer it down while other trappings of office, the cap and robe, were similarly removed. A touching detail of this final disgrace was provided by one of the senators present, whose compassionate glance caught the old man's eye. 'Whose son are you?' he asked. 'The son of Marin Memo,' came the answer. 'Well, tell my dear friend your father to visit me as a precious comfort. We shall take a gondola and visit the monasteries together.' Leaving the palace the next morning he refused to go down a private staircase to the waiting boat, announcing 'I shall descend by the very same stairs up which I came when I was first made doge.'

Francesco Foscari died a week later, amid the anger of ordinary Venetians at the shabby hypocrisy exhibited by the Senate's proclamation declaring that their late doge had been 'allowed to renounce his office through incapacity occasioned by advancing old age'. His wife Marina Nani remained thoroughly disgusted at the pantomime now laid on by a guilty and embarrassed Signoria in the shape of an elaborate funeral, with her husband's body taken to Palazzo Ducale to lie in state, before a procession to the Frari under a golden canopy. She declined to attend the ceremony, saying that she was ready to spend the dowry that, according to custom, had been returned to her as Foscari's widow on a private funeral for a man whom the Republic had so blatantly wronged.

The tragedy of the doge's last years was avidly seized on by artists of another age, the nineteenth-century Romantic era, for its cruel pathos and inherent irony. Byron's verse drama *The Two Foscari* (1821) dwelt on what he called its 'suppressed passions, as opposed to the ranting of the present day', Verdi's opera of the same title, first performed in Rome in 1844, gave Jacopo much greater depth of character than he possessed in actuality, while the great Italian history painter Francesco Hayez brought the scene of father and son's agonized parting vividly to life. Venetians of Francesco Foscari's own day had always respected his energy and firmness of purpose, as if Venice itself were in some sense unthinkable without him at the helm. Most potent symbol of his centrality to the concept of La Serenissima triumphant is the Porta della Carta, forming the principal entrance to Palazzo Ducale from Piazza San Marco. Begun in 1438 by the master architect Bartolomeo Bon, it was probably completed about five years afterwards and represents one of the most flamboyant examples of the highly idiosyncratic Venetian Gothic style.

A sublime gesture of political propaganda, the work incorporates figures of four cardinal virtues, Temperance, Fortitude, Prudence and Charity, beneath the dominant female form of Justice. The surrounding furniture of columns and crockets was all originally picked out in blue and gold. In a panel above the doorway, facing the winged lion, kneels Doge Francesco Foscari himself, as characterful and authoritative a figure as we should expect. The original sculpture, by Antonio Bregno, was destroyed by the French in 1797 and only replaced a century later by the present copy. The act of stamping so forcefully personal an image for all eternity on what is by its very nature a public palace was one of quite shameless hubris at this very moment in Foscari's career, yet nobody seems to have questioned the impropriety and there it was allowed to remain. In office for forty-three years, he was perhaps the nearest Venice ever came to having a king.

overleaf   Francesco Hayez's depiction (1852) of the last meeting between Francesco Foscari and his son Jacopo. The downfall of 'the two Foscari' in the 1450s would spawn a verse drama by Byron and an opera by Verdi.

AN AGE OF
UNCERTAINTY

Doubtless old Tommaso Mocenigo, on his deathbed, had been wise in warning the Venetian Senate not to choose Francesco Foscari as its doge, given the near-continuous state of war with mainland powers in which the Republic quickly became involved during his long reign. The drive towards mastery of the Veneto, Friuli and eastern Lombardy, whatever its ultimate success, had left the economy in a parlous condition, needing to be buoyed up by a series of forced loans, a weightier tax burden and a depression of trade and industry for which the gracing of a score of gateways to captured cities with a stone plaque proudly bearing Saint Mark's lion with his open book was an inadequate compensation. The responsibility was not Foscari's alone, but in his autocratic, quasi-monarchical style he had been among the principal advocates for this shift of focus from sea to land.

Whatever blame might attach to the doge for empire-building, there was one major international catastrophe he had no chance to prevent even if he and the Signoria must long have seen it looming. Since the fifteenth century began, the Ottoman Turks had started advancing into Byzantine territory, across areas of Anatolia and along the Black Sea coast. By 1420 they had gained possession of southern Bulgaria and moved southwards from thence into the Greek province of Thrace, crossing the Dardanelles and eventually throwing a hostile ring around the city of Constantinople itself, the sacred metropolis of eastern Christendom. It was in a desperate attempt to counter this growing Turkish threat that Emperor John VIII Palaeologos had paid his visit to Italy in 1438, seeking to forge a doctrinal bond between the Roman Catholic and Orthodox churches that might provide the basis for a Western crusade. The initiative grounded almost immediately on a total rejection by the Greek ecclesiastical community in Constantinople and the defeat, at Varna on the Black Sea, of a Catholic army from

Hungary, moving against the Turks in response to a summons from Pope Eugenius IV, himself a Venetian. The old crusading impulse of previous ages was effectively dead across western Europe or else, in the case of the Spanish kingdoms of Aragon and Castile, focused on conquering and Christianizing what remained of Moorish domains in Andalusia. For Byzantium in its final incarnation no further help was forthcoming.

The young sultan of the Ottomans, Mehmet II, succeeding his father Murat in 1451 at the age of nineteen, was well aware of just how vulnerable the Greek capital had now become but realistic in assessing the practicalities of laying siege to it. First of all he devoted his attention to raising a fortress at Rumelihisarı, on the European shore of the Bosphorus, designed as a counterpart to an already existing Byzantine castle on the other side of the strait, recently captured by the Turks. Not for nothing was this stronghold nicknamed 'Throat-Cutter', since now any passing vessels headed to or from Constantinople could be stopped by a battery of heavy guns, to be searched or sent back. This was a crucial manoeuvre in cutting off the last supply lines to the city while Sultan Mehmet gathered his own fleet together so as to ensure a swift end to the coming assault.

Within Constantinople, bracing himself for the siege, Emperor Constantine Palaeologos wrote a defiant message to the sultan. 'As it is plain that you wish for war rather than peace, so let it be according to your will. Now I turn to God, I close the gates of my city and I shall defend my people to my last drops of blood. May you reign in happiness till the Righteous and Supreme Judge summons us both before his judgment seat.' An immense Turkish army, conservatively reckoned at around 80,000 men, surrounded the walls defended with ferocious courage by a Byzantine force of barely more than 7,000, constantly heartened by the apparently unsleeping Constantine as the siege wore on through the first weeks of April 1453. A chain stretched across the Golden Horn looked likely to prevent Turkish ships from breaking through and a landward assault on 18 April was successfully beaten back via a sortie from the Saint Romanus gate.

Much nevertheless depended on the arrival of relief in the form of a fleet from Italy, more specifically from Venice, eight of whose galleys now lay within the Golden Horn. As regarded the siege La Serenissima's position was a delicate one. She had no additional resources beyond those already committed to the continuing conflict with Milan and she depended in any case on friendly relations with the Ottomans so as to keep her eastern trade routes open. There had been

The Porta della Carta, ceremonial gateway to Palazzo Ducale, begun in 1438, features the sculpted image of Francesco Foscari.

an ugly episode the previous year when a Venetian ship, refusing to halt at Rumelihisarı and submit to a search, was pounded by Turkish cannon and its captain sentenced to death by impalement as a warning against any further such defiance. No matter what outrage was induced or the sense that Venice might have some sort of moral duty to rescue what remained of a Christian empire in the East, certain practical imperatives surrounding commerce with the dominant Islamic power in the Levant could scarcely be ignored. In Constantinople itself the mood of the Venetian merchant community was distinctly combative during the months immediately before the Turkish siege began. Led by their chief spokesman, known as the *bailo*, Girolamo Minotto, they seem genuinely to have believed that the Greeks had a chance of survival, perhaps with help from some of that seasoned diplomacy for which the Republic was internationally commended. Thus they were prepared to stay and fight, buoyed up by an expectation that some sort of naval backup was on hand from Venice.

In response to Minotto's increasingly gloomy reports the Signoria sent a squadron of fifteen galleys and two troopships able to land 400 men, but these were not properly prepared and provisioned until May, by which time Sultan Mehmet had brought a host of his own vessels overland, via a system of rollers and specially excavated trenches, so as to bypass the chain across the Golden Horn. In desperation at the non-appearance of their own fleet, a group of courageous Venetian merchants, disguising themselves as Turks, took a ship out into the open sea to reconnoitre for a possible sighting of the relief force but headed home after a fortnight's fruitless search, bringing their grim tidings to Emperor Constantine. Urged by his counsellors to slip away so that he could raise an army to recapture the city, he answered, 'How could I leave the churches of our God, their clergy, my throne and my people in such misfortune? Whatever would the world say of me? Never will I do this. I am resolved to die here beside you.' After which he dissolved in bitter tears.

A striking contrast in attitude becomes obvious at this point between the Venetian community within Constantinople, loyal to what they must by now have judged to be a hopeless cause, and the government at home in Venice, apparently ready to take advantage of the worsening situation so as to secure the best deal with the Turks when Byzantium inevitably fell. As various historians have pointed out, the naval force, its dispatch essentially a public relations exercise, was privately financed rather than funded by the state and its voyage across the Mediterranean involved halting at Corfu, Negroponte and the

Sultan Mehmet II, portrayed by Gentile Bellini in 1480. Following Mehmet's capture of Constantinople in 1453, Venice became a place of refuge for Greeks fleeing the city's Ottoman conquerors.

Venetian fortress island of Tenedos before it could actually sail up the Bosphorus.

Had the fleet arrived a week or so earlier the Turks might just have abandoned the struggle, so vigorous was the resistance put up by Constantine and his defenders, but it is unlikely that this would have put off by very much Mehmet's iron resolve to become master of the Greek empire in Asia or, with this behind him, to begin manoeuvres against Venetian ports in the Aegean and the Peloponnese. When his offer of honourable surrender terms to Constantine was rejected, the Turks made ready, on 28 May, for a final onslaught, while Constantine went to take the Eucharist in the great church of Hagia Sophia, the Holy Wisdom, before making ready for the end. The following morning, as Ottoman troops swept through the very gate of Saint Romanus which had seen them beaten back a month earlier, the last Byzantine emperor died fighting and his head was cut off to be carried to the sultan. Within Hagia Sophia the thousands of his subjects who sought shelter there and prayed for divine intervention were either slaughtered or dragged away to slavery while the Turks ransacked and desecrated the entire sacred space. Sultan Mehmet, on entering the building, ordered a halt to such barbarity and assured the Greek clergy of his protection but made sure that the Holy Koran was read from the pulpit in his presence.

During the siege the Venetian merchants, led by their *bailo* Girolamo Minotto, had fought with conspicuous gallantry alongside Emperor Constantine's defence force. This was in notable contrast to their old commercial rivals the Genoese, who, with a few heroic exceptions, had preferred sheltering in cosy neutrality in their residential quarter of Galata, on the opposite side of the strait, and were vilified by the Venetians for making peace with the sultan. Minotto, who had ordered a desperate last stand on 29 May, was taken prisoner and beheaded. Many others of his force were either drowned as they sought to escape to their galleys in the Bosphorus or else cut down as the Turks poured into the city. The ships, soon crowded with refugees, made for the open Aegean, only managing to evade their Turkish counterparts because the latter's crews had swarmed on shore to join in the looting.

It was a month before tidings of the fall of Constantinople arrived in Venice, carried by a small craft able to sail up the Grand Canal as far as the Rialto bridge, then a wooden structure whose two halves could be raised to allow masted vessels to pass through. From the deck came the dire news that the Greek capital had been taken amid appalling carnage. Along the canal there echoed 'despairing laments, crying and

The interior of the Byzantine metropolitan church of Hagia Sophia as the Muslim mosque it became after the fall of Constantinople. This lithograph (1853) is based on an original painting by Gaspare Fossati.

groaning, the people beating their breasts, tearing their hair at the likely death of family members or the loss of money and goods'. The Grand Council sat thunderstruck at the realization of what had happened. It was an event which marked the end of a relationship stretching back a thousand years, almost to Venice's foundation, a symbiotic connexion it was inconceivable could ever be effaced, let alone with such brutal suddenness.

Was it, as has been suggested, La Serenissima's own fault? Had the catastrophe of 1204, the sack of Byzantium, the hour of 'old, blind Dandolo', the squalid Crusader regime that followed, all found their historic consummation at this signal moment? The claim for such a cyclic resolution seems much too glib, the more so because of what the Signoria chose to do next. Shakespeare observes in *The Merchant of Venice* that 'the trade and profit of the city / Consisteth of all nations' and this remained La Serenissima's guiding principle. Its merchants had been doing business with the Turks since their appearance during the thirteenth century as a force to reckoned with in Levantine affairs. If money was to be made and commercial enterprise was to survive as the *raison d'être* of the Republic, then the new reality of an Islamic state impervious to Christian crusading would have to be confronted. 'The Turk', that generic label for a novel species of otherness, now provided the focus of Venice's curiosity, fear and speculation. Almost at once an embassy was dispatched to Sultan Mehmet in the hopes of restoring the rights and privileges of Venetian merchants and affirming the agreements made with his father, Murad II.

Venice itself had already become a place of refuge for Greeks fleeing from Turkish invasion as Mehmet, driven by strong religious convictions and a sense of his own destiny, began planning further incursions into the territories of Christendom. Though Byzantium itself had notably failed to renew the traditions of Greek antiquity in terms of its culture, formulaic and undistinguished as so much of this appears, it had remained the invaluable guardian of many of those texts through whom the inheritance of a classical past was transmitted to European civilization during the Renaissance. 'Brown Greek manuscripts' became part of the cargo on fifteenth-century Venetian ships, while the rediscovery of humane value systems and ideologies predating Christianity was enabled through the teaching of the Greek language itself, a key element in the new learning that formed part of civilized aspiration across Italy at this time.

One obvious beneficiary was the University of Padua. Its freedom in comparison with other Italian schools was already earning it an international reputation, since the Venetian Republic allowed no kind of pedagogical interference here from either the Holy Office or the Roman church establishment more generally. Thus Greek Orthodox scholars could study here without being pestered with accusations of heresy and they brought with them a wealth of classical texts and related commentaries. The earliest university chair of Greek in Western Europe was founded in Padua in 1463, while in Venice Greek printers began to publish editions of the ancient authors, including the earliest attempt at a complete Plato. As a result, a wholesale revision became necessary of the Aristotelianism hitherto mediated through transmission from Islamic sources in earlier centuries.

Foremost among the learned Greek fugitives and exiles was an erstwhile monk from Trebizond named Vassilios, who had taken the name Vissarion when entering the cloister. A dedicated student, he sought instruction further afield, in Mistras in the Peloponnese where he became a pupil of the highly influential Yorgos Gemistos, known as Pletho, who schooled him in the liberal disciplines of Neoplatonist philosophy, abstract and speculative. Both master and student would carry its ideas with them to Italy in 1437, when they accompanied Emperor John VIII Palaeologos on his visit to the Council of Ferrara. Vissarion was the official spokesman for a body of Greek clergy who favoured the union of Orthodox and Catholic churches debated at the congress and found himself gradually moving towards a theological acceptance of Catholicism, for which he was soon appointed a cardinal by Pope Eugenius IV.

He had meanwhile made the acquaintance of Cosimo de' Medici, ruler of Florence, who listened eagerly to what he and Gemistos Pletho had to say about Neoplatonism and went on to found a Florentine academy for promoting the new philosophy. Cardinal Bessarion, as the distinguished proselyte now became known, settled in Rome and took every opportunity to promote Greek studies, sheltering refugee scholars, sponsoring translators but never straying doctrinally from the Western rite he had now embraced. Given further appointments within the church, Bessarion was employed as a papal diplomat in France and Germany and finally named Cardinal Patriarch of Constantinople in 1463. The title was of course honorific but it testified to the high regard in which this spiritual renegade was held among senior Roman clergy.

Bessarion never forgot the impression made on him by his earliest visit to Venice in 1437. For him the place was essentially a Greek city in the western Mediterranean, marked by the presence of Byzantium in its architecture and sheltering a lively Hellenic community. It seemed

BESSARION. CARD^s

the obvious destination for a most remarkable gift, the library of 482 Greek and 264 Latin manuscripts chiefly assembled during his thirty years spent in Italy. Not long before his death in Ravenna in 1472, Bessarion presented this collection to the Venetian Senate. 'Though nations from almost all over the earth flock in vast numbers to your city,' he told them, 'the Greeks are the most numerous of all; as they sail in from their own regions they make Venice their first landfall and have such a tie with you that on disembarking within your city they feel as if entering a second Byzantium.' He had gathered the books together, as he said, 'for the sake of those Greeks who are left now, as well as for those who may enjoy a better fortune in the future'. Through this precious gift, later forming the nucleus of what some decades later became the great Biblioteca Marciana, one of Europe's major libraries, Bessarion had an ulterior design, that of encouraging the Latin West to redeem the Greek-speaking lands now under Turkish rule.

Before the donation of manuscripts and books to Venice there came another treasure with equally significant associations for Cardinal Bessarion. Much impressed by the work of the charitable *scuole* in the life of the city, he was happy to find himself elected, on 29 August 1463, to the Scuola della Carità, housed in the building which now contains the Accademia art gallery. His presentation to the confraternity marking this occasion was a gorgeous reliquary left to him by the priest Gregorios, former confessor to the Byzantine imperial court. It took the form of a Greek cross, silver-gilt on a decorated enamel background, flanked by panels adorned with gemstones and featuring painted icons. Within the central sections, under glass, were two fragments of Christ's robe and two pieces of the True Cross. Once again the gift embodied an admonition to Venice, as with the library, that she should stand firm against the infidel, protect the Greeks and restore them to their rightful inheritance.

A feeling had grown ever stronger among Venetians, following Constantinople's fall, that meekly yielding to the sultan's demands in exchange for trading privileges was no longer enough. Swiftly Mehmet's restless combativeness had led him to plan fresh campaigns across the Balkans, aimed at destroying the last Christian states in mainland Greece, while he also seized hold of islands in the Aegean. When it looked as if Turkey would force its way down through Bosnia and Albania onto the Adriatic, the Senate made ready for outright war but only if other Italian states were ready to mobilize as well. Pope Pius II, the romantic Sienese humanist Aeneas Silvius Piccolomini, was poised to proclaim a crusade, supported as he was by Cardinal

The Byzantine Greek humanist Cardinal Bessarion, in a portrait attributed to Antonio Maria Crespi. Bessarion, who gifted his magnificent library to the Venetian Senate, saw the city as another Byzantium.

Bessarion, and in 1464 he journeyed to Ancona where, theoretically at least, the princes of Christendom would be sending fleets to fall, as of old, on the detested paynim hordes.

Like so much else in Piccolomini's extraordinary career – he had written an epistolary love story, fathered a bastard child while on an embassy to Scotland and become bishop of Trieste almost by accident – reality and expectation never quite kept pace with each other and his life seemed to be going in every direction at once. Already a semi-invalid, he was seriously ill by the time of his arrival in Ancona, where all that awaited him was a small squadron of Venetian galleys. Burning August in the busy port fostered the spread of disease, soon carrying off this most arresting occupant of Saint Peter's chair. The crusade, which many considered a mere *ignis fatuus*, was rendered more unlikely by the fact that almost all Italy's other powers had hurried to make their peace with Sultan Mehmet. When the pope had sought to rally them, their response was a not unreasonable complaint that even if they did join forces with Venice, it would be sure to take the lion's share of reconquered territories. 'Everything won in Greece', warned a Florentine envoy, 'will become Venetian property, so that afterwards they may seize hold of Italy itself.'

As it happened, the ambassador was wrong. The Republic at this moment had no choice in the matter and all too soon it would become plain to Florence, Naples and the lesser states that they and their citizens were seriously threatened by the manoeuvres of that very same Ottoman power whose favours their diplomacy now solicited. The sultan in any case had his eye on a specially prized piece of the Venetian *Stato da Mar*, the island of Euboea, known as Negroponte. After a desultory four or five years of war in the Balkans against Greeks, Serbs and the Albanian forces led by the heroic Johannes Kastrioti, known by his Turkish nickname Skanderbeg, Mehmet began assembling a fleet and an army to overwhelm Negroponte's defenders. 'The Republic's safety is threatened,' wrote the merchant Geronimo Longo to the Senate from Corfu. 'With the loss of Negroponte the whole of the Levant will be in peril. Now our Signoria must show its strength, sending at whatever cost, all the ships, money and resources it can muster.' Taking his message seriously, the Signoria ordered the fitting out and provisioning of thirty galleys with the help of forced loans from its newly acquired mainland cities. Commanding the fleet, Nicolò da Canal, a diplomat turned admiral, sailed first towards Crete, then northwards to the island of Skiathos, commanding the Euripus, the stretch of water running between Negroponte and the Greek mainland.

By the time Canal's fleet hove into view, the Turks had launched their siege of the principal stronghold, originally called Chalcis, whose Venetian name Negroponte – 'black bridge' – had become affixed to the entire island (or semi-island, since Euboea remains attached to the mainland by a narrow isthmus). Mehmet's army had raised its pontoons further south to carry the troops across, easily surrounding the city and starting to pound its walls with cannon fire. The garrison commander Paolo Erizzo issued a spirited rejection of the sultan's offer of generous surrender terms, knowing full well that these would not be honoured, and infuriated Mehmet still further by telling him to 'go and eat pork'. Like everyone else within the walls, Erizzo had pinned his hopes on the Venetian armada's arrival and was overjoyed when at length, on 11 July, Canal, after what seemed an unconscionable delay, ordered his ships to move down the Euripus towards the beleaguered town.

Excitement turned to horror and despair among the watchers on Negroponte's ramparts as the fleet, borne on seemingly irresistibly by wind and tide and apparently aiming to shiver the pontoons to pieces, suddenly checked its advance and dropped anchor. Against all the entreaties of his officers, Canal had lost his nerve, unwilling to run the gauntlet of Turkish gunfire or risk losing any of his ships. In a frantic effort to hearten him again, Erizzo ordered the great banner of Saint Mark to be raised as a token of their shared allegiance, while a colossal crucifix was hoisted aloft, 'so that the fleet's commanders might be moved to pity us in ways they might imagine for themselves'. On land the Turks, preparing to abandon the siege altogether, could hardly believe their luck. A gleeful Mehmet gave orders for an all-out attack, the city was taken and most of its male population put to the sword, while the women and children were carried off as slaves. Paolo Erizzo, fighting to the last, was brought before the sultan, whom he proudly asked to spare him a beheading. Mehmet, who had not forgiven the governor's earlier defiance, ordered that he be sawn in half at the waist. As for Canal, having volunteered a belated assault on the pontoon, he once again changed his mind and abandoned his compatriots to their inevitable fate.

The loss of Negroponte on 12 July 1470 had an even more traumatic impact on Venice than the fall of Constantinople. 'The entire city,' reported a Milanese diplomat, 'is so smitten with horror that its inhabitants seem dead.' Though the Signoria resolved initially to tough out the catastrophe, proclaiming its readiness to carry on the struggle in the guise of Christendom's frontline champion, the wound ran far too deep for any immediate remedy. War with the Ottomans now shifted from an all-out conflict between two imperial powers to one of attrition, where the Venetian fleet, aided by ships from Naples and Ancona, raided ports along the Turkish coast and Mehmet's troops struck back at Venetian strongholds in the Peloponnese and Albania. In 1475 the first moves towards a peace treaty were made, but it took another four years, with Turkish attacks on Aegean island fortresses and forays into Friuli, before an exhausted and demoralized Republic sought favourable terms from Sultan Mehmet.

These were not forthcoming. Venice was forced to yield substantial possessions in Greece and Albania, together with the island of Lemnos in the Dodecanese, and to pay 'the Great Turk' an annual indemnity of 10,000 ducats for the privilege of being able to maintain a trading community in Constantinople. All this, however, was preferable to sustaining the role of a new crusading power which had increasingly been thrust on her by other Italian states, so that when in 1480 the Turks raided the port of Otranto in Apulia, belonging to the King of Naples, the attack was viewed as being somehow the fruit of Venetian perfidy in having made so unworthy a compact with the sultan during the previous year. Brewing around this event was a more general resentment of Venice throughout Italy, based on little more than outright envy of her business acumen, her wealth and her repeated ability to bounce back from adversity. Political exceptionalism counted further against her. In an age when great princely families – Sforza, Medici, Este, Gonzaga or Borgia – were establishing a ruthless grip on those cities and territories whose communal governments they had challenged or subverted, La Serenissima, administered not by tyrants but through councils and committees, was in various senses a reproach to their despotism and use of *force majeure*. However clannish and oligarchic the management of a Venetian state, whatever the openings which still offered themselves to figures like Francesco Foscari for a forceful and hyperactive personality as doge, this was a different polity to those elsewhere in Italy, one which, as regarded professional loyalty and an ultimate subservience to the rule of law, seemed remarkably – or dangerously – effective in the way it functioned. Partly because of this, Venice, during the fifteenth century's closing decades, began assuming the position of a presumptuous, overmighty competitor which, sooner rather than later, would need taking down and teaching a lesson.

Venetian arrogance was unlikely to be checked by the news, in 1460, that a young daughter of La Serenissima, Caterina Cornaro, was about to be made Queen of Cyprus. That great island, easternmost in the Mediterranean, had been ruled for over two hundred years by members of the French noble house of Lusignan, to whom it had been sold in 1192 by Richard Coeur de Lion, King of England. Alméric de Lusignan, its second king, had married a princess from the Crusader kingdom of Jerusalem, who had brought her father's titles (he was also nominally King of Armenia) with her and it was these which successive Lusignan kings of Cyprus inherited. The Cypriot court was a sophisticated one, as its architecture, music and poetry suggest, but in order to survive, its monarchs had needed to place themselves under the protection of the Mamluk sultans of Egypt. In 1432 a succession crisis threatened when King Jean II ascended the throne. His ambitious consort Elena, a princess from the Greek Palaeologos family, was determined to cut out all challengers to the rights of her daughter Princess Charlotte and made plans to neutralize or else exterminate anyone who stood in the way.

Her husband's mistress Maria Patras was the first to suffer. Made a captive, she was hideously mutilated on Elena's orders, having her nose slit and both ears chopped off. In this state she was exhibited to King Jean as a dire warning. Next in Elena's sights was a more problematic victim in the shape of King Jean's bastard son Jacques, handsome, talented and highly popular, a prince in everything but name and likely to be named his father's heir. The difficulty for Elena was how to exclude him from the succession without antagonizing the Cypriots en masse. She managed to persuade the pliable king to make the boy a priest, appointing him Catholic archbishop of Nicosia, the island's second city – not a perfect solution, but it would keep this child of the detested Maria Patras out of the way for the time being.

For Elena's daughter Princess Charlotte she now made what at first seemed an ideal arrangement by marrying her to a son of the King of Portugal, Prince João. The plan seems to have been that João would act as a kind of royal factotum to his wife while Elena managed the principal business of the kingdom from her advantageous position as consort to the idle, pleasure-loving King Jean. Nothing turned out quite as intended. João, a member of Portugal's ambitious and highly respected ruling house of Avis, was not at all content with being Elena's puppet and started making his own bid for power in Cyprus. He was duly put to death at her orders while she hurriedly sought another husband for the hapless Charlotte, this time in the shape of the inoffensive-seeming Prince Louis of Savoy. Early that summer of 1458, however, the inveterate schemer herself was finally carried off by a malignant fever, after which King Jean hastened to bring his beloved Jacques home to the court at Famagusta. A few months later the doting father died, whereupon a genuine succession crisis overtook the Cypriot throne.

As the legitimate heir, Charlotte was expected to claim the crown. Louis of Savoy, her new spouse, had not yet arrived in Cyprus but she had support from the Knights Hospitaller governing the nearby island of Rhodes and from the Genoese merchant community in Famagusta. Young Jacques, having pledged his fealty to her, returned to Nicosia, where his winning personality had made him many friends among a powerful group of Venetians trading in the island. When Charlotte, following her late mother's example, determined to have him killed, he escaped just in time to Alexandria, casting himself on the mercy of Egypt's Mamluk sultan, Sayf al-Din, who commanded him to be robed and crowned as King of Cyprus. Returning to Nicosia with money, munitions and a Mamluk guard, he was able to drive Charlotte and her supporters from the island and in 1463, aged twenty-four, he was acknowledged as King Jacques II.

Charlotte, not her mother's daughter for nothing, wasted no time in rallying financial backers in Genoa and Rome. Her glamorous rival, meanwhile, looked increasingly to his Venetian friends for assistance. One of these was Andrea Cornaro, whose brother Marco held estates in the island and had followed Jacopo's career with special interest as regarded its political advantages to Venice. The Cornaro had a niece, Caterina, who had arrived at the marriageable age of fourteen. Their family was among the Republic's richest and most securely established (one of them had been elected doge at the time of Marin Falier's conspiracy) and for young King Jacques an alliance this solid must have seemed an ideal solution as regarded bolstering his credit and status in the Mediterranean. By birth Caterina had the additional asset of a descent, through her mother Fiorenza Crispo, from Johannes Komnenos, Emperor of Trebizond, the breakaway Byzantine state on the Black Sea.

A proxy betrothal ceremony took place in 1468 in the presence of the Doge Cristoforo Moro and the Grand Council, with the bride being carried in procession down the Grand Canal on the Bucintoro. 'Her lovely eyes glistened like stars,' wrote the Cypriot ambassador Filippo Mastachelli to his royal master, 'her abundant fair hair seemed

Titian's posthumous portrait of Caterina Cornaro as Saint Catherine of Alexandria, 1542. The martyred Saint Catherine's wheel is visible in the background.

made of gold and her fine features proclaimed her noble blood.' The truth was that even as his engagement went ahead, Jacques de Lusignan had been busy seeking a better deal elsewhere in terms of money and munitions, so that it was to be another three years before Caterina actually set eyes on her husband and his realm. Venice meanwhile had been busy putting diplomatic pressure on the young king and emphasizing the benefits of La Serenissima's protection once his share of the bargain was properly fulfilled. Finally, with the eighteen-year-old girl officially named as an adopted daughter of the Republic – essentially a warning to Jacques not to renege on the agreement – she was brought to Cyprus with an escort of Venetian galleys.

Initially all the omens seemed good to her uncle Andrea Cornaro, broker of the match and counsellor to the king. Jacques was captivated by his wife, Caterina had enough shrewdness and good sense to match her charm, easily winning the islanders' hearts, and it was soon announced that she was carrying his child. The palace at Famagusta nevertheless remained a snake pit, containing as it did the king's bastard offspring, two sons and a daughter, and his mother, the disfigured Maria, whose resentment of the new queen quickly turned to loathing. When in July 1473 Jacques died, supposedly of a fever caught while out hunting, poison was immediately suspected and Caterina, giving birth to a son the following month, took stock of her vulnerability. Bad blood had risen between the Cypriot nobility and Venetian merchants, the exiled Charlotte de Lusignan still retained a malcontent following and, most dangerous of all, the powerful Louis Fabrègues, Archbishop of Nicosia, was busy intriguing with King Ferdinand of Naples to marry the latter's son to Jacques's bastard daughter and seize control of the island.

The archbishop's supporters struck on 13 November, breaking into the palace at midnight, killing the royal physician and hacking Andrea Cornaro to death before stripping his body and flinging it into the moat to be eaten by dogs. Caterina's baby boy, named after his father, was snatched from her and she was forced to write a letter to the Grand Council declaring herself happy with the Neapolitan marriage. An instant reaction from Venice was inevitable. By the time a punitive expedition arrived, the captive queen had gathered genuine sympathy among the common people across the island, so that while Archbishop Fabrègues and a few other leading rebels managed to escape, it was easy enough to round up the rest and put them to death. Caterina now reigned with the help of Venetian arms and money. For the Republic the process of adding Cyprus to the *Stato da Mar* was about to begin.

Nominally Caterina remained Queen of Cyprus, but her situation was not exactly enviable. Though little Jacques was returned to her, he died soon after his first birthday, encouraging the exiled Charlotte to press her claims as legitimate pretender to the throne. To avoid further trouble Maria Patras and her children were packed off to Venice, yet this made things no easier for Caterina, treated more and more by the Republic's chief agents as a distinguished prisoner under house arrest rather than as the free woman her sovereign status entitled her to be. Soon all the great offices of the realm were occupied by Venetians, further souring her relations with the Cypriot nobility, several of whom had their own designs upon the crown. For a decade this uneasy arrangement prevailed, while care was taken to prevent Caterina, still young and able to bear children, from seeking a new husband.

When in 1488 the Signoria got wind of a plot whose different strands involved a fugitive conspirator in Archbishop Fabrègues's earlier coup, one of Caterina's ladies-in-waiting and agents of the King of Naples, it became time to end the increasingly shaky and implausible status quo. The queen's brother Giorgio Cornaro sailed with a Venetian fleet to Cyprus, charged with the task of persuading her to abdicate. Should she fail to accept, La Serenissima would simply annexe the island by force. Initially Caterina put up a stout resistance but Giorgio appealed both to her sense of Cornaro family honour, still strong in the queen after sixteen years' absence from Venice, and to the distasteful realities of her current situation. A further incentive was added with pledges that she would be hailed as a faithful daughter of the Republic, that her rank as queen would be respected by the government and that she would be given the financial wherewithal to sustain her unique social position after returning home.

To this bizarre and unprecedented solution Caterina assented and in March 1489 she boarded a ship for Venice. The Signoria was as good as its word, greeting her, once arrived off the Lido, with a personal welcome by the doge and his counsellors and a triumphant journey on the Bucintoro before her abdication was solemnized at a high mass in San Marco. Thereafter, following a reunion with her extended family in their palace on the Grand Canal – still called Palazzo Corner della Regina following the brief time she spent there – the queen retreated to the castle assigned to her in the little town of Asolo in the hills north of Venice. In essence this delightful place (later favoured by the English poet Robert Browning, who made it the setting for his verse drama *Pippa Passes*, and by the Italian actress Eleonora Duse), became the capital of Caterina's miniature kingdom, where she dispensed laws and justice, handed out provisions to impoverished families and set up a pawnbroker's business for others in need.

For the next twenty years the court at Asolo attracted distinguished visitors from all over Italy, fascinated by its cultural sophistication and by such touches of exoticism as parrots, monkeys and Egyptian slaves. The Venetian Senate viewed all this with a wary eye. There was an enduring whiff of scandal – did the Queen of Cyprus take lovers? – and a more general suspicion of the royal palace, known as Il Barco, as being too much of a distraction from Venice itself for its high-end habitués. Caterina was mostly able to ignore this, enjoying her newest incarnation as a well-deserved reward for everything in the way of stress and heartache she had been made to endure while still in her island domain.

Perhaps her greatest good fortune at this moment, around the turn of the fifteenth and sixteenth centuries, lay in being able to catch hold of the Renaissance as its aesthetic values and creative dynamism spread throughout the smaller courts of Italy, such as Ferrara, Mantua and Urbino. An archetypal representative of this trend arrived in the person of Pietro Bembo, son of a Venetian diplomat at the Medici court in Florence. Imbued with the new learning in Latin and Greek, he had become a particular friend of the great printer Aldus Manutius, who in 1505 issued one of Bembo's first major works, *Gli Asolani*, a poetic dialogue on romantic love, set at Queen Caterina's court. Its three speakers, Perottino, Gismondo and Lavinello, share their varied experiences of passion, the last of them espousing a Platonic idealism exalting beauty in different earthly forms. The presence of such an accomplished *littérateur* at Il Barco was a distinct coup for the queen (though the work is actually dedicated to another patroness, Lucrezia Borgia, Duchess of Ferrara). Bembo, who went on to become a cardinal and a prince of the church, certainly enjoyed his sojourns with her, coining the term *asolare* to mean 'having fun in Asolo'. This was later taken up by Robert Browning to provide a title for his very last collection of poems, *Asolando* (1890).

Politics, the bane of Queen Caterina's life, would ultimately put an end to these pleasures. In 1509 the strife occasioned by the League of Cambrai in its efforts to crush the Republic (see chapter 11) drove her back to Venice and the safety of her brother's palace. Asolo was occupied by the troops of Emperor Maximilian of Austria, who looted and burned Il Barco so completely that only one forlornly elegant arcade survives to give us some idea of its splendour. The following year Caterina Cornaro, Queen of Cyprus, died at the age of fifty-six and was given an elaborate state funeral, her coffin carrying the very same crown which she had earlier renounced, and taken for burial in her family chapel at the church of Santi Apostoli, close to the Rialto.

Where Venice was concerned, the faithful and honoured daughter of Saint Mark had served her purpose magnificently in delivering the gift of a large, prosperous, fruitful domain to compensate for losses elsewhere in the *Stato da Mar*. The Signoria would soon discover how difficult Cyprus honestly was to administer internally, its surly, factious islanders reluctant to accept either the notional blessings of La Serenissima's control or the realities of the growing tax burden needed to sustain and defend this. Meanwhile the Turks awaited their moment to snatch the prize. It would not be long in coming.

THE POLITICS
OF ENVY

So many of those who enriched the cultural life of Venice across the ages were visitors, incomers, foreigners whom the city captivated or, in the best sense, arrested, to the extent that they gladly made themselves adoptive Venetians. One of the most outstanding examples of this willing surrender was that of the great printer and bookseller Aldo Manuzio, known to history by his Latin name of Aldus Manutius. His home town, Bassiano, lies deep in the Latian countryside south of Rome, but he soon left it behind to learn Latin and Greek at Ferrara, whence he journeyed to nearby humanist courts at Carpi and Mirandola before settling in Venice in 1490 as a printer. Joining forces with Andrea Torresano, whose daughter he married, Aldus dedicated himself to the diffusion of classical Latin and Greek texts in versions whose scrupulous editing matched the clarity and elegance of their production. Pietro Bembo became his friend and patron, giving him the ancient Roman coin bearing the image of a dolphin wrapped around an anchor which Aldus adopted as his personal and professional emblem. Under this sign a whole sequence of editions, beginning with five volumes of a complete set of Aristotle's works and including Bembo's own presentation of Petrarch's collected verse, emerged from the Aldine press, which had its premises in the *sestiere* of San Polo, close to the Frari and the now vanished church of Sant'Agostino. The sheer volume of the printshop's business rose rapidly enough for a notice to be set up that enjoined visitors: 'Whoever you may be, Aldus constantly desires to know what you want from him. Briefly state your business, then go away at once.'

The Aldine press made Venice a magnet for humanists, whether from Italy or across the Alps, and in 1502 Aldus founded the so-called New Academy to further the study, writing and speaking of Greek. His major achievement was to make the wisdom and creativity of the

overleaf   A page from Aldus Manutius's 1499 printing of
Hypnerotomachia Polifili, an anonymous allegorical romance.
Distinguished by its typography and woodcuts, this is one of the
most sought-after of all incunabula.

lute trece sopra il pāno soppresso, inundáte, la forma rugata, ou
cata dil inglomato panno, gli subtilissimi capegli æmulauan
erano ancora debitamente pulpidule cum gli carnosi genui
mente alquanto ad se ritracti, monstrando gli sui stristi petali ii
ponere la mano & pertrectarli & strengerli. Et il residuo dil for
corpo, prouocaua chi fortuito simigliante ella ritrouato se fus

Vno frondoso di non decidue foglie di Memerylo poscia
la testa degli molli & rotondi Vnedi copioso, & di auiculetti, c
no garrire, & inducere causa di dolce somno. Ad gli pedi staua
ro in lasciuia pruriente & tutto commoto, Cum gli pedi capre
il buccamento ad naso adhærito, capreato & Simo, Cū la barb
to distincta in due irricature di Caprini Spirili, & cusi ad gli hi
Et per questo pari modo alla testa, cum pilate auricule, & di fro
nato, cum effigie tra caprea, & humana adulterata. Excogitai ch
cutissimo ingegnio il lithoglypho habilissimamente & al libi
lo pificio dilla natura præsente nella Idea.

Il dicto Satyro haua larboro Arbuto per gli rami cum la si
no uiolente rapto, & al suo ualore sopra la soporata Nympha
lo, indicaua di farli gratiosa umbra. Et cum laltro brachio trah
tremo di una cortinetta, che era negli rami al tronco proximi
Intra larboro comaro, & il Satyro, assideuano dui Satyruli inf
cum uno uaso nelle mano, & laltro cum le sue inuilupate
cumuoluti serpi.

Non potria sufficiente exprimere, quanto delicato, quanto
& perfecto era questo figmento, accedeua & alla uenustate illu
la petra quale striso eburo. Miraua summamente ancora l
optimo & peruio tripanato degli rami & foliatura cedrina
le auicule cum gli pediculi sui di tutta exactura & exp
so, & per il simigliante dil Satyro. Sotto di questa ta
le & mirabile scalptura, tra le gulature, &
undule, nella piana fascia, uidi in-
scalpto, questo mysterioso di
cto di egregio Chara-
ctere Atthico.

ΓΑΝΤΑ
ΤΟΚΑ
ΔΙ

✳

ΠΑΝΤΩΝ ΤΟΚΑΔΙ

Per laquale cosa io non saperei definire, sila diuturna & tanta acre se-
te pridiana tolerata ad bere trahendo me prouocasse, ouero il bellissimo
suscitabulo dello instruméto. La frigiditate dil quale, inditio mi dede che
la petra mentiua. Circuncirca dunque di questo placido loco, & per gli
loquaci riuuli fioriuano il Vaticinio, Lilii conuallii, & la floréte Lysima
chia, & il odoroso Calamo, & la Cedouaria, Apio, & hydrolapato, & di
assai altre appretiate herbe aquicole & nobili fiori, Et il canaliculo poscia

c

ancient world accessible in the form of portable printed books, whose typefaces he himself had painstakingly designed and whose texts in several cases were those of hitherto lost fragments of classical authors recently brought to light by pioneering scholarly investigators. The fact that so many of these volumes were in small format, an octavo easily carried in the hand or slipped into a pocket, meant that the ideas, value systems and literary techniques of their writers became central to the culture of the Renaissance, not in Italy alone but throughout the whole of Europe. In Venice itself, newly enriched by what Greek refugees had brought with them in the wake of Byzantium's fall, a crucial shift in tastes, attitudes and lifestyle among urban households began taking place, partly as a result of Aldus Manutius's remarkable success, as an impassioned incomer, in diffusing the new learning from his shop in San Polo.

A key figure in cultural history, his genius perhaps not celebrated emphatically enough by writers on this period, Aldus might seem a little eccentric in choosing Venice as a fulcrum for his work when we look at the fortunes of the Republic in the fifteenth century's final decades. Her resources stretched by campaigns on the *terraferma*, her merchant empire shrinking rapidly as the emboldened Ottomans pushed westwards across the Mediterranean, her economy weakened by a series of banking failures, Venice's back, ostensibly, was against the wall. A miraculous resilience nevertheless enabled her to thrive as a city of marvels at which the world beyond the lagoon gazed with deepening envy. Knock-backs, wherever they sprang from, could somehow always be transcended. Too much, in this respect, has perhaps been made of that moment in 1501, dreadful as it truly seemed at the time, when news arrived from Portugal that Vasco da Gama, rounding the Cape of Good Hope, had crossed the Indian Ocean to reach the port of Calicut, a mart for the spices of southeast Asia. 'On receiving these tidings,' wrote the diarist Girolamo Priuli, 'the city was struck dumb and wisest heads judged them the worst they ever heard.' Venetian trade, Priuli believed, would be seriously damaged, 'since foreigners came here from everywhere to purchase such large quantities of spices as were brought by our sea voyages'. Now, he supposed, the Portuguese would knock down the prices and the European market among Germans, French, Flemish and Hungarians would shift its centre to Lisbon.

Priuli was not wrong and neither was the Portuguese merchant who judged that 'He who controls Malacca has his hand around Venice's neck,' but the consequent impact on trade was gradual rather than dramatic. Two centuries later Venice still had merchant colonies in the Levant, a *bailo* in Istanbul and a spice market on the Rialto, even if commerce was not nearly so vigorous as it had been in the glory days of the Middle Ages. During the sixteenth century in any case, thanks partly to miscalculations by the Portuguese and to various reverses suffered while they sought to extend their power in the East, this aspect of Venetian commerce would enjoy a prolonged period of recovery, bringing renewed prosperity and wealth to the city.

In the crucial decades when Aldus Manutius set up his business in Venice as printer and bookseller, he found himself working in a context where a book as artefact or visual object had almost as much a claim to attention as the text which it flourished before the reader. At the century's turn the city had embraced the values of Renaissance humanism as part of a civic and spiritual ethos, manifested in everything from Tullio Lombardo's nobly proportioned church of San Salvador (1507) to the marble screen giving access to the courtyard of the Scuola Grande di San Giovanni Evangelista, the work of his father Pietro, begun around 1481. The *scuole* in general responded fervently to this mood of revitalized idealism, manifested by architecture and sculpture, as witnessed in the grandeur of the Scuola di San Rocco by Bartolomeo Bon and Antonio Scarpagnino or by the amazing decorative banquet laid out for us by the Lombardo family on the Scuola di San Marco, finished off in a sequence of lunettes designed by their brilliant contemporary, the architect Mauro Codussi. A footstep away from this archetypally Venetian Renaissance eye-catcher is Pietro Lombardo's most astounding achievement in the shape of the church of Santa Maria dei Miracoli, a perfect synthesis, in its structural and decorative discourse, of Venice as a city at the crossroads between Rome, Byzantium and the Muslim East, transfigured by a visceral Venetian fondness for variety, parade and display across its marble planes.

Appropriate spaces in which to display the artworks, antique statues, coins and medals which became status indicators for the patrician class in Renaissance Venice were created amid the extraordinary wealth of palaces built or rebuilt in the early years of the new century. Mauro Codussi was among the most favoured architects for this marmoreal enrichment, in buildings like the Ca' Corner Spinelli (subsequently enlarged by Michele Sanmicheli) and the imposing Ca' Loredan, now known by the name of its later occupants, the Vendramin Calergi family. Palaces like these had few if any rivals elsewhere in Europe in terms of the harmony, elegance and dignity of their proportions and their cumulative impact on the Venetian townscape helped in shaping an image of the city's power and riches that endured even as its actual

overleaf The gorgeous interior of Pietro Lombardo's Santa Maria dei Miracoli, built 1481–9 to house an icon of the Virgin Mary.

resources started to diminish. '*Venezia, Venezia, chi non ti vede non ti prezia*' – 'Venice, Venice, whoever hasn't seen you can't measure your worth' – ran an Italian saying. It was the knockout vision of these massive structures, uncompromising in their handsomeness, rising so abruptly from the water that surrounded them, which asserted the Republic's supremacy as well as underlining the entitlement, sophistication and exceptionalism of its governing elite.

Not surprisingly, such palpable manifestations of beauty and wealth fuelled a growing envy among other Italian states. The need to bring Venice to heel, to humiliate the Most Serene Republic, to plunder its wealth and choke its arrogance was not new, as we have seen, but this particular hunger demanded satisfying more strongly than ever before as the new century got into its stride. A wider context for this general longing to see an appropriate nemesis visited on the overmighty Serenissima had arisen from events shaking the whole of Italy in 1494, when Charles VIII, King of France, encouraged by several of his fellow sovereigns, resolved to claim what he deemed his rightful inheritance in the shape of the Kingdom of Naples. Leading an army of nearly 50,000 men over the Alps, he had advanced, largely unopposed, into the heartland of his new realm, entering Naples itself on 22 February 1495 amid jubilant crowds. The ease with which the whole operation had been carried out was unnerving to Italian rulers, the more so since the actual Neapolitan sovereign, Alfonso of Aragon, had preferred to abdicate rather than stand and fight. If the French king could swoop so successfully on one portion of the peninsula, what was to prevent him from snapping up the rest?

Swiftly a hostile alliance was formed that included the Republic of Venice, Pope Alexander VI, Ludovico Sforza, claimant to the Duchy of Milan, and Emperor Maximilian of Austria, with the stated objects of defending Italy against Turkish invasion and, much more ominously, that of protecting their own territories in the process. King Charles's ambassador to Venice at this juncture was Philippe de Commines (encountered in an earlier chapter) who watched in disgust as the new compact was celebrated on the Grand Canal with fireworks and fanfares. He took Doge Antonio Barbarigo's assurance for what it was worth that the king could return to France unharmed, provided his progress across Italy was made in pure friendship. With very different intentions Charles moved northwards, bent on testing the forces of the alliance, but the inevitable confrontation, taking place at Fornovo di Taro, south of Parma, was a stalemate. The king scattered his enemies, poorly led by Francesco Gonzaga, Marquis of Mantua, yet wholly failed to follow up the victory, overtaken by the speed of events elsewhere in Italy combining to wreck his dreams of conquest. News of the fight at Fornovo reached Venice in a garbled report that indicated a thorough trouncing of the French army. Everyone on the Rialto spoke of victory and kissed each other for joy, while little boys waved Saint Mark's banner as they ransacked the market's fruit stalls. There was no ultimate reason to regret the more sober accounts later revealing Gonzaga's incompetence and the battle's dubious outcome. Winning or losing made less difference to Venice than the position La Serenissima had achieved at the forefront of an international alliance. Whether this particular partnership would survive its immediate purpose, that of ousting a tiresome foreign interloper, was not so important as the chance to take a significant place alongside some of the most potent figures currently bestriding the European political stage.

Such an enhanced status threatened danger as a newly emboldened Senate started plotting a revised strategy calculated to burnish Venice's image as one of Italy's key players. France, so lately the enemy, was now to be courted as an ally. In 1498 King Charles died from a fatal concussion on his way to watch a game of tennis. His successor Louis XII was someone the Signoria felt it could do business with, more particularly as regarded the Duchy of Milan, to which he claimed inheritance rights. Having supported Ludovico Sforza only a few years earlier, Venice now found it opportune to back the new king in his plans to annexe the duchy, in return for certain long-coveted towns in western Lombardy and access to ports on Italy's Tyrrhenian coast. By the autumn of 1499 Milan had effectively become a dependency of the French crown, with the Serene Republic seeking to stretch an arm from one side of the peninsula to another.

Gripped by the fever of expansionism, the Grand Council turned its focus on what seemed like Venice's most vulnerable neighbour, the States of Holy Church, that slew of fiefdoms and domains in central Italy on which the popes grounded their political authority. The basis of such a pretention was the so-called 'Donation of Constantine', a totally fraudulent document supposedly issued by the Roman emperor of that name, assigning power over the city of Rome and the lands surrounding it to the papacy in perpetuity. Probably fabricated during the ninth century, it had been exposed as a forgery by the lawyer and scholar Lorenzo Valla in 1440, for which the Holy Inquisition duly anathematized him, though he managed to avoid trial and imprisonment. Now, fifty years later, in the current climate of jostling aggression among Italian states, questions of territorial ownership and

validation of sovereignty had become still more important to the popes. A new pontiff, Julius II, elected in 1503, was determined to give fresh life to the spirit of the Donation.

Ironically, in view of what soon transpired, Venice had been among the strongest supporters of the sixty-year-old Giuliano della Rovere in his candidature for the throne of Saint Peter. Though best known to posterity as the man who commissioned Michelangelo's frescoes for the Sistine Chapel and Raphael's *Stanze* in the Vatican, Pope Julius was more familiar to his own era in the guise of a restless, thuggish bully, a warrior manqué, insatiably ambitious, the slave of impulse and sudden mood swings, yet at the same time passionately devoted to advancing the dignity and standing of Holy Church in a world where the Reformation's earliest ripples were making themselves felt. Well disposed towards Venice initially, he had invoked its aid in working against the power and influence of the Borgia family, headed by Pope Alexander VI and his son Cesare. It was Julius, as Cardinal della Rovere, who encouraged the Signoria to pursue its advantages in the Romagna region south of the Po delta, where the Venetians were quick to seize the cities of Rimini and Faenza from under Cesare Borgia's nose.

To their obvious alarm, the complaisant cardinal whom his Roman rivals had labelled '*Il Veneziano*' for his partisanship, vanished from view on becoming an omnipotent Pope Julius II. The diarist Marin Sanudo, a rich source for historians of Venice at this period, tells us that the new pontiff aimed at being 'lord and master of the world'. If so, then to achieve this he required the immediate restitution of those very same towns and castles he had urged Venice to seize hold of only a year or so previously. Such gains were part of the Donation of Constantine (interpreted at its most liberal) so what belonged to the church must remain with it, as part of Julius's grander design for re-establishing that dignity and primacy in world affairs that it had lost under the notoriously corrupt Pope Alexander. It was in this spirit that he told the historian Nicolò Machiavelli, sent to him as an envoy from the Florentines, that even though friendly to Venice, he was ready, should the Republic not be willing to renounce its conquests in Romagna and the Marche, to rouse all the princes of Christendom against it.

Which was what Julius proceeded to do, having clinched an agreement with King Louis of France and Emperor Maximilian at the former's chateau of Blois in the autumn of 1504. The fact that both monarchs, after signing the treaty, immediately started quarrelling with each other over an entirely different issue, bought a little time for the Venetians. They were ready to challenge the emperor when, a year

Raphael's portrait of Pope Julius II, the warrior pope for whom
Venice was by turns a deadly menace and a valued ally.

or so later, he sent an army into Friuli and thence into the Veneto. His main aim was to establish control over Verona and Vicenza before moving on to gain territory from the Republic of Genoa, closing in on Milan and adding the whole of Lombardy to his empire. Aware of his grand game, Venice outflanked Maximilian with consummate success, invoking the leadership of seasoned *condottieri* to force him to negotiate with her, that very same power he had earlier singled out as 'Austria's arch-enemy'.

To crush La Serenissima in revenge was not good enough for the emperor and his allies. She would first need to be utterly humiliated and thereafter expunged from among the great powers of Italy, her conquests over the last hundred years on *terraferma* to be parcelled out, not just between the neighbour duchies, Ferrara, Mantua and Milan, but also to France, Hungary and Savoy, all of whom cherished resentments against her. From the era's propagandists, led by Nicolò Machiavelli, came an image of Venice as a behemoth, a monstrous political aberration, consumed by 'lust for dominion', a state which, in the words of the great Florentine, 'had resolved, within her deepest soul, to create an empire like that of ancient Rome'. It hardly needs saying that Pope Julius, full of his own schemes for ruling Italy, took a central role in fomenting the aggressive alliance, gleefully anathematizing the Venetians' insatiable greed and their lust for power, along with their 'tyrannical usurpations', their violence and brutality, so that any kind of revenge for all these was to be justified as 'the extinguishing of some great fire'.

The town of Cambrai in eastern France was a prosperous centre of clothworking, famous for a kind of fine white linen material called 'cambric' in English, used for making shirts and handkerchiefs. Standing on the River Scheldt, a natural frontier between the French king's lands and those of the former Duchy of Burgundy, recently annexed by Emperor Maximilian, it was an ideal spot for ambassadors to converge in the last weeks of 1508 for the ceremony of signing the document which sealed the fate (as it then seemed) of Venice and her presumptuous oligarchy. The whole grand alliance would not in fact move into action until the following March, when King Ferdinand of Spain, scenting advantages both mercantile and territorial, added his support.

Only now was Pope Julius ready to offer a direct commitment to the scheme his own zeal, indignation and sense of entitlement had been so effective in fostering. Driven to further rage when news reached him that the Signoria had rejected his candidate for the vacant bishopric of Vicenza in favour of its own, he vowed that he would return the city of Venice to its origins and make a town full of gorgeous palaces into a fishing village. In Palazzo Ducale meanwhile, the doge, Leonardo Loredan, whose portrait by Giovanni Bellini is among the most striking images in world art, faced the Grand Council with the stark choice which lay before its members. 'Either bury your personal differences and join together in defending the state or else confront your own extinction and the perpetual loss of your freedom.'

On 17 April King Louis's official herald, dressed in his tabard adorned with the lilies of France, arrived in Venice to throw down the symbolic glove representing a declaration of war. A few days later, as French troops poured into the Veneto, the pope issued a scarifying bull of excommunication against the Republic, allowing her less than a month to come to heel and tender him the appropriate submission. Having had, in Shakespeare's memorable phrase, 'a kind of light what would ensue', the Signoria gallantly rejected this very considerable threat, banning all issue of it within the confines of the state. Though in recent weeks they had sought to fend off the unavoidable conflict through offers of cash and concessions to the League of Cambrai's various signatories, they were brave enough, at this knife-edge moment, to confront reality in the shape of the most formidable opposition Venice had faced in a thousand years of its history. It was another of those episodes, like the War of Chioggia or the great Austrian siege of 1849, in which the concept of what their city meant in terms of freedom and communal solidarity brought out the best in the Venetians, with their backs against the wall and defeat seeming to stare them in the face.

Catastrophe broke out in earnest when, on 14 May 1509, the armies of the League confronted the forces of the Venetian Republic at the Lombard village of Agnadello, close to the town of Lodi, south of Milan. Even under pouring rain the Venetians seemed to enjoy an initial advantage, though their Roman *condottieri* generals, the cousins Nicolò and Bartolomeo Orsini, were at loggerheads over strategy and the various corps of troops were spread too thinly along a dangerously extended front. A key failure by Nicolò to mobilize his men in support of Bartolomeo meant that a pincer movement by the French army under King Louis could easily overwhelm the main Venetian infantry regiments and scatter the cavalry brigades. Four thousand men were killed fighting for La Serenissima and with them went any dreams she might still have entertained of dominance over the western area of Lombardy. News of the defeat at Agnadello, sent to Venice by the governor of Brescia, reached the Signoria while preparations were in train for Ascension Day, '*la Festa della Sensa*'. The annual festival of the Sposalizio, the marriage of the Serene Republic to the sea, was normally such a joyful occasion with its gala dress, fanfares and pomp on board the Bucintoro but now, when the fatal letter was read aloud to Doge Loredan and his counsellors, Marin Sanudo tells us, 'they looked as if they had been struck dead by the greatest sorrow. Everybody wept, none dared go out into the Piazza, the senators seemed utterly lost, our doge most of all who could not speak for sadness.' The next day's traditional celebrations, says the diarist, were set aside in favour of a modest procession to San Marco, in which the nobility pointedly left off its robes of gilt brocade. 'There were few people present. Instead the whole city was desperately seeking about for further news.'

As more information arrived, the scale of the disaster at Agnadello became horrifyingly apparent. At one point it was seriously proposed by certain Council members that an envoy be sent to the sultan in Istanbul to beg his assistance in clawing back the lands currently being overrun by the League. Fifty thousand ducats' worth of fine textiles and another fifty thousand in precious stones would be offered to the Grand Turk as security. Even as the Senate frantically cast around for anybody in the shape of an ally, Emperor Maximilian, Duke Ercole of Ferrara and an exultant Pope Julius were falling greedily on towns and cities across the Veneto and the Bassa Padana, the lands around the estuary of the River Po. It honestly looked, at this stage, as though Venice would indeed return to its modest beginnings among the *barene* and marshes of the lagoon.

Yet the victory gained by the League of Cambrai on that rainy May afternoon in Lombardy was not, after all, quite so decisive as it at first appeared. Agnadello was a significant engagement but its impact was delayed, indirect and unforeseen, one not achieved solely with swords, pikes and gunpowder, a battle which, as matters transpired, would yield almost nothing of real value to the winners. For no sooner had the League's chief players claimed their various prizes in the shape of towns and villages than their inhabitants began fretting beneath the constraints placed on them by these new overlords. It has been noted earlier that in most, though not all, of the Venetian empire (Crete, Šibenik and the Peloponnese offer telling exceptions) the rule of La Serenissima was gratefully and tranquilly accepted. The lion of Saint Mark above fortified gateways was a badge of belonging, an emblem of disinterested authority, relative absence of corruption and dependable permanence in local government. This very same sense of attachment was what now served to rescue the Republic at a major crisis point in its survival.

Earliest to throw off its new masters, in the shape of Maximilian's imperial lieutenants, was the city of Padua, by now among Venice's most devoted mainland satellites. On 17 July a Venetian force easily retook the town, amid jubilant crowds who, Marin Sanudo tells us, 'cried out "Marco! Marco! Praise be to God that we see our Venetian masters in command once again, whom the traitors wished to destroy!"' Sanudo later uses the word *marcheschi*, a generic term for supporters of La Serenissima in all the provinces invaded by the League. In Friuli it was taken up by the peasants who worked on the estates of the region's nobility, the latter being rather too keen, just now, to curry favour with the emperor. For these labouring folk the presence of a Venetian government had guaranteed stability and fair dealing, both of which the war had overturned. Elsewhere, in Treviso for example, the imperial presence was simply shrugged off as a tiresome interruption: the town's *marcheschi* stood firm in their allegiance to the lion and his open book. Soon enough a slew of captured towns proclaimed their loyalty, so that by the autumn everywhere from Montagnana in the Euganean hills to Bassano on the edge of the Dolomites had returned to Venetian control.

Things were made easier by the fact that the League was finding itself overstretched both militarily and administratively. Pope Julius had in any case grown steadily more mistrustful of his allies, whether French, Austrian or Italian. He was not inclined to move in step with them where imposing a peace settlement on Venice was concerned. Furious at the loss of Padua, followed as this soon was by those of Verona and Vicenza, he resolved to teach the Senate a lesson by publicly humiliating its envoys. When these appeared before him in Rome, they were treated as disgraced excommunicates by the papal officials and made to perform due acts of penitence, as well as having to receive the pope's surrender terms without demur. These included a swingeing financial indemnity for all losses incurred by the church within the disputed territories being reclaimed and a total forfeit of privileges and legal sanctions relating to the appointment of bishops and jurisdiction over the clergy. An elaborate ceremony of submission and obeisance concluded with the Venetians kissing the papal slipper, listening, while on their knees, to an hour-long catalogue of La Serenissima's malfeasances and accepting symbols of their chastisement in the shape of wands used for scourging repentant sinners, as a choir intoned the *Miserere*. Only after such an elaborate pantomime was Pope Julius content to pronounce absolution.

Other members of the League, unhappy with the pope's ever more ambiguous stance towards it, took pains to restore cohesion, managing to sustain the war in the Veneto for at least another year. Venice, true to form, had already made up its mind that if indeed the Republic was to be humbled in the fashion ordained by a choleric tyrant, the process should be accepted by the Signoria purely as a formality. In their official register the Council of Ten entered a declaration that the surrender had been unjustly exacted and that Venice now yielded to His Holiness 'not of her own free will but because compelled to do so, through grievous threats, superior force and fear'. Since there was no adequate moral basis for yielding to such conditions, the Ten's minutes implied, the Signoria was not bound to honour them.

What the Venetian ambassadors could not have foreseen, as they knelt before an exultant pontiff in the porch of Saint Peter's basilica, was the speed with which his original commitment to the League would start to shift during the early summer of 1510. Perhaps recalling Charles VIII's Italian expedition made a decade or so earlier, Julius's wariness of French involvement in the ongoing campaign deepened to an outright hostility. The pope was that familiar species of leader whose validation needs the continuing presence of an enemy, regardless what kind. With Venice apparently brought low, his enduring fretfulness focused on King Louis and what might be his further designs for mastery over the whole of northern Italy. With Emperor Maximilian, whose heart had gone out of warfare anyway, he had no quarrel, but Louis, from his reading of events, now represented a menace that must be dealt with for the greater good of Italy in her role as the nurse of Holy Church. To get rid of the French became a sacred cause and it was opportune for Julius to represent his former allies as little better than the savage hordes that had pulled down the Roman empire centuries earlier. '*Fuori i barbari!*' – 'Away with the barbarians!' – became his famous rallying cry of 1512, as he started pulling together another alliance, a so-called Holy League, this time involving King Ferdinand of Spain, the young King Henry VIII of England and the Republic of Venice. That very same once-detested enemy was currently busy with rebuilding its mainland empire through a series of largely successful operations across the Veneto against Louis's forces. Now it became the banker of the Holy League as a fresh international conflict broke out across northern Italy.

For almost two decades more the marches, counter-marches, battles, sieges and spoliation would continue, following Pope Julius II's death from a malignant fever in 1513. His final year had been wracked by the zigzags of war, culminating in a brief, blood-soaked triumph for the French outside Ravenna, which encouraged them to discredit the pope at a special church council in Milan, with a view to barring him from office altogether. When at last Emperor Maximilian agreed to join the League, bringing his Swiss mercenaries to the fray, King Louis, further menaced on home territory by an invasion from England, had ordered a sudden withdrawal of all his troops from Italy. Yet peace seemed a mirage as Maximilian stuck to his claims, established under the terms of the League of Cambrai, to be overlord of the Veneto's chief cities. As a result, the newer alliance began to fragment. Even as Julius lay on his deathbed, Venice was in the process of striking a fresh agreement with her erstwhile foe Louis of France to challenge imperial pretentions.

A last lunge at Italy on the part of the French monarchy was made not by Louis XII but by his youthful and glamorous successor King François I, culturally an ardent Italophile, whose victory over the emperor's troops at Marignano in 1516 brought the exhausted combatants to peacemaking later that year. The new pope, Leo X, a Medici with his own territorial and dynastic ambitions, was prepared to clinch a deal just as long as his nephew could become Duke of Urbino and the young King Carlos of Spain was to be assured of succession to the empire on Maximilian's death. In favouring this remarkable figure, whose reign as Emperor Charles V would make him in essence the most powerful man in the world, Leo could not foresee the ultimate downfall of that very same temporal supremacy he represented, when in 1527 his relative and successor Clement VII was driven from Rome and the city was sacked by an imperial army.

For Venice the treaties concluded in Brussels and at the northern French cathedral town of Noyon resulted in the restitution of nearly all her lost cities across the *terraferma*, including Brescia, Vicenza and, through a diplomatic sleight of hand allowing Emperor Maximilian to save face, the prized possession of Verona. The aim of the League of Cambrai had been to crush and humiliate the Republic so that her role as '*La Bella Dominante*' would be seen as, at best, a hollow pretence. Such an enterprise had failed and Venice was once again that bloody but unbowed survivor she had been at the time of the War of Chioggia a century earlier. The city itself remained abundantly rich, vigorous,

Giorgione's *La Tempesta*, painted in 1507, is the artist's best-known
work, but its imagery has never been definitively interpreted.

busily at work, densely populated with around 160,000 inhabitants by the opening of the new century. The experience of prolonged warfare, far from breaking her confidence as one historical viewpoint suggests, had if anything emboldened Venice to display herself to the world with even greater extravagance and splendour.

For we should remember that this very same period had witnessed the rise of that stupendous artistic impetus which gives Venice her position of major significance in the visual culture of the Italian Renaissance. While the Republic's back was against the wall, while its towns and territory were being lost and won and lost again, while its armies were in disarray and its liberty at stake, the city was emerging as a focus of patronage for painters, sculptors and architects. Giovanni Bellini, among the longest-lived of Renaissance painters, had become so respected for works such as the altarpieces at San Giobbe (1487) and San Zaccaria (1505) that the Signoria granted him special privileges as well as entrusting him with supervision of the paintings contained within Palazzo Ducale. His studio became a training ground for nascent genius. Giovanni Cima da Conegliano studied here, mastering the older artist's feeling for colour and the beauty of background landscape, and so in later years did the more wayward figure of Lorenzo Lotto. Giorgio da Castelfranco, known by his nickname Giorgione, spent some time as Bellini's pupil before rejecting the older artist's style (according to Vasari) as 'arid' and going on to evolve his own more lyrical idiom. Among the last – and surely the greatest – of Bellini's students was a young man from the village of Pieve di Cadore, up in the Dolomites, named Tiziano Vecellio, Titian to us, numinous and incomparable in his handling of paint, an innovative sense of colour and design and the free play of a boundless imagination across a career spanning some seventy years.

Interestingly, none of these masters – except Titian in an altarpiece for a church in Ancona, implicitly celebrating the end of the League of Cambrai war – actually portrays the Venetian cityscape in his work. For this we turn to one of the era's truly astounding achievements, the great map by the artist Jacopo de' Barbari, taking the form of a colossal print, made up of half a dozen woodblocks across as many sheets of paper, bearing the title '*VENETIE MD*' and issued, as its Roman numerals imply, in 1500. The panorama shows not just Venice itself but the surrounding islands, Murano, Burano and Torcello, and is adorned with images of various winds familiar to Mediterranean sailors such as the Sirocco, the Libeccio and the Mistral. Classical deities lend assistance. Neptune of course is here as king of the sea, but so too is

overleaf Jacopo de' Barbari's panoramic map of Venice, issued in 1500, set a benchmark in urban cartography with its astounding wealth of detail.

Mercury, patron god of commerce and travel – a Latin hexameter line translates as 'I, Mercury, shed my favourable light upon this place above all other markets.'

The detail in the actual mapping of Venice is so amazingly precise that de' Barbari's print remains in use today as a reference point for topographers. Though the architectural proportions of certain buildings are somewhat distorted and the street layout has been tweaked and modified in different areas, this is nevertheless the Venice we still recognize, even if the artist (for every map is, from one or other aspect, a work of art) has laid distinct emphasis on the city's identifiable resemblance to a dolphin swimming in the Adriatic. De' Barbari did not sign the work – issued that same year of 1500, with authorization from the Signoria, by Anton Kolb, a German printer busy in Venice – but the achievement is credited to him from the

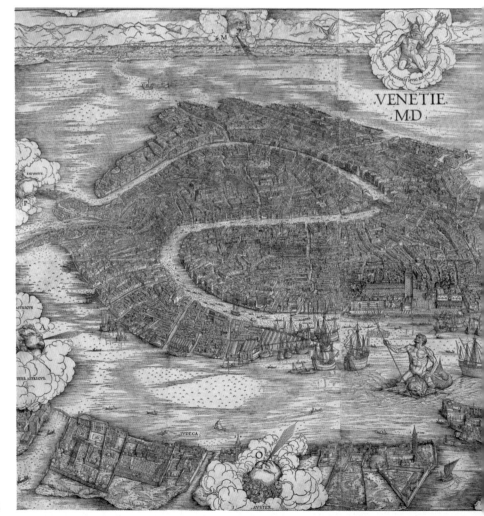

presence of Mercury's magic wand, the caduceus, used by the artist as a signature in his paintings. The map, whose woodblocks survive in the Museo Correr, proclaims the robust confidence of a Venice nurturing the initiatives of culture, politics and creativity on every level, a place which, notwithstanding auguries of its imminent decline, was very much open for business with the world.

LEPANTO

VICTORY THROUGH ILLUSION

Ow to lose an empire is trickier, in its way, than the process of acquiring one. For certain states the business is fraught with pain, aggression and contingent disgrace, from which the home country will emerge as a very different, almost unrecognizable nation from the arrogant, self-deluding avatar that preceded it. For others the issue looks easy on the surface – a graceful, phased withdrawal, managed with a good deal of condescension, accompanied by reassuring noises about shared values and happy memories – until, that is, history chooses to bite back at the complacent imperialists with its bitter truths. Later generations will force the erstwhile superpower to confront its most cherished myths and measure them against relentless actuality. Losing an empire takes time. Hauling down the flag and handing authority to the natives may look simply like the work of an afternoon, but even acts such as these leave a long wake behind them. Getting used to the loss is sometimes easier for those with hands-on experience of governing and managing the occupied territories than for those at home, to whom the imperial project gave a national identity and a sense of belonging. Its absence creates an enduring trauma.

All these aspects formed part of Venetian experience throughout the long sixteenth century, as La Serenissima's empire began slipping from her grasp. What we can scarcely fail to admire in the story of Venice between the settlement of Italy created by the triumph of Emperor Charles V in 1530 and the beginning of the long struggle for Crete some hundred years later is the vigour and conviction with which the Republic sustained its public performance on the world stage as an independent power, believing firmly in the value of punching above what constituted its genuine weight. The state and the city at its core became – paradoxically, given what started to happen – a focus of greater amazement and admiration than ever before among foreign

overleaf   Completed around 1534, Titian's *Venus of Urbino* is one of Renaissance art's most compelling and controversial images, though both the background to the commission and the model's identity remain mysterious.

visitors and commentators. Intense interest became concentrated on the governmental structures of the Signoria, on the nature of its administrative councils and the role of the doge in comparison with that of other heads of state. Curiosity grew as to its finances, its commercial resources, its maritime trade and the management of its land empire. How could Venice itself survive as a physical entity on its lagoon, wondered travellers, as the crowded hub of what was still a wealthy trading network in the Adriatic and across the wider Mediterranean?

They needed to go there and see for themselves. It was during this late Renaissance epoch that Venice first took on the role it has played ever since as a tourist resort, a place to be enjoyed for its pleasures and amusements and as a market for luxury goods. Visiting the city during an extended trip to Italy in 1580, the French essayist Michel de Montaigne, one of his age's most incisive minds, remarked on 'the very large number of foreigners here'. Some years later, the English dramatist and poet Ben Jonson, in his Venetian comedy *Volpone*, brought three such travellers onto the stage in a way which suggests that the author himself may have spent some time in the city. Young Peregrine – his name means 'wanderer' – meets up with a rich, self-important English couple, Sir Politic and Lady Wouldbe, both desperate to pick up a little sophistication in Venice and show it off while there. While Lady Wouldbe torments the wealthy Volpone with her cultural pretentiousness, Sir Politic gravely tries to teach Peregrine (who in fact already knows a thing or two) about Venetian manners:

> Then must you learn the use
> And handling of your silver fork at meals,
>   The metal of your glass (these are main matters
> With your Italian) and to know the hour
>   When you must eat your melons and your figs.

At some point during the mid-1580s Ben Jonson's younger contemporary William Shakespeare probably paid a visit to Venice, as his knowledge both of the town itself and of places on the mainland under Venetian sway is much too specific to have been gathered solely from books or travellers' reports. His comedy *The Merchant of Venice*, written around 1598, and the tragic story of *Othello*, whose source novel he seems to have read in its original Italian, both make use of authentic aspects of Venetian life which give each play a powerful sense of local colour and atmosphere. Shakespeare was obviously aware, for example, of the *colleganza* system central to Venetian commerce, since his Antonio, the eponymous merchant, depends on this to finance Bassanio's expedition to seek the hand of the fabulously rich heiress Portia. He also seems to have made close observation of the thriving Jewish community in the Venetian ghetto. It can be argued that Shylock, the play's most compelling figure, rather than being a vulgar antisemitic caricature, appears as an observant and devout Jew, a careful father to his ultimately callous, disobedient daughter, and someone with a perfectly valid reason for loathing the gentiles who abuse him even as they avail themselves of whatever he can supply as a moneylender.

Smaller details in the play, such as Portia's 'sunny locks', that blonde hair so favoured among Venetian women in the paintings of Titian, Veronese and Carpaccio, the basket of pigeons brought by Lancelot Gobbo's peasant father for Shylock (whose religion would of course not have allowed him to eat them), the gondola in which Lorenzo elopes with Jessica and the *traghetto*, 'the tranect... the common ferry / Which trades to Venice', all these contribute to a sense that Shakespeare was actually present in the world he evokes, rather than assembling it from material supplied him by travellers among his acquaintance or from the very few books available from which he could extract information on Venice.

In *Othello* such features also play their part and it is worth noting that in converting his source, a novella by Giraldi Cinzio which he read in its original Italian, into a stage play, Shakespeare enhanced the Venetian atmosphere. The first act, with its nocturnal setting, its mention of the 'special officers of the night' – only someone who had actually lived in Venice would know about the *Signori di Notte* – and its emergency session of the doge's council, is an authorial add-on, as indeed is the whole aspect of a Cyprus in stand-off against the encroaching power of Ottoman Turkey. 'So let the Turk of Cyprus us beguile,' says the doge to his senators in a cynical aside. By 1604, when Shakespeare wrote the play, this was exactly what had happened. If, as we may believe, he spent some time in Venice two decades earlier, the wound thus administered to La Serenissima as an imperial power would still have been raw and painful.

Since Queen Caterina Cornaro had conceded government over the island to her native Venice in 1489, the Republic had ruled Cyprus in the same style as one of its mainland provinces or large towns. There was a lieutenant governor, assisted by two rectors and a council formed from the local aristocracy together with members of the various Venetian grandee families that had put down roots there. Their administration, unusually for Venice, had never been noted for probity, fairness or altruism. Instead of dismantling the old feudal system developed in medieval centuries under the Lusignan monarchs, the Signoria had chosen to collude with it, so that the loyalty which ought to have transformed ordinary Cypriots into devoted *marcheschi* of the kind to be found in Dalmatia or the Ionian islands was dangerously lacking at a moment when most required.

This arrived when, on 28 March 1570, Sultan Selim II of Turkey sent an envoy to the Signoria to demand the immediate cession of Cyprus. The ambassador's message was cast in the form of a cold-blooded threat. 'If you are bold enough,' he informed the doge and Grand Council, 'not to yield the kingdom of Cyprus to us as is our right, then we shall come against you with all our powers on land and sea, so that you will be unable to prevent us from destroying you, leaving you dead, scattered or humbled, for so our Holy Prophet has promised us.' The doge at this time was Pietro Loredan, whose age, eighty-five, on being summoned to the position had made him reluctant to accept it. Now he mustered sufficient courage to answer the sultan's envoy in fine style. 'Justice will give us the sword with which to defend our rights,' he declared, 'and God will lend us his blessed aid with which to resist force with reason and bring our own strength to the business of resisting your unjust violence.'

The ambassador's mission formed a culminating stage in the series of hostile moves that had begun three months earlier in Constantinople, when the *bailo* of the Venetian community was apprised of Sultan Selim's designs on Cyprus. Arrests were then made among the merchants, ships were prevented from sailing and property was confiscated. Such acts were a calculated provocation, deliberately breaking a treaty made some twenty years earlier with the sultan's predecessor Suleiman the Magnificent, who had been sedulous in honouring its provisions. Selim saw things in a different light, more especially as regarded the island's strategic usefulness in controlling the eastern Mediterranean. With its capture, Venice's last major imperial outpost, in the form of Crete, would be left more vulnerable, making the Serene Republic's historic role as the maritime bulwark of Christendom almost impossible to sustain for much longer.

An early attempt by the Republic to set something like a crusade in motion among the various European states had met with a lukewarm response. When at length King Philip of Spain, Pope Pius V and the Knights of Malta agreed to join the expedition, the result was as dismally unproductive as the Turks might have wanted. Disagreements among the admirals, a *fainéant* Venetian commander in the shape of Captain-

General Girolamo Zane and a sequence of missed opportunities for the fleet brought the whole enterprise to an early and unworthy end in the November of 1570. By now the Turkish fleet was moored in the harbour of Larnaca, Sultan Selim's troops were swarming through the island and the city of Nicosia had been besieged, looted and sacked. All that remained was the great fortress at Famagusta, defended by its small garrison under the leadership of Marcantonio Bragadin and Lorenzo Tiepolo, with the *condottiero* Astorre Baglioni, a nobleman from Perugia, by their side.

In the hands of this redoubtable trio the defence of Famagusta pulled the Turks up short. For an astounding eleven months the Venetians held firm, until the Ottoman pasha Lala Mustafa organized a lethal network of mines and constructed extra siege towers to reduce the town to submission. The defence force, originally standing at nearly 8,000, had been reduced to a hard-pressed remnant of 500 men, for whom hopes of a relief force arriving from Crete were fast dwindling. Gallantry was no real substitute for lack of provisions and on 1 August 1571 the guns on both sides fell silent. In the sultan's name Lala Mustafa offered a truce permitting safe passage onto their ships for Venetian troops and any Cypriots who wished to follow them. The soldiers were allowed to take their weapons and baggage as well as their wives and children. Any citizens staying behind in Famagusta were allowed the space of two years in which to decide whether or not to remain subjects of the Sublime Porte or to leave the island. As surrender terms went, these conditions appeared strikingly magnanimous, as if intended to honour the courage of the defenders.

It was when Marcantonio Bragadin offered to present himself in person to the pasha, however, that everything changed. Dressed in the patrician robes appropriate to his status as a Venetian *provveditore*, bearing the keys of the fortress and accompanied by Baglioni and Tiepolo, his fellow generals, Bragadin was politely received at first. What seems to have angered Lala Mustafa, so much indeed that his whole manner changed abruptly, was the defeated governor's remark as he handed over the keys: 'Bear in mind that I give you these not as a proof of my cowardice, but through pure necessity.' Flying into a rage, the pasha accused Bragadin of having killed Turkish prisoners and failing to hand over all the weapons of war. With his dagger he slashed off the Venetian's ear and ordered that the other one be removed along with his nose. He then commanded his guard to slaughter the entire military escort, numbering around 300 men, and himself oversaw the beheading of Astorre Baglioni and the hanging of Lorenzo Tiepolo. In

D O P
M. ANTONII BRAGADENI
CVM PRO FIDE ET PATRIA
BELLO CYPRIO SALAMINÆ
CONTRA TVRCAS CONSTAN
TER FORTITERQ. CVRAM
PRINCIPEM SVSTINERET
LONGA OBSIDIONE VICTI
A PERFIDA HOSTIS MANV
IPSO VIVO, AC INTREPIDE
SVFFERENTE DETRACTA
PELLIS
ANN. SAL. CIƆ IƆ LXXI XV. KL. SEP. I.
ANTON. FRATRIS OPERA, ET
IMPENSA BYZANTIO HVC
ADVECTA
ATQVE HIC A MARCO, HER
MOLAO. ANTONIOQ. FILIIS
DILIGENTISS. AD SVMMI DEI
PATRIÆ. PATERNIQ. NOMI
NIS GLORIAM SEMPITERNAM
POSITA
ANN. SAL. CIƆ IƆ LXXXXVI.
VIXIT ANN. XXXXVI.

the streets of Famagusta meanwhile, those generous treaty terms were gleefully violated as the Turks rampaged through the city in a spree of rape and carnage.

For Marcantonio Bragadin a more hideously protracted ending was ordained. Flung in prison, he was later made to stagger around the walls of the fort under heavy sacks full of earth, before being taken out to a ship full of enslaved Christians, stripped naked and tied to the mainmast as a jeering Turkish crew called out, 'Can you see your fleet arriving? Can you see the great Jesus Christ coming to help Famagusta?' Hauled down again, he was tied to a column and flayed in the pasha's presence. Already suffering grievously from gangrened facial wounds, Bragadin died as the knife stripped the skin from his stomach. The body, with its head removed, was cut into quarters and distributed for display among the army. As a grisly final gesture, the skin, stuffed with straw, was mounted on the back of a cow and paraded through the streets of Famagusta, a fur hat grotesquely doing duty for the wretched governor's head. Later this trophy was taken back to Constantinople, where after some time two Genoese merchants managed to get hold of it in return for money and took the skin to Venice. What remains of Bragadin is now in the marble urn on top of his memorial plaque on the south wall of the church of Santi Giovanni e Paolo.

The invasion of Cyprus was all that Venice needed in order to reignite the impetus for a fresh expedition against the Turks. They seemed lucky, at this juncture, in being able to secure the necessary spiritual backing. Pope Pius V, a learned theologian and devout promoter of church missions to South America and the Far East, had become fired with an extra zeal as a cardinal attending the Council of Trent, during whose eighteen-year-long sessions the Roman Catholic church had engaged in redefining its essential dogmatic foundation and reforming and purifying its fundamental structures and practices. During a papacy lasting only six years Pius's achievement was vital in restoring a sense of purpose to his church and he was subsequently made a saint, a deserved honour for one of the most visionary and dynamic holders of Saint Peter's throne. Having tried in 1570 to foster the ultimately abortive combined operation against Sultan Selim, Pius was happy to use the dire accounts of the catastrophe at Famagusta so as to set a crusade in motion once more.

In May 1571, an alliance was formed in Rome between the Republic of Venice, the Kingdom of Spain and the Holy See. During the next three months an immense armada was gathered together in the Sicilian port of Messina (the island was then in Spanish hands) under

The urn surmounting Marcantonio Bragadin's monument is said to contain the skin flayed from him, while still alive, following his surrender of Cyprus to the Turks in 1571.

the triple command of Don Juan of Austria, bastard brother of King Philip II, Marcantonio Colonna, Duke of Paliano, leading the papal squadron, and the Venetian admiral Sebastiano Venier. A triple portrait of them painted around this time implies an atmosphere of dignified co-operation among the trio, yet such was never entirely the case, since the three powers had different objectives for joining the alliance. Venice wanted Cyprus back – at this stage the siege of Famagusta was still in progress – and with it perhaps some further recovery of her lost dominion over the Aegean. Spain, on the other hand, was more concerned with keeping the Turks from aiding Muslim rulers in Tunis, Algiers and Morocco, whose pirate fleets were a continuing menace to her south-eastern seaboard. The pope appears to have seen the whole international compact as guaranteeing an ongoing Christian presence in a beleaguered Mediterranean, where the various partners would undertake regular onslaughts against Ottoman fleets, to be planned during an autumn or winter conference in Rome.

For Venice this joint operation could scarcely come too soon. The Turks were already launching raids on the Dalmatian ports and menacing the Ionian islands. The focus of naval action must therefore be on the coast of western Greece, more particularly in the Gulf of Patras, being used by the Turkish fleet as a convenient bolthole in its forays up and down the Adriatic. After six weeks spent rallying the different squadrons at Messina, the three commanders and their staff met in council. The Spaniards prove the most pessimistic, ready with doubts and disadvantages, so much so that Sebastiano Venier, commanding the Venetians, threatened to abandon the league altogether and make a lone attempt with his galleys at recovering Cyprus. It was Marcantonio Colonna, ever the diplomat and conciliator, who brought the others back to the table, so that they finally agreed to sail into the Adriatic and deal once and for all with the Ottoman navy before it could return to Constantinople.

Amid the ensuing flurry of preparation the religious aspect of the expedition was not forgotten. Each vessel in the fleet carried a friar of the Capuchin order of Franciscans. Senior clergy had already insisted that none among the ships should bring with them 'persons of corrupt manners' and that there should be no women or boys on board, whose presence might compromise the purity of the enterprise. We know, however, of at least one female participant in the forthcoming battle. A certain Spanish girl, known to history as Maria la Bailadora, 'the Dancer', had followed her lover to the wars, dressed as a man – the classic type of escapade enshrined in the old English ballad of *Sweet*

Polly Oliver. Maria fought valiantly, it seems, and lived to claim her sweetheart.

Surveying the whole prospect of the ships lying at anchor in the harbour at Messina, Colonna's brother-in-law Onorato Caetani was moved to declare that 'altogether this is the finest armada that has ever been known in Christian times'. On Sunday 16 September, the grand fleet, numbering over 200 ships, was ready to lift anchor, seen off by jubilant crowds on the quayside, priestly benedictions and a salvo of cannon fire from the citadel. Morale was high and almost every natural phenomenon – the flight of a bird, the reddish colour of the moon, the brilliance of the sunset – was hailed for a lucky omen as the galleys rounded the promontories of Calabria and Puglia. At Cephalonia news arrived of the capture of Famagusta and Bragadin's appalling end, both of which served to inflame the atmosphere of crusading zeal among the crews.

At Igoumenitsa, on the Greek coast, unwelcome tensions started to arise between the Venetians and Don Juan's Spanish contingent. 'A great disorder', as Caetani discreetly calls it, occasioned by an argument over the availability of crossbows among Venier's staff and some of Juan's officers on a visit to the admiral's flagship, ended with weapons being drawn and several men killed. When Venier hanged four or five of the Spaniards from his vessel's yardarm, the enraged young prince refused any further communications with him, demanded his expulsion from the council of war and dashed off an angry letter to the Signoria demanding condign punishment. Colonna once again poured oil on troubled waters – 'he was up half the night with the whole business' – and the fleet could return to its mission.

On 6 October the Turks left the port of Nafpaktos, known in Italian as Lepanto, and sailed out into the open Adriatic. Its admirals looked for a direct engagement in preference to sheltering any longer within the capacious gulf between the coast of Epirus and the northern Peloponnese. Next morning, around half past ten, the two immense navies had their first encounter, in which Agostino Barbarigo, Venier's second-in-command, led a squadron at the northern end of Don Juan's extended battle line against Mehmet Saulak in a swift and ferocious combat. Barbarigo was mortally wounded by an arrow but his officers succeeded in driving the Turks to shore, where they were pursued and cut down.

Don Juan, meanwhile, had marked the Ottoman admiral Ali Pasha as his particular prey. Impulsive and arrogant the young Spaniard may have been but even the most critical among Venetians alongside him found much to admire in his conduct of the battle. Gerolamo Diedo, whose account of the fight in a long dispatch sent to Venice from Corfu is one of the most dependable, says that Juan 'showed in both his face and his words that he resembled his father, the unconquered Emperor Charles V of glorious memory'. His flagship, the *Real*, bore down inexorably on that of Ali Pasha and the pair of vessels became a battlefield as the troops on board staged a desperate struggle across blood-soaked decks. When the pasha's head was struck off by a cannonball fired from Colonna's galley, a Spanish soldier waved it high on the end of a pikestaff, striking terror into the Turks, whose ships began a headlong retreat. 'The Venetians', says Diedo, 'had fought like a miracle and their volunteer crews rowing the galleys were as brave as any soldiers in the battle'. Out of 240 Ottoman vessels, he reckoned, only 50 had made a clear getaway.

Even if the southernmost wing of the Christian battle line had been rendered more vulnerable through the tergiversations of the Genoese admiral Gian Andrea Doria, serving King Philip as a watchdog over Don Juan, the Knights of Malta, in their small fleet, had kept the Turks busy enough until more Spanish galleys eventually arrived to scatter the enemy. By evening the victory of Lepanto, the fiercest naval battle of its era, looked certain and Don Juan as its undaunted strategist had justified Diedo's assessment of him as '*animosissimo*', a word almost impossible to translate except as 'super-active'. He had been able to set free some 15,000 Christian galley slaves and distribute an immense spoil from plundering the vessels they rowed, though several of the victorious captains felt that the dithering Gian Andrea Doria deserved precious little share of this. The impact of Lepanto on a world hitherto gloomily resigned to the Turkish advance into Europe as inexorable was massively significant. 'As for lordship over the sea,' boasted Onorato Caetani, writing to his uncle, a Roman cardinal, after the battle, 'these dogs of Turks have lost it without any doubt. For everything we must render infinite thanks to Our Lord God, from whose hands we have received so great a victory, conceded to the whole of Christendom.'

The news was brought to Venice a week after the battle by a galley captained by Onofre Zustinian, who had taken care, on entering the lagoon, to drape his ship's sides with captured Turkish banners. On that day, 18 October, Doge Alvise Mocenigo was sitting in council, pondering various imminent problems created by the loss of Cyprus. Zustinian, bursting in with the glad tidings, initially met a cool reception owing to his lack of ceremony, before announcing: 'Serene Prince, I declare to you the noblest and most wondrous victory. The

Turkish fleet is beaten and scattered. May yours be the glory and the happiness!' Solemnity among the doge and senators at once dissolved into tears of joy as the news rippled out into the Piazza and the city was soon in a riot of jubilation. Shopkeepers put up their shutters with the notice 'Closed for the death of the Turks', the Rialto was decorated with triumphal arches and the next few days were given over to banquets, music and dancing. A thanksgiving mass and Te Deum at San Marco heralded the proclamation ordering 7 October, date of the battle, to be kept as an annual feast, with the doge visiting the church of Santa Giustina (almost next door to San Francesco della Vigna) and distributing money to the nuns at its convent. An image of the saint herself, the Roman martyr whose day this was, later adorned the great portal of the Arsenale.

A famous victory Lepanto undoubtedly appeared and on the strength of his leadership Sebastiano Venier found himself elected as doge six years later. Yet what, in a final analysis, did it achieve? The League so earnestly desired by Pope Pius V soon broke up amid recriminations chiefly directed at Gian Andrea Doria for his distinctly dubious conduct on the battle front's southern wing. It was suspected by some that King Philip of Spain had all along been playing a double game, intriguing with the Turks while posing as the champion of Christendom. Even if Don Juan, flushed with triumph, had wanted to continue the great enterprise, his brother, profoundly suspicious of the Venetians, greeted the news of the victory without enthusiasm. When Pius died on 1 May 1572, attempts by the Republic to engage his successor Gregory XII (Ugo Buoncompagni) were productive up to a point, with Marcantonio Colonna proving as reliable a champion as ever, but the new pontiff was honestly more interested in the fate of the Roman church at the hands of French Huguenots or under England's Protestant Queen Elizabeth than in reviving a holy war with Islam.

Though the battle became an indispensable element in that increasingly elaborate superstructure of myth and symbolism with which Venice strove to emphasize her particularity, a distinctiveness from other states in birth, evolution and essence, its results were of no lasting consequence in halting a slow but unavoidable process of decline. In 1573, with Cyprus firmly in Turkish hands and the Holy League dissolved, La Serenissima, under the scornful gaze of its former allies, returned to making peace with the Ottomans. There was, after all, too much for Venetian merchants to lose, given the competition now being offered them by English vessels of Queen Elizabeth I's newly chartered Levant Company and by a surge in activity from the little Dalmatian maritime republic of Ragusa (modern Dubrovnik), whose traders were proving more nimble in bidding for cargoes. Thus a treaty with the Sublime Porte was sullenly confirmed, in which Venice renounced all her claims to Cyprus and agreed to a payment, staggered but all the same immense, of 300,000 ducats to the sultan, besides continuing to pay him a forfeit for possession of the Ionian island of Zante (Zakynthos).

Anybody visiting Venice at this period would scarcely have recognized a state in crisis or confronting failure. Image-building mattered just as much as myth-making to La Serenissima in its current predicament. Throughout the sixteenth century's middle decades a remarkable transformation had taken place within the central nexus of buildings adjacent to the Basilica of San Marco and Palazzo Ducale, more especially in the very character of the Piazza itself. Much of this was owing to yet another talented refugee, the Tuscan architect and sculptor Jacopo Sansovino, who had fled to Venice in 1527 following the sack of Rome, where he was at work, by the army of Emperor Charles V. Appointed *Proto Magister*, chief architect, to the government and encouraged by the discerning and philanthropic Doge Andrea Gritti, Sansovino set to work on the completion of the Procuratie Vecchie, on the Piazza's north side, begun thirty years earlier by Mauro Codussi and Bartolomeo Bon. This was an arcade above which was a range of palatial dwellings for the Procuratori di San Marco, Venice's senior magistrates, with Codussi's clock tower, the Torre dell'Orologio, standing at its eastern end.

The Piazza forthwith became a life's project for Sansovino, inspired as he already was by the buildings of ancient Rome and now convinced that a classical grandeur of the kind he envisaged might transform the square into the noblest forum of any Italian city – which indeed it has remained. The great and good of Venice were there to encourage him, including Pietro Bembo, Queen Caterina's poet, now a cardinal, and the illustrious Daniele Barbaro, humanist, diplomat, patriarch of Aquileia and translator of Vitruvius's *Ten Books of Architecture*. What both these patrons were glad to see was a realization, at Sansovino's hands, of the long-delayed scheme for a Biblioteca Marciana, a library worthy of housing Cardinal Bessarion's collection of manuscripts, the building's white marble frontage topped by obelisks and mythological statues. Within it an ample staircase, with carvings and decorations by master sculptor Alessandro Vittoria, led to a space originally meant as a lecture room, over which Titian's serenely imagined representation of Wisdom held sway. Beyond this lay the library hall itself, its painted

An anonymous depiction of the naval Battle of Lepanto (1571), fought off western Greece, in which the Spanish–Italian Holy League defeated the fleet of the Ottoman Empire. Venice contributed most of the Christian ships.

ceiling panels displaying an omnium gatherum of the Virtues, the Arts and the Seasons, featuring some of Paolo Veronese's earliest Venetian works.

From here Sansovino went on to design Palazzo della Zecca next door, housing the mint for Venetian coinage, a sturdy and assertive contrast to the delicacy of his library building, and to create the miniature triumphal arch in red marble that forms the Loggetta of the Campanile, adorned with his own statues of Pallas Athene, Apollo and Mercury and an all-important figuration of Peace. Within the Piazza he added a graceful façade to the church of San Geminiano standing at its western end (demolished by Napoleon in 1805) and planned a new colonnade along the south side, the Procuratie Nuove, carried out after his death in 1570 by Vincenzo Scamozzi.

This incomparable ensemble made the perfect backdrop for welcoming one of those powerful European allies of whom Venice was seriously in need, in the shape of King Henri III of France, on his way home from Poland, where he had been elected sovereign in February 1574 before receiving the joyful news that he had succeeded, through the death of his brother Charles IX, to the French throne. A week of glittering festivities now awaited him, with the entire city donning gala costume for the occasion. It was a moment of political theatre which no other state at this period could honestly rival and it set a pattern for similar (if less costly) events in places like London, Paris and Antwerp later in the decade. A gorgeous triumphal arch designed by Andrea Palladio was raised for the king's arrival on the Lido, complete with decorations by Tintoretto and Veronese, every available musician in town seems to have accompanied his progress on the Bucintoro, escorted by barges of the different civic guilds, to the Riva degli Schiavoni, and still more music heralded that evening's dazzling firework display on the Grand Canal. Three thousand guests sat down to a banquet in the Sala del Maggior Consiglio, where a ball was later given to which two hundred of the fairest noblewomen were invited. On other days His Most Christian Majesty (a title conferred on French kings by the pope) was treated to acrobatic displays, bull-running, masquerades and an exhibition, mounted on a raft, of glassblowing by experts specially brought over from Murano's island furnaces.

To certain members of the doge's council this last demonstration probably mattered more than the superstructure of pomp and circumstance designed to impress Henri on his entrance to the lagoon. What Venice needed to underline to her visitors at this moment, given the implicit note of desperation struck by her separate peace with the Turks, was that she remained a busy centre for making luxury goods, fine fabrics and those very ships in which they could be exported for trading. Accordingly Henri found himself roused early one morning, to be rowed to the Arsenale, where he watched the initial stages in the construction of a galley. Taken then to an exhibition of the weapons, banners and other trophies seized at the battle of Lepanto, followed by yet another banquet, he was brought back to the yards at the end of the afternoon, to be shown the whole craft assembled, with its masts, sails and tackle complete. The numerous publications in Italian or French commemorating the royal visit are notably silent as to whether the whole presentation was in fact a kind of flat-pack assembly exercise, but the monarch, inheriting the shrewdness of his Florentine mother, Catherine de Medici, was surely aware of what was going on and what the Venetians wished him to understand by it. The truth was that shipbuilding in Venice was now undergoing a decline as available supplies of forest timber from Alpine woodlands started to dwindle, so that it became correspondingly important for the Signoria to mount such a demonstration, accentuating the positive, for its own benefit, let alone the entertainment of a prestigious potential ally.

However Venice might have prided herself on such consummate showmanship during that hectic July week in 1574, nothing prepared her for a visitor of another kind altogether during the winter of the following year. Epidemic outbreaks were a commonplace in cities as tightly packed and densely populated as this one, but not since the Black Death had there been such a virulent wave of plague infection as swept across the lagoon during the next eighteen months. Matters were made worse by the Signoria's frantic denials, anxious as it was to dampen rumours among merchant communities elsewhere in Italy. Giambattista Castagna, the papal nuncio to Venice, was among those not to be fooled. 'Anybody declaring there to be no plague here just at present', he told Pope Gregory XII, 'is merely telling a colossal lie.' All prophylactics, miracle nostrums and conventional safety measures, which included the compulsory fumigation of letters from outside the city, proved useless. Houses were sealed up by dozens on suspicion of sheltering the sick and quarantine periods of the required forty days often resulted in deaths from thirst and starvation. The Lazzaretti, the isolation hospitals in use on several lagoon islands, became 'like Hell itself, full of a disgusting and unendurable stench, with three or four sick persons sharing a bed and the air thick with smoke from burning corpses'. In the space of a year, between the spring of 1576 and the

early months of 1577, Venice lost more than a quarter of its population. Among them was the venerable presiding genius of contemporary artists Tiziano Vecellio – Titian – who died of a 'fever' which may or may not have been the plague.

Well before the whole traumatic experience was over, the Senate, led by Doge Alvise Mocenigo, took a collective vow during a mass at San Marco to raise a votive shrine to Christ the Redeemer on the island of Giudecca, with friars of the Capuchin order as its guardians. Architect of this new church, begun in 1577 when the worst of the epidemic had passed, was Andrea Palladio. His imprint on Venice and the Veneto had effectively served to fashion a built environment whose harmony, grace and decorum have never been surpassed. As an experiment in contrasted forms and volumes, the Redentore is, in the best sense, a rejoinder to the more elaborate statement proposed by its majestic companion only a short space away, the Benedictine church of San Giorgio Maggiore, designed by the same master a decade or so earlier.

Palladio, delighting as he did in the abundant opportunities given him to realize his own reading of ancient Roman architectonic discourse, had spent much of his professional career creating country villas for the Venetian nobility on the *terraferma* around cities like Vicenza and his native Padua. During the plague of 1575–7, these superb structures would inevitably assume additional importance as places of refuge for their owners, where spacious interiors and the open stretches of surrounding farmland could check the spread of contagion. Palladio never lost sight of the fundamental concept, in planning his villas, of such buildings not just as rustic pleasure palaces but as farmhouses with stores for produce of various kinds and direct links to the agriculture flourishing around them. In a description of his very first such work, Villa Godi, near Vicenza, he takes care to indicate the presence of a granary and of an area for making wine. Elsewhere in the same book, his *I quattro libri dell'architettura* (1570), writing of his work on Daniele Barbaro's villa at Maser, its central building flanked by arcades connecting to the *barchesse*, agricultural wings, the architect is at pains to mention its nearby dovecote and fish ponds. The painter Veronese, working here in 1560 on what is surely the most captivating secular fresco sequence ever painted, drew obvious inspiration from his surroundings, bringing the country into the house with his scenes of woods, avenues, picturesque ruins and the occasional *trompe l'œil* figure to lend scale and humour to the fictive prospect inside the villa, matching the leafy pastoral reality outside.

Andrea Palladio's Villa Rotonda, begun in 1566, was conceived as a belvedere on a high hilltop outside the city of Vicenza.

Several of the classic Palladian villas, such as Villa Foscari at Mira, known as La Malcontenta, and Villa Almerico Capra, 'La Rotonda', were designed as belvederes or pleasure pavilions, but the majority were connected to the work going on amid surrounding fields and farms. The key mover in this shift of patrician interest from the sea to the land as a source of profit was Alvise Cornaro, born in Padua in 1484, an early patron of Palladio and a pioneering agriculturalist, who believed that farming was just as vital to the civilized life of a decently evolving community as scientific research, literature, music and the fine arts. He was among the first writers, what is more, to promote the virtues of careful dieting and fresh air as contributors to a long life.

Work had already started in the Veneto on land reclamation and draining extensive stretches of marshy terrain when Cornaro began his own experiments in hydraulic engineering, published after his death in 1566. At his villa at Este in the Euganean Hills he began devising a new kind of magistracy for the Venetian Signoria, to be added to its other government departments. This was the *Magistrato dei Beni Inculti*, which took care of the development of unused land for farming and promoted the need to keep estates in good heart, with adequate drainage and irrigation. From its foundation in 1545, landowners all over the region took a fresh interest in getting the best from what was, after all, one of northern Italy's most fertile and potentially productive areas. Several of them published their own books on the subject. The translated title of Agostino Gallo's 1564 essay, *Ten Days of True Farming and the Pleasures of the Villa*, says it all, in a work embracing everything from proper weeding and pruning to methods for training vines, the importance of cleaning ditches and how to choose the best kind of seed for a good harvest. Three years later his near neighbour in the countryside around Brescia, Camillo Tarello, in his *Ricordo d'agricoltura*, was groundbreaking, both literally and metaphorically, in being the first to propose, long before it was pioneered among farmers in northern Europe, a system of crop rotation so as not to exhaust the earth's bountiful yields. Both writers had taken their cue from Alvise Cornaro, who himself became regarded as the founding father of a Veneto villa culture that now became part of La Serenissima's seasonal rhythm – at least for those who could afford it.

A young member of the Barbaro family peeps round a *trompe l'oeil* door in one of Veronese's brilliant frescoes in Palladio's Villa di Maser.

TRIALS
OF FAITH

Venetians continually prided themselves on the steadfastness of their religion and the reputation of their city as a defender of the Christian faith. The calendar of the Serene Republic was set out according to a sequence of major feast days, on which the doge, his counsellors and other dignitaries visited individual churches across the city for services and ceremonies marking moments of special importance in the historic evolution of the state. Such occasions were understood by everyone as offering a chance to connect a parish and its people with the wider community, thus reflecting the abstract concept of Venice as being an exceptional place, cherished by God and blessed in its patron Saint Mark, whose symbolic lion was everywhere visible. Sacred imagery of this kind enriched the entire fabric of the city, from the intricately detailed medieval capitals of the arcades surrounding Palazzo Ducale to the stone facings on the western side of the Rialto bridge, begun in 1588 under the patronage of the saintly Doge Pasquale Cicogna to a design by the aptly named Andrea da Ponte. Carved in relief on either end of the arch span is an Annunciation with figures of the Virgin Mary and the Angel Gabriel.

There were churches, chapels and oratories to accommodate every sort of Catholic devotional practice or commitment. Anyone seeking an ideal contrast with the gorgeous gold mosaic interior of the Basilica of San Marco, the doge's palatine chapel, could take a gondola and journey into the poorest quarter of the town to visit the little church of San Nicolo dei Mendicoli – 'Saint Nicholas of the Beggars' – which acted as a cathedral for the locality, whose inhabitants, mostly working folk and fishermen, were known as Nicolotti and had their own doge, who wore a straw hat rather than a *corno dogale*. Elsewhere charitable institutions like the Scuola dei Picai, in Campo San Fantin, whose black-hooded brethren were tasked with accompanying condemned persons to execution and ensuring that they 'made a good end', had their own consecrated places of worship or otherwise made use of an adjacent church. All the *scuole*, large or small, laid emphasis on the essentially religious character of their activities, whether paying out pensions, offering dowries to poor girls or providing social housing, known as *casa per amor de dio* – 'a house through the love of God'.

Training a keen eye on the grandest of the *scuole*, that of San Rocco, in its looming premises behind the Frari, was the painter Jacopo Tintoretto. From an early stage in his career he had spotted a profitable source of employment here, first of all in the next-door church, where in 1549 his strikingly expansive *Saint Roch Healing the Plague-Stricken* could furnish a kind of business card advertising his skills to the institution's members. Any commission from them seems to have been thwarted by Titian, scenting a potential competitor. Fifteen years would pass before the younger artist was asked to paint the central ceiling panel of the Scuola di San Rocco's Chapter Hall and a few months afterwards he became an associate of the charity. His *The Apotheosis of Saint Roch* had already been allowed to win, by a majority vote, what was supposed to be a competition among 'three or four of Venice's choicest masters' but had actually been fixed via an agreement between Tintoretto and his supporters on the committee that he would do the work for nothing. Now he was assigned the task of decorating the so-called *Albergo*, the small conference chamber on the building's upper floor.

His *Crucifixion*, dominating the room and forming a natural climax for visitors to the Scuola di San Rocco, is one of the most eloquent, complex and moving realizations of this scene ever painted. The play of colour, particularly among different shades of red, the compositional freedom of experiment, the use of episodes from the Gospel Passion narratives shown happening simultaneously around the crucified Saviour, make this work an incomparably dramatic statement of Venetian Renaissance art in its compelling final phase. Over a decade later, with Venice still reeling from the terrible plague visitation of 1576–7, Tintoretto offered his services here at a reduced fee, 'to show the great love which I bear to our honourable scuola and my devotion to Saint Roch', for the execution of a whole stupendous sequence of epic canvases filling the building's two great halls. Inspired partly by German and Netherlandish woodcuts and imbued with his own evident penchant for storytelling and the play of a restless fancy, these works, among them a stunning *Annunciation*, a *Flight into Egypt* set in a romantic landscape and a quasi-abstract *Massacre of the Innocents*, reveal

The interior of the church of San Nicolò dei Mendicoli, 'the cathedral of the poor'.

a specifically Venetian spirituality, transporting us through its powerful grounding in a humane, everyday world.

In Tintoretto's Venice what may seem extraordinary to us, given the limited space allowed for the town to grow and flourish on its huddled archipelago, was the number of convents and monasteries sheltered within it. Nowadays almost all of them are given over to other uses: the Franciscan cloisters of the Frari have become the great Archivio di Stato, containing a treasury of documents from the days of the Republic and afterwards, the Augustinian convent of Santa Caterina is a state high school and the former Jesuit college around the corner, having long done duty as a military barracks, was recently given over to student accommodation. A few, such as the friary at San Francesco della Vigna and the commandery of the Knights of Malta in the Castello district, remain dedicated to their original purpose, survivors from what was once a city whose fevers of commerce, pleasure and luxury were emphatically counterbalanced by lives of prayer, contemplation and self-denial.

Nevertheless, despite the popular fervour of Catholic devotion, the status of the clergy in Venetian society seemed a fairly humble one. Venice was under no circumstances a priest-ridden city, even allowing for the fact that many more churches and parishes existed than we find there today. Cardinal Alberto Bolognetti, papal nuncio to the Republic in 1580, complained to Pope Gregory XIII that 'ecclesiastical persons' were held 'in less esteem than is appropriate', noting sourly that 'when the gentlemen of this city don the priestly cassock, the affection of their fellow patricians grows cold towards them, as if they had joined a faction that stood as a rival to the greatness of the Republic'. More alarming to Bolognetti was the particular way in which the Senate chose to discuss any matters pertaining to the church. 'Before doing so, they make everyone leave the chamber who has the slightest connexion with a priest, whether through his family or in the way of lawful business.'

The oblique and uneasy relationship between La Serenissima and Holy Mother Church, more particularly with the popes and their senior clergy, was in essence an irreconcilable struggle between two extreme forms of entitlement. On the one hand stood the papacy, perennially absorbed with the problem of asserting its universal authority, not only over Roman Catholics, but in respect of emperors, kings and governors throughout the world. On the other, defiant, overreaching, buoyed up by its own exceptionalism, stood the free Republic of Venice, historically dedicated to the pursuit of its own

previous pages   Tintoretto's *Annunciation*, 1583–7; from his cycle of frescoes for the Scuola Grande di San Rocco.

advantages in the name of survival and convinced, whether justifiably or not, of its right to exercise laws and privileges exactly as might seem fit. The results of this enduring stand-off down the ages were plain for all to see. Yes indeed, the great porch of San Marco had provided a memorable setting for the day in 1177 when Pope Alexander III and Emperor Frederick Barbarossa had been reconciled under Doge Sebastiano Ziani's eirenic sponsorship. Three Venetians, what is more, had occupied the papal throne, the latest of these, Paul II (1464–71), conspicuous for seeking to assert the papacy's territorial claims in central Italy. Yet there was also a history of tensions, stretching back over three centuries, that included no fewer than four papal interdicts, the last of them that ferocious anathema against Venice issued in 1506 by Julius II and resulting in the League of Cambrai.

In the wake of the Counter-Reformation and the Council of Trent, engrossing the Roman church as the various forms of Protestantism gained ground during the sixteenth century, successive popes grew ever more wary of what they took for signs of a lukewarm and ambiguous attitude on the part of Venetians towards a reawakened zeal in promoting Catholic orthodoxy. It scarcely sat well with Rome that Venice had seemed to support the Huguenot King Henri of Navarre during the prolonged religious wars in France, besides taking a generally friendly and pacific attitude towards Queen Elizabeth of England and her successor King James I. The presence of what the church loosely defined as 'heretics' in the city and its mainland towns was disagreeably obvious and the Signoria's nonchalance in this respect puzzled the faithful elsewhere in Italy. This problem was especially marked at the university of Padua, where liberal attitudes prevailing in the faculties of medicine and philosophy attracted students, scholars and teachers from all over Europe. These were the schools which nourished the great Flemish anatomist Andreas Vesalius, the pioneering embryologist Girolamo Fabrizi and the prescient surgeon and medical polymath Gabriele Falloppio, from whom the fallopian tubes receive their name. In the next generation it was that arch-heretic among scientists Galileo Galilei who considered his Padua professorship as having embraced the happiest, most fortunate period of his career.

For a while it had seemed as if whatever difficulties the church might have as regarded Venice's waywardness could be solved through the advent of the Jesuits. Founded in 1540, the order of the Society of Jesus had swiftly made itself indispensable to Rome as a species of religious commando regiment, a shock troop ready to enforce Catholic orthodoxy by whatever means but equally becoming synonymous, even among true believers, with every kind of subversive operation and intrigue in the name of enforcing official dogma and rooting out heresy. For a time the Jesuits had gained control over teaching in the Paduan schools and their influence in Venice itself had been powerful enough at one point to prevent stage plays being acted. Many such performances took place privately within the palaces of the nobility – as yet there were no public theatres in the city – but the order was no respecter of rank in this instance.

Its activities were specially encouraged by that sector of the government labelled the '*vecchi*', 'the old men', seasoned politicians, diplomats and public servants, all from the best patrician families, who saw themselves as guardians of Venetian traditional values, earnestly Catholic and always eager to cultivate closer relations with the pope and the King of Spain, self-appointed generalissimo of the Faith. Opposing them were the so-called '*giovani*', 'the youngsters', not necessarily young in years but far more open to new ideas, favourable towards strengthened links with rising commercial powers like England or the newly liberated Dutch Protestant provinces and deeply suspicious of Spanish meddling in Italian affairs. Since Spain at this time effectively boxed in the entire peninsula of Italy with its control over the Duchy of Milan and its viceroyalties in Naples and Sicily, their wariness was not unjustified, as we shall see. The *giovani* watched the Jesuits, whom they saw as simply an arm of Spanish political interests, with deepening anxiety over the course of the sixteenth century's closing decades. Among this echelon of the Signoria there was, in addition, a genuine sense that by countenancing the Society's work the *vecchi* were betraying that basic patriotism, a loyalty to the central concept of the Republic and what it stood for, which was both a privilege and a duty for all true Venetians.

The *giovani* were proud, by the same token, of their state's reputation as a bastion of liberty, at least as interpreted by commentators and intellectuals during this period. Venice was the last major free republic to have survived after the fall of Florence to Cosimo de' Medici (made grand duke for his pains) in 1539 and his extinction of an independent Siena in 1554. Genoa, however rich it had grown from international banking operations, was no longer a convincing rival and the image of Venice could now be burnished with the concept of it as a lone champion of freedom, a refuge for those harassed by bigots and tyrants, 'that fair seat whither Liberty repairs', as a contemporary Italian poet called it.

To this Venetian climate of liberal opinion and expression the official institution in 1559 of the *Index of Forbidden Books* by the puritanical Pope Paul IV had dealt a serious blow. Still a leading centre of printing and book production half a century after the great days of Aldus Manutius, Venice boasted some five hundred printers' shops, amounting to almost half of publishers throughout Italy. Even though the Council of Ten did its best to defend their interests commercially, the influence of the *vecchi* against them was too powerful at this stage. Ideologues such as the Jesuit diplomat and polemicist Antonio Possevino began recommending a thoroughgoing surveillance, not just of the presses themselves but of their catalogues for the already well-established Frankfurt book fair, and encouraged periodic inspections of private libraries and their owners' purchases and sales. His use of the verb *disciplinare*, to discipline, was ominous: 'Reading', he declared, 'must be confined to the cultivation of virtue rather than to whatever might sharpen the intellect to a greater subtlety.' The Holy Office, the Inquisition, established in Venice since 1249, played its part in the work of censorship and suppression, overseeing the various public burnings of doctrinally suspect works which took place at the Rialto and in Piazza San Marco, including those of Jewish texts issued by Christian printers. At the root of such zeal lay the simple fact that Venetians tended to read more than most other Italians, with such a high literacy level not confined to patricians or *cittadini*. The Inquisitors regularly received information that this or that workman was given to the habit of reading or actually owned books, deemed indicative of possible subversion or at least considered an inappropriate activity. By the year 1600, not surprisingly, the number of printers in Venice had shrunk to around forty as its primacy as a centre of the book trade shifted to Antwerp, Amsterdam and Geneva.

Equally alarming to Rome were those heretical communities which La Serenissima, by the very nature of its internationalism, was happy to shelter as long as they kept themselves apart from the religious life of a Catholic city. Why, argued successive popes, should Venice have sanctioned the building, in 1539, of a Greek Orthodox church, San Giorgio dei Greci, even going so far as to allow its worshippers to establish their own *scuola*, which embraced members from Serbia, Montenegro and Bosnia, in flight from the Turks? Still worse, in the view of the Roman Curia, was the freedom which the Republic seemed to allow to its various Jewish communities, whether in Venice itself or in the mainland cities of its Italian empire. Almost every little

town up and down the Veneto, Friuli and eastern Lombardy could boast a ghetto with a synagogue and Jews engaged in the trades and businesses to which they were legally confined. Their rights were scarcely those enjoyed by Christian citizens, their privileges were fairly few and they were confined to residence within their cramped quarter, their comings and goings regulated by local officials. Nevertheless these 'aliens' were tolerated and mostly experienced rather less in terms of oppression than their co-religionists in Rome, living beside the Tiber amid squalor and annual flooding only to be humiliated by the church hierarchy for the sin of not being Christian.

Only when things were going badly with the Turks did the Signoria seem inclined to treat its Jewish subjects with less of a half-hearted shrug and view them, considering their peripatetic links with the East, as a potential security risk. When Cyprus was well and truly lost in 1572 the whole community was briefly in danger of expulsion, before wiser heads on the Grand Council restored equanimity in the light of economic needs. The fact that in 1589 a whole new sector of Jewish trade within Venice was opened up via the Senate's admission of Sephardi 'New Christians' from Spain served to bolster the image of the city as a veritable nursery of heretics. The sober reality of Venetian controls over the Ghetto and its inhabitants made no difference to Rome's growing suspicion and hostility.

The situation grew more heated on the accession to the papacy in 1592 of Cardinal Ippolito Aldobrandini as Clement VIII. An earnest, cultivated intellectual, anxious to distance himself and his advisers from overmuch Spanish political interference, Clement was equally determined, in the manner of his predecessors, to assert the church's authority wherever this involved the special rights of the clergy or anything which looked like a gratuitous insult to the dignity of the office God had conferred on him. A notoriously short temper hardly helped. 'The pope issues forth thunders and lightnings,' complained Venice's ambassador in the course of dealing with Clement over matters as varied as a vacant bishopric, customs dues imposed on merchant ships and the fate of a bandit seeking refuge in Venetian territory from papal justice.

What provoked His Holiness still further was a dispute arising after the death in 1600 of Venice's cardinal patriarch, Lorenzo Priuli. For Pope Clement, editor of liturgical texts and promulgator of the official Latin Vulgate Bible known thereafter as the 'Clementina', a thorough theological grounding was an essential requirement in his senior clergy. Thus he made it necessary for all those newly appointed to travel to

The iconostasis in the Eastern Orthodox church of San Giorgio dei Greci, on which construction began in the 1530s.

Rome for an oral examination in the presence of expert interrogators. Nomination of the late cardinal's successor as patriarch lay in the hands of the Pregadi, the executive nucleus of the Venetian Senate. They had been quick to choose Matteo Zane, whose principal experience had been as an ambassador and previously as *bailo* of the merchants in Constantinople.

Zane, duly summoned to Rome, contrived to pass his exam and was then invested, but Pope Clement had been unsatisfied by what he considered Venice's truculent attitude to the whole procedure. La Serenissima, for her part, had not been happy with his encroachment on her borders when in 1598 he took possession of the Duchy of Ferrara, invoking the pretext that its new duke, Cesare d'Este, was born out of wedlock and had no lawful claim to the realm. Though Cesare was eventually given another duchy, that of Modena with its surrounding territories, and the Republic sent envoys to congratulate the pope on his triumphal entry into Ferrara, Venetian discontent was palpable. The Vatican's itch for control seemed to be developing exponentially as its genuine powers weakened among nominally Catholic states, whatever the piety of their respective sovereigns. Where Venice was concerned, it was her own business as to whom she allowed to settle within her borders and exactly how much freedom she allowed to heretics for practising their own religion. It angered Venetians furthermore that Rome should automatically question their devotional sincerity. 'We are Christians, as good as the pope himself, and Christians we shall die, whether others like it or not,' declared Leonardo Donà, leader of the *giovani*, on being elected doge in 1606.

Some years earlier Donà had been part of a diplomatic mission to Rome, where one of the leading cardinals, Camillo Borghese, grew particularly irritated by his intransigence over issues of ecclesiastical authority. 'If I were pope,' said Borghese, 'I should excommunicate the Venetians.' 'And if I were doge,' came Donà's immediate rejoinder, 'I should throw that excommunication back in your face.' In 1606 both men's challenges caught up with them. Donà now wore the *corno dogale* and ermine tippet, while Borghese had indeed been chosen pontiff as Pope Paul V. For him the death of Pope Clement the previous year had left incomplete the serious task of forcing the Republic of Venice to bow to the Holy Church's domination. There was work to be done and Paul, as an expert canon lawyer with the needful instruments to hand, was the man to finish the job.

His chance arrived earlier than anticipated. When Matteo Zane, the new Patriarch of San Marco, died unexpectedly, his successor

Francesco Vendramin, appointed according to custom by the Senate, was immediately summoned to Rome for the required theological screening. This time the Venetian authorities demurred, needing time to ponder the matter, not something Pope Paul was ready to allow. Almost at the same time Venice played into his hands over the lingering issue of the clergy's legal status within the Republic. Were priests to be tried by civil courts or should they remain solely under the jurisdiction of the church? In the autumn of 1605 two test cases had arisen from denunciations made to the Council of Ten. A canon of Vicenza cathedral, Scipione Saraceni, was accused of trying to rape his niece, whom he afterwards slandered, covering her house door with excrement. Meanwhile Marcantonio Brandolin, abbot of a monastery at Nervesa in the Dolomite foothills, had been taxed with crimes against his own family, including fraudulent alienation of property and the attempted murder of a nephew. As if both these were not cause enough for a scrap with Rome, the pope chose to pursue a further quarrel with the Signoria over ecclesiastical ownership of real estate within Venice itself and a new law limiting further space allowed for religious buildings of whatever kind.

With Leonardo Donà just elected as doge and the *giovani* on fighting form, the Senate was not inclined to back down on all this. During February and March of 1606 the *froideur* between Venice and Rome intensified and on 17 April Pope Paul issued his expected ultimatum. The Republic was given a period of twenty-four days in which to humble itself before him, to abrogate the offensive legislation and hand over the two criminal clerics to the justice of the church. If none of this happened, then a full papal interdict would come into force and the entire population of Venice's domains, from Brescia and Bergamo to Corfu and Crete, would suffer excommunication, with the churches, chapels and oratories closed to all.

A lesser state than Venice at this time would have reeled beneath the threat and submitted dutifully enough to the pope's peremptory demands. Other powers across Europe, both Catholic and Protestant, were now looking on, suddenly mesmerized by the confrontation and exactly what it might seem to imply. Even if La Serenissima was not the unimaginably wealthy and powerful Mediterranean arbiter of a hundred years previously, she remained prosperous, confident in the validity of her greatness and, for many, a unique example of how a community could thrive successfully under a government of committees and an elected head of state with no executive capacity. Her oligarchy, what is more, perceived the value of their city's cosmopolitanism to its survival and were not inclined, for the most part, to be hectored at by a foreign autocrat – which was what the Holy Father in this instance amounted to. Liberty was once again too precious for Venetians to let go.

They were fortunate just now to have found a native spokesman for their cause who happened to be one of the most remarkable figures of his era, a man of genuine grit, depth and substance, a herald of the European Enlightenment, someone whose name should be far better known in the history of intellectual freedom across the world than it currently is. Paolo Sarpi has his statue in Venice, next to the church of Santa Fosca, close by the bridge where those who most feared his candour and integrity sought to have him assassinated. They knew, as nowadays we have forgotten, how potent his armoury of concept, argument and discourse was against bigotry, obscurantism, tyrannical self-aggrandizement and the rule of unreason.

Born to bourgeois parents in Venice in 1552, Sarpi was destined by his pious mother Isabella Morelli for the priesthood and his precocious bookishness confirmed this. 'We were always at play while Paolo was at his books,' recalled a school friend. Aged fourteen, however, instead of entering a seminary, he joined the Servite friars, the Order of the Servants of Mary, remaining a member for the rest of his life. A natural teacher, he spent some time giving lessons in Mantua and Padua and developed a passionate interest in science, medicine and philosophy, besides studying theology and canon law. The English ambassador to Venice, Henry Wootton, who got to know him well, described Sarpi as 'excellent in scholastical and polemical divinity, a rare mathematician, even in the most abstruse parts thereof... and yet withal so expert in the history of plants, as if he had never perused any book but nature.' His pupil and early biographer Fulgenzio Micanzio says that 'his whole life was devoted to three things – the service of God, his own studies and learned conversation with others'. Fra Paolo's cultivation of a wide international circle made him vulnerable to censure as a heretic from fellow churchmen throughout his career. Among valued friends he numbered Wootton's successor as ambassador, Dudley Carleton, and the embassy chaplain William Bedell, both of them Calvinists in the colour of their Anglican Protestantism yet each acknowledging the Servite friar's spiritual inspiration. His interest in the Torah, nurtured through meetings with Jewish rabbis in the Ghetto, attracted equal suspicion. Hostile eyes were always on him and the church establishment was busy fingering his work for 'errors' of different kinds. Not for nothing, while living in Padua, had Fra Paolo become a close associate of Galileo.

The title page of Galileo's *Sidereus Nuncius*, published in Venice in 1610. The publication, challenging official scientific teaching, showed Venice still defying the Pope four years after the papal interdict of 1606.

SIDEREVS
NVNCIVS

MAGNA, LONGEQVE ADMIRABILIA
Spectacula pandens, suspiciendáque proponens
vnicuique, præsertim verò

PHILOSOPHIS, atq̃ ASTRONOMIS, quæ à

GALILEO GALILEO

PATRITIO FLORENTINO
Patauini Gymnasij Publico Mathematico

PERSPICILLI

Nuper à se reperti beneficio sunt obseruata in LVNÆ FACIE, FIXIS IN-
NVMERIS, LACTEO CIRCVLO, STELLIS NEBVLOSIS,
Apprime verò in

QVATVOR PLANETIS

Circa IOVIS Stellam disparibus interuallis, atque periodis, celeri-
tate mirabili circumuolutis; quos, nemini in hanc vsque
diem cognitos, nouissimè Author depræ-
hendit primus; atque

MEDICEA SIDERA

NVNCVPANDOS DECREVIT.

VENETIIS, Apud Thomam Baglionum. M DC X.

Superiorum Permissu, & Priuilegio.

M VIIII ㄴㄴ. ㄴん.

In 1601, while trouble with the Vatican was brewing, Sarpi had offered his services to the Signoria as its 'reverent and devoted servant'. Now, five years later, his reputation for sage authority already so well established in Venice, he seemed an obvious choice to lead the formidable cohort of jurists, university teachers and experts from the various monastic orders who could be relied upon to give the Senate the advice and arguments it needed on which to base an official protest against the grievous sentence handed down by the pope. The latter could certainly not take the loyalty of churchmen within the Republic for granted, Fra Paolo's least of all. To him as to others what mattered was the sacred integrity of Venice, her laws and institutions, and this he was now ready, with all his wisdom and shrewdness, to defend. A whole sequence of lethally skilful polemics now issued from Sarpi's pen and were duly committed to print, emphasizing the crucial distinction between that spiritual supremacy to which the pope, by the very nature of his office, was entitled and the temporal sovereignty over Christian monarchs and governments which he wrongly believed to be his by right. In the international arena, as in Venice itself, the two Pauls, the pontiff and friar, now faced up to one another while a ferocious pamphlet war between their respective partisans began raging around them.

Sarpi's judgment on the pope, set out in a book he later wrote on the whole episode of the Interdict, was extremely astute. It was hardly an exaggeration to claim, as he did, that 'Paul V, from his childhood years, was dedicated to those studies which taught him that his final goal must be the acquisition by the Roman pontificate of rule over the whole world, both spiritual and temporal'. His Holiness was the sworn enemy 'of anybody who seemed to offer an obstruction to his free exercise of ecclesiastical licence and the arbitrary use of excommunication'. The writer himself, it hardly needed saying, had been early anathematized after this fashion. Above all, claimed Sarpi plausibly enough, the pope's greatest hatred 'was turned upon the Republic of Venice, both because she alone sustains the dignity and true qualities of an independent prince and because she totally excludes ecclesiastics from participation in her government'. Added to which, says Fra Paolo with a flash of pardonable cynicism, 'she does not, unlike other sovereigns, keep Roman cardinals in her pay'.

Any notion that La Serenissima would simply crumple into a suitably abject posture of decorous humility before Saint Peter's throne was set at naught by a response, issued on 6 May 1606 and known as the *Protesto*, from the doge himself to the Interdict, in the form of a charge to the clergy across the Venetian domains. In the name of preserving the peace of the Republic, claimed Leonardo Donà, he had set out before the pope the lawful aspirations of Venice, receiving in return a document that outraged holy scripture, the wisdom of the Church Fathers and the entirety of canon law. It was 'prejudicial besides to secular authority as bestowed by Almighty God and to the freedoms of our state'. On such dubious foundations the pope's threats should be reckoned worthless and the course of religious life must be allowed to continue as before. Venice's firm resolve was 'to remain within the Holy Church and the Apostolic Faith'. A last majestically insolent flourish from Donà, who almost certainly composed the letter himself, with advice from Sarpi and others, consisted of a prayer to God that the pope should be freed from his vanity, enough to make him aware of the harm he was doing to the Republic and lead him to understand the true righteousness of Venice's cause. When the papal nuncio arrived before the Grand Council to take his leave, the doge gave him short shrift. 'As for your interdict, we think nothing of that: it is a thing of no value.'

So indeed it proved, partly as a result of firm measures by the government but also through the steadfastness of Venetians at every social level. The Jesuits were immediately expelled from the state, requiring an armed escort in various places to see them off, so unpopular had they become. With them went two other religious orders, Theatines and Capuchins, whose superior clergy had been unwilling to accept the *Protesto*. A few other wavering priests were soon made aware of who exactly was in control. One Venetian parish went so far as to install a gallows to remind its shepherd of souls where his duty lay. In Padua, when a senior cleric not unreasonably told the city governor that he preferred listening to the Holy Spirit as to whether or not to say mass, he was sternly informed that the Holy Spirit had brought instructions from the Council of Ten to hang anyone who disobeyed the order. Customary seasonal processions and saints' day festivities went ahead, weddings and funerals took place and the churches were as full as before. As so often, a communal pride among Venetian citizens in their singular inheritance as sons and daughters of Saint Mark set all other considerations at naught.

Pope Paul had of course imagined another scenario altogether, one in which an abject populace, denied the Eucharist, confession or any other sacraments, would force the Signoria to its knees before the throne of God's Vicar. Instead, the sound of a stable door being flung wide open and the rattle of bolting hooves was each of them distinctly audible. In addressing the papal nuncio, Leonardo Donà had concluded with the sinister warning: 'Only think to what our resolution might lead were others to follow our example.' In France, Spain and Austria, wise heads had begun thinking just this. What Paul and his consistory, far behind the curve, had not bothered to consider was the way in which the relationship between the church and secular governments was starting radically to change. It would take the full horrors of the Thirty Years' War, soon overwhelming Europe, to make this shift a permanent one.

The excitement or unease experienced internationally by those observing Venice's robust opposition to the Interdict, under Paolo Sarpi's indefatigable championship, soon made other governments ready to act as intermediaries between the pope and La Serenissima, but as much for their own advantage as for any special motives of eirenic altruism. Perhaps not surprisingly, given his apparent success in peacemaking between his country's warring factions, King Henri IV of France, most dynamic political figure of the age, was eager to lead the way. Cardinal François de Joyeuse, Archbishop of Rouen, was formally dispatched to Venice as ambassador and in April 1607, almost exactly a year after the issue of the Interdict and the corresponding *Protesto*, a settlement was concluded.

Who had actually won the contest? Since the Signoria now showed itself ready to hand over the two offending priests, Saraceni and Brandolin, to the cardinal on the understanding that they would both be sent to Rome for justice, it might have looked as though Pope Paul was the ultimate victor. The gesture, however, was hardly one of submission, since it implied that France rather than the Vatican had the only genuine validity as negotiator. What was more, the Republic refused to petition the pope for an official lifting of the Interdict, declined to readmit the Jesuits – they were not allowed back for another fifty years – and would under no circumstances issue an apology for the *Protesto*, though ready to cancel it as soon as the papal ban was set aside. In the world's eyes the whole episode had damaged the authority and dignity of the Holy See almost beyond repair. Pope Borghese's vanity project was destined never to be repeated, as elsewhere his dreams of worldwide Catholic primacy were shattered. In England the failure of the 1605 Gunpowder Plot had served to further demonize an already vulnerable Papist minority; in France the Huguenots, bolstered by Henri IV's Edict of Nantes, swaggered with new confidence; the breakaway Protestant Dutch provinces were becoming a European power to reckon with and an attempt by the Jesuits to advance a Catholic

Paolo Sarpi, polymath, polemicist and passionate defender of Venetian freedom. His statue stands in the Campo Santa Fosca, close to where he was attacked by papal assassins in 1607.

PAOLO SARPI

pretender, the so-called 'False Dimitri', as Tsar of Russia, came to nothing. Paolo Sarpi meanwhile remained vocal and unpunished. He had gained international celebrity as a public intellectual and Venice was suitably grateful for his courageous spokesmanship on her behalf. The Senate began turning to him for advice on a whole range of key policy issues, on which his individual papers, known as *consulti*, were deemed invaluable, more especially where they might involve any kind of dealings with the Vatican. For this very reason he became, in the wake of the Interdict, a marked man.

The streets of Venice after nightfall were no safer than those of other cities. Thomas Coryat, during his visit here, had cause to note 'certaine desperate and resolute villaines called Braves [Bravoes] who at some unlawfull times do commit great villainy. They wander abroad very late in the night to and fro for their prey, like hungry Lyons, being armed with a privy coate of maile, a gauntlet upon their right hand, and a little sharpe dagger called a stiletto.' Sarpi must have been aware that his homeward journey to the Servite friary in Cannaregio from a day's work in government offices was always fraught with danger. On the evening of 5 October 1607, crossing Campo Santa Fosca towards the bridge over the canal at its eastern edge, he was attacked by a band of armed men who stabbed him twice in the neck and once on the side of his head, leaving a knife embedded in his cheek bone before they ran off, supposing him dead. Amazingly he recovered from his injuries, but though the Signoria, suitably alarmed, offered him lodgings in Piazza San Marco and his own gondola, he refused both, faithful always to his spiritual calling among the Servites.

The scars from the attack were Fra Paolo's honourable war wounds. While being patched up he remarked, with typical dry wit: 'I recognize the style of the Roman Curia,' expecting further attempts on his life, which duly followed. To his enemies the friar was maddeningly resilient, a redoubtable polemicist and campaigner for the Republic, 'a person of singular learning, valour and virtue' as one official document hailed him. In January 1623, however, he fell ill but refused to take to his bed, sitting upright in his chair, eating and drinking little, saying: 'I must give back to God what He has given me.' He rejected all traditional last rites except the Eucharist and died (said a friend in a letter to Dudley Carleton) 'like a lamb, very peacefully, with no regrets at leaving this world'. Fra Paolo's last words were addressed to Venice herself. '*Esto perpetua,*' he murmured. The Latin words mean 'May she live for ever.'

DAUGHTERS
OF SAINT MARK

Cities are traditionally represented as female and in many languages the word for a town or even for the smallest settled community belongs to the feminine gender. In visual art, poetry and song, a city is always 'she'. Think, for example, of London as represented on the Monument, Sir Christopher Wren's column commemorating the Great Fire of 1666, where the city appears, in a relief sculpture by Caius Gabriel Cibber, as a disconsolate reclining maiden baring her ample bosom to King Charles II, perhaps a little too eager, after his fashion, to stretch forth a comforting arm. Think, on the other hand, of Paris as evoked by the popular French *chanteuse* Mistinguett in a music-hall song of 1926:

> Paris, c'est une blonde
> Qui plaît à tout le monde.

The spirit of place is forever a woman and so it remains with Venice. Among the most memorable realizations of this concept are the various decorative allegories painted for Palazzo Ducale by one of the most gifted and engaging of all Venetian Renaissance painters, Paolo Veronese. In the mid-1570s disastrous fires wrecked the most important council chambers of the palace, so that a major rebuilding programme needed to be initiated as soon as possible. The commission for the Sala del Collegio, the biggest of these conference halls, was awarded to Veronese, who devised a spectacular ceiling, its gilded wooden panels featuring three large canvases surrounded by a sequence of allegorical images cleverly contrasting chiaroscuro ovals with rectangular sections displaying a brilliant luminosity.

Central to the narrative in this magnificent sequence is the idea of Venetian values – justice, peace, religion, faith and that special bond with the sea – as serenely triumphant. La Serenissima here is exactly what her name implies, a maturely beautiful woman, relaxed, confident and benign in her majestic domination under the tutelage of the pagan gods Neptune and Mars, yet simultaneously blessed by Christ, the Blessed Virgin and the saints. Some years earlier, in a painting for a church on the island of Murano celebrating the victory at Lepanto, Veronese had portrayed Venice as an armed female warrior, sword in hand, being presented to the Virgin by Saint Mark, a cloud-borne ensemble above a vigorous battle scene showing the ships in furious combat. In the Sala del Collegio by contrast, the city is a soft-eyed young damsel, clad in brocade and ermine, half shadowed by the gorgeous *baldacchino* under which she sits. A still later image, *The Triumph of Venice*, shows an older woman, fuller of figure, more elaborately costumed but still imbued with the calm self-assurance of her other avatars.

Interestingly Venice, like Mistinguett's Paris, is forever blonde. It was a colour Veronese favoured for his many different representations of women, whether the goddess of Love or the mother of God, and some of his most striking female portraits, such as the famous *La Bella Nani* now in the Louvre, are of fair-haired sitters whose peaches-and-cream complexion complements the flaxen curls above. Not for nothing does Shakespeare say of Portia, the rich heiress in her country villa in *The Merchant of Venice*, that 'her sunny locks / hang on her temples like a golden fleece'. The particular colour was not always achieved without a little help from elsewhere. One of the most easily available bleaching agents was urine, used to soak long tresses which were then stretched over a special headdress and dried in the sun.

What non-Venetians remarked on was just how much of the panache and vitality of the city's social life was owing to its womenfolk, even given the notable contrast between extremes of protectiveness in some households and a general freedom of conversation prevailing in others. From this aspect, the wife of a doge – the dogaressa (or 'ducissa' as early medieval Venetians called her) – found herself accorded a special kind of public profile as soon as her husband took office. Her own coronation, known as a *trionfo*, came complete with a cortege of decorated boats, train-bearing ladies-in-waiting, ringing of bells and volleys of cannon fire, a procession through the Piazza and a Te Deum sung in San Marco. There she was required to swear to the *Promissione*, the solemn oath taken by her husband on his election.

In the palace which now became her home the dogaressa had to listen to a special admonition delivered to her by a senior member of the Grand Council. This indicated, with uncompromising precision, what would happen to her after her death. 'Since Your Serenity has

Veronese's *The Triumph of Venice, Crowned by Victory*, a ceiling painting (1582) in the Palazzo Ducale.

taken possession of the palace while alive, be aware that once dead, your brain, your eyes and your entrails will be removed from your body and you will lie in this very place for three days before your burial.' The dogaressa was then required to answer: 'We are well content with what you say, and let it happen according to the disposition of Almighty God.' Not surprisingly, in the wake of such a macabre reminder, there followed three days of non-stop festivity, with banqueting, receptions for the patricians' wives and those of leading citizens, and a regatta on the Grand Canal. This queen of Venice, which was essentially what she became, could further console herself with the reflection that if she survived her husband, the state would award her enough in the way of a pension and servants for her to enjoy a comfortable widowhood.

Typically Venetian was the seriousness surrounding this material provision. Most marriages during the Republic's 1,300-year existence were arranged according to contracts and settlements and an important feature, here as elsewhere, was the offer of a dowry by the bride's family. On becoming a widow, the wife had a claim to anything that she herself might have brought into the house as part of her jointure, which itself might have increased in value since the time of her wedding. In addition, if she belonged to a property-owning family she had the right to reclaim possession of any land or houses which her father had specifically settled on her at the time of the engagement. Even if Shakespeare's Portia hands over the villa at Belmont to the handsome gold digger Bassanio as soon as he chooses the leaden casket –

> This house, these servants, and this same myself
> Are yours, my lord

– they will be hers again by law should he predecease her. Portia is an educated and cultured woman, as she amply goes on to prove (with some help from her Paduan uncle's legal know-how) in the great trial scene that forms the fourth act of *The Merchant of Venice*. In a state which prided itself on its success as a centre of book production, with a correspondingly high level of literacy among its citizens, ignorance was not viewed as an essential virtue in a wife. It is probable that Renaissance Venice boasted a larger proportion of learned women than could be found anywhere else in Italy. Wives were expected first and foremost to be bearers of children and dutiful supervisors of the household, but this did not bar them from a life of the intellect or from developing considerable skills in the various arts for which La Serenissima was renowned.

In this chapter we look at the careers of three distinguished Venetian women during the period from 1540 to 1630. It was the age of Lepanto, of the Interdict, of the worst plague epidemic to overtake the city and the beginning of a long and finally fruitless struggle to defend the island of Crete from conquest by the Turks. Though the era witnessed a gradual loss of power and prestige for the Republic, the image of Venice as a prosperous, successful and well-ordered commonwealth continued to hold firm. Its diplomats went on playing a key role in European affairs as brokers and intermediaries and in 1648 their intervention would help to bring about the historically crucial Peace of Westphalia that brought an end to the Thirty Years' War. The lives of these three women were thus led against a restless and troubled background, yet each of them in her different way transcended such a context, finding fame among contemporaries in the process.

First in our frame is Gaspara Stampa, a poet of true distinction, who renewed the great traditions established by Petrarch and Michelangelo in the hallowed form of the sonnet, managing in the process to fashion a genuinely striking species of autobiography from her lofty, elegantly crafted verses. She was not from a particularly affluent or socially exalted background, as the daughter of a shopkeeper in Padua who had moved his business, selling trinkets and articles of jewellery, to Venice, even if her father was believed to have connexions with the Milanese nobility. He died early, leaving the family comfortably off, and his widow Cecilia did her best to give the children a decent education. Gaspara and her sister Cassandra learnt music and soon became sought after as singers, while their brother Baldassare was a talented poet. The three of them were often invited to patrician households where cultured gatherings known as 'academies' took place, prefiguring the salons of eighteenth- and nineteenth-century Paris. Here Gaspara could meet influential figures from the world of the arts, including writers like Ludovico Ariosto, author of the wildly inventive romantic epic *Orlando Furioso*, the virtuoso lyricist Benedetto Varchi and his fellow Tuscan, the perennially witty, scabrous, sometimes positively sulphurous Pietro Aretino, who had settled in Venice and become a friend of several of its leading painters, Titian and Sebastiano del Piombo among them. No portrait of Gaspara from life has yet been identified but it is possible that she appears, along with her sister, in a painting by Bonifazio de' Pitati now in the Accademia gallery, illustrating Christ's parable of Dives and Lazarus. Here we see a richly-garbed female lutenist – with a blonde coiffure naturally – singing from a score held up for her by a

overleaf Detail from Bonifazio de' Pitati's *Parable of Dives and Lazarus*. The figures in the painting may well include representations of the poet Gaspara Stampa and her sister.

little black page boy, while an equally well-dressed young woman looks pensively on at the scene.

This was the age when the first of the many learned societies throughout Italy were being established and Gaspara became a member of the Accademia dei Dubbiosi, 'the doubters', originally founded in Brescia by Count Fortunato Martinengo Cesaresco, who later moved it to Venice. Members of such groups always took pseudonyms and hers was Anaxilla, from the Latin name Anaxus given to the Piave, one of the Veneto's biggest rivers. Soon the Stampa household itself became a cultural forum, with Gaspara's beauty, liveliness and versatility drawing a throng of admirers. Was she, as is sometimes suggested, nothing more than a courtesan, the equivalent of a Japanese geisha purveying sophisticated entertainment to a select group of clients from the Venetian nobility? The reality was surely somewhat more nuanced. No direct evidence for such a status exists: among the Dubbiosi she was definitely not of a dubious reputation. Yet the fact that she was a citizen's daughter, with only a questionable link to the aristocracy of another town altogether, would soon count against her at the very instant when she most needed a guarantee of respectability.

In 1544 her brother Baldassare died, aged only twenty, of a broken heart, it was said, through love for a woman who had rejected him. Gaspara, deeply shaken by the loss of a sibling who was also a fellow poet, could hardly have guessed that a similar destiny lay in wait for her. Four years later she first encountered the attractive young nobleman Collaltino di Collalto, from a family with a clutch of castles in the Marca Trevigiana, the country surrounding the city of Treviso. He too was a rhymer of sorts. This age of Baldassare Castiglione's *Il Cortegiano* (1528), a style bible for the Renaissance man, expected its courtly paragons to show off in verse with the same *sprezzatura* – nonchalant grace – as they might choose to display in sword-fighting, tennis games or riding a horse in the manège.

Collalto's impact on Gaspara Stampa was devastating. She must have known, though she was unlikely to want to acknowledge it, that he could never stoop socially to taking her as a wife. What in contemporary England was called 'marrying within his degree' was an automatic assumption among nobles of the young man's class and his parents were already in search of a bride for him from out of the limited circle of their fellow landowners across the eastern Veneto. It was flattering nevertheless to be courted and taken seriously by a woman whose gifts as a poet, musician and conversationalist were so highly regarded by Venice's cultural elite. Soon enough the pair of them became lovers. What Collalto could not know – maybe indeed he never knew it – was that the whole bittersweet experience of her passion for him inspired Gaspara to create one of the most potently expressive of all the great Renaissance sonnet sequences.

Published posthumously by the devoted Cassandra, the 245 poems, in the prescribed Petrarchan rhyme scheme, offer a perfect exemplar of that ageless literary genre, the you-hurt-me narrative. Such is their quality that the collection rises far above the commonplaces of self-pity to address the true rawness and complexity of the writer's emotions, so that we end up feeling like privileged eavesdroppers on the relationship as it progresses. Gaspara's emotional lurches and zigzags are fundamental to the impact of the entire sequence. The fact that nothing in the affair is remotely predictable adds to the fascination of what is essentially the logbook of a voyage across dangerous and uncharted waters. 'Life and death, joy and sorrow, fear and trust,' says the poet accusingly, 'by your agency, Love, all derive from a single place.' Collalto's heart may be 'hard as an Alpine mountain, cold as the snow which covers it', but from certain aspects Gaspara finds this easier to deal with. 'Love's flowery meadow is not perfect, in my judgment, unless mixed with its opposite, when annoyance sharpens the edge of pleasure.' The pair get to spend the night together – more than one, it may be assumed – and the poet pays ecstatic tribute to those dark hours, 'brighter and more blessed by me than all the bright and blessed days, worthy of praise from the rarest genius, let alone mine'. As Collalto lies in her arms, Gaspara hails the night as 'faithful minister to my joys' and wishes she were the mythical Alcmena in the embraces of Jove, who could order Phoebus to delay the onset of dawn.

The whole scenario unfolds as bitterly as its creator might have expected. It becomes obvious that Gaspara was warned against the attachment by her mother and sisters but chose instead to luxuriate in the inspirations which its muddle and cruelty afforded her. Off went Collalto in 1549 to France in the suite of Prince Orazio Farnese of Parma, to spend several years as a captain for King Henri II of France in a war against England and Spain. As far as we know, he never bothered to write to Gaspara. Would he ever come back? If so, as Gaspara must have suspected, it would only be to cast her aside for good. In 1554, worn out by longing and despair, she seems to have had a premonition that not much of existence was left to her. The final sonnets were addressed not to the heartless beloved but to a suffering Christ, from whom she begged forgiveness for 'wasting my life in vain love affairs'. Perhaps the very last line of verse she ever wrote runs simply: 'Sweet

Lord, do not let me perish.' Shortly afterwards she died of a fever, aged only thirty-one. Three years later Collaltino di Collalto married a marchesa from Mantua. They had five children.

It was Cassandra Stampa who saw justice done to her sister by having all the poems, including song texts, elegies and occasional verse, published in a complete edition. By way of a preface she decided to add the singularly poignant prose address headed *Allo illustre mio signore*, which Gaspara had written to introduce the heart-wrenching sonnet sequence. 'Since my letters and poems have made no impression on you whatever,' she tells Collato, 'I decided to gather them into a single volume to see whether that would work.' She bids him read 'these records of that anguish and sorrow endured in love by your most faithful, most unhappy Anaxilla'. The very rooms and furniture of her house, 'the beds, the chambers, the halls', will tell him of 'the laments, groans, sighs and tears' that she has poured out both day and night. Perhaps, she says, 'on receiving this little book, you will grant me the courtesy of a sigh, so as to refresh the memory of your forgotten and abandoned Anaxilla'. Gaspara Stampa had the sweetest of revenges. Except among his aristocratic progeny, Collaltino di Collalto is history, known to the wider world only as the undeserving lover of one of Venice's greatest poets and the Italian Renaissance's most arresting female voice.

Certain commentators on Gaspara Stampa's career and social background, as we have already noted, tend to view her as not much better than a high-status sex worker, someone whose family saw distinct advantages in encouraging her free association with libertine artists, musicians and intellectuals. This assumption is made the easier by the notoriety of sixteenth-century Venice as a major centre of prostitution, a tax on whose profits might furnish a continuing revenue stream for the coffers of the Republic. One of the most famously rewarding descriptions of the city and its inhabitants during this period derives from the pen of the eccentric and opinionated Englishman Thomas Coryat, whose *Coryat's Crudities: Hastily Gobbled Up in Five Months Travels in France, Italy &c* describes his tour across Europe in 1608. After visiting Venice, he estimated the number of working prostitutes in the area of the Venetian lagoon as being 'at the least twenty thousand'.

While deploring 'a toleration of such licentious wantons in so glorious, so potent, so renowned a city', Coryat was at pains to offer two good reasons for this. One, however paradoxical, was a need on the part of Venetian husbands to protect their wives from dishonour by visiting brothels so as to indulge their own casual cravings and not need to pay

Thomas Coryat visits a Venetian courtesan in an engraving from *Coryat's Crudities*, a vivid and informative account of his journey to Venice and back in 1608.

unwelcome attentions to respectable women as a means of satisfying such urges. The other, rather more convincing given all we know as to the constant search for fresh sources of money among Venetians, was as a source of public funding. 'The revenues which [the women] pay unto the Senate for their toleration', says Coryat, 'do maintain a dozen of their galleys (as many reported to me in Venice) and so save them a great charge.' From this aspect the prostitutes were a profitable visitor attraction. A growing part of Venice's international reputation was as a capital of worldly pleasures, a Vanity Fair rich with different kinds of entertainment, sophisticated or otherwise, of which the courtesans formed a key component. 'So infinite are the allurements of these amorous Calypsoes that the fame of them hath drawn many to Venice from some of the remotest parts of Christendom, to contemplate their beauties and enjoy their pleasing dalliances.'

Coryat, who himself visited one of the 'amorous Calypsoes' while in Venice, either to enjoy her pleasing dalliance or pick up some local colour, describes their houses as 'very magnificent and portly buildings fit for the entertainment of a great Prince'. He frames his account of the whole experience as a warning to the curious reader (presumably male): beware of the fine rooms, decked out in 'most sumptuous tapestry and rich leather', the makeup compounded of 'famous apothecary drugs' with which these women 'adulterate their faces', the silk stockings, the red petticoat, the perfumed bed linen and 'the heart-tempting harmony of her voice'. And take care that you pay on the nail for hospitality of whatever kind, otherwise 'she will either cause thy throat to be cut by her Ruffiano [pimp] if he can after catch thee in the City, or procure thee to be arrested (if thou art to be found) and clapped up in the prison, where thou shalt remain till thou hast paid her all thou didst promise her'.

Somewhat bizarrely, superior prostitutes like these were sometimes identified with the name *cortigiana onesta* – honest whore – to distinguish them from the type of common harlot – *cortigiana di lume* – whose services were sought by sailors, gondoliers and market porters. Most illustrious in this top grade was surely Veronica Franco, a woman whose life was not very much longer than that of the hapless Gaspara Stampa but altogether more rewarding in terms of experience and personal fulfilment. Veronica was born in Venice in 1546, to Paola Fracassa, herself a whore and listed in one of the available directories as living in the parish of Santa Maria Formosa in the *sestiere* of Castello. Paola was determined that her daughter should enjoy the advantages of a decent education, the kind which might prepare her, if marriage

The well-connected courtesan and poet Veronica Franco (1546–91), in a portrait from Tintoretto's studio.

opportunities were lacking, to make a successful career as a courtesan. Veronica was accordingly given the same humanist schooling as her brother, learning to read and write and acquiring considerable skill as a poet. In her *Lettere familiari* (1580), a collection of elegant epistles she addressed to assorted friends, lovers and eminent personages, she tells one of them: 'You well know that among all those who seek to win my favours, the very dearest are those who practise the different academic disciplines and the fine arts, of which I, as a woman of scant learning, am devoted by inclination and desire. So eager for those things am I and so delighted to speak of them with those who know, in order that I may learn even more, that if my fortunes allowed me, I should spend my whole life in the company of cultivated men.'

A glance at her group of friends as mirrored in her published poems, the *Capitoli*, all in the *terza rima* form standardized by Dante in his *Divina Commedia*, suggests that Veronica's wishes in this respect were very substantially fulfilled. Her circle included Jacopo Robusti, nicknamed 'Tintoretto', 'the little dyer', who seems to have used her as a model in at least three remarkable female portraits, though none of these is firmly acknowledged as a likeness. She grew acquainted with the poet Orsatto Giustinian, whose translation of the *Oedipus Rex* of Sophocles formed the libretto for the inaugural opera staged at Teatro Olimpico in Vicenza, its music provided by Andrea Gabrieli, doyen of Venetian composers and organist at San Marco, with designs by Paolo Veronese. In addition she was evidently in contact with several Italian princes, such as Guglielmo Gonzaga, Duke of Mantua, and Cardinal Luigi d'Este, brother of the last Duke of Ferrara. Franco was, in short, an expert networker and it was not for nothing that her likeness was included in an album of miniature portraits of Venice's most beautiful and accomplished courtesans shown to King Henri III of France on his visit to the city in the summer of 1574. La Serenissima, as we have seen, pushed the boat out both figuratively and literally on this occasion and the week of frenetic festivity included a visit to Veronica. Given Henri's known predilection for good-looking young men and his reluctance to marry, it may be that the pair simply spent the time discussing art and literature. He took home a portrait of her by Tintoretto and she later addressed two of her poems to him.

We need to understand Veronica in the context of her own era and, more specifically, within that of late sixteenth-century Venice. There is no evidence that she was forced into prostitution, even if her mother had followed this kind of career. It is likely that the superior education she received – classical Latin authors like Catullus, Propertius and Ovid formed part of her reading – encouraged her to embrace the role of *cortigiana onesta* as a means of liberating herself from the narrow domesticity imposed on an average Venetian girl as soon as she married. As somebody decidedly and determinedly not average, Franco preferred instead to follow the more socially ambiguous path trodden by women whose sexual freedom, whatever it cost them in terms of reputation, brought valuable opportunities for engaging with writers and intellectuals, challenging that conventional outlook which denied them a life of the mind and an adequate creative fulfilment. 'Women, by their very nature, are no less agile than men', declares one of Franco's poems. 'When we have weapons and learn to use them, we shall prove we have hands, feet and hearts just like yours.' The fact that she sent a copy of her book to Montaigne on his visit to Venice in November 1580 underlines her serious intentions as a writer. While there, he never actually met the '*gentifemme vénitienne*', as he calls her, but gave a tip to the servant who delivered the volume. His *Essais* had been published earlier that year, with a dedication to King Henri. Had the monarch stayed in touch with Veronica over the intervening period since their evening together, so that an early edition might have reached her from his hands?

She had, of course, a living to earn and as a Venetian the business of driving a trade was hardwired in her. Beauty and its commercial advantages left Veronica vulnerable to the spite, resentment and hypocrisy of men who saw her rejection of them as unpardonable insolence or else, as so often happens, were genuinely afraid of her spirit and talent. The defiance at the heart of the verses quoted above was aimed at a fellow writer and former lover, the young dialect poet Maffio Venier, a creature of damaged brilliance. Nephew of the senator Domenico Venier under whose artistic patronage Franco flourished, Maffio had turned on her for reasons still not altogether clear, in a savage rant at the violation of nature inherent in the act of giving money to a prostitute for her services. Elsewhere he called her 'a contemptible bastard, spawned below stairs', accused her of spreading the pox and compared her salon to a stable. In a far more dignified poetic strain she threw everything back in his face: 'No more words: let us take to the field of combat. To arms! I am ready to die so as to free myself from these hateful insults. Acknowledge your wrongdoing, ingratitude and faithlessness, otherwise with these same hands of mine I shall pluck the living heart from your breast.' And this, you feel, is exactly what Veronica would have done if offered the chance.

Living constantly above her income, needing to sustain a

handsome domestic establishment so as to foster the kind of clientele whose company she herself could enjoy, Veronica was anxious that others in her line of work should not be left to beggary and neglect. Her proposal to the Signoria of a scheme for a house of refuge for prostitutes and their children got little further, alas, than a brief flutter of pious headshaking from the saintly Doge Pasquale Cicogna. The effects of the devastating plague epidemic in 1577 had reduced many of her fellow sex workers, whether *onesta* or *di lume*, to penury and Franco's own finances never properly recovered in its wake. On 22 July 1591 she died, aged only forty-five, of an unspecified fever and was buried in the church of San Moise.

Like so many other high-living Venetians, Veronica Franco had needed, at intervals, to negotiate financial loans from the Jewish moneylenders who furnished such a vital element in La Serenissima's commercial activity. During the sixteenth century their presence had considerably increased and in 1589 the merchant Daniel Rodriguez persuaded the Senate to allow a new group of Jews to take up residence within the Ghetto. Known in Venice as 'Daniele Rodriga', he was a *Marrano*, the name given to so-called 'New Christians', those Spanish Jews whom legal sanctions in Spain and Portugal had obliged to convert to Catholicism but who in many cases still practised their faith in secret. When further religious bigotry drove them from Spain, many had settled in Ottoman Greece and Turkey and it was Rodriguez whose persistent lobbying of the doge and various Council members finally assured this Sephardic refugee group – *la nazione ponentina* – of a permanent place within the city and the chance to erect their own synagogue.

The new arrivals had inevitably to accept the traditional limitations imposed upon Jews under Venetian law. Scarlet caps or yellow turbans identified them as 'Hebrew' or 'Israelite', they were forbidden to practise as doctors except within their own community (though since everyone knew that Jewish doctors were the best, many Christians, including the doge himself, regularly broke this prohibition) and every night their Ghetto gates were locked and guarded. The reality was, however, that Venice had long ago perceived the advantages of maintaining a Jewish population, consistently challenging the official antisemitism enshrined in various papal edicts or in meddlesome supervision by the Holy Inquisition. Not surprisingly this tolerance towards the Jews, motivated by sheer practicality rather than any preternaturally humane impulse though it was, had been viewed by successive popes with suspicion and disapproval. In the period leading up to the Interdict of 1606 it became a genuine bone of contention between Venice and Rome, the whole issue being subsequently exacerbated by Paolo Sarpi's shrewdly legalistic championship of the *Marranos* as, in essence, a refugee community shielded by a state which stood to gain from its presence.

Life within the Ghetto was not made easier by occasional contention between the different Jewish 'nations', each with their separate synagogues. Desperate overcrowding offered a further problem. A major conservation project taking place while this book is being written will enable modern visitors to understand just how cramped, airless and windowless so many of the dwellings here became as their storeys stacked up and their spaces were necessarily divided and subdivided. At the same time the Ghetto was also home to a tenacious, energetic and intensely focused ethno-religious grouping within the Venetian cosmopolis, attracting curious foreign visitors from whose home countries Jews had long ago been expelled. Thomas Coryat was one of these, as we might expect, and was able to attend a synagogue service, where he listened to 'the Levite that readeth the law to them... pronounce before the congregation not by a sober, distinct and orderly reading, but by an exceeding loud yaling, undecent roaring... as it were a beastly bellowing of it forth'. The Jews seemed to him 'to bee such goodly and proper men, most elegant and sweet featured persons'. As for their womenfolk, 'some were as beautiful as ever I saw, and so gorgeous in their apparel, jewels, chaines of gold, and rings adorned with precious stones, that some of our English Countesses do scarce exceede them'. A discussion in Latin with a passing rabbi on basic doctrinal questions grew embarrassingly heated 'after there had passed many vehement speeches to and fro between us', so that Coryat was forced to flee across a bridge into Cannaregio when a 'swaggering' Jewish crowd gathered to defend the faith. As luck would have it, 'our noble Ambassador Sir Henry Wotton' just happened to be passing in his gondola, 'espyed me somewhat earnestly bickering with them' and rescued his compatriot from a tricky encounter.

Female members of this Venetian Jewry were often better educated than their Christian counterparts. For example, the arrival of Daniel Rodriguez's fellow Sephardim during the 1590s meant that their polyglot skills in Spanish, Greek, Turkish and Arabic could be turned to various uses by the government. A number of Jewish women took on the valuable role of go-betweens during particularly delicate negotiations with the Ottoman court in Istanbul. Others were admired in Venice for their musical, literary or technical gifts. For these and other reasons the Ghetto, regardless of official disapproval and periodic efforts, more especially on religious grounds, to limit or constrain the resident community, took its place alongside the Arsenale, the Rialto bridge or the Merceria, Venice's major shopping street, as one of the city's chief curiosities, an institution that set it apart from other metropolitan centres in early modern Europe.

During the seventeenth century's opening decades, such a distinctive identity was enhanced by the presence of Sara Coppio Sullam, perfect exemplar, at that period, of a cultured Jewish woman who looked beyond her traditional destiny as wife and mother in pursuit of intellectual freedom. Born around 1590 into an affluent family originally from Mantua, she showed ability both as a singer and as a poet, yet was not content simply to pass for the kind of accomplished girl who could be married off to provide some wealthy husband with a quiverful of children, as approved by the Psalmist. Engaged and wedded Sara certainly was, in 1612, to the banker Giacobbe Sullam. We know relatively little about him except that he seems to have understood her need for a life of the mind and the conversation of the learned. Other husbands might have sought to smother the impact of the education given her by a proud father, Simon Coppio, who went so far as to send his daughter for instruction to Leone da Modena, the city's most eminent rabbinical teacher and a major figure in Italian Jewish life of the age. Giacobbe nevertheless encouraged Sara's aspirations when she started hosting an 'academy' in their house on the edge of the Ghetto, close to the church of San Girolamo, welcoming writers, scholars and musical virtuosi.

'Radiantly beautiful, blonde-haired, her glance full of tenderness' is how one Venetian historian portrays her, 'an authentic *femme savant*, a lively conversationalist, an elegant improviser, a gifted musician' says another – Sara Coppio Sullam's fame began to spread beyond the confines of Venice itself and in 1618 she initiated a singular intellectual correspondence with one of her distant admirers, a man she would never actually meet. The Genoese poet and dramatist Ansaldo Cebà had recently published an epic treatment of the story, as told in Jewish scripture, of Esther, whose successful intercession with the Persian king Ahasuerus on behalf of her fellow Jews, menaced by the wicked Haman, is honoured each year in the spring festival of Purim. Fascinated by the poem, Sara wrote him a laudatory letter. Cebà, who seems already to have heard something of her from friends in Padua, his old university, replied eagerly enough, voicing a hope that she might now think of converting to Christianity. His answer was accompanied with a sonnet,

The *Manifesto* of the Jewish writer Sara Copio Sullam, in which she defended herself against Christian charges of heresy.

elegantly penned but decidedly ambiguous in both language and direction. Attractive Sara no doubt was, but her outward allure, so he feared, might be a mask for impiety and ignorance of the true faith. 'In the darkness of her Hebrew rites she cannot apprehend the light which opens my Christian eyes.'

Was Cebà afraid that Sara might seduce him? There's a faint suggestion that at the age of fifty-three, 'at the extreme edge of life', he found something almost too engaging in the notion of a fan letter from a woman thirty years younger and Jewish to boot. The pair of them exchanged portraits and an intense correspondence ensued. Letters sped back and forth between Venice and Genoa for at least four years as Cebà, with growing desperation, strove to draw Sara closer to what he conscientiously maintained was the only true illumination, that of the Holy Gospel. Sara had absolutely no intention of converting. Steadfast in her Jewish beliefs, she evidently enjoyed the intellectual exchange with the ageing poet, but that was to be all. Cebà, unable to relish the epistolary dialogue for its own sake, at length conceded defeat,

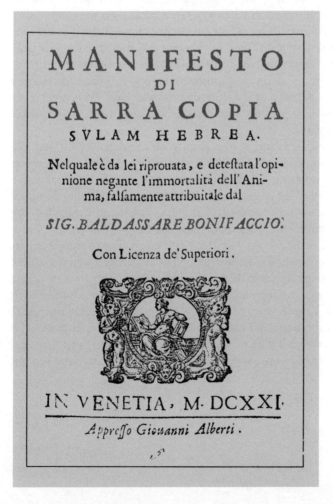

admonishing her rather peevishly: 'If you cannot think of converting, then you had better lay aside your pen, since without such an end in view I cannot think of using mine.' His share of the correspondence was published in Genoa in 1623. Sara's letters have all disappeared.

Contemporary readers of Cebà's book were able, all the same, to piece together her ideas and religious principles from his own reactions to them. There seems to have been a general unwillingness to accept that a mere woman could have held her own so adroitly in the field of theological argument and several people supposed that Sara was simply expressing concepts formulated by her teacher, Rabbi Leone da Modena, ventriloquizing, as it were, from within the Venice Ghetto. That Sara Coppio Sullam was perfectly capable of voicing her own rational opinions (though Rabbi Leone may well have helped to develop certain ideas more fully) became obvious a year or so later when she found herself drawn into a potentially risky, perhaps even mortally dangerous spiritual controversy. Her salon at San Girolamo had attracted gentile visitors as often as Jews and among the former was Baldassare Bonifacio, an earnest young cleric who later became an archdeacon in the diocese of Treviso. In a treatise on the immortality of the soul, Bonifacio, for whatever reason, chose to turn against his former friend and accuse her of denying the fundamental principle on which the essay was based. Effectively this amounted to a serious charge of heresy and the Inquisition, scenting a chance for combat following the debacle of the Interdict, would have every excuse to arrest, imprison or perhaps even torture Sara were such an accusation to be substantiated.

She was quick to spring into print with her defence, entitled *The Manifesto of Sara Coppio Sullam the Jew*, in which the opinion denying the soul's immortality, falsely attributed to her by Signor Baldassare Bonifacio, is rejected as detestable. Published in Venice, the *Manifesto* was dedicated to the memory of her late father, implying that she would have made him proud and that something of his immortal soul lived on in his daughter. As with the Cebà letters, poetry played its part here; these seventeenth-century pamphlet wars were nothing if not courtly and elegant. Just as Bonifacio had prefaced his treatise with a scatter of sonnets ruefully attacking Sara, so she enjoyed hitting back with her own neatly turned verses. The ensuing preface (in prose) suggests that she knew her audience and felt entitled by now to some measure of respect. 'I dare to suppose, dear readers, that you may find it strange to see my name, very well known within this city and beyond it, in print for the first time and associated with material quite different from what usually flows from my pen.'

Sara goes on to put Bonifacio through the wringer of her irony and indignation. Yes, he has indeed a soul, 'incorruptible, immortal and divine', something both Jews and Christians can believe in, 'which makes your calumnies cruel and reprehensible'. Contemptuous of his scholarship – 'you need more than a degree in canon law to ponder the immortality of the soul' – she is equally scornful regarding his command of Hebrew and knowledge of the scriptures. Resounding through Sara's manifesto is that very same kind of certainty which had at last vanquished Ansaldo Cebà in his efforts to bring her over to Catholicism. Whatever the smart gentile company she kept, however broad those intellectual perspectives encouraged by the discourse among the habitués of her academy at San Girolamo, she remained unshakeable in her Judaism and such firm conviction makes her response to Bonifacio the more devastating. Her magnanimity becomes an edged weapon as she plays wittily on the double meaning of the Italian word *pietà* as both 'piety' and 'compassion' in saying '*La pietà della mia legge mi fa pietosa della vostra simplicità.*' 'The holiness of my law makes me pity your ignorance' goes only part of the way towards translating this complex statement. How indeed could the archdeacon hope to survive?

Left unmolested by the Holy Office, Sara died in 1641. The inconsolable husband Giacobbe Sullam turned to her old teacher Leone da Modena for her Hebrew epitaph, which runs as follows:

> This stone commemorates the eminent Signora Sara, wife of Giacobbe Sullam, yet living. The exterminating angel let fly his dart, mortally wounding Sara. Wise among women, a support to the distressed, a companion and a friend to the wretched. If now she is a prey to the worms, then on the destined day the Good Lord shall say: 'Return, return, o Shulamite!' She ceased living on the sixth day (Friday) 5 Adar 5401 of the Jewish calendar. May her soul enjoy eternal beatitude.

How Sara Coppio Sullam would have loved Rabbi Leone's affectionate tribute, with its gently humorous play – Shulam/Sullam – on her married surname in quoting from the *Song of Solomon*: 'Return, return, o Shulamite: return, return that we may look upon thee!' In her, in Veronica Franco and in Gaspara Stampa we can hear the authentic voice of Venice at her most vigrous, free and inspiriting.

A LAST
HURRAH

During the Ascension week festivities of 1645, when the doge, according to custom, was rowed out into the lagoon in the Bucintoro on the Festa della Sensa to perform the ceremony of marrying the sea, one of those watching the hallowed ritual was a young Englishman named John Evelyn. Together with some friends he had left his native country, plunged in the horror and confusion of civil war, to go travelling across France and Italy, spending the best part of two years away and taking detailed notes of everything he saw. These were written up on his return, to form one of the most fascinating records of European travel in the early modern era, as part of a personal diary Evelyn kept for the next sixty years.

The Venice which he visited during that early summer of 1645 may have been the capital of a state now entering upon a major period of political and economic decline, but the diarist himself picked up very little evidence of such an imperial downturn. 'This famous Emporium, which is always crowded with strangers' was to all intents and purposes thriving, prosperous and productive, its inhabitants 'a frugal and wise people, and exact observers of all sumptuary laws'. The latter aspect made a strong impression on this serious-minded young traveller. Venetians, it seemed to him, were happy to play by the rules in following a seasonal calendar which governed both their amusements and the garments they donned in order to pursue them. At the Festa della Sensa, Evelyn was careful to note, 'the doge's vest is of crimson velvet, the Procurators' &c of damask, very stately'.

One feature of this highly enjoyable week was completely new to Evelyn and his friends and would consequently never be forgotten. On the evening of that same Ascension feast day 'we went to the Opera, where comedies and other plays are represented in recitative music by the most excellent musicians, vocal and instrumental'. They looked in amazement at the sumptuous painted sets and marvelled at their perspective effects, together with the 'machines for flying in the air and other wonderful notions'. The work itself was Giovanni Rovetta's *Ercole in Lidia*, performed at Teatro Novissimo, Venice's first purpose-built opera house, standing next to the church of Santi Giovanni e Paolo. It starred the Roman soprano Anna Renzi, earliest incarnation of that stellar and notorious species, the prima donna – but, says Evelyn, 'there was an eunuch who in my opinion surpassed her; also a Genoese that sung an incomparable bass'. His brief account of a night at the opera is one of the earliest testimonies we have to the impact of the seventeenth century's hottest new entertainment form. 'Taken together', concludes the diarist, 'it is one of the most magnificent and expensive diversions the wit of man can invent.'

Opera was not itself invented in Venice but its earliest evolution as a major musical genre belongs essentially to this city and no survey of Venetian culture and history would be complete without some acknowledgment of its significance in the life of the urban community over what is now almost four hundred years. The first public performances of lyric theatre would take place here during the 1630s, with a benchmark being set by the era's most distinguished composer, Claudio Monteverdi, choirmaster of San Marco. Originally from Cremona, Monteverdi had gained early success with his published books of madrigals before seeking employment at the Gonzaga court in Mantua, becoming the duke's chapel master and making a spectacular impact with his *Vespro della Beata Vergine* of 1610. Here his first opera, *L'Orfeo*, was produced, but it was only in Venice, to which he moved in 1612 as director of music at San Marco, that the promise of this early lyric masterpiece could substantially be built on. By 1640 a taste for opera had started to engross the Venetians, with performances at Teatro San Cassiano leading the way, followed by the Novissimo and another opera house at San Moise. Monteverdi, while busy supervising the Basilica's musical activities, had also found time to compose some dozen dramatic works for staging in Venice, Mantua and Parma, most of them, alas, now lost. What luckily survive are two of his operas written for these newly opened Venetian public theatres, *Il ritorno di Ulisse in patria* and *L'incoronazione di Poppea*, each of them focused on music's power to mediate human emotion, the guiding motivator, of Monteverdi's entire creative output.

By the end of the century as many as ten different opera houses, from Castello and Cannaregio to San Polo and Santa Croce, were presenting seasonal programmes, mostly of new and specially com-

A portrait (*c.*1640) of Claudio Monteverdi, multifaceted musical
genius of seventeenth-century Venice,
by Bernardo Strozzi.

missioned works in which nearly every Italian composer of note was involved, writing arias for a roster of outstanding vocal artists. Monteverdi's mantle had been inherited by Francesco Cavalli and Antonio Sartorio, as the Venetian operatic style gathered eager imitators in other Italian cities and travelled beyond the Alps to Vienna, Munich, Hanover and Hamburg. Whatever La Serenissima might be losing in terms of commercial success and international standing among European nations was offset in some degree by her continuing importance as an apparently inexhaustible nursery of musical talent in this most elaborate and sophisticated of art forms. The paradox of opera is summed up for us in Evelyn's two adjectives 'magnificent' and 'expensive'. With few exceptions no operatic enterprise has ever been exactly a dependable source of profit, yet this has never deterred composers, performers, managements and audiences from a desire to realize its all-encompassing splendour as a genre.

A view of Senj, Istrian stronghold of the Uskok pirates who preyed on Venetian merchant ships in the early seventeenth century.

Quite how aware the Venetian audience was of the disjunct between the lavishness of this new entertainment and the actuality of what was happening to their republic we have little means of knowing. The story of La Serenissima in the seventeenth century follows a depressing trajectory of hard knocks, baffled expectations, loss of face and a correspondingly desperate attempt to preserve some sort of dignity and composure while her status continued to diminish and she became a sideshow, something of a curiosity even, within Italy or across the broader European scene. Forfeiting her right to be taken seriously was perhaps the most tragic aspect of what happened to Venice during this period, but it was all made harder for her by that very same sense of entitlement and complacency with which she confronted the wider world. Nothing, as it seemed, was wrong with La Serenissima until things actually went wrong, by which time it was nearly always too late to put them right.

Others apart from the Turks, her habitual predators and trading partners, wanted their share of Venice's advantages in the Mediterranean. Habsburg Austria, by 1600 a major power in central Europe, had seen its chance to gain control of the upper Adriatic by encouraging Christian fugitives from Ottoman conquests in the Balkans to settle along its south-eastern frontier. Known as 'Uskoks', from a Serbo-Croat word meaning 'those who make an ambush', they based their operations at the port of Senj on the Istrian coast, whence they ran a piratical enterprise focused on attacking merchant ships with fleets of small, swift galleys. It was the plunder rather than the manpower they were after and their whole economy ran on shares in the booty gathered on sea and land, since they also made regular raids among towns and villages along the Ottoman frontier.

The Uskoks – *gli Uscocchi* – became the bane of Venetian shipping during the early years of the seventeenth century. Their piracy among Turkish vessels added an extra problem for the Signoria, as the Turks had their own trading *fondaco* in Venice and peace with the Sublime Porte was crucial in this respect. Since the Uskoks were nominally Austrian subjects, Venice remonstrated with the Habsburg Archduke Ferdinand, controlling the imperial frontier, as to keeping a firmer hand on the pirates. The Republic, increasingly mistrustful of Habsburg intentions regarding her own territory in Friuli, had begun the creation of an entirely new stronghold in the region, named Palmanova, to a plan by local engineer Girolamo Savorgnan. Ostensibly built as a citadel against Ottoman incursion, this perfect example of a Renaissance 'ideal city', begun in 1593 and employing the talents of major architects like Vincenzo Scamozzi and Baldassare Longhena, was in essence a warning to any power, whether Muslim or Christian, not to meddle with a still potent Serenissima.

The ultimate outrage came in 1613 with an Uskok attack on a Venetian galley, whose crew and passengers were treated with more than usual barbarity before being put to the sword. Its captain, Cristoforo Venier, was then dragged on shore and decapitated, after which, according to witnesses among the oarsmen kept alive to row the ship, his heart was cut from his body and eaten while the miscreants sopped his blood with slices of bread. Exaggerated in the telling or not, news of this jolted the Senate into action and when further Uskok raids on Friuli seemed to be taking place under the archduke's benign gaze, Venice, for the first time in almost a hundred years, found herself at war with a neighbouring state.

The so-called 'War of Gradisca', named for a major fortress town on the Austrian frontier, was one of attrition between two sides bolstered by allied forces, Archduke Ferdinand's from his Habsburg cousin Philip III of Spain, and Venice supported by brigades of Dutch and English volunteers. In 1617, after two inconclusive years, a peace was finally signed in Madrid, forcing the Republic to return its various captured fortresses in return for Austria agreeing to move the entire Uskok community off the coast of Istria and sufficiently far inland not to pose any further threat to Venice's command of the Adriatic. Glory for the Republic there was little or none, since piracy still threatened from others prowling these waters, but for a brief period the Grand Council could resume what was fast becoming its default position of a studious neutrality in the affairs of an increasingly storm-tossed Europe.

What mattered to Venice, as it had always mattered, was to keep trade routes and supply lines open, more especially those crossing Lombardy and the western Alps, menaced as these were by the knock-on impact of the Thirty Years' War, now in its opening phase among the states of Germany. The dominant military power in northern Italy was that of Spain, whose viceroyalty of the Duchy of Milan made it an awkward neighbour for the Republic. Venetian mistrust of Spain as a paymaster for Roman cardinals had been a contributory factor to its robust stance throughout the Interdict, with Paolo Sarpi keeping this wariness alive in several of his *consulti* for the Senate. The presence of Spanish ships had emboldened the Uskoks in their sea raids from Senj and Spain's embassy in Venice was fingered as a continual source of intrigues against the state. In 1618 the ambassador himself, Alfonso de la Cueva, Marquis of Bedmar, was found to be plotting, under direction from the Viceroy of Naples, to overthrow the Republic, having (to use Shakespeare's phrase) 'shark'd up a list of lawless resolutes' to help him. Most of these were footloose Frenchmen with vague ambitions either to become soldiers of fortune for different Italian states or else to follow a nefarious career among bravoes of the kind who had earlier knifed Fra Paolo. Their leader, a Norman named Jacques Pierre, had at one stage taken them all up to the top of the Campanile of San Marco to point out, as they watched the crowd in the Piazza below, just how easy any kind of terrorist activity might be. 'A handful of stout men with sticks might make themselves masters of it all and drive this herd of pantaloons into the water,' he claimed. 'Is it not a wonder that Venice has remained so long a virgin?'

He had reckoned without the singular effectiveness of those multiple intelligence services operated by the Council of Ten. Quickly the whole scheme started to implode. Details passed to the Senate from a French traveller led to the entrapment of one of the conspirators, Gabriel de Moncassin, whose information suggested that the plot's true source lay far off in Naples, where the Spanish viceroy, Pedro Giron, Duke of Ossuna, was busy fomenting it as part of his wider personal ambitions on the Italian political scene. No concrete evidence emerged to validate this, but the Ten grew sufficiently worried as to use Moncassin as a spy at gatherings of the conspirators. Promptly rounded up, two of them were tortured, then hanged between the infamous columns on the Piazzetta, two others were carried out to sea, bundled inside weighted sacks and drowned, while a fifth was shipped off to the citadel at Zara to be shot. As for the Marquis of Bedmar, with his direct complicity made palpable King Philip could do nothing but recall him.

'The Spanish Conspiracy', as the event was afterwards known, delivered something of a propaganda coup to the Senate and gained an international resonance. Half a century later it offered an ideal subject for the English dramatist Thomas Otway's tragedy *Venice Preserved or A Plot Discovered*, a triumph with audiences in Restoration London, more especially for certain topical parallels drawn with the ongoing hysteria over the Popish Plot. Though certain historians, notably Pierre Daru in his *Histoire de la République de Venise* (1821), have since sought to dismantle the whole episode in terms of pure panic and exaggeration on the part of the authorities, the fact that government agents were ordered to arrest, interrogate and eventually execute 300 others in addition to the chief suspects would seem to suggest that the Spanish Conspiracy presented a rather more serious threat than might appear to the overall stability of the Republic.

Yet again Venice had come through unscathed, but her survival was hardly watertight in the wider context of an Italy starting to experience the fallout, from across the Alps, of the Thirty Years' War. If religion, more particularly the rise of Protestant powers resistant to traditional Catholic supremacy, had triggered the initial stand-off, other interests, dynastic and territorial, were now drawing fresh participants into the fray. Duke Carlo Emanuele of Savoy was one of these, keen to exploit the volatile situation along his frontiers with France and the Republic of Genoa so as to expand the duchy and gain for himself the title of king he had always coveted. Having given support to Venice in the War of Gradisca, he could make her part of his designs on controlling northern Lombardy, more specifically the Tyrolean mountain area of Valtellina. Keeping the passes open here mattered equally to the Spanish viceroy and the Republic, whose fortresses guarded their eastern approaches. In 1624, when the viceroy sought to outflank Venice by transferring his authority over Valtellina to the pope, a hasty alliance between the Republic, France and Savoy sent an army of occupation speeding to the mountains. Since both French and Spanish troops were needed in campaigns on the other side of the Alps, it proved more opportune for their leaders to patch up a truce, leaving Duke Carlo Emanuele and the Venetian Signoria abruptly in the lurch, with no option but to accept terms. It seemed as if La Serenissima's military enterprises of two centuries earlier, in the days of the *condottieri*, were now repeating themselves, but with no obvious advantage on the present occasion.

That neither the fudge after Gradisca or the failed intervention in Valtellina had taught her any lessons was proved by what happened when Vincenzo Gonzaga, Duke of Mantua, died without a direct heir in 1627. His state was a dual fiefdom, since, as well as their original Mantovano domains, whose borders marched with Venice's own, the Gonzaga also ruled over the Marquisate of Monferrato in distant Piedmont. Here at Casale they had raised a citadel so well-armed that possession of it had become central to the conflicting plans of France and Spain for annexing the surrounding territory, while an ever-restless Carlo Emanuele of Savoy was making his own envious calculations. What counted most for Venice, however, was keeping the Habsburgs, Spanish or Austrian, away from Mantua itself, so in 1629 she chose to support the French claimant to the duchy, Charles, Duc de Nevers, even as Spaniards and Savoyard forces began separate moves on Casale. By the following summer the graceful city of Mantua, on whose defence the Republic had laid out immense resources, was in Austrian hands, sacked, burned and thoroughly pillaged of its Gonzaga art treasures. Though France had driven Carlo Emanuele's forces out of Monferrato, the greedy duke subsequently got most of the lands he wanted through the terms of a peace treaty drawn up in the autumn of 1631. By the same agreement Charles de Nevers became Duke of Mantua – that much Venice had achieved – but the venture had come at a massive cost and it was scarcely comforting for the Signoria to reflect that he was there on sufferance and that Austria might pounce on the duchy again whenever she chose.

In driving Venice to the conference table an older enemy than the Habsburgs had played its part. The closing months of 1630 saw the whole of northern Italy visited by a major plague epidemic, whose surge was intensified by the ongoing war and its kindred insecurities. Within several cities a belief took hold that somehow the infection was being spread by secret agents as a kind of germ warfare between different states and in Milan, where this induced a general panic, two men were actually arrested and executed for such a crime. To the credit of the Venetian Signoria, any notion of plague-diffusers working out of secret laboratories was quickly talked down, even if some innocent Frenchmen engaged in alchemical experiments found themselves briefly investigated as subversives by the authorities. Altogether more serious was the pandemic's long-term effect on the city's commercial activity. By the summer of 1631, when danger from infection had largely subsided, almost one third of Venice's population had been carried away, a blow from which the lagoon economy, as well as that of the *terraferma* towns, could never properly recover.

Venetians still kept their pride intact. The passing of what would be the last serious epidemic outbreak in the Republic's history was deemed worthy of a commemorative gesture which could stand for eternity and make a permanent change to the city's profile. Proposed was a basilica dedicated to the Blessed Virgin both as patron of the state and as a bringer of health to the ravaged populace. The commission fell to the architect Baldassare Longhena, overseeing a project ampler and more elaborate than anything carried out in Venice for almost a century. Taking some fifty years to accomplish, Santa Maria della Salute, with its ample volutes around a triumphant dome, an Istrian stone exterior, a floor of polychrome marble and lavish Baroque altars, represents a masterstroke in the creation of a dramatic cityscape, a heart-stirring flourish with which to begin or end a journey along the Grand Canal. Perched on a platform composed of over a million wooden piles, the work enshrines a singular kind of permanence that defies the practical or prosaic in both concept and execution.

overleaf   Santa Maria della Salute, Baldassare Longhena's Baroque masterpiece; as viewed by Canaletto in his *Entrance to the Grand Canal*, a classic Venetian *veduta*, c.1730.

A lacerated Venice now focused its attention on whatever remained of the once-great *Stato da Mar*. On the Dalmatian coast, in the wake of Uskok depredations, the harbour of Spalato, modern Split, had been transformed into an entrepôt for eastern merchandise carried overland through the Balkans, with the former spice trade starting to experience something of a revival. The mover and shaker here was that same Daniel Rodriguez who had persuaded the Senate to admit the Marrano Jews and whose enterprise had now helped to fashion a thriving port city out of the ruins of the vast imperial palace raised by the Roman emperor Diocletian in the fourth century CE. Further south in the Adriatic, the seven Ionian islands were major producers of olive oil and chief exporters of currants and raisins to the rest of Europe, with a distinctively Venetian imprint visible in the look and layout of towns and villages on Corfu, Zante and Cephalonia.

For the time being La Serenissima's most daunting foe would leave these imperial possessions unharmed. The Turks had a bigger prize in view, the island of Crete, which ever since Lepanto and the loss of Cyprus the Venetians had transformed into a marine fortress. Its chief cities, Canea, Candia (Heraklion) and Rethymno perfectly bristled with sophisticated defensive installations of the type that culminated, at the century's close, in the great citadels of France and Flanders built by military architect Sebastien de Vauban. Smaller islands girdling Crete itself were given similar fortifications, more than a mere token in each case of the Republic's resolve to keep what it had gained here from Byzantium four hundred years earlier and so laboriously striven to Venetianize in the intervening ages.

Relations between the islanders and their overlords had never been specially harmonious. Spasmodic rebellions against Venetian rule had become a trope in the rhythm of Cretan life and the Signoria had shown itself arrogant, insensitive and at times wantonly oppressive in its lordship over the freedom-loving Cretans. After Byzantium's fall in 1453, however, the island became a refuge for Greek fugitives, witnessing the rise of a rich hybrid culture which fostered scholars and artists. Out of this Veneto-Hellenic world, let us recall, there sprang one of the sixteenth century's most compelling talents, that of Doménikos Theotokópoulos, a young icon painter born in Candia in 1541. Moving first to Venice, thence to Rome, he absorbed influences from Titian and Tintoretto and, later on, Mannerist touches of Parmigianino and Correggio, whose sinuous, elongated figures would offer him a key inspiration. Finally, in his thirties, he journeyed to Spain and settled in Toledo, acquiring the nickname 'El Greco', 'the Greek', by which we now know him. The unmistakable style he developed in the polychromatic beauty of works like *The Burial of Count Orgaz* or *The Opening of the Fifth Seal* has its wellsprings in an intense but always uneasy fusion of late Renaissance Italy with the Cretan school of Orthodox icon painters, nuanced by the sombre austerity of Catholic Spain under the Habsburg kings.

El Greco died in Toledo in 1614, apparently still in touch with his Cretan friends and family, though he had long ago embraced Roman Catholicism. By now it would have been obvious to the islanders that the Turks were patiently awaiting the opportune moment for a full-scale invasion, though reluctant, for the time being, to face a handsomely equipped expeditionary force sent from Venice. The flashpoint arrived in 1644 when, after a Turkish ship carrying pilgrims to Mecca was captured by vessels under the Maltese flag of the Knights Hospitallers, the sultan, Ibrahim I, chose to blame the Venetians, still officially at peace with the Sublime Porte, for the attack. On 25 June 1645, an Ottoman armada landed troops at Canea and began a siege of the town. Frantic attempts by the Signoria to reignite the international Holy League initiatives of the Lepanto era were a failure, the relief expedition reached Canea too late and the Turks gained a firm foothold on the island.

During the next few years they gradually established control over almost every other Venetian stronghold on Crete. The single exception, which has given its name to the lingering struggle carried on over two decades, was the mighty fortress harbour of Candia, 'Candy' as English merchants called it. Somehow, with the help of constant raids on Turkish shipping and forays into the Dardanelles by gallant Venetian naval squadrons, the garrison sustained a heroic resistance, amounting to the longest siege in recorded history. The Republic hastened in the meantime to deploy one of its more dependable resources, diplomacy, in an effort to secure assistance from Christian powers, Catholic or Protestant. Yet as things turned out, a shared faith was no longer the cast-iron guarantee of support that it had been at the time of Lepanto. The pope, the King of Spain and the Austrian emperor each either made their adherence conditional or else pleaded the excuse that they had signed non-aggression pacts with the Porte. King Louis XIV of France, showing form as Europe's most slippery sovereign, made compassionate gestures while happily intriguing with the sultan so as to gain greater mercantile privileges in Constantinople in the wake of a Venetian defeat.

From England La Serenissima felt she might legitimately have hoped for more. In 1650 Charles II, exiled heir to his newly beheaded father, had sent an ambassador to Venice in the shape of the playwright, poet and virtuoso Thomas Killigrew. The Senate was not impressed, either by his inadequate command of Italian or, more broadly, with the suggestion the envoy's presence seemed to carry that they should be backing the losing political cause of English Royalism, something Charles's defeat at Worcester the following year only served to reinforce. So as to finance his mission, Killigrew opened a butcher's shop in the parish of San Fantin, exploiting his ambassadorial tax privileges in the selling of cheap cuts of meat. This embarrassed the Signoria, who dispatched their legal secretary Francesco Busenello – librettist, incidentally, of Monteverdi's opera *L'incoronazione di Poppea* – to give him notice of dismissal. Since it happened that King Charles had already sent Killigrew a letter of recall, face was saved on both sides.

Attempts in the meantime at persuading Oliver Cromwell, then ruling Britain as Lord Protector, to join the struggle against the Turks got no further than a few well-meaning words. To Venice's ambassador Giovanni Sagredo it quickly became obvious that Cromwell, whatever his characteristic claim, during their interview, to have 'frequently felt the pricks and goads of zeal for the service of God', was rather more responsive to pressures from the anxious merchants of London's Levant Company, keen not to lose flourishing markets in Aleppo and Istanbul. When, in 1660, King Charles was restored, things proved scarcely more promising. Strapped for cash, the king, whose fleet was being readied for wars with the Dutch, simply could not afford a Mediterranean expedition and found Venetian overtures wearisome. His naval secretary, the diarist Samuel Pepys, derided the gondolas – 'ridiculous gundilows' – sent as a present to the king and launched on the pond in St James's Park.

And yet Venice, characteristically dogged in the face of mounting adversity, went on daring to hope that her defence of Candia would become a beacon of inspiration for the Christian world. The Turks, after all, under the active leadership of a new grand vizier in Istanbul, Ahmed Köprülü, had begun to present a graver threat to the states along her land borders in eastern Europe. Morale in the Cretan garrison, on the other hand, had improved with the appointment of a new and genuinely capable commander, Francesco Morosini, a hardened campaigner who had seen service on land and sea and was passionately committed to the Republic. His acceptance of the post was unwavering. 'Always disdainful of danger, taking risks and valuing honour, I have had the happiness of finding myself with sword in hand on more than 200 occasions,' he told the Senate.

Morosini was born into one of Venice's most ancient and illustrious families, whose members had included an elector of the very first doge, Orso Ipato, and three more of whom had themselves been appointed to the office. His childhood had been scarred by a traumatic episode which took place on the River Brenta during the annual summer *villeggiatura*. Out boating, his mother Maria Priuli fell into the water and drowned. It was rumoured afterwards that little Francesco's father, Pietro Morosini, who had married the rich heiress for her money, either pushed her under or else failed to make sufficient efforts to drag her to the riverbank. The boy, who had witnessed the whole episode, seems to have withdrawn thereafter from any kind of emotional engagement, dedicating himself to a career in the armed services as a naval officer and an army colonel and remaining unmarried throughout his long life. His sole attachment, other than to Venice and the profession of arms, was to his pet cat Nini, whom he carried with him on all his campaigns and whose mummified body, together with that of a rat she caught, is nowadays exhibited beside Morosini's leather buff coat in the Museo Correr.

Once instated as captain-general of Venetian forces in and around Candia, the new supremo reorganized the garrison and planned a series of mostly successful sorties that emboldened him to prepare an attack on Canea with a view to recovering the town. Morosini was not helped, while finding his feet at this stage, either by the attitude of the Grand Council, headed by Doge Domenico Contarini, which demanded a continuing narrative of triumphs and victories to feed the Venetian public, or by the bickering that went on among various government departments. At one point he was subjected to an ignominious inquiry into his claims for expenditure on armaments, at another he was accused of overcaution in deploying his various forces. When foreign reinforcements were eventually forthcoming, the Captain-General needed all his resources of tact and management skill to establish an effective level of operational harmony among the different naval squadrons and bodies of troops. The Signoria was in any case critical of Morosini's favoured strategy, an amphibious warfare using naval support to undertake surprise troop landings along the Cretan coast, so that in the end it was only his unshakeable resolve in sustaining Candia's resistance that kept the city from falling to the Ottomans earlier than it did.

overleaf A view of the fortress harbour of Candia under siege by the Ottomans. From 1645 the Turks took control of nearly every Venetian possession on Crete, but Candia (modern Heraklion) held out until 1669.

A belated intervention by combined French and papal forces during the autumn of 1668 made little difference to what the Captain-General saw coming in the shape of an unavoidable surrender. 'The condition of this town of Candia', noted a French officer, 'was a dreadful sight: its streets were littered with cannonballs, bullets and fragments of shot. Not a church, not a single building but was riddled with holes or reduced to rubble. The houses had become wretched hovels, the stench everywhere was sickening and all around lay dead and rotting bodies.' After a last disastrous sortie on 13 May 1669, Morosini offered surrender terms to the Turkish commander, with the aim of salvaging any slightest advantage possible for the Venetian Republic. Thus it was agreed that surviving troops and any citizens who wished could leave on Venetian vessels, while Venice was allowed to retain its forts on the island of Gravosa at Crete's north-western tip. The defeated force was also permitted to remove any guns not in place at the start of the war

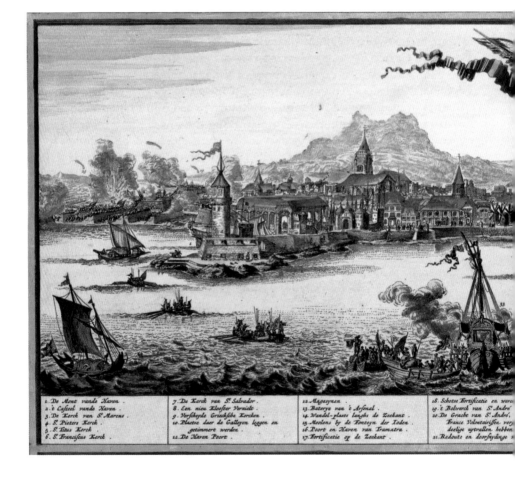

twenty-two years earlier. In the overall character of the truce there is a strong sense that Ahmed Köprülü's magnanimity was meant as a tribute to an adversary for whom he had developed a genuine respect.

None of this was likely to cut much ice with the Senate. The loss of Crete was the bitterest of wounds to La Serenissima's self-esteem. Costing over 4 million ducats and partly paid for by allowing nouveau-riche merchants to buy themselves a coveted place in the aristocratic Golden Book, the War of Candia was the most expensive operation of its kind undertaken by the Republic. Thirty thousand Venetian troops had perished, either of wounds or disease, including nearly three hundred patricians, amounting to about a quarter of the Grand Council. Perhaps not surprisingly, Francesco Morosini was greeted, on returning to Venice, with a mixture of furious recrimination and glum acceptance that he had done the best he could under the circumstances. As so often happens, an impeachment process was launched, with his

339

inveterate critic Antonio Correr portraying the Captain-General's actions as dishonourable, contemptible, those of 'a violator of his country's laws and a usurper of sovereign power'. Morosini's defence was undertaken by Giovanni Sagredo, the same ambassador who had formerly sought to win support from Oliver Cromwell. He took the brief, he said, 'so that the hangman should not kill him whom so many thousands of Turks had spared'. By the end of 1670 Morosini, following an investigation evidently more focused on shielding the patrician caste from blame and opprobrium than getting at the truth, was pronounced innocent by the State Inquisitors.

Venice, nursing its injuries from the war, had certainly not finished with the Turks. Emboldened by their Cretan conquest, the latter had carried forward campaigns in the Ukraine, Poland and Lithuania, and the leadership of Ahmed Köprülü's brother Kara Mustafa Pasha brought their armies to the gates of Vienna. Here at last, on 12 September 1683, Ottoman forces were decisively overwhelmed by the Polish king Jan Sobieski and Emperor Leopold I of Austria, a victory that not only marked the first stage in removing a threat to the Christian world launched over a century earlier but awoke fresh longings in Venice to avenge the loss of Crete. The proposed Holy League spurned twenty years earlier suddenly assumed a genuine urgency, driven on as it was by the active engagement of a strong-willed pope in the shape of Innocent XI. It took some months for his envoys, in the wake of Jan Sobieski's success, to persuade the Grand Council but further pressure was added by Emperor Leopold and a treaty of alliance was concluded by the four powers in 1684.

The natural choice as commander of Venetian forces was Francesco Morosini, who had spent the past few years quietly serving the state as a regional magistrate in Friuli. He resisted all suggestions that his first duty should be to recapture Crete. It had become obvious that Ottoman military power in the Balkans had overextended itself and that any effective strike ought to aim at the ill-defended strongholds of Epirus and the Peloponnese, forts which Venice herself had built and held until Sultan Mehmet's conquest two centuries earlier. With an army made up substantially of loyal Dalmatian regiments and troops hired from the Protestant dukedoms of north Germany, the Captain-General (it was Morosini's third such appointment) set off for the Ionian islands to launch his first momentous expedition into northern Greece.

Here over the next two years he could put into practice those tactics earlier frustrated in Crete by the Signoria's ill-timed interference. Swift and efficient naval landings, well-managed infantry attacks, artillery support directed by expert gunners, all brought desired results. Preveza fell, followed by the great Venetian-designed citadel at Koroni and the fortress of Kalamata. At Igoumenitsa, as Morosini reported in one of his daily dispatches to the doge, 'the enemy fled from their defences in cowardly fashion up the nearby mountain slopes. Our determination, protected by God's omnipotent hand, at length saw the venerable conquering flags of Your Serenity displayed in triumph on the infidel walls.' By the summer of 1686 almost the entire Peloponnese, including the key city of Nafplion – called Napoli di Romania by the Venetians – was in the hands of La Serenissima.

Aware as he always was of the campaign's historic significance for Venice and of that 'legacy' element it enshrined, Morosini would have wished to move on towards the real prize represented by Evvia, that Negroponte whose loss in 1470 was still a burning affront to the Republic's honour. He was persuaded instead to focus on the small, thinly-peopled town of Athens, where the Turks had concentrated their defence within the Acropolis atop its lofty crag. Here the magnificent Parthenon had been turned into a refuge for their womenfolk, while one end of the former temple was being used as a powder magazine. Morosini's Swedish artillery commander, Count Otto Wilhelm von Königsmarck, had ordered a gun battery of six cannon into position to pound the fortress into surrender and on 26 September 1687, 'we were happy to see one of these achieve a lucky hit, setting light to a goodly store of gunpowder'. The unfortunate Turkish women were all killed in the blast, which blew the roof off the building and started a fire that ravaged the whole area 'with notable damage and grievous effects'. These included dislodging the splendid carved metopes of the Doric frieze decorating the space between the triglyphs above the Parthenon's colonnade. Hence Lord Elgin, a century later, was able to buy whatever of these had not already been used for construction work elsewhere or ground down for mortar, and remove them to London, where they are currently on view in the British Museum.

Morosini prided himself that 'the renowned and illustrious fortress of Athens has fallen into Your Serenities' possession, along with its famous city, adorned with noteworthy buildings and the ancient vestiges of history and learning'. By the end of 1688 the Ottomans were in thorough disarray, following crushing defeats in Hungary and their conspicuous failure to hold on in the Peloponnese. That autumn a revolt broke out in Constantinople, Sultan Mehmet IV was deposed by his Janissaries and the first tentative peace feelers were extended by Grand Vizier Bekri Mustafa. Venice, cock-a-hoop with her

recent victories, saw no reason for now to accept these. When Doge Marcantonio Giustinian died that same year, there was really only one obvious candidate for his vacant office. Francesco Morosini was happy to accept the Grand Council's unanimous vote, while remaining on manoeuvres in the Morea for another eighteen months before making a triumphal return to Venice in January 1690.

The old man, aged almost seventy-one, was loaded with honours, including the exceptional tribute, from Pope Alexander VIII, of the ceremonial baton and decorated bonnet 'with which our predecessors, the Roman pontiffs, have been accustomed to distinguish famous champions'. While the Senate conferred on him the title of *Il Peloponnesiaco*, a bronze bust of the Captain-General was commissioned from the sculptor Filippo Parodi, to be placed in the armoury of Palazzo Ducale, and after the doge's death a triumphal arch in his memory was raised inside the Sala dello Scrutinio. Significantly, neither of these artistic tributes was made accessible to ordinary Venetian citizens. Memories of ducal vainglory on the part of a Falier or a Foscari, peacocking in front of the commonalty, were still powerful.

Not that there was any real danger of the elderly doge seeking to outrage the susceptibilities of a Venetian state whose devoted servant he had been for the whole of his life. If he had a 'significant other', apart from the Nini the cat, it was La Serenissima. For her dignity and standing in the world Morosini had risked his safety, his military reputation and his personal honour and he was happy to do so again. In 1692 he received for a fourth time the title of *Capitano Generale da Mar*, being required on this occasion formally to confer the office, as doge, on himself. A handsome new galley was duly fitted out in the Arsenale, equipped with 'whatever may seem decent and decorous for His Serenity', and on 24 May 1693, following a solemn mass 'in the ducal church of our protector Saint Mark', off he went to war once again, in no very good state of health. A lingering fever set in and from Nafplion, early the following year, Morosini sent a deeply moving deathbed letter to the Senate. 'With pious humility of heart,' it concludes, 'we have received the Holy Eucharist, resigned to God's will. Informing Your Excellencies of the sickly state to which we have been reduced, we beg you to understand that we experience no other discomfort than that of not having been able to serve the Republic as well as we desired or it deserved.'

News of his death on 6 January 1694 reached Venice a few weeks later and grief was universal. Yet towards this last and greatest of Venetian paladins, one nurtured at home rather than a hired mercenary, the

The warrior doge Francesco Morosini, leader of *La Serenissima's* forces on land and sea, in a portrait by Bartolomeo Nazari.

state which owed him so much appeared, from one aspect, inflexibly mean. Morosini had wanted to raise for himself a suitably imposing monument, either in the Gothic church of the Augustinians at Santo Stefano or in his parish church of San Vidal. While the Barbaro family, his old enemies and rivals, had been allowed to plaster the façade of Santa Maria del Giglio with effigies of themselves in full-bottomed periwigs and senatorial togas, this was on a basis of having made substantial donations to the church. In Morosini's case the Senate remained wary of turning its servants, however 'comely and pleasant in their lives' they might have been, into heroes, thus aggrandizing the feats of one patrician family at the expense of another's. Hence his memorial, apart from those reserved tributes in Palazzo Ducale mentioned earlier, is a simple decorated bronze roundel set into the nave floor at Santo Stefano, all too easily ignored by visitors to the church.

Il Peloponnesiaco had nevertheless served Venice well. The Turks, further shaken by news of the adherence of Tsar Peter I of Russia, 'Peter the Great', and Elector Friedrich August of Saxony, 'Augustus the Strong', to the Holy League, were brought at length to the conference table. Forty years of conflict were ended for now by a treaty signed on 26 January 1699 at Karlowitz (Karlocza) on the estuary of the Danube, which transferred the Morea in its entirety to Venice as well as establishing the Republic's lordship over the entire Ionian archipelago, even if the sultan managed to retain control over those very areas of central Greece, including Athens, where Morosini had earlier validated his military prowess. For the present, nevertheless, La Serenissima could resume her role as a Mediterranean imperial power with – who could tell? – the possibility, at some not very distant date, of regaining Negroponte and ousting the Ottomans from Crete.

This was not to be. Lacking both in realism and nuance, the Signoria fell on its suddenly enlarged Greek empire with a conspicuously heavy hand, whether in the form of an insensitive engagement with the Greek clergy in communities across the Morea or in suffocating local enterprise with bureaucratic controls and increased tax burdens. Swiftly enough a Venetian presence among the Greeks became even more distasteful than that of the Turks had been and the suspicion arose that at any moment a swarm of Franciscans and Capuchins would arrive to enforce Catholicism among a Christian population for whom Orthodoxy meant national identity as much as religion. Thus in 1714, when Sultan Ahmed trumped up a pretext for reopening the war, there was little enthusiasm for resistance as, one after another, the great citadels at Nafplion, Corinth and Methoni surrendered and the islands of Tinos and Aegina were overrun. Only on Corfu were the Turks at last driven back, largely by the tenacity and military genius of the German *condottiero* Mathias Johann von der Schulenburg, taking a leaf or two from Morosini's book during a long Turkish siege which he was able to round off through a masterly sortie, aided by the hand of God in the form of a tornado that devastated the Ottoman galleys in the harbour of Kerkyra. Though Venice's own navy had belatedly managed to salvage something of honour for the Republic with victories in the Aegean, a peace settlement in 1718 left the Peloponnese in the sultan's hands once more and the last hurrah of imperial Venice died away.

Irrepressible during all this time, on the other hand, was the exuberant noise made by opera. By the end of the seventeenth century the number of Venetian theatres was around a dozen, while several others flourished briefly before straitened finances or conflagration shut them down. A special new government department, the *Magistrato alle Pompe*, was formed by the Council of Ten to supervise theatrical managements, ticket prices, payment of artists and the dress and conduct of audiences. Wars might rage beyond the lagoons, the state's honour and credit might hang in the balance, but the ideal world of the Venetian lyric stage could still thrive on a willing suspension of disbelief, as goddesses flew through the air, princely palaces changed places with enchanted forests in grand transformation scenes and a happy ending was always guaranteed.

Censors monitored each libretto carefully to ensure it contained nothing which outraged public decency and Catholic dogma or undermined the dignity of the governing class. Writers were at pains to point out that not everything in the stories represented was true to the facts, and the formula '*Il resto si finge*', 'the rest is made up', was added to the introduction of many a printed text. Nevertheless a shrewd observer might have detected some analogies between so-called fiction and contemporary actuality. The opera John Evelyn and his friends attended in 1645 was *Ercole in Lidia*, based on the Greek myth which tells of Hercules, the mighty champion and warrior, being seduced by the Asian queen Omphale, who made him give up his sword and shield, dress himself in women's clothes and take to the female arts of weaving and embroidery. Would some of the audience have seen this as a metaphor for what was about to happen – or what, indeed, was already happening – to the once-proud Republic of the Lion?

16

WHERE JOY
RESIDES

In his mock-epic poem *The Dunciad* the poet Alexander Pope satirizes
the dullness and mediocrity of cultural life in the eighteenth-century
England of his day. The last and most scarifying of its four books, a
vision of encroaching darkness and anarchy as the lights of art, science
and morality all flicker out, includes a vignette of a young nobleman
setting off on the Grand Tour of Europe, which at that period formed
the culminating phase of an aristocratic education. The gilded youth
visits Paris,

> where the Seine, obsequious as she runs,
> Pours at great Bourbon's feet her silken sons,

goes to Rome,

> Vain of Italian Arts, Italian Souls

and ends his tour in Venice,

> chief her shrine where naked Venus keeps,
>   And Cupids ride the Lion of the Deeps;
> Where, eas'd of Fleets, the Adriatic main
>   Wafts the smooth Eunuch and enamour'd swain.

By the time Pope published his final version of *The Dunciad* in
1742, most of its readers would have savoured the deftness with which
the writer summed up, in a mere four lines, what everybody knew had
happened to Venice during the past half-century since the war with
the Turks in Greece and the two treaties of Karlowitz and Passarowitz.
Though the Republic still sent its ambassadors to European courts,
though Venetian diplomats had lent their skills to negotiating the
Treaty of Utrecht in 1712, though La Serenissima could still mount the

most splendid of shows and pageants for distinguished guests visiting the city – a Danish king, a Saxon prince, a Russian grand duke – the performance did nothing to obscure the reality of advancing decline and political insignificance. Her role was now that of a neutral spectator as the great powers, France, Spain, Austria, Prussia and Britain, renewed their struggles for predominance both in Europe and across the wider theatres of global empire. For seventy years at least, the Most Serene Republic had little choice but to enjoy a genuine serenity, one forced on her by the fact of being marginalized or ignored by bigger players on the world stage, depending as she increasingly did on their indulgence and civility.

The real problem for Venice was the familiar one among great nations reluctant to come to terms with their decay, a profound complacency rooted in the sense that its constitutional settlement was still the envy of Europe and that its former imperial authority somehow still carried a certain resonance, even if a physical reach across the eastern Mediterranean had notably shrunk during the past hundred years. The city itself still prospered. Though France, under Louis XIV's enterprising chief minister Jean-Baptiste Colbert, had managed, via bribery and industrial espionage, to steal the specialist technology behind glass-blowing on the island of Murano and the art of lace-making on neighbouring Burano, there was still a busy textile trade and silk-weaving flourished on the mainland. Fewer ships might now have been assembled in the yards and workshops of the Arsenale, but seaborne traffic was carried on, the port thriving and merchants still clinching deals on the Rialto and the Riva degli Schiavoni.

What the Republic lacked most sorely was an adequately empowered bourgeoisie to challenge the sclerotic conservatism and narrowness of vision among the patriciate. The latter relied mostly on rents from their landed estates, in whose practical management they took far too little interest. The spirited ruralism of Alvise Cornaro and Camillo Tarello was a distant memory. There were agricultural academies in the Veneto towns, earnestly studying new kinds of animal husbandry and soil economy, but little of this attracted serious interest from Golden Book landlords happy to let old, wasteful farming practices continue as long as a summer at the villa remained an annual fixture. Country houses themselves continued to be built and adorned, works on a grand scale like Villa Loschi Zileri outside Vicenza, with its 'English park' and stuccoed atrium frescoed by Tiepolo, the austerely classical Villa Pompei Carlotti near Verona or, most ostentatious of them all,

Villa Pisani at Stra, raised as a kind of Versailles on the Brenta by Alvise Pisani to celebrate his election as doge in 1735.

Any serious questioning of the status quo in Venetian government and society would need to come from within that very same oligarchy which chose to spend its money on these rustic pleasure-domes, but such constructive reaction was destined to arrive far too late for it to do any real good. The calm of Venice's eighteenth century muffled an interior crisis among the patrician class that gathered momentum with succeeding decades. Too many of the 'good families' in the Golden Book, the Barbarigo, Mocenigo and Pasqualigo, the Contarini, Foscarini and Querini, the Zen, the Sten, the Tron and their ilk, in all their historic tribal branches, found themselves with too little money and not enough to do. All the offices of state, whether in the lagoon, on the *terraferma*, or across whatever might remain of the Stato da Mar, the governorships, captaincies, magistracies and assessorships would barely furnish enough to support a grand lifestyle or, more important, to maintain a family. A mushrooming echelon of unmarried aristocracy, the younger brothers and sisters of a designated heir to this or that great house, often became priests or nuns *faute de mieux* or else ended up among the *barnabotti*, those noble families living in genteel poverty in accommodation provided for them by the Republic in the area around the church of San Barnaba on Dorsoduro.

What such a situation inevitably encouraged in Venice was an atmosphere, palpable enough to foreign visitors, of calculated triviality, a sense that serious initiatives and major political concerns had to all intents and purposes evaporated in a society most of which enjoyed no active share in the government. Pope's ironic assessment in *The Dunciad* proved strikingly accurate. 'The Lion of the Deeps' no longer roared, 'the Adriatic main' belonged to La Serenissima mostly as a diplomatic courtesy and the rhythms of the city were governed largely by ceremony of various kinds. The lagoon had indeed become 'her shrine where naked Venus keeps', a realm of easy erotic indulgence and sensual amusement. Not for nothing did Venice's carnival season, heralding the beginning of Lent, somehow seem livelier, more abandoned in its hedonism than ever before.

The figure most powerfully identified with this nowadays perhaps rather too hackneyed image of eighteenth-century Venice as Europe's seaside fun palace, an amalgam of Xanadu, Sodom and Las Vegas, is the always controversial Giacomo Casanova. Born in 1725 to two opera dancers from the San Samuele theatre, he made a career for himself as

overleaf The arrival of the French ambassador Henri-Charles Arnauld de Pomponne at the Palazzo Ducale, 1705; by Luca Carlevarijs, pioneer of the cityscape or *veduta*.

a fixer, gambler, go-between and charlatan which is almost impossible to characterize. This took him to almost every great city in Europe, introducing him to figures as various as Empress Catherine of Russia, Wolfgang Amadeus Mozart and Benjamin Franklin. On the way he tried his hand as an actor, a priest, an orchestral violinist, a diplomat and a spy. He fought a duel in Poland, opened a silk factory in Paris, became a freemason, flirted with Frederick the Great, embarked on a translation of the *Iliad* and collaborated with Lorenzo da Ponte on the libretto of *Don Giovanni*. While the European *grand monde* was captivated by this restless creature, its governments and their officials were less easily charmed and Casanova found himself 'moved on' most inopportunely at different phases of a life which was already, through his own choice, that of a supremely gifted vagabond.

Attempts to keep him under surveillance, on the other hand, were singularly unsuccessful. The most famous of these, his incarceration in the prison next to Palazzo Ducale for 'public outrages against the holy religion', failed the more spectacularly because his escape, risking life and limb in a midnight scramble over the roofs of Venice, was something nobody had ever contrived before. It was an exploit he revisited in the voluminous memoirs composed at the end of his life, having already published a separate account of the episode and refined its details with frequent retelling.

The leitmotif in Casanova's memoirs – most of which there is really no adequate reason for us to doubt – was his genuine fondness for the company of women. Though his name is synonymous with that of a seducer and sexual athlete, and while his contribution to Da Ponte's *Don Giovanni* libretto is sometimes taken for professional input, he was as unlike the wicked, cynical 'Trickster of Seville' as we could possibly imagine. Women cherished his company because he was clearly fascinated by their emotional lives, by the nature and quality of their expressive faculties and depth of response in comparison with those of his own sex. Again and again while reading the memoirs we find indications that Casanova preferred female society to that of men, creatures who often bored, irritated or merely frustrated him through the narrowness of their sensitivities when contrasted with those of women.

Casanova's Venice was a densely peopled planet, something painters of this period never allow us to forget. The city at this time shakes off its previous pictorial incarnation as an occasional backdrop to portraits or religious scenes, becoming instead the subject in view, chief focus of attention as a built environment whose inhabitants do rather more than simply lend scale to palaces, churches, a bridge or a canal. Just as landscape painting had evolved in northern Europe in the form of an independent genre, so a uniquely Venetian equivalent, the urban *veduta* – 'prospect' – began emerging, to make a powerful impact on contemporary taste and connoisseurship, circulated as it easily was through collections of engravings made by its chief exponents.

Leading the way was Luca Carlevarijs, a mathematician from Udine for whom painting probably began as a sideline. His *Fabriche e Vedute di Venezia*, published in 1703, were intended, some art historians believe, to enshrine a political statement at a time when the Serene Republic was trying, not always effectively, to sustain her neutrality during the ongoing War of the Spanish Succession. The hundred or so engravings of the *Fabriche*, enormously successful in their various editions, emphasized what really mattered to the Signoria, the promotion of an image of substance, grandeur and permanence in Venice's structures of brick and marble, underlining that sturdy singularity in the city's fashioning which the ephemeral vicissitudes of politics could never destroy. 'He created works unequalled in their skill,' says a contemporary of Carlevarijs, 'in the elegant movement of the figures, in their novel grouping, in the beauty of the open air and gleaming waters.' The people in these prints – two women and a little boy walking to church, boatmen heaving a load onto the quay, carpenters at work in a *squero*, a street vendor with his basket – have as much to say, from this aspect, as the splendid marble façades of Palazzo Balbi, the Scuola di San Rocco or San Giorgio Maggiore in front of which they move. These glimpses of Venice are about La Serenissima's continuity and endurance as much as anything else.

As a painter, the first truly gifted *vedutista*, Carlevarijs was moved to celebrate the pomp and ceremony of the Venetian state as well as its multitudinous vitality. The French ambassador Henri-Charles Arnauld de Pomponne arrives at Palazzo Ducale in 1705 in a scene that realistically flings together the Republic's need to be taken seriously as an Italian power in the land with a less colourful but similarly major imperative, that of Venice still very much open for business. Thus the envoy's gilded barge in the left foreground, where one of its oarsmen has stripped off to cool down, is moored alongside jostling gondolas and an array of cargo boats, their sails furled, their decks shaded by tarpaulins from the June sunlight. Crowds have gathered outside the palace and on its balconies to watch Arnauld, with his handsomely garbed suite, enter the building, but in the background, where the artist, helped maybe by a camera obscura, has deployed a powerful depth of field, the ordinary bustle of Venetian life proceeds unconcerned.

Carlevarijs's inspiration – he was also a gifted landscape painter and a creator of so-called *capricci*, fantasy fusions of the manmade and the natural in scenic juxtaposition – transmitted itself to a rising generation of Venetian artists led by his near-contemporary Marco Ricci and the younger, more impressionistic talent of Michele Marieschi. There was one painter, however, whose acute eye for rhythm and tonality in the daily prospect along the city's canals and across its open spaces would render him the acknowledged master of this entire genre. It is probably just a legend that asks us to believe that the skills of Antonio Canal, known to us as Canaletto, caused Luca Carlevarijs such consuming envy that he dropped dead of a heart attack, but we can understand how such a story might have gained hold. The son of an operatic stage designer, Canaletto focused his theatrical training on the actuality of that Venice which surrounded him. 'His excellence lies in painting things which fall immediately under his eyes', noted an expatriate English observer in commendation of his talent. Canaletto's treatment of the Venetian scene is more bright-hued, sophisticated and fluent than that of Carlevarijs, but he shares the older artist's command of detail in the placing of figures, their connexion to one another and their relationship to the surfaces of water and stone over which they move. He is essentially a narrator, dispensing his own recorded truth as a context for the Venetian story, always realistic but never pedantically exact, since once he had sketched the master drawing of a particular view he seems not to have wanted to alter this, whatever changes might later be carried out on the principal buildings featured. Sharp contrast between areas of light and shadow in the townscape plays a significant role, as does the cloud conformation in the sky above it. And we are never alone. In *The Stonemason's Yard*, for example, the artisan hammering at a block of marble has his back turned as his wife reproves their little son who has fallen over, while another child demurely watches at a distance. Elsewhere, in a view from Campo San Vio down the Grand Canal towards the Salute, a ferryman in scarlet breeches brings his gondola to the landing steps while an old man stalks, hunched and purposeful, past a couple gossiping nearby.

During the War of the Austrian Succession (1740–48) Canaletto's business in Venice was badly hit, prompting him to set off for England, encouraged by his devoted patron, the British consul Joseph Smith. Here he spent nearly a decade, training a memorably Venetian glance on London and on several country houses (most notably Warwick Castle) belonging to admirers of his work. 'Canaletti', as they called him, had his reputation confirmed via this clientele, meaning that his particular glance at Venice has since set a benchmark against which visitors over three centuries have tested their visual experience of the city.

What we witness in eighteenth-century Venice is a transformation, leisurely but palpable, of a predominantly commercial metropolis into a tourist destination. Pope's young sprig of the nobility in *The Dunciad* was among an affluent international crowd flocking to the lagoon in search of pleasure among theatres, casinos, brothels, shops and artists' studios. Its presence, for some, was too noisily emphatic. Mary Wortley Montagu for example, settling here in 1739, bewailed the number of 'boys and governors' – young gentlemen and their tutors in the process of making the Grand Tour. 'Inundations of them broke in upon us this carnival and my apartment must be their refuge... I look on them as the greatest blockheads in nature; and, to say truth, the compound of booby and *petit maitre* makes up a very odd sort of animal.' The following year we find her complaining yet more loudly of 'this town being at present infested with English, who torment me as much as the frogs and lice did the palace of Pharaoh'.

Other tourists managed to steer clear of such society. Young Duke Friedrich Franz of Anhalt-Dessau, travelling to Venice with his cultural mentor, the architect Friedrich Wilhelm von Erdmannsdorff, in 1765, took serious stock of Venetian buildings and decorative styles before returning to Germany. There, on his estate at Wörlitz, he raised his own version of a Palladian villa, in which he created a charming series of guest suites whose décor evoked the different Italian locations that had inspired him, Venice among them. Another German visitor, the poet and dramatist Johann Wolfgang von Goethe, arriving in 1786, was equally enthralled by Palladio, of whom he wrote, 'There is something godlike in his talent, comparable to the power of a great poet, someone who, from worlds of truth and falsehood, shapes another universe whose borrowed existence charms us.' Elsewhere Goethe beautifully and justly notes that anyone entering one of Palladio's buildings immediately feels uplifted, as if the work itself brought out the best in those lucky enough to find themselves there.

Goethe's profound engagement with the totality of Venetian experience – he was among the first foreign travellers to observe the problematic relationship between the city and its maritime environment – made him interested in getting to hear the legendary antiphonal

overleaf The Stonemason's Yard, by Canaletto, *c.*1725.
The open space in the foreground is the Campo San Vidal, while the façade of the Scuola Grande della Carità can be seen across the Grand Canal.

singing of the gondoliers chanting stanzas from Torquato Tasso's great Renaissance epic poem *Gerusalemme liberata* to one another along the canals. By this time the custom was starting to die out, but the poet was lucky enough to meet two boatmen who could oblige with a performance, and extremely moving he found this. 'The sound of their distant voices was quite extraordinary, a kind of lament, only without anything sad in it, and I was moved to tears.' The presence of a full moon on a mild October evening may have helped, but this was clearly an unforgettable moment. 'The simple melody', he wrote, 'is the cry of a lonely human being flung into the wide world until it strikes the ear of someone else, similarly alone, who can be moved to answer it.'

The gondoliers' chant was made use of in several sonatas by the violin virtuoso Giuseppe Tartini, born a Venetian subject in the Istrian port of Pirano (Piran in modern Slovenia) and spending most of his career in Padua. Music was what drew so many travellers to Venice at this period. The opera houses continued to showcase those Italian singing stars who went on to make their fortunes in courts and capitals across Europe, so that talent-spotting impresarios and composers took their places in the audience each season. When the musicologist Dr Charles Burney arrived here in 1770, it was with 'very sanguine expectations from this city with regard to the music of past times as well as the present'. He soon found that 'my expectations were well grounded'. Voices and instruments reverberated along streets and canals. If the Tasso recitations were fast becoming a lost art, the gondoliers could sing plenty of anything else while plying the oar, every open space seemed full of itinerant performers during the day, while in the evening the whole city was vibrant with music. 'Harmony prevails in every part', says Burney. 'If two of the common people walk together arm in arm, they are always singing and seem to converse in song.' He was enchanted, one warm August night, to find a barge on the Grand Canal carrying an entire orchestra, including 'horns, bases, and a kettle-drum', accompanying 'a pretty good tenor voice', intended as 'a piece of gallantry at the expense of an *inamorato* in order to serenade his mistress'. Whether this had the desired effect Burney feels unqualified to say, but 'the symphonies seemed to me to be admirable, full of fancy, full of fire'.

Like every music-lover on a trip to Venice at this time, he was enthralled by the talents assembled in the orchestras of the charitable *ospedali* of the Mendicanti, the Incurabili and the Pietà. These were orphanages for girls, maintained at state expense and essentially conservatoires where the children, as well as being given a good basic education, were taught singing and offered practical music tuition by professional instrumentalists. The French traveller Charles de Brosses was suitably impressed by their versatility. 'The largest instrument of music holds no terror for them. They are treated like nuns... I can assure you there is nothing more charming than to see a young and pretty nun dressed in white with a bunch of pomegranate flowers in her hair, conducting the orchestra and beating time with great care and precision.' Some of the era's finest composers, including Baldassare Galuppi, born on the lagoon island of Burano, and the immigrant German Johann Adolf Hasse, buried in the church of San Marcuola, became music directors at these prestigious institutions, where their artistry was richly complemented by the prowess of those for whom they wrote.

The master who seems to have drawn most from his orphan pupils in the way of skill and expressiveness was Charles de Brosses's friend Antonio Vivaldi, 'a topping fellow in those days', as Burney puts it, and now regarded as one of the Baroque's most original creative spirits. *Il Prete Rosso*, 'the red-haired priest', kept a mistress and wrote operas for Venetian theatres as well as composing music for the Ospedale della Pietà. He revolutionized the concerto form and clothed everything from a cantata, a psalm setting or an oratorio to solo sonatas or works for mixed chamber ensemble in his unique and unmistakable sound world. For many listeners this has a hauntingly local register to it, as if encapsulating the very air, light and water of the lagoon. Vivaldi's professional career, however, was a chequered affair, culminating in his decision, in 1740, to quit Venice for Vienna, where he hoped to direct the opera season at the Theater am Kärntnertor. For a variety of reasons the move came to nothing and the composer died in modest circumstances the following year.

Tempting Venetian 'creatives' away from their native soil was nothing new. Painters were as susceptible as musicians to the offer of a prestigious commission from a foreign enthusiast and proved ready, as in the case of Canaletto, to travel the necessary distance in search of this. Most famous and triumphantly successful of all La Serenissima's image-makers at this time was Giambattista Tiepolo, long-lived, pro-ductive, precocious, a virtuoso gifted as a draftsman and colourist, the acknowledged master of grand designs in fresco on a church ceiling, in the halls and saloons of a piazza or on the walls of a country villa. Born in Venice in 1692, the son of a ship chandler in the parish of San Pietro in Castello, he swiftly acquired the grand manner of Renaissance artists like Veronese and Tintoretto while making it very much his own through touches of playfulness, fantasy and romance. He has been called 'operatic' on account of his lavish, expansive treatment of scenes and characters in the decorative fresco cycles he painted, such as the opulent episodes from the story of Antony and Cleopatra in Palazzo Labia or the dramatic series devised for Villa Valmarana outside Vicenza. The term is somewhat misapplied, since opera at this period, serious or comic, had become a good deal more intimate or austere in its proportions when compared with the visual amplitude of Tiepolo at his most assertive and idiosyncratic.

Resistless in its impact, Tiepolo's work was coveted abroad, but he was a shrewd businessman – his sister Eugenia expressly declared in her will that she was leaving him nothing because he had quite enough already – and drove a hard bargain. Late in his career, nevertheless, he accepted an invitation to fresco the staircase and grand saloon, the Kaisersaal, of the Residenz of the Prince Bishop of Würzburg, Karl Philipp von Greiffenklau, creating in the process one of the true masterworks of Rococo art, symphonic rather than operatic in the satisfying grace and deftness of the design adorning each of the two spaces that awaited him. Indefatigable even at what was then the fairly advanced age of sixty, Tiepolo returned to an impressive scatter of commissions in Venice before a personal invitation to Madrid from King Carlos III of Spain sent him on his travels again. This time he chose to linger after his grand ceiling in the newly built Palacio Real was finished, dying while still at work on a sequence of altarpieces conceived in a more sombre, emotionally intense idiom than he had used in earlier paintings.

Though a gifted caricaturist and fond of making on-the-spot drawings of details from the locations where he worked, Tiepolo is seldom interested in giving us the flavour of that everyday Venice which surrounds him. This is the realm, instead, of Pietro Longhi, neither a great painter nor an especially good one, but fascinated enough by the Venetian scene to have registered it in the kind of affectionate detail which seems positively to invite the viewer to join the company portrayed on canvas. Thus we sit down to a card game, go duck-shooting in the lagoon, kneel at confession with a priest, hurry to gawp at novelties such as an Irish giant or an African rhinoceros, listen to a concert or pay a visit while wearing the *bauta*, that classic eighteenth-century Venetian ensemble made up of a black tricorn hat, a white mask and the long black cloak known as a *domino*. What arrests Longhi's eye is the normality of all this, the plain fact of these people caught in the process of living their daily lives, indulging their

The Charlatan (1757), by Pietro Longhi, a painter who brought an observant eye to his depictions of members of Venetian patrician society as they go about their daily business.

leisure among a scatter of children, friends, servants and dogs. Longhi is an observer rather than a satirist or critic, yet by the same token a highly plausible mediator between us and the social world he explores, with its unquenchable appetite for novelty and amusement, as skilful an operator, in his way, as the puppeteer pulling the strings in the marionette show which figures on one of his canvases.

If the stream of visitors to La Serenissima paid good money for Longhi's little paintings or engravings of them, such travellers looked to another hand altogether for images of themselves as they appeared while on holiday. The most distinguished Venetian portraitist during the century's early decades was Rosalba Carriera, doyenne of pastel artists, whose technique in her chosen medium has never since been equalled. Foreign clients flocked to her studio, especially the French, some of whom invited her on a highly profitable visit to Paris in 1720. While she flattered her sitters during the course of a long career, she could also slyly capture their vanity, their wistfulness and a hint or two of private longing or discontent. A cosmetic perfection of surface and shading in her Grand Tour portraits can mislead us at first glance. There is always more to Rosalba's sardonic scrutiny than the subject may have wanted or guessed at.

Her autonomy as a professional portraitist, managing her own business affairs, was not especially remarkable among Venetian women. They seemed to enjoy greater social freedoms than those allowed elsewhere in Italy, a feature especially notable among working-class communities of small tradesmen, artisans and gondoliers in areas like Cannaregio or San Niccolo. At the higher end of the scale, patrician ladies cultivated what appeared to be a deliberately transgressive independence from their husbands in favouring the attentions of a *cicisbeo* or *cavaliere servente*, a male admirer who, wearing his mask and domino, accompanied a woman of fashion to the opera, the gambling room or a ball, each on terms of limited gallantry in which no open physical displays of affection were tolerated and intimacy was never taken to an extreme. This in its turn allowed the development in Venice of salons, places of the kind which flourished in contemporary Paris, where elegant women of culture could welcome writers, intellectuals and figures from the world of the arts in what were known as *casini di conversazione*.

Leading the way here were the ladies of the Sagredo family, patrons themselves of Pietro Longhi, in whose little group portraits they appear. Caterina Sagredo, a precocious reader and book collector as a girl, amassed a library of two thousand volumes, attracting inconvenient attention from the *Inquisitori di Stato*, a subcommittee of the Ten whose task, among many others, was to censor the press and monitor the book trade. Her younger sister Marina was also under suspicion for reading works of philosophy and theology, as well as for taking what was deemed to be an inappropriate – perhaps because unladylike – interest in architecture. Both sisters married husbands who encouraged their literary interests and activity as salon hostesses, while being fully aware of the risks run by each woman from hypervigilant government surveillance.

Almost inevitably, each of their *casini di conversazione*, Caterina's on the Giudecca and Marina's near the church of San Giuliano, found itself closed down by interfering officials. While either still flourished, however, a welcome visitor was the dramatist who, more than any other writer, brings us into direct and joyous contact with eighteenth-century Venice's inhabitants. Carlo Goldoni, the son of a doctor from Modena, was intended by his father for the law and actually practised as an advocate till he was forty, when the theatre at last proved too much of a lure. His earliest plays included subtle attempts at giving shape and outline to the rich Italian tradition of the *commedia dell'arte*, the popular improvised theatre, with its stock characters, known as 'masks', and reliance on farcical situations enhanced by quick-fire dialogue exchanges. In Goldoni's hands, through works like *Il servitore dei due padroni* (1746), known in one recent modern English version as *One Man, Two Guvnors*, this hallowed medium took on a greater sophistication, with standard figures like the rascally, ever-resourceful Truffaldino, busy swapping masters, the old codger Pantalon de' Bisognosi and the pompous Doctor Lombardi, gaining greater substance through the playwright's presentation of them.

Quickly enough Goldoni began turning his attention to a different kind of comedy altogether, one which he largely created himself, centred on a bourgeois world of merchants, shopkeepers, café proprietors, their wives and daughters, thoroughly naturalistic in its plotlines, in the exchanges between characters and in the destinies they embrace. Soon his plays were being performed all over Italy, generating a demand he could hardly keep pace with, so that in one amazing year, 1750, no fewer than seventeen comedies sprang from his pen. Works like *Il ventaglio* (The Fan), *La locandiera* (The Hostess) and the superb *Villeggiatura* trilogy, portraying bittersweet relationships among the guests at a country villa, became stage classics, bringing Goldoni an international reputation for his benevolent perspectives on the foibles and obsessions of ordinary folk. Many of his best plays, *I rusteghi*, for

overleaf *The Banquet of Cleopatra*, 1743–4, by Giambattista Tiepolo: part of a fresco cycle in the ballroom of Venice's Palazzo Labia, featuring encounters between Cleopatra and Mark Antony.

example, or *Sior Todero brontolon*, were written in Venetian dialect, capturing the rhythms and nuances of life among the working people in the town around him through the visceral energy of their colourful, unpolished speech.

Like Vivaldi before him and Tiepolo afterwards, Goldoni chose to forsake his birthplace and carry his talents abroad. His success in Venice was increasingly a target for envious critics and professional rivals, so that an invitation to direct a resident company of Italian actors in Paris was too good to resist. The last thirty years of his life were spent in this voluntary French exile, but he never forgot the Venetian world that had nourished his genius so lavishly. His last play for Venice, *Una delle ultime sere di Carnovale*, produced at Teatro San Luca in February 1762, features a most touching farewell to the city, voiced in dialect by the young fashion designer Anzoleto:

> Shall I ever forget this town, my adored homeland? Shall I ever forget my patrons or my friends? I carry the name of Venice engraved in my heart, ever mindful of the grace and kindness I have received here. Keep your love for me alive, dear friends. May heaven bless you, I wish it with all my heart.

The first-night audience, moved to tears, cried out: '*Buon viazo! Torne presto!*' – 'Come back soon!' He never did.

The Venice to which the dramatist was bidding farewell had itself not much longer left in the way of survival. We can all be wise after the event about what was soon to overtake La Serenissima and start hunting for ominous *memento mori* signs in the plaintive slow movements of Vivaldi concertos or search for decay behind the crepuscular beauty of Francesco Guardi's haunting images of the Venetian lagoon, offering such a potent contrast with those of his fellow *vedutista* Canaletto. The truth was that despite warnings and jeremiads from such radically-inclined patricians as Giorgio Pisani, a continuing critic, during the 1770s, of the more ossified among the various governmental insti-tutions, and Carlo Contarini, who berated the Grand Council on key issues of inflation and the cost of living, their own ruling caste still held complacently to its belief in Venice's exceptionalism, a Panglossian politics of 'Everything is for the best in the best of all possible worlds.' It was deemed desirable therefore, in the summer of 1780, to arrest both men, sending Pisani to gaol on the mainland in Verona's fortress of San Felice but dispatching Contarini to the dungeons of Cattaro (Kotor) in distant Montenegro. In both cases the agency involved was that of the *Inquisitori di Stato*, effectively managing the administration of justice within the city and across the empire. Their severity was miscalculated, fuelling resentment of the status quo which had begun gathering momentum among the citizenry and the impoverished nobles, those *barnabotti* to which Pisani himself belonged. Staying in Venice in 1788, the pioneering English agronomist Arthur Young saw the writing on the wall for the government. 'The first real shock that happens will overturn it', he concluded.

The outbreak of the French Revolution in the following summer did not initially furnish the needed wake-up call. A posture of neutrality came so naturally to Venice by now that invitations from other sovereign states, led by Austria, to join in an alliance against France's new regime were easily brushed aside. The issue was as much practical as political. La Serenissima had almost nothing left of any practical use in the way of a defence force which might adequately challenge the French army bracing itself for war with Austria. The latter's Italian territory included Milan and the whole of surrounding Lombardy. Fearful that the poison of liberty, equality and fraternity might cross a permeable frontier and seep into the Venetian body politic, the government stepped up its watch on suspected liberals and dissidents, while adopting a warier stance towards foreigners. What emerges at this juncture, with the Revolution gathering ever more rapid momentum, is the sheer bonelessness of the regime in the face of a need to formulate a clearly defined policy which should ensure both its survival and that of La Serenissima's integrity as a free and independent state. Diplomacy, that old staple of Venetian success, might have helped at this stage to carry her through, the more so since she repeatedly turned aside from proposals for a defensive alliance with Naples, Tuscany or Sardinia (the former Duchy of Savoy) besides refusing to join an international coalition with Austria, England and Spain. Her ambassador in Paris, however, Alvise Pisani, had been so shaken by the savagery of the *sans-culotte* mob that he fled with his wife and children to London, where he remained till after the execution of King Louis XVI and Queen Marie-Antoinette in 1793. The Senate's relations with the French ambassador Jean-Baptiste Lallement, former French consul in Naples, were frosty but always polite, but the situation grew more hazardous when King Louis's brother, the Comte de Lille, chose to settle in Verona and the Venetian authorities there were asked to move him on. News that an Austrian army had been allowed to march unhindered across the Veneto drew the strongest protest from France's Directoire government, to which the Signoria returned feeble excuses while continuing to insist on its neutrality.

The most lethal development came with the Directoire's appointment of twenty-seven-year-old Napoleon Bonaparte as commander of its forces in Italy. Astounding speed and brilliance of execution characterized the young Corsican's handling of his campaign during the spring of 1796, as he knocked Sardinian armies easily out of his way, humiliated the Austrians in Lombardy and seized their key city of Milan. For Napoleon the Republic of Venice represented a mounting inconvenience in his attempts at driving Habsburg regiments back towards Tyrol and his style of dealing with La Serenissima grew more obviously impatient and contemptuous. Venetian envoys, what was more, never fully grasped how much he could rely on bluster and posturing when it suited him. The Signoria was becoming all too well aware, with Lallement still in place as ambassador, of how much Bonaparte was getting to know from him as to its unreadiness for serious armed resistance should he choose to invade. Yet when, during August and September 1796, Lallement suddenly offered a proposal for a Franco-Venetian alliance, apparently Napoleon's own idea, the government chose to reject this, shuddering with patrician horror at associating with a crew of upstart foreign regicides.

Having taken possession of Mantua, Austria's most sizeable stronghold in eastern Italy, and moved troops into Venetian cities on the *terraferma*, the general now sped north into Habsburg heartlands across the mountains. When serious anti-French demonstrations kicked off in Verona during April 1797 – the so-called '*Pasque Veronesi*', 'Veronese Easter' – these discontents took hold in the surrounding countryside, needing immediate action if he was to face down any remaining resistance from the Austrians. Suppression of the uprising was swift, brutal and exacting. As Bonaparte's lieutenants squeezed a massive indemnity from the Veronese and executed almost a hundred leading rioters, he himself had resolved on an armistice with the Austrian high command whose terms should present him to the world as a magnanimous victor, allow further time for calming the restive situation in the Veneto and overshadow the achievements of his professional rival, General Lazare Hoche, currently leading the Directoire's forces to victory in southern Germany.

Napoleon's patience with the Venetian government, whom he held partially responsible for fomenting the *Pasque Veronesi*, had run low and he was prepared, in making a truce with the Austrians, to offer them a sizeable portion of its mainland territory, together with Istria and Dalmatia. Only two days after the accord was drawn up, an episode took place which convinced him that this partial dismemberment of

La Signoria was by no means enough. On 20 April 1797 a small French naval patrol, sailing from Ancona, entered the lagoon, headed by the ominously named *Libérateur d'Italie*, under its captain Jean-Baptiste Laugier. By now the Signoria was desperately signalling its neutrality by forbidding access to all foreign warships, but Laugier seems to have been genuinely unaware of this measure. As his flotilla neared the fort of Sant'Andrea, on the Lido, its commander, Domenico Pizzamano, ordered warning shots to be fired. The *Libérateur*, intercepted by a Venetian vessel whose crew of *fanti da mar*, amphibious marines, then climbed aboard, offered surrender and was taken under escort to the Arsenale, but in the struggle five French sailors had been killed, among them Laugier himself. When ambassador Lallement protested at the violent outrage, an answer came that the government had issued an official tribute to Pizzamano's heroism, accompanied by a pay increase for his men.

The attack on the *Libérateur* was the pretext Napoleon needed for dealing once and for all with the Republic of Venice as an autonomous authority. His order that Lallement should leave the city was a sign that outright hostilities were in preparation. Venetian envoys sent to treat with the general at the Austrian city of Graz were roundly told that unless the Signoria released all its political prisoners and pursued justice against Pizzamano and his crew, their entire state would be summarily eradicated. 'I shall tolerate no more Inquisition, no more Senate,' fumed Bonaparte. 'I shall be a very Attila to Venice.' Thoroughly cowed by this and several more ferocious tirades, the Venetians returned, across a *terraferma* where La Serenissima's rule had been largely swept away by occupying French troops, to inform the doge and Grand Council of what they and their fellow citizens might now expect.

Venice's 120th and last doge, Lodovico Manin, has been treated more than a little meanly by certain historians, possibly, one supposes, for his notable lack of *physique du role* – portrait artists could clearly do nothing with his drooping, chinless countenance – but also because he came from a nouveau-riche background, belonging to a family of minor Friulan aristocracy that had been added to the Golden Book as recently as 1651. The implication seems occasionally to be that if only someone from the smarter patrician clans, a Grimani, a Pesaro, a Mocenigo, say, had been appointed doge, the leadership so badly needed by La Serenissima at this moment might somehow have been forthcoming. As it was, the speed with which events overtook the Republic, especially following Bonaparte's invasion of its territory and given its chronic state of military unpreparedness, was scarcely to be

overleaf   The Grand Canal with Santa Lucia and the church of the Scalzi, 1780s, by Francesco Guardi. The church of Santa Lucia was demolished in 1861, and its location is now the site of Venezia Santa Lucia railway station.

countered by a simple adrenalin rush of ancestral pluck. The days of Enrico Dandolo, Vettor Pisani or Francesco Morosini were long gone and there was no indication that anyone in their heroic mould now waited his hour to rescue Venice from political dissolution.

On the morning of 1 May, as Napoleon, who had reached Treviso, prepared a lengthy series of conditions to be met before he withdrew a threatened declaration of war against the Republic, the doge recommended to the Grand Council that it should agree to existing French demands for the punishment of Domenico Pizzamano, the liberation of political prisoners and the dismantling of the office of *Inquisitori di Stato*. Manin's caution that unless this happened, 'Tonight we shall none of us be safe even in our own beds' was always held against him, though he was merely being realistic under the circumstances. The Council accepted, but a week later Lallement's secretary Joseph Villetard returned with the list of fresh stipulations, including admission of a French garrison, the placing under its command of Venice's own fleet, a democratic vote for all citizens to elect representatives to a new municipality, the erection of a Liberty Tree (that archetypal revolutionary symbol) in Piazza San Marco and the establishment of a free press.

It may seem extraordinary that the Grand Council should have shown itself suddenly so abject in bowing to all this, yet we need to remember the profound trauma induced among Europe's various oligarchies by news of the recent Reign of Terror in France, with its calculated extermination of so many aristocrats and those accused of aiding or sympathizing with them. On 12 May 1797, as a large crowd started to gather in the Piazza, the doge presented Napoleon's demands to the assembled Council in its immense chamber within Palazzo Ducale, suggesting that in the name of preserving civic order, life, property and religion, its historic powers should be handed over to a newly constituted democratic administration.

Just at that moment the noise of gunshots became audible from the Riva degli Schiavoni, beyond the palace. By a cruel irony, this happened to be a salvo of respect towards Venice and its government, fired by a battalion of loyal Dalmatian troops as they prepared to leave the city in obedience to French stipulations. The debate which might have taken place broke up at once, as the senators, fearful at the prospect of what they imagined was open revolt breaking out in the streets around them, hurriedly voted by a huge majority – only twenty against and five abstaining – to accept Napoleon's terms. Flinging off their official togas, they fled from the palace, leaving a hapless Doge Manin to contemplate the outcome and adjourn to his private apartments to be divested of his regalia. He was a lonely widower nowadays. His wife Elisabetta Grimani, who never wanted to be dogaressa and preferred to spend her time in reading and spiritual exercises, had died of a lingering illness five years earlier. At this moment, as his valet lifted the *corno dogale* from the doge's head and removed the linen cap beneath, Manin said quietly: 'Take it, I shall not be needing it again.'

Thus, in a mere half hour and amid an atmosphere of unseemly panic, the longest-lasting state in world history was allowed thus abruptly to implode. There is a touching footnote, however, to this whole episode, provided by some of those same Dalmatian soldiers who fired the salute that scared the senators. In the little Adriatic port of Perasto, on the gulf of Kotor, the garrison stayed faithful to Venice for as long as it could, holding out against the French until late summer that year. On 22 August 1797 the governor, Count Giuseppe Viscovich, hauled down the Venetian flag, with its lion of Saint Mark, in the presence of a tearful populace. The banner was solemnly carried to the church of the Holy Cross and placed in a casket beneath the high altar. Over two succeeding centuries Perasto, modern Perast, has been subject to three other regimes, Austria-Hungary, Yugoslavia and Montenegro, but still proudly remembers its loyalty to La Serenissima.

AFTER
THE FALL

If the departing Dalmatians, on that fateful morning of 12 May 1797, had not fired their respectful salute and frightened the Grand Council into self-extinction, how would the debate have gone and what might the result have been? The answer is that even without such an accidental stimulus, the vote would still have been influenced by the powerful current of sympathy for the French and their revolutionary ideals which had already gained ground among Venice's patrician elite. Only the previous day, for example, Alessandro Balbi, from one of the Republic's most distinguished clans, had found himself officially prohibited from publishing a rousing summons to his fellow nobles to cast off their hallowed privileges. 'Send home your Dalmatian troops, call in your ships of war,' he had urged them. 'Trust in the magnanimity of a great nation [meaning France], set fire to all systems of antediluvian politics and inapplicable laws recorded in decaying archives.' Styling himself 'Citizen' and claiming, however implausibly, always to have been 'a democrat, one of the people, a despiser of oligarchs', Balbi assured his fellow Venetians that 'the French bring you neither destruction nor death. Fear nothing, trust in Bonaparte and follow the voice of destiny which guides you towards taking your place upon the universal stage.'

While evidence suggests that Balbi may later have regretted this effusion, others like him saw which way the tide was flowing, more especially given the presence within the city of a sizeable number of French troops under the command of General Louis Baraguey d'Hilliers, whom Napoleon had appointed military governor. On 16 May a body of sixty citizens, their names approved by the ever-vigilant Joseph Villetard, was summoned to form a municipal administration, designed to operate, as far as possible, according to completely different principles from those of the vanished Serenissima. They included, it was true, several aristocratic names, a Bembo, a Gritti, a Mocenigo, a Cornaro, but from other aspects this new committee was more authentically representative of ordinary Venetians than any that had governed Venice before. There were merchants, bankers, lawyers, two apothecaries and a fisherman on the list, notable furthermore for including three Jews. In a brief while the gates of the Ghetto would be torn down and a limited portion of civil rights be granted to its community. Though such gestures by no means guaranteed safety or acceptance for the Jews in Venice, the ceremonial destruction and burning of the gates on 12 July, accompanied by music and dancing as they mingled with Christians in Campo del Ghetto Novo, was a portent of just what or how much was set to change within the city as the century drew to a close.

Very swiftly the municipality assumed control of civic administration in all its most significant areas. Committees were formed to oversee finance, education, health, justice and what was referred to by that already notorious French Revolutionary euphemism 'public safety', which included policing, the postal service and relations with foreign governments. None of these briefs and portfolios was especially easy to manage, since the French and Austrians now controlled La Serenissima's former mainland provinces and the imperial territories along the Adriatic, including the Ionian islands, so that any revenue deriving from these was no longer forthcoming and straitened public resources remained a constant problem. What mattered above all at this stage was that some sort of order and sense of continuity should be taken as guaranteed. In this respect the new government of Venice must do its best to appear firm, fair and resolute as Bonaparte and his French myrmidons looked inexorably over its shoulder.

What clearly mattered to many during these summer months in a suddenly-achieved atmosphere of social equality was the open and systematic denigration of that old order which had prevailed until 12 May. Propaganda now encouraged a scenario of rebirth for Venice, evoking the concept of a purely democratic republican state supposedly existing during the early Middle Ages until the patricians had destroyed it with the *Serrata del Maggior Consiglio*, the closing of the Grand Council in 1297. This notion of mythic levelling was not unlike that of 'the Norman yoke', supposedly violating fine old Anglo-Saxon egalitarianism, which diehard republicans in England had developed during the Civil War. For a certain kind of Venetian, correspondingly, the chimerical golden age needed bringing back to life.

With this in mind it was decided by the French, under General Baraguey d'Hilliers's direction, that this newly-regained identity, whatever it was actually supposed to be, should have its own celebration in the form of a so-called *Festa Nazionale*, after the manner of those that various revolutionary governments in Paris had mounted for the citizens in their capital's public gardens and squares. On 4 June 1797 therefore, in Piazza San Marco where a Liberty Tree had already been installed complete with a symbolic Phrygian bonnet, a crowd assembled to watch a pageant whose various cortèges were designed to illustrate the blessings of freedom on the different generations from infancy to old age. A bonfire had been stacked up in the Piazza and on it were placed Doge Lodovico Manin's *corno dogale* and one of the various copies kept of the now iniquitous *Libro d'Oro*, the Golden Book recording the accession to oligarchy of respected families in their several branches. To this pyre Baraguey d'Hilliers now solemnly applied the torch and the Venetians looked on at the emblematic destruction of what, until a fortnight previously, had been their immemorially constituted government. Except possibly for Baraguey, a few of his staff and the saturnine secretary Villetard, what none of those present could guess was the future which Bonaparte had already sketched out for Venice. Liberty, with or without her Phrygian bonnet and green leaves, was decidedly not part of the deal the Corsican had in mind.

Members of the newly-instituted municipal administration clung in the meantime to a hope that they and their city would sooner or later be incorporated into the so-called Cisalpine Republic, a puppet state on republican principles which Napoleon established in Milan that summer. Thus some sort of dignified autonomy might be salvaged for Venice, even if her wider territorial independence could no longer be validated, given the continuing presence of the French. Their expectations were dashed when, in the early autumn, Bonaparte, accompanied on this occasion by his wife Josephine de Beauharnais, took up residence in the enormous villa (belonging as it happened to Ludovico Manin) at Passariano, near Udine, to meet with the latest delegation from Vienna. Each side was happy to consolidate the agreement made earlier that year which should bring an end to Franco-Austrian hostilities throughout the region. For both parties Venice was merely a bargaining chip in calculations requiring just a touch more in the way of detail so that they could be set out as the terms of a treaty, signed on 17 October and always referred to by the name of the nearby town of Campoformio.

The arrangement was a singular foreshadowing of similar events taking place a century and a half later at Yalta, when Roosevelt, Stalin and Churchill met to decide the destiny of Europe once the Second World War was brought to an end. For nations like Hungary, Poland and Czechoslovakia, 'Yalta' came to mean far more than the name of a seaside resort in the Crimea. Equally, 'Campoformio' became synonymous for Venetians with their ultimate humiliation as a free people. Representatives of the municipality attended the peace conference and in the name of securing a more favourable outcome there had been an attempt to bribe Bonaparte, while Josephine for her part was offered a *douceur* in the form of a jewelled bracelet. Instead the two great powers abruptly sealed Venice's fate according to the deal made six months previously. According to the Treaty of Campoformio the entire empire of La Serenissima was to be divided into French and Austrian spheres of influence. The Ionian islands would become a French naval base, while the western Veneto, including the cities of Bergamo and Brescia, was absorbed into the Cisalpine Republic. Austria, in return for surrendering territory in Lorraine and the Netherlands, would take control of Friuli, Istria and Dalmatia. As for Venice itself, the city and its surrounding lagoon now became part of the Habsburg domains, its townsfolk made subject, at the stroke of a pen, to Emperor Francis II.

Determined, as it seems, that Venice should suffer materially as well as politically and eager not to hand over a fully functioning naval base to the Austrians, who might use it to obtain mastery of the Adriatic, Bonaparte now embarked on an exercise in asset-stripping that should fulfil his earlier pledge, that of being La Serenissima's second Attila. At the time of the Serene Republic's dissolution, the Arsenale, whatever the decrease in its shipbuilding activities, was still an efficient, well-stocked and properly maintained naval dockyard. A French report now took note of what lay within its walls, including 'an immense quantity of bronze artillery, a magnificent rope walk, excellent workshops and large stores of wood, iron, brass and tiles'. Bonaparte's successor as commander in Italy, General Alexandre Berthier, lost no time in ordering all available armaments to be removed by his troops, 'so that when we hand Venice over, not a single cannon must remain'. Whatever ships were moored in or around the yards were to be sunk and the soldiers were instructed to complete their task by vandalizing the entire area thoroughly enough to make it useless to the incoming Austrians.

One vessel in particular, berthed within the Arsenale, was a special target of this destructive spree, since it seemed to symbolize everything the French most detested about the extinct Signoria. The Bucintoro, that great ceremonial barge on which the doge annually married Venice to the sea on Ascension Day, was now towed out to the Bacino di San Marco, between the Piazzetta and San Giorgio Maggiore. Its gilded Baroque splendour was much reduced, since care had been taken beforehand to unscrew or prise off as many of the boat's decorative features as possible, leaving it an immense, distressed hulk. Now, in full view of those for whom it had been a unique emblem of the vanished state's sovereignty and continuity, what remained of the Bucintoro was put to the torch and left to burn over the course of three whole days.

Another kind of spoliation, one to which Venetians would need to grow accustomed over coming decades, was set in train as a result of secret clauses agreed by Bonaparte in the wake of Campoformio. The first haul of the city's astounding profusion of art treasures was removed to Paris, in the shape of paintings, sculptures, a selection of precious manuscripts and, most wounding of all to Venetian *amor patriae*, the four antique bronze horses on the front of the Basilica and the ancient Iranian winged lion gracing one of the two tall columns in the Piazzetta. Efforts had already been made by the Municipality to expunge, in all its forms, the lion as a symbol of the old regime, but this particular act of desecration appeared a needless excess. As for the four horses, they would remain abroad as trophies of French victory for the next seventeen years. Not the least insulting aspect of this theft was a smug propaganda announcement from Paris, declaring that after several centuries of captivity the statues were 'at last in a free country'.

The Municipality was dissolved in readiness for the Austrians' arrival. In spite of the sneers aimed at it then and since, this hastily assembled authority had managed as best it could under exceptionally trying circumstances. The point has been well made, what is more, that involvement in running the administration gave Venetians a taste of genuine freedom, democratic decision-making and social interaction they were not likely to forget. Yet for the general community the overall experience of the past two years had scarcely been encouraging. Returning to Venice in 1799, Lorenzo da Ponte, Mozart's librettist, born a Venetian subject in the Jewish ghetto of Ceneda in Friuli, recorded the views of a friend: 'We are surrounded by hordes who, through fear and hatred, have destroyed both trade and industry here, cutting off all means of earning money. A thousand opinions have been created, a thousand bickering factions, inducing rivalry, hatred and bad faith and reducing us all to the necessity of finding ways to survive.'

Things would not change dramatically for the better once Austria's imperial authority was instated in January 1798. Stricter, more rigorously puritanical policies of censorship and surveillance were now put in place, driving many to quit the city for a more liberal atmosphere on the mainland, and the drain on the city's population which had begun during the French takeover became still more noticeable. An increasing sense of neglect and marginalization started overtaking Venice as the Habsburgs chose to focus on developing Trieste as its principal port in the Adriatic. Though the patrician class, reduced after the fall of the Republic to the status of 'former people', found the new regime more sympathetic towards it, fresh financial problems beset this old nobility, beginning a process of selling off items of family heritage, such as paintings, libraries and archives, that would continue throughout the approaching century. Amid the larger urban community, meanwhile, a sense of purposelessness began taking hold. There was no obvious indication that rule from Vienna would restore that powerful identity, that self-esteem, that share, small as it might be, in something special whereby the Serene Republic's existence had provided its citizens with an inalienable birthright, however lowly their status. 'La Bella Dominante' had become a backwater, in as broad a sense as the term allowed, flagging commercially, failing to keep pace with Trieste and fast losing any sense of what kind of a city it wished to be, now that it was no longer an imperial capital, the august metropolis of a free state.

The peace between France and Austria which Campoformio was meant to seal grew increasingly frayed at the edges as the nineteenth century began. Napoleon's stellar trajectory carried him from first consul to emperor while his conquering armies overwhelmed the different states of Germany, challenging the Austrians in open war and inflicting a signal defeat on them at Austerlitz in 1805. The resulting Treaty of Pressburg effectively handed Italy in its entirety to Bonaparte, whose directive of 17 March established the peninsula as a kingdom, to be governed in its various regions by members of his family (or in one case a loyal field marshal) named as viceroy, king or queen wherever he saw fit. Hence the Veneto and Friuli became part of a northern Italian viceroyalty under the emperor's stepson Eugene de Beauharnais, who was later given the title 'Prince of Venice'. Napoleon made his intentions perfectly plain regarding his new realm. Venice, he decreed, was to be handled as a conquered country. 'Now my victory is established, I shall treat the place as its good sovereign, provided the Venetians are good subjects in return.'

His triumphal visit in 1807 was partially designed to confer an official blessing on modernization schemes begun in response to pleas from prominent Venetians who had journeyed in a deputation to Paris the previous year. The devastated Arsenale was rebuilt and newly equipped, key channels within the lagoon were dredged and lighthouses installed. Public gardens were to be laid out at the northern end of Riva degli Schiavoni and behind these, through one of the Castello *sestiere*'s poorest areas, a grand boulevard, named Via Eugenia after the viceroy, would be driven. On the Piazza itself, which Napoleon is traditionally said to have dubbed 'the finest drawing room in Europe', the French passion for order and system now imposed itself in a scheme uniting the two Procuratie, Vecchie and Nuove, via a new palatial wing, since always known as the Ala Napoleonica, sweeping away in the process Sansovino's elegant little church of San Geminiano.

Ecclesiastical Venice would indeed be the biggest sufferer during the eight years of Bonaparte's imperial annexation. Almost as soon as the viceregal government took over, an order was given for the suppression, across the city and among the lagoon's many islands, of thirty-four monastic foundations and nine churches. A further twenty-six convents and monasteries, together with fifteen more churches, were closed down during the next few years. Some of these became military barracks or public offices, others were left empty or half-ruined, many are simply remembered today through the appearance of their names – San Provolo, San Paternian, San Severo, San Basegio – on the black-and-white street signs among the different *sestieri*. In consequence a wholesale reorganization took place of the parishes across the urban community, a significant change in the life of what was still a devoutly religious population.

During such a drastic shakeup, the French could scarcely ignore the opportunities afforded for further looting of art treasures. Paintings in their thousands, including that most celebrated booty of all, Veronese's panoramic *Wedding Feast at Cana* from the refectory at San Giorgio Maggiore, were carted off, either to the new Brera gallery in Milan or to the massive exhibition spaces created in Paris's new museum at the Louvre. Not a few, on the other hand, were kept to enrich the newly enhanced Accademia di Belle Arti, now installed in the premises of the former convent, church and *scuola* of Santa Maria della Carita on the Grand Canal. Like several of those teaching Venetians how to love their birthplace and what best to value within it, Leopoldo Cicognara, the academy's president, was not himself from Venice. Born in Ferrara, this visionary and determined character, who did more than anyone to foster the city's sense of its artistic heritage, now raised the art school's status and profile as a teaching institution, himself producing major studies of Venetian architecture and sculpture to inspire its students.

The collapse of Napoleon's empire in the wake of his disastrous Russian campaign of 1812 had its own devastating impact on Venice. By the autumn of 1813 the lagoon was being blockaded by British ships while an Austrian army had gathered on the mainland, food prices rocketed and the first deaths occurred from starvation. The emperor's defeat at Leipzig and subsequent exile to Elba meant that Austria could once again establish mastery over the city, a hegemony that was to remain secure – with, as we shall see, a brief but heroic interval – for another fifty years. By now a state of chronic decline was painfully visible, more especially for those who remembered Venice as it had been twenty years previously, during those last fragile days of the Serene Republic. The population at that time, estimated at around 140,000, had fallen by almost a third. At least half of those who hung on were in dire financial circumstances, dozens of buildings stood empty or had been allowed to decay, trade and industry were at a standstill and the overall mood of the citizens was one of gloomy resignation. How exactly was Habsburg Austria, victorious in the wake of Waterloo and Bonaparte's dispatch to Saint Helena, prepared to tackle the problems of its reacquired trophy?

Among the earliest priorities was reckoned to be the recovery of that vast artistic booty that the French had carried away, not just from Venice but from all over Italy, during the previous decade. This act of restitution had been supported from the outset by the art-loving Duke of Wellington, who had enforced on the British foreign secretary Lord Castlereagh his conviction that 'the Allies could not do otherwise than restore [the art treasures] to the countries from which, contrary to the practice of civilized warfare, they had been torn by the tyranny of Bonaparte'. Appropriately, the chief agent in organizing the programme of return was the era's finest sculptor and a leading figure in Venice's artistic life, Antonio Canova. Working in Rome at the time, he was sent to Paris under the auspices of Ercole Consalvi, a secular cardinal working as secretary of state for Pope Pius VII and anxious to retrieve the myriad art objects looted from the Vatican collections. Backed by Wellington and the Allied sovereigns, Canova successfully oversaw the restoration of most, if not all, the stolen patrimony, to the indignation of the French themselves, whose argument was that by placing these

Napoleon as Mars the Peacemaker, Antonio Canova's nude statue of Napoleon Bonaparte, dating from 1806, is now on display at the Duke of Wellington's London residence, Apsley House.

works inside a public museum they had rendered a service to world culture. As somebody to whose training and early career Venice had provided the crucially nurturing background, Canova was happy to be able to bring home the totemic horses of Saint Mark and the Piazzetta's bronze lion, both of them restored to their places in 1815.

An often-reproduced painting by Vincenzo Chilone of the ceremonial occasion at which the four horses were drawn into the Piazza prior to being hoisted once again onto the church façade has another narrative strand entwined with what, on the surface, was intended as a benign gesture by the new regime towards its Venetian subjects. To the right of the prospect, in the shadow of the Campanile, stands a crowd of civilian spectators, but the overall view, comprising the Basilica, Palazzo Ducale and (at this stage) a single column on the Piazzetta, is dominated by triple files of troops wearing the white uniforms of Habsburg imperial infantry regiments. The message here would seem to be plain. You Venetians may have your emblems back but do not expect, by any means, a restoration of that ancient republic whose enterprise brought them as symbols of power and conquest six hundred years ago from Byzantium. We are your masters now and your destiny is in the gun barrels of those serried ranks of musketeers.

Once the city became part of a unified Italian nation state after 1866, the officially promoted image of Austrian rule in Venice was one of a generally oppressive colonialism, hostile to enterprise or initiative, intolerant of criticism or dissentient voices and sluggish in addressing any kind of administrative reform. In recent years an inevitable current of historical revisionism has sought to turn this round, seeking to emphasize the fundamentally benign and positive aspects of the Habsburg imperial regime and laying suitable stress on the fact that a number of its bureaucratic structures were readily absorbed within the new Italian kingdom's workings. Frankly, the revisionists are keen to point out, there had been little of any real importance in the way of abuses for Venetians to complain of. It is true, of course, that the stirrings of what is loosely labelled the Risorgimento were afoot, subversive concepts of unification for an Italy which, contrary to the view famously expressed by Austria's long-lived chief minister Prince Clemens von Metternich, was more than just 'a geographical expression'. Yet against this broader framework of discontent, resentment of alien interference and a belief that Italians might manage their own affairs without continual oversight from Vienna, none of these things, say the revisionists, should blind us to Austria's genuine achievements as ruler of Venice during most of the early nineteenth century.

The Habsburg government indeed presided over a gradual if somewhat belated economic recovery for the city, mostly taking place in the wake of an imperial concession of free-port status in 1830. By the end of the decade Venice had become the third busiest Italian port after Genoa and Livorno, a direct Mediterranean competitor with Marseille and Constantinople. An active chamber of commerce included thriving enterprises linked mostly to shipping, maritime insurance and a trade in commodities such as glass, fine fabrics and leather goods. The town was one of Italy's first to be illuminated by gas (metal frames of the earliest cylinders are preserved next to the church of San Francesco della Vigna) and attempts were made at improving the overall sanitation of streets and waterways. More bridges, mostly in cast iron, were put in place, while many canals large or small were filled in and built over, occasioning serious changes in the urban infrastructure. A further number of churches was swept away, but since the Austrians viewed the religious establishment as an essential bulwark of the conservatism they had championed at the Congress of Vienna, care was taken to reopen several others closed during the Napoleonic era and the Patriarch of San Marco was given a fine new palace on the northern flank of his basilica.

previous pages   *The Return of the Bronze Horses to San Marco,*
by Vincenzo Chilone. Looted by Napoleon from St Mark's
Basilica in 1797, the horses came back to Venice in 1815, following
the emperor's final defeat.

Palatial real estate, more especially on the Grand Canal and along Riva degli Schiavoni, had become a marketable commodity for the numerous patrician families brought low with the Republic's collapse. Several palazzi, such as the Gritti at Santa Maria del Giglio, became hotels, others were divided for rented accommodation or occupied by government offices and still more were bought by affluent foreigners who could afford either to restore them or instead to reconfigure them according to individual whims and needs. A notable casualty in this respect was the Ca' d'Oro, built during the mid-fifteenth century by Marco Contarini, Procurator of San Marco, employing the Bon family of masons and carvers, in what has come to be regarded as a brilliant final flourish of that Venetian Gothic style familiar to us from the architecture of Palazzo Ducale, which clearly influenced aspects of its design. In 1843 it was acquired by Prince Aleksandr Trubetskoy, a Russian nobleman, who presented it to his mistress, the internationally famed ballerina Maria Taglioni, who at once set about an entire refurbishment, vandalizing, in the process, many of its most exquisite carvings, mouldings and capitals.

By now Venice had achieved a fresh incarnation, one which would soon dominate its seasonal pulses and rhythms, as a tourist resort. Painters from beyond Italy grew enthralled by the waterborne city's singular light effects. To this period belong some of the most compelling – because most dreamlike – Venetian images, those created by J.M.W. Turner and Richard Parkes Bonington. Meanwhile, the entire area comprising the Piazza, the Piazzetta and the Molo, that waterside esplanade outside the Biblioteca Marciana and the new range of palatial apartments inhabited by the Austrian governor and his family, became the focus of fashionable promenades where smart society could gather, listen to music from café orchestras and military bands or board a gondola for tours of the city. The gondoliers, though greatly reduced in number since 1797, were still a vocal echelon and their anger was audible when in 1843 the railway, that ultimate symbol of contemporary progress, was brought from Padua to Marghera, where oared omnibuses were waiting to carry passengers the short distance across the lagoon to the head of the Grand Canal. Worse where gondola traffic was concerned came with the building, three years later, of a fine white marble viaduct carrying trains into a terminus on the site of the former church of Santa Lucia, whose name the station still bears. Keeping pace with all of this was a hotel trade which took its standards from the Albergo Danieli, opened in 1826 by Francesco Dal Niel inside a former Dandolo palace on Riva degli Schiavoni, where a

overleaf   The Piazzetta San Marco by Moonlight,
by Ippolito Caffi (1809–66).

scatter of rival establishments were soon catering to the richer end of an increasingly varied tourist clientele.

What exactly did the tourists come to see? The keynote had been struck in 1817 by a poet, no less a figure than Lord Byron, leaving England under a cloud of gossip and scandal surrounding his divorce case and eventually taking up residence in a rented palace on the Grand Canal. It was Byron's moralizing on the fall of La Serenissima, first of all in an ode inspired by Venice's tragic destiny, then in a more fulsome tribute paid in the fourth canto of his autobiographical travelogue *Childe Harold's Pilgrimage*, which set the tone for visitors thereafter, intrigued by the forlorn grandeur and stateliness of a city which, having lost its metropolitan role, seemed destitute of any identifiable future.

> Oh! agony – that centuries should reap
> No mellower harvest! Thirteen hundred years
> Of wealth and glory turn'd to dust and tears;
> And every monument the stranger meets,
> Church, palace, pillar, as a mourner greets;
> And even the Lion all subdued appears

Ironically, though Byron loathed the Austrian colonial regime and all that its presence seemed to imply, he was in some sense assisting its propaganda efforts by emphasizing the image of Venice's fallen greatness as a punishment for its sins. There grew up, during this period, what has become known as 'the Black Legend', the idea that the extinct Republic had thoroughly deserved to perish through its callous pursuit of material wealth and a total contempt for the lives of its subjects. This had been strenuously promoted by the former Napoleonic secretary for war Pierre Daru in his influential *Histoire de la République de Venise* (1816), a work which aroused understandable fury among its Venetian readers. His portrayal of the Signoria's system of government via a series of closed committees, the use of torture and the imposition of dreary prison sentences – typified, in the Black Legend, by the Bridge of Sighs and the dungeons of Palazzo Ducale – was invoked by the Austrians as a counterweight to any nostalgic notion that the old regime could somehow have been preferable to that of the Habsburg police state. The latter's secretiveness and obfuscations, its use of spies and informers to maintain surveillance of suspect individuals through their friendship networks, their reading habits or even their overheard remarks in conversation, needed to be understood simply as provident and well-intentioned measures for the protection of ordinary citizens. It suited Metternich's government, if not actively to foster, then certainly not to stifle a view of the vanished Serenissima as a realm of tyrannical oppression and the rule of fear.

Venice could thus easily be marketed to the imaginative traveller as a species of elegant graveyard, where outmoded systems, foiled aspirations and the hubristic 'pomps and vanities of this wicked world' could accomplish their decay amid empty palaces, crumbling churches and stagnant canals. What imperial Austria, under Metternich's smug stewardship, failed to grasp until too late was the crucial change in temperature taking place in Italy as a whole, not to speak of a Venice revived and economically energized by a newly empowered bourgeoisie. An observation by a modern American historian seems apposite here. 'The primary problem of politics', he declares, 'is the lag in the development of political institutions behind socio-economic change.' By 1840, some sort of clash between the new Venetian oligarchy on the one hand, represented by lawyers, merchants, entrepreneurs, shipping agents and bankers, and on the other a sclerotic Austrian governing echelon dominated by aristocrats and army officers and served by a nervously pedantic bureaucracy, was more or less inevitable.

The Risorgimento provided the perfect context for this show-down. Agitation in the various states was now gaining momentum for some kind of liberty for people to bond together as Italians, without police interference, press censorship or, in the background, the looming obstructiveness of diktats from Vienna. In Venice an increasingly volatile atmosphere made everywhere a forum for this political unease, from a 'patriotic' café like Florian in Piazza San Marco to Teatro La Fenice, recently rebuilt after its destruction by fire but, like many another Italian opera houses, suspect to the authorities as a crucible of dissent. In January 1848, when first of all the lawyer Daniele Manin and soon afterwards the author and ideologue Niccolò Tommaseo dared to criticize

Daniele Manin, leader of Venice's 1848 revolution against the Austrians, overlooks the *campo* bearing his name.

aspects of Austrian government policy, requesting the abolition of press controls, the curtailing of police powers and a form of home rule for the two imperial provinces of Lombardy-Venetia, both men were arrested, tried for subversion and imprisoned in the gaol next to Palazzo Ducale.

Such a move came far too late. The first of a wave of revolutions eventually sweeping across the whole of Europe in this extraordinary year had broken out that same month in Palermo, then part of the Kingdom of the Two Sicilies, followed by similar uprisings in France and Germany. In March it was Austria's own turn, with the elderly Prince Metternich driven into exile and a complete breakdown of that artificial tranquillity – defined by one Italian revolutionary leader as 'the peace of the tomb' – over which he had presided as magus and ringmaster for the past thirty years. In Venice the civil governor's release of Manin and Tommaseo, carried in triumph through the Piazza amid jubilant crowds, heralded a panic-stricken withdrawal of the heavy Austrian troop garrison and, as a result, the sudden restoration of freedom to the city to do as it pleased. The date of this momentous event, 22 March, is commemorated nowadays in the name of one of Venice's principal thoroughfares.

'We are free, we belong to nobody but ourselves, we have our own motherland and can speak those sacred words "We are Italians". Courage has vanquished strength and words have blunted the bayonet's power.' These ringing sentences from the lead article in Venice's principal newspaper *Gazzetta privilegiata* heralded an astounding episode in the history of the city, one still insufficiently known, not just to non-Italians but to Venetians themselves. During the spring and summer months of 1848 Venice, under a democratic government, managed its own affairs amid the zigzags, muddles and disappointments of revolution and warfare in other Italian states. Only when Austria, by force of arms, succeeded in restoring control over much of the peninsula and returning its flustered sovereigns (including Pope Pius IX, mistakenly hailed at an earlier stage as the apostle of liberty) did the Venetians find themselves well and truly alone before the onslaught of reactionary battalions.

It was at this stage that Daniele Manin stepped forward as the hero of resistance. A tubby little man in thick spectacles and suffering from asthma, he was at first glance an implausible leader, but the Venetians grew to love him deeply as he guided them through the nine gruelling months of a siege led by Austria's most experienced commander, the eighty-one-year-old Field Marshal Johann Josef Radetzky. Many

Italian patriots forced into exile by the failure of their own revolutions arrived in Venice to join the struggle, admiring the fervour and courage of the besieged population. During 1849 the city was under constant bombardment, with several of the honourable wounds from this being visible in its fabric to the present time. The entire community, from an aristocratic ladies' nursing service and the bakers who, when food supplies fell short, devised a species of 'patriotic bread' to fend off hunger, to priests, beggars and those little boys carrying spent Austrian cannonballs to the rebel gun batteries who could fire them back, threw itself into the initiative, vain as some of them knew this must finally be. Cholera and typhus spread through the city, starvation threatened, but, as a French naval officer observing events was moved to declare, 'The calm, the patience, the strange determination to resist among most of the population subject to such grim ordeals is, in my opinion, one of the most incredible and extraordinary things it is possible to witness.'

With every resource, human or material, pushed to its limit, Manin and his Venetian government were reduced to surrender to the Austrians on 24 August 1849. He went into exile with his family, dying in Paris in 1857. The unredeemed Venice, a Habsburg imperial colony once again, was divided between a minority of *austriacanti*, who had welcomed the besiegers for restoring peace, order and decorum, and a resentful majority unwilling to set memories of their earlier sacrifice aside and ready to make their feelings known through various kinds of silent demonstration. These might include regularly leaving the Piazza whenever an Austrian military band played, boycotting any official occasion on which senior Austrian dignitaries were present, attending memorial masses sung to mark the deaths of exiled patriots, most notably Daniele Manin, and refusing to appear during visits to the city by members of the imperial family, including Emperor Franz Josef and Empress Elisabeth. When the war of 1859 between France and Austria enabled the creation of a unified Kingdom of Italy, Venice and the Veneto were left in Habsburg hands. It was only with the military humiliation of the Austrians in the struggle with Prussia towards which Bismarck had lured them in 1866 that they were forced to yield their Adriatic trophy to Italy via a face-saving operation which briefly transferred the city and its province to the French emperor Napoleon III, who then bestowed it as a present on King Victor Emmanuel. The latter was given a jubilant reception in Venice on 7 November 1866 and his equestrian statue later replaced that of Radetzky which the Austrians had installed on Riva degli Schiavoni. Venice's destiny, from now on, for better or worse, was Italy's own.

overleaf　Fire breaks out at the church of San Geremia during
the Austrian bombardment of 1849, as depicted
by Luigi Querena (1824–87).

VENICE
TRANSFORMED

In 1885 the prolific Scottish author Margaret Oliphant published a work entitled *The Makers of Venice: Doges, Conquerors, Painters & Men of Letters*. To the book's distinguished roster of figures from the Venetian past she could easily have added someone who was still alive when it appeared. An elderly Oxford professor of fine art, he had recently become involved in an absurd and degrading libel action brought against him by the American artist James McNeill Whistler, whose series of 'Nocturnes' he had damned with the words '[I] never expected to hear a coxcomb ask two hundred guineas for flinging a pot of paint in the public's face'. His mental state, already uncertain, entered on a further period of decline as he started work on *Praeterita*, a survey, muddled and muddling, of his career, convictions and enthusiasms. By this stage he was nevertheless regarded, whatever his moments of eccentricity or spells of genuine madness, as one of the nineteenth century's truly numinous and influential figures, teaching his contemporaries how to look at and meditate on art, architecture and sculpture and appreciate why these mattered in a civilized society. At the heart of his searching and restless understanding of such matters lay the various inspirations, infinite as they seemed, which had been offered to him by Venice.

John Ruskin made his first visit to the city in 1835, accompanying his parents on a picturesque tour of Europe when still an adolescent and deeply responsive to the poetry of Byron. This first encounter moved him profoundly. He wept on having to leave and felt grateful to the poet for helping him to make the imaginative connexion between the fabric of the built environment surrounding him and the actual experience of those who had lived there in past ages. 'Byron told me of, and reanimated for me, the real people whose feet had worn the marble I trod on.' This way of engaging with art, conditioned as it was besides by the young man's Christian evangelical upbringing, introduced a moral dimension that transcended purely aesthetic considerations. Such intensity of focus, through the power and eloquence with which Ruskin later expressed it in his published studies, his letters and private diaries, had a permanent impact on the critical gaze that our culture has trained on art ever since.

This kind of immersive experience was Venice's everlasting gift to her most dedicated interpreter. On his return ten years later, Ruskin became overwhelmed through his encounter with the work of Tintoretto – 'Tintoret' as he insists on calling him – whom he now placed 'at the top, top, top of everything, with a great big black line to stop him off from everybody' and who, as he felt, 'swept me away at once into the "*mare maggiore*" of the schools of painting which crowned the power and perished in the fall of Venice'. The great 'Crucifixion' in the Scuola di San Rocco had essentially given Ruskin a life's vocation

as aesthete, writer and ideologue. In his book *Modern Painters* he evokes 'Tintoret here, as in all other cases, penetrating into the root and deep places of his subject', identifying Christ's agony as being 'told by this and this only, that though there yet remains a chasm of light on the mountain horizon where the earthquake darkness closes upon the day, the broad and sunlight glory about the Head of the Redeemer has become wan, and of the colour of ashes'. On a further visit in 1850, this time bringing his wife Effie Gray with him, he concentrated more fully on Venetian medieval architecture, using his exceptional gifts as a draughtsman and watercolourist to capture the vernacular Gothic of palaces and churches. The fruits of this trip and those that quickly followed it appeared in *The Stones of Venice*, published in three volumes between 1851 and 1853, in which Ruskin's connexions and extrapolations, made in the ampler contexts of Venetian architecture and history, would make their mark on buildings, streets and cities across the entire world.

The potency of his arguments is not just that of a simple conviction linked to his view of art and architecture as transformative forces in our lives, but derives also from his skill as a prose stylist. Those opening paragraphs of *The Stones of Venice*'s second volume, contrasting a prosaic 'rush of arrival in the railway station' with a journey from the mainland by gondola 'in the olden days of travelling, now to return no more', are a bravura exercise in re-enacting the experience of Ruskin's own early encounters with his beloved city. Equal virtuosity characterizes his superb account of visiting Torcello, on its 'waste of wild sea moor… lifeless, the colour of sack cloth, with the corrupted sea-water soaking through the roots of its acrid weeds'. For the writer the place becomes the mother of Venice itself, its two churches expressive of 'a simple and tender effort' by the earliest lagoon communities 'to recover some form of the temples which they had loved, and to do honour to God by that which they were erecting'.

Ruskin's impassioned relationship with Venice thereafter was lifelong. He went on learning from it, gaining in the process a somewhat more nuanced perspective of the Renaissance architecture he felt had corrupted the city, while he fell completely beneath the spell of 'Paul Veronese', a painter whose sensual worldliness in handling the sacred we might have expected him to shy away from. The whole place became symbolic for him of that archetypal sequence in the story of peoples, empires, communities and individuals whereby the finest of their creative instincts and energies are sapped away through greed and moral degradation. He could see this at work in what was happening

John Ruskin (1819–1900), for many the most influential interpreter of Venetian medieval and Renaissance art.

to the nineteenth-century Venice surrounding him and was devastated by the coarse philistinism underlying the processes of rebuilding and restoration. The Austrians' whitewashing of Palazzo Ducale and Maria Taglioni's assault on the façade of Ca' d'Oro were followed, to his horror, by scraping 'all the glorious old weather stains' off the front of San Marco and then by a drastic restoration of the whole Basilica during the 1870s under the direction of the city's chief architect Giovanni Battista Meduna. In Ruskin's view and that of his growing number of followers and admirers, there had to be more to rescuing whatever was of value in the fabric of Venice than this kind of blinkered concentration on its surfaces, as opposed to the multifaceted narrative retailed by its colours, materials and designs. His own absorption with the singularity of Venetian architecture – in *The Stones of Venice* he identifies almost forty different varieties of medieval window – inspired a new approach to looking at the city and trying to grasp the complexities involved in preserving it.

Just as an earlier generation, including Ruskin himself, had looked to Byron as their guide, now its children and grandchildren would arrive with *The Stones of Venice* in their luggage. What he had obviously not chosen to prepare them for was the physical actuality of a historic town battered by siege, neglect and depopulation and unable to accommodate or keep pace with demands for some sort of modern infrastructure. Others besides Ruskin had been anguished at the advent of a railway link. Similar horror was manifest with the arrival in the lagoon, more especially up and down the Grand Canal, of the bus boats which, though their steam power was long ago replaced by motors, are still called *vaporetti*. First introduced by the Compagnie des Bateaux Omnibus de Venise in 1872, they began regular service on the Canal in 1881, triggering protests by the gondoliers, many of whom were later driven to find alternative jobs in the boatyards of the Arsenale or the mills and factories springing up in the Santa Marta district at the extreme west of the town.

Employment was an abiding problem for at least half of the city's population at this time. One major source of work arrived with the erection, in 1895, of the gigantic Molino Stucky on the western edge of Giudecca, whose gaunt crenellations dominate the prospect from the Zattere. Giovanni Stucky, half Swiss, half Venetian, came from an enterprising family of flour millers based in Cannaregio but running several other mills on the mainland. Using steam power to grind Russian grain imported from the Crimea by the Dalmatian shipowners who now played a key role in Venice's economy, Stucky commissioned

A Quiet Canal, an etching (1886) by the American artist James McNeill Whistler.

Ernst Wullekopf, a German architect with whom he had got into casual conversation on a train journey, to design the whole striking range of towers, silos and workrooms which by the century's end had become one of northern Italy's most successful business ventures.

Profitable modernization as represented by the *vaporetto* and the Stucky mill was altogether less congenial to a certain type of nineteenth-century visitor than the picturesque 'simplicity' – or rank poverty, to call it by its true name – in which so many Venetians lived. A tendency to romanticize all this was easy enough. Already in 1834 the French author George Sand in her *Lettres d'un Voyageur*, could be found extolling a Venice 'so decayed, so oppressed and so impoverished, refusing to allow time or mankind to mar her beauty and serenity'. Enraptured at 'this tribe of fishermen who sleep on the pavement with no other mattress than a tattered coat, no other pillow than a granite step', Sand found them 'admirably philosophical'. A resource that by the 1870s they were forced to fall back on even further, given the execrable state of public hygiene and sewerage in the city, its exposure to epidemic disease and the run-down, verminous conditions of housing in the poorer areas of Cannaregio and Castello.

Such aspects, along with the lingering cultural phantom of the *leggenda nera*, tended to foster a growing preoccupation among a certain type of northern European visitor with a notion of Venice as a place of decadence, morbidity and death itself. Thomas Mann's Aschenbach in the eponymous *Death in Venice* was at this point a cloud no bigger than a man's hand on the literary horizon but the trope during the nineteenth-century's concluding decades was already flourishing. Robert Browning, who died in Ca' Rezzonico in 1889 (the palazzo bought by his son with his daughter-in-law's money), had given it an early utterance in his poem 'A Toccata of Galuppi's', mediating the fall of La Serenissima through the music, entirely forgotten by the time the poet was writing, of one of its most versatile eighteenth-century composers.

> As for Venice and her people, merely born to bloom and drop,
> Here on earth they bore their fruitage, mirth and folly were the crop:
> What of soul was left, I wonder, when the kissing had to stop?
> 'Dust and ashes!'

Others viewed the whole Venetian context as an elegantly bedecked stage set for their particular distillations of pleasure or melancholy or an amalgam of them both. In *The Wings of the Dove*, a novel by Henry James published in 1908, a death in Venice allows the beautiful

American invalid Milly Theale to cheat the predatory British pack of spongers and fortune-hunters closing in on her. Earlier he had based *The Aspern Papers* on a true story which similarly involved deviousness and dishonesty in an expatriate community, but shifted the original location from Tuscany to Venice. Both works offer subtle analyses of misapplied energy and baffled aspiration for which the city on the lagoon furnished him with an ideal backdrop.

Just before *The Aspern Papers* achieves its lethally abrupt climax, James's super-unreliable narrator sums up for us the impact of this unique urban atmosphere on the type of tourist represented by the author himself, who paid his first visit here in 1869, thereafter adopting Venice as very much his own city of the heart. 'Without streets and vehicles, the uproar of wheels, the brutality of horses and with its little winding ways where people crowd together, where voices sound as in the corridors of a house, where the human step circulates as if it skirted the angles of furniture and shoes never wear out, the place has the character of an immense collective apartment, in which Piazza San Marco is the most ornamented corner and palaces and churches, for the rest, play the part of great divans of repose.' Like many another fanciful visitor James sees the city as essentially a theatre where 'the Venetian figures, moving to and fro against the battered scenery of their little houses of comedy, strike you as members of an endless dramatic troupe'.

To several movers and shakers among Venetians themselves such a performative or merely decorative view of their city was not specially congenial. In 1886 the mayor, Count Dante di Serego Alighieri, set out a serious project for improved living conditions and new development schemes, most of which were based on practical expediency rather than a wish to convert the urban ground plan into something more like a conventional modern metropolis along the lines of Paris or Vienna. By now, however, a powerful traditionalist lobby, with prestigious international support, had become vocal enough to see off this kind of initiative. Its chief spokesman, the painter and historian Pompeo Molmenti, issued a furious polemic in the periodical *Nuova Antologia*, blasting the installation of a new fish market at the Rialto, warning that before long carriages would be bowling down Via 22 Marzo and that Venice, 'picturesque, poetic, full of fascination and mystery', would lose its quintessential particularity just for the sake of making something new. 'Who wants to reduce Venice to a boring, monotonous, modern city?' he fumed. At a time when all over Europe and America a drive towards the provision of decent housing was seen as essential to the economic survival of settled communities, Molmenti was identifying himself as an active opponent of slum clearance for the sake of preserving Venice's *venezianita*, its 'Venetianness'. In this attack on Serego's project we can discover the beginnings of a major and hitherto unresolved conflict over the city's future between well-intentioned progressives on the one hand and reverential conservationists on the other. Outflanking each of these factions has been a third, composed of commercial opportunists and dangerously plausible promoters of short-term solutions to age-old Venetian problems.

Backing the conservationists, for the most part, was a growing and influential expatriate caucus whose Ruskin-inspired affection for what it felt Venice best embodied as a species of cultural time capsule made an indelible mark on the city's sense of its own identity and immediate destiny. Most of these foreign residents had originally arrived as tourists before deciding to stay on and settle down in the lagoon and the majority of them were British or American. During the Risorgimento years the existence of the United States had been a beacon lamp for revolutionary Italy. Not for nothing had the newly formed Venetian government of 1848 decreed a 4 July celebration of American independence and the presence of a US consul was taken as a reciprocal gesture of fraternity and good faith. Edmund Flagg, who occupied the post following the return of the Austrians in 1849, published his own account of the siege, gathered from those who lived through the whole harrowing episode, but it was the journalist and novelist William Dean Howells, spending four years as consul here between 1861 and 1865, whose book *Venetian Life* still ranks as one of the shrewdest, most sympathetic and enjoyably detailed studies of its subject. Howells made a deliberate effort to dispel the myth-history of Pierre Daru's *leggenda nera*, to emphasize, like the good American he was, the desire for liberty on the part of 'a nation in mourning' under Austrian rule, and, most important of all, to capture the essence of an ordinary modern Venice through its moods, voices and social rhythms. Going into several editions, *Venetian Life* was an obvious inspiration for his compatriots to try Venice for themselves, which was what so many of them hastened to do once the trauma of the American Civil War had ended.

Passionate Veneto-Americans were Daniel and Ariana Curtis, who in 1885 rescued Palazzo Barbaro, on the Grand Canal, from imminent ruin and began a tradition of welcoming distinguished writers and artists to the house. Henry James, who finished *The Aspern Papers* here and used it as a background for *The Wings of the Dove*, became a frequent visitor, while John Singer Sargent, in a group painting of the Curtis family in their grand *salotto*, contrived a classic image of patrician expatriates thoroughly at home in a Venetian setting. Like Howells, whose book he read, Sargent grew intrigued by a world far removed from this, a workaday ambience of artisans and labouring folk in the town's obscurer quarters, his glance trained on a group of girls in black shawls crossing a *campo* after leaving church, a pair of boatmen paddling a barge down a narrow canal or the women known as *impiraresse*, whose job was threading beads and pearls.

To the Italian government it seemed entirely appropriate that Venice's continuing stimulus for artists should be rewarded with a national exhibition, and in 1887 a section of the public gardens originally laid out by Napoleon was assigned to what was envisaged, to start off with, as a one-off event, with works displayed in a varied assortment of pavilions among the paths and plane trees. The show's success became a spur to a fresh enterprise developed over the next decade, involving civic patronage and a specially invited fine art commission. Thus the Venice Biennale, an international display staged every two years, drawing on the work of featured painters and sculptors from all over the world, came into being and has remained a major fixture in the cultural calendar ever since. From this aspect the city was able to reacquire its predominance as a centre of contemporary creativity rather than a repository for sentimentality and historical cliché. Along with the evolution of the Biennale came further debates over enlarging Venice's potential as a port and adding to the dockyards and workshops of the Arsenale, which now belonged to the Italian navy. By the late 1880s the massive high-walled enclosure was growing at least as busy as it had been when, three centuries earlier, the Signoria had proudly shown off the expertise of shipwrights, chandlers and ropemakers in assembling and equipping a galley for the edification of France's King Henri III in the space of a single day. The latest cranes were purchased from England, at the Tyneside works of Armstrong Mitchell – one gaunt survivor has remained an established feature of the Venetian skyline – so that Italy could construct and launch her own battleships here in an ongoing bid for recognition among Europe's major powers.

Venice had meanwhile embraced the modern in another form altogether, that of the significant change in the lifestyle of sophisticated Western societies represented by the vogue for sea bathing and the enjoyment of a beach culture linked to the opening of large, handsomely furnished hotels. At least until 1870 the long, narrow island known as the Lido had been a semi-wild stretch of scrub to which bathers, mostly

overleaf *An Interior in Venice* (1899), by John Singer Sargent. The wealthy American Curtis family, depicted here at Palazzo Barbaro, acquired the seventeenth-century palazzo in 1885, making it a gathering-spot for artists and writers.

male, resorted purely for the purpose of swimming in the Adriatic, its waters untainted by the raw sewage polluting the canals to produce the smells routinely remarked on by travellers visiting at the height of summer. Byron and his poet friend Percy Bysshe Shelley went riding here in 1817 (the latter's *Julian and Maddalo* recalls the scene) and enjoyed the spectacular clarity of the prospect across the lagoon towards the mainland and the snow-clad Dolomites. It was a spot cherished for its loneliness and a chance to get some kind of distance from the noise, bustle and bad air of a close-packed town. Apart from a line of Austrian forts, the old Jewish cemetery and a scatter of fishing villages, including whatever remained of the once-important medieval port of Malamocco, a human imprint here was blissfully slight.

All this changed with startling abruptness during the 1880s when the first important provision of bathing facilities began turning the Lido into what it has since remained, an elegant, well-managed seaside resort, complete with esplanades, tree-lined avenues, villa residences, manicured beaches and a scatter of cafés and restaurants. Hotels on a grand scale, the Excelsior, the Grand Hotel des Bains and others, spread themselves along the seashore, directly connecting to the sands with their ranks of sunshades and beach chairs. By the end of the century the Venice Lido, made fashionable in any case by Italy's Queen Margherita, who had brought her son there in hopes that sea air and bracing sunshine would make him grow just a little taller (he never quite managed this), had become one of the smartest destinations in Europe. As a result, the word 'lido' became synonymous, in certain countries, with a public swimming pool and in Paris was given to a successful nightclub.

Sunbathing, if it did nothing to transform the diminutive Crown Prince Vittorio Emanuele, was a draw for a different kind of traveller altogether. Among loungers on the Lido beaches was the writer Gabriele D'Annunzio, whose life, from its very outset in the deeply provincial Adriatic town of Pescara, was devoted to the kind of high-voltage celebrity which becomes positively tyrannical in its addictive need to be indulged as flamboyantly as possible. It was not enough for D'Annunzio to be famous as a poet, novelist and playwright. He had to be a central character in the narrative of Italy as Europe's newest nation, vibrant in its embrace of whatever was most eye-catchingly modern yet at the same time cannily repurposing elements of a national past so as to embrace and burnish its profile in the context of a present rich with limitless possibilities.

D'Annunzio's relationship with Venice was typically opportunistic. During the 1890s it formed the background to a skilfully publicized affair with Italy's greatest actress. Born in Chioggia, Eleonora Duse had learnt her craft in the Venetian theatrical tradition stretching back to the days of Goldoni and beyond. By now, in the wake of sensational world tours, she was a goddess of the stage, thus an inevitable trophy to be snatched by D'Annunzio, who made Venice his centre of operations for this purpose. Duse was ready to be impressed. 'I see the sun,' she told him, 'and thank all the powers in the world for having met you.' He was nothing like the sun, a little simian creature with premature baldness and halitosis from his decaying teeth, but his impact on women was infallibly galvanic and for the next six years he and Duse carried on a liaison which, because of who each of them was, appeared never less than dramatic. Shamelessly exploiting the actress's histrionic talent in his plays, he managed at the same time to make her carry most of the production expenses as well as keeping him in the style he felt appropriate for an artist of his calibre. Running through her money, serially unfaithful yet always somehow managing to depict himself as Duse's innocent victim, D'Annunzio finally took a step too far in his portrayal of her as the actress heroine Foscarina in his Venetian novel *Il Fuoco*, where she figures, in all her posturing vulnerability, as almost a caricature of the real woman he had so intently pursued. For Duse this treacherous exposure ended the affair and the rawness of the whole experience endured for the rest of her life.

Venice, as has been pointed out by students of D'Annunzio, is the book's protagonist even more genuinely than poor Duse. It is impossible to imagine the city, at the turn of the nineteenth and twentieth centuries, without the dimension which, for better or worse, his continuing presence accorded it. Its recompense lay in fostering, through a mixture of atmosphere and experience, his toxic reveries of a quasi-mystical union between art and energy, furnishing an imagined source of renewal for creativity at its most instinctual and intense. At least some of those chimerical delusions which led eventually to the rise of Fascism were spawned in D'Annunzio's Venice and it was during his years of closest association with the city that his rhetoric helped many of these notions to take root among his fellow Italians. Just as Venice had vitally shaped and cemented John Ruskin's ideology, so equally it provided the frame around D'Annunzio's hectic fantasizing. A parallel between the two must obviously end there, while testifying at the same time to the grip exerted by Venice on the responsive incomer.

overleaf A view of the Piazzetta around 1900. Note the *vaporetto* arriving and the fishing boats on the Giudecca Canal.

Whether the place which nurtured the two writers in such radically different ways could survive in the purely physical sense defined by bricks and mortar was another matter altogether. During the 1890s more attention was being focused by the civic authorities on the fragility of the various church *campanili*, that scatter of bell towers which punctuated the townscape, most of them dating from the early Middle Ages. US consul Edmund Flagg may have sought to assure readers of his *Venice, City of the Sea* in 1853 that 'the edifices of Venice, even the humblest, seem constructed for eternity, not time', but by the century's end others were not so sure, more especially as regarded the great Campanile of San Marco. In the summer of 1902, while restoration work was being carried out on Jacopo Sansovino's graceful Renaissance Loggetta at the base of the tower, a series of cracks began appearing in the brickwork above it and in a few days the whole surface became ominously fissured. The café orchestras below were ordered to stop their selections of popular ballads and operetta numbers in case vibrations from their playing hastened the collapse which now seemed imminent. Around half past nine on 14 July 1902 walkers in the Piazza hurried to find safety as clouds of dust began puffing out of the Campanile's lowest section, followed by the rapid fall of the entire structure, scattering a powdery deposit across the Procuratie on either side. No one, by good fortune, was hurt and relatively little damage befell the surrounding buildings, apart from the façade of the Biblioteca Marciana. An enormous heap of rubble, most of which could not be reutilized in any form, now stood almost as high as Palazzo Ducale and included fragments of that big bell known as *La Marangona*, 'the stonemason's wife', which is rung by tradition every midnight and whose haunting, plaintive call floats across the whole of Venice with the poignancy of a disembodied voice.

The process of rebuilding, which would take almost a decade, introduced the Italian phrase '*Com'era e dov'era*', 'As it was and where it was', that has furnished a bone of contention for conservators in Venice ever since. A powerful trend of opinion among international architects favoured a new tower in a thoroughly modern style, with Vienna's Otto Wagner as its chief advocate, proposing the use of locally made mosaics to cover the surface and thus implicitly forge a bond with the Byzantine decorative scheme within the Basilica. *The Builder*, a British architectural review, was distinctly censorious of the Venetian authorities' preference for a mere replica, whose staring orange brick would need many years of weathering before it assumed the mellow hues of the original Campanile. 'In any previous period, if an important building fell down, the immediate desire would have been not to "restore" it but to erect something better and finer in its place'.

Others would have been happy to see not just the Campanile vanish but to watch the entire city disappear into the lagoon, beneath the waves whence it had sprung. In 1909 the poet and publicist Filippo Tommaso Marinetti published his *Futurist Manifesto*, a deliberately grandiloquent and hysterical paean to the beauties of speed, mechanization and technological novelty as agents of cultural change, a dizzying vision of 'multicoloured, polyphonic tides of revolution in the modern capitals... shipyards blazing with violent electric moons, greedy railway stations that devour smoke-plumed serpents'. For a few heady years Marinetti and his followers were able to hijack the dawning twentieth century in a parade of headline-grabbing exhibitions, concerts and performance events, giving a brand identity, as it were, to the era. Training their stentorian attack on art's abject thraldom to the past, the Futurists found in Venice a sitting target and made the replacement Campanile now under construction a prime culprit.

Active fulfilment of this loathing came in 1910, when Marinetti, accompanied by his fellow Futurists, the painters Umberto Boccioni and Carlo Carra, ascended the Torre dell'Orologio, the clock tower in the Piazza, to scatter copies of a leaflet entitled *Contro Venezia passatista* on the crowds beneath. 'We repudiate ancient Venice, exhausted by centuries of pleasure,' it declared, 'the Venice of the foreigners, market of antiquarian fakers, magnet of snobbery and stupidity, bejewelled hip-bath of cosmopolitan courtesans, this rotting city, gilded plague-sore of the past... Let us fill the stinking little canals with rubble from tottering, diseased palaces. Let us burn the gondolas, those rocking chairs for imbeciles, and raise up instead the majestic geometry of metal bridges, smoke-crowned factories [and] the reign of divine electric light, to liberate Venice from her moonlight in obscene hotel rooms'. An anti-Ruskinian subtext here is not hard to detect. The Futurists grasped all too well the damage, as they saw it, done by the Victorian sage's worship of the past – *il passatismo*, as they called this – and Marinetti had already vilified him to shocked or fascinated audiences in London as 'a deplorable figure with his hatred of machinery, steam power and electricity', corrupting the English with 'sickly nostalgia for rusticity and the simple life', a maniac 'who would have wanted to reconstruct that absurd Campanile of San Marco like someone presenting a little girl whose grandmother had died with a cardboard doll which looked just like the dead woman'.

No Futurist demonstration marred the self-congratulatory atmo-

sphere at the opening of the new tower (more or less '*com'era e dov'era*') which took place on 25 April 1912, in the presence of Italian royalty, the mayor of Venice Count Filippo Grimani, foreign diplomats, church dignitaries and representatives from the armed forces. In his address, the mayor emphasized the 'moral harmony' existing between the building now on view, 'speaking with the ancestral voices of God and the Motherland', and present-day Italy, which 'affirms in various ways the splendid rebirth of our people'. Whether the British ambassador Sir James Rennell Rodd could find more in this rhetoric than ceremonial hot air was questionable, but he added his own tribute by identifying the Campanile as 'a virile symbol of the good blood that belies itself not' and applauded the occasion's culminating gesture, involving the dispatch of a huge flock of carrier pigeons from the top of the tower to bear the good news to different cities throughout Italy.

The expatriate British community represented by Sir James formed a notable social element in Venice during this period. Nowadays there is a temptation to see this group as inherently 'colonial', accused of treating the native inhabitants with the same kind of dictatorial arrogance as it might have used in one of Britain's imperial domains across the globe. Surely the Futurists' animus against the blinkered snobbery of Anglo-Venetians, it might be argued, was not altogether groundless. The reality nevertheless appears more nuanced. Not all of those who decided to settle in Venice had come, Ruskin in hand, to gaze misty-eyed at the wonders of 'Tintoret', 'Giambellino' or 'Paul Veronese'. The attractions of a bare-chested gondolier clinched the loyalties of the aesthete John Addington Symonds to the place, as they almost certainly did for the more circumspect Horatio Brown, a cash-strapped Scots laird who become one of the Venetian past's most dedicated chroniclers and researchers. Meanwhile Frederic Rolfe, sustaining a bizarre literary career as 'Baron Corvo', lived out its final phase in Venice 'as a sponger and sodomite'. A sexual double-entendre in the title of his last novel, *The Desire and Pursuit of the Whole*, is designed to tease those respectable and well-meaning members of the British community, led by their doyenne Enid, Lady Layard, who had earlier sought to help him financially and now found themselves cruelly satirized in the book. They had not been overmuch bothered by Corvo's penchant for Venetian youths. Similar tastes on the part of Symonds and Brown were evidently forgivable in the light of both men's achievements as interpreters of Venice to the world. Their writings forged a strong, sympathetic bond with the city's unique past, showed a closer engagement with what made Venetians different from

A tabard in embroidered silk, created around 1912 by the Spanish fashion designer Mariano Fortuny, who lived in Venice from 1889.

other Italians and expressed a genuine anxiety as to how the modern city might find a valid means of survival without losing her sense of identity and definition.

What expatriate Venice never let herself become, during the twentieth century's first ten years, was just another 'sunny spot for shady people'. Thomas Mann's novella *Der Tod in Venedig*, 'Death in Venice', published in the same year as the opening of the new Campanile, may look superficially like a neat crystallization of the city's more noxious aspects as a realm of decadence and corruption, sapping Gustav Aschenbach's spiritual integrity through its siren improvisations on the theme of forbidden desire. Yet the work can also be read as in some form a tribute to Venice's undimmed potency in freeing imprisoned senses and suppressed emotions. All this takes place, it needs to be said, against a background of insistent modernity, with the epiphany of young Tadzio before the hapless Aschenbach imagined via the *mise-en-scène* of a smart hotel on the Lido and the pitiless actuality of a cholera epidemic claiming another victim.

For many who looked back later on at those closing seasons of the decade, Venice had managed to achieve an imperishable air of smartness, elegance and excitement. It was the place, after all, where the Spanish artist Mariano Fortuny y Madrazo had come with his wife to live, originally for the purely prosaic reason that he had an allergy to horses which made finding a town without them especially desirable. Once settled in a Gothic palace close to Campo Sant'Angelo, Fortuny began his new career as a fabric designer and couturier, creatively inspired by historic Venetian textiles and opening his own workshop for production. The astounding pleated silks made there radically altered the discourse of contemporary fashion through the deftness with which their weave, patterns and luminescence fused elemental modernism with a historic inheritance from the days of La Serenissima at its zenith. A Fortuny tea gown, legendarily capable of being pulled unscathed and entire through a wedding ring, offers yet another proof of Venice's inexhaustible capacity for engineering the miraculous.

For anyone with the least whisper of style or imagination at this instant, the lagoon had become an enchanted lake and the city a realm of desire, Gustav Klimt dazzled patrons of the Biennale, Claude Monet transfigured the light dappling the Grand Canal, Igor Stravinsky mesmerized Sergei Diaghilev at the Hotel des Bains with his earliest musical sketches for *The Rite of Spring*, Rainer Maria Rilke, in a Venetian winter, went searching, as so many continue to do, for that elusive creature known as 'the real Venice', Hugo Von Hofmannsthal sought to bring Casanova back to life and Marcel Proust, who could quote entire pages of Ruskin by heart, dressed his fugitive Albertine in a Fortuny gown 'that seemed to embody the tempting phantasm of an invisible Venice'. This latest incarnation was not to last, as perhaps something in each of them intuited. A more dismal and anarchic reality was on hand to destroy it.

BETWEEN
TWO WARS

Feeding the pigeons in the Piazza one afternoon in 1910 were a tall, soldierly-looking man with an extravagantly curled moustache and his wife in a hat positively overgrown with artificial flowers. Knowing observers might easily have identified them as Archduke Franz Ferdinand, heir to the throne of Austria–Hungary, and Countess Sophie Chotek, whom in 1900 he had defied imperial convention by marrying, since she was not from a royal or princely family. In four years' time the murder of them both by a political activist during a visit to the Bosnian city of Sarajevo would trigger a seemingly unstoppable sequence of reactions that led, in the space of a few weeks, to the outbreak of the Great War.

Our wisdom after the event, when looking back at this cataclysmic episode, delights in spotting all the different indicators, large or small, of its looming advent on the historical horizon. Venice, at the close of the twentieth century's first decade, had several such pointers handy. For example, it may be that the opening of the new Campanile in 1912, Mayor Grimani's allusion to Italy's ongoing war with Turkey as one of the factors which 'affirms in various guises the splendid rebirth of our race' offered a grim foretaste of the national self-delusion and eventual annihilation which would form a common inheritance for Italians over the next thirty years. The Futurists' appeal, at the same time, to a notion of their newfangled Venice as 'strong, industrial, commercial and military, thrusting into the Adriatic to convert it into a great Italian lake' could be viewed as similarly baleful in its implied hankering after territorial expansion. During this epoch of apparent progress and prosperity, Italy was wracked with civil unrest, including a series of strikes by factory and farm workers. Thus a war like the trumped-up conflict with the Ottoman empire, resulting in the acquisition of Libya, proved useful for the government as a distraction.

There was a nationalist fever abroad, what was more, for 'redeeming' Italian-speaking sectors of Austria-Hungary such as Istria and Dalmatia, both of them former possessions of La Serenissima's *Stato da Mar*. In this context we should certainly not have been surprised at hearing the voice of Gabriele D'Annunzio resonating at its most theatrically strident.

Not until the Great War had run its course for at least a year was Italy persuaded to renounce an earlier alliance with Austria and Germany, made in 1882, and lured instead into a pact with France and Britain that would assure her of enlargement in the shape of the two Habsburg provinces of Trento and South Tyrol. By this same agreement, the Treaty of London, she would gain full control of Libya and the Dodecanese islands through a destined breakup of the Ottoman empire and take over most of Dalmatia. Whatever damage this might do to the country's international reputation, in the wake of a longstanding policy of appeasement and neutrality, the headlong rush to combat suited the mood of the hour, at least where D'Annunzio was concerned. His inflammatory rhetoric in speeches to Roman crowds and a set of bellicose polemics in his newspaper *Il Popolo d'Italia* helped to raise the temperature on behalf of intervention. Such a pitch of enthusiasm was equally accommodating to Italy's relatively new class of affluent industrialists, mostly based in Turin and Milan, whose factory production lines could easily be converted to the matériel needed for speeding Italian forces on their way towards what was anticipated – and so much of the Great War was fought on a basis of abundant anticipation – as an easy victory over the Austrians, after fifty years the enemy once again.

Venice now found herself in the eye of whatever perfect storm was about to break. An uncomfortable proximity to battle lines opening in Friuli and the Dolomites meant that artworks needed either moving to safer locations or else to be wrapped up and padded against the impact of an expected bombardment. Accordingly the great Titian *Assumption* in the Frari was trundled off across the railway bridge, the four bronze horses were lowered from their plinths on the façade of San Marco and taken into hiding, while the Basilica itself was boarded up entirely. There were still elderly folk alive in the city who remembered the siege conditions of 1849. On that occasion the Austrian attempt to bomb the rebel Venetians into submission with explosive balloons had been a laughable failure. Now, on the other hand, that most thrilling component of the Futurists' mechanized nirvana, the aeroplane, brought outright and relentless devastation via a full-scale assault unleashed on the very day, 24 May 1915, that Italy entered the war. The places where Franz Ferdinand and his Sophie had fed the pigeons and where Gustav Klimt's gold-bedecked neo-Byzantine sirens had stunned the Biennale would now be treated without pity or piety, in a grim foretaste of those 'Baedeker raids' which were to flatten European art cities in the next world war.

One specially ferocious attack was unleashed later in the year. By this time the *sestieri* of Castello and Cannaregio had taken a serious drubbing from enemy bombs, to which the zone behind Madonna dell'Orto bears witness in the range of grim, barrack-like apartment blocks raised there after the war was over. On the evening of 25 October the church of Santa Maria di Nazareth, known as the Scalzi (literally 'without shoes', referring to its link with the order of Discalced Carmelites), received a direct hit, shattering much of Baldassare Longhena's Baroque interior, inflicting damage on the eighteenth-century façade by Giuseppe Sardi and utterly wrecking Giambattista Tiepolo's ceiling fresco *The Transport of the Holy House of Loreto*, of which a few fragments and a preparatory oil sketch are preserved in the Accademia gallery. A remark by Venice's patriarch, Cardinal Pietro La Fontaine, as he surveyed the devastation, that it represented 'God's summons to a humanity perverted by sin' appeared strikingly malapropos.

Other notable buildings, such as the church of Santi Giovanni e Paolo, the campanile of San Francesco della Vigna and the big cotton factory near San Nicolo, were also damaged, though not quite as drastically. The general impact of the raids fell more obviously on the Venetians themselves than on the city which surrounded them. A tourist economy which, for at least thirty years, had generated such a promising revival for the whole community dwindled rapidly enough, even while Italy still remained neutral through the winter of 1914–15 and the activities of the port and the Arsenale slowed almost to nothing. Poverty, habitual on the town's outer residential fringes, whatever its role as a playground for the rich, bit the sharper as desperate crowds of refugees arrived from areas overrun by Austrian forces and workers in hospitality, shipping and textile manufacture lost their jobs. A naval governor, Admiral Paolo Thaon de Revel, was placed in charge of maintaining public order, overseeing the city's transformation into what was effectively a fortress island, complete with curfews, blackouts, censorship and rationing. Many of those with places to go to and the means to do so began leaving: by the war's end, it was reckoned, as many as 60,000 out of a population of 150,000 had slipped away.

overleaf Porto Marghera, developed after World War I, offers an eloquent contrast with historic Venice.

Fear as much as anything else had inspired this exodus. For Italy, so wretchedly underprepared to engage with an enemy whose fighting resolve was being stiffened by support from its German ally, the course of the war went swiftly from bad to worse. When in 1917 the Russian front collapsed, allowing the two powers to send further reinforcements into Istria, Friuli and the Trentino, it looked as if a full-scale invasion was poised to overwhelm the entire north-eastern region, with Venice, which Thaon de Revel had already designated as a naval base, more exposed than ever to frontline assault. The sheer incompetence and wastefulness of the Italian high command at this stage fostered a surge of discontent within the civilian population, let alone amid the ranks of ill-equipped conscripts sent to do battle in muddy shell holes along the River Isonzo or in freezing trenches high up on the Asiago plateau. At Caporetto, over several October days during 1917, an Austrian advance succeeded in routing almost 100,000 Italian troops and the defensive line on the Piave was only held by prompt action from the French, British and American brigades sent to bolster Italian resistance. What eventually enabled Italy to emerge from the struggle with some scrap of honour which might justify the excessive levels of posturing and rhodomontade inflating military propaganda was a victory gained the following year at Vittorio Veneto, resulting in Austria's surrender and

leaving Venice bruised, half empty, impoverished, yet as ever unbowed.

While Italian delegates to the peace conference at Versailles haggled over what they felt was their proper share in the spoils of victory – a British diplomat called them 'the most odious colleagues and allies to have at a conference, the beggars of Europe, well known for their whining alternated by truculence' – Venetians looked to make the best of fresh commercial advantages brought them by a project for a new port at Marghera, on the lagoon's western edge. Its guiding spirit was that of Count Giuseppe Volpi, identified by one modern historian as 'the most important and influential Venetian of the twentieth century'. A restless entrepreneur with expansive ideas, Volpi was worthy, from this single aspect, of those who had raised La Serenissima to pre-eminence in an earlier age. The initial plan for the port had been put forward in 1902, drawing in, as this developed, a small but highly significant group of leading Italian capitalists that included the banker Piero Foscari, the influential industrialist Vittorio Cini and the engineer Achille Gaggia. Large-scale corporate interests soon came on board in the shape of steelworks, shipping companies and chemical producers and electrical enterprises. The advent of the war naturally rendered the whole operation more urgent and by 1917 a vast new installation was planned which would embrace a petroleum

Giuseppe Volpi in a studio portrait, *c.*1925: businessman, politician
and a mover and shaker in the making of twentieth-century
Venice.

port, commercial docks and the creation of a residential zone for the workforce.

Necessary excavation of a new canal, seven metres deep, linking Porto Marghera (as it became known) with the Giudecca and the Lido, was an augury, had anyone at the time realized this, of worse times approaching. At this period there was little or no awareness of any long-term damage likely to be inflicted on the uniquely delicate ecosystem of the Venetian lagoon. Such protests as were raised seem mostly to have derived from disgruntled mercantile interests within Venice's Chamber of Commerce. With these easily brushed aside in the name of national needs and the importance of competitive capitalism in asserting Italy's primacy among the victorious powers settling the world's affairs at Versailles, Giuseppe Volpi, as president of the *Società Porto Industriale*, was keen to promote the concept of a new kind of Venice altogether, a vast industrial hub, more ruthlessly assertive of progress and technology than anything conjured up by the noisier Futurist fantasies before 1914. The old town on its three islands was to form part of this complex through the building of a road bridge that would run parallel with the historic railway viaduct of 1846, bringing motorized traffic and pedestrians to a forum, Piazzale Roma, close to what had been the church and convent of Santa Chiara, at the head of the Grand Canal.

By the time this new point of entry and its road access were completed in 1933, Italy had spent ten years under a Fascist regime dominated by Benito Mussolini. Its triumph in 1922 had been assured, following the so-called 'March on Rome', by the concession of dictatorial powers to Mussolini by King Victor Emmanuel III, still nominally the head of state but hereafter reduced to a cipher. Support for Fascism came from every quarter of society, more especially the business community, the lesser bourgeoisie and the type of conservative aristocrat and army officer who saw the social unrest of the immediate post-war years as a harbinger of Communism, with the dangers of a Russian-style revolution on the political horizon. Words like 'order' and 'discipline' dominated the regime's discourse. Mussolini himself, as *Il Duce*, 'the Leader', assumed major ministerial roles, press censorship was imposed, local government was purged of dissident voices, trade unions were to be state-controlled and strikes became illegal. Democracy effectively disappeared under a series of ordinances which turned the Duce, his henchmen, apparatchiks and militias into the executive power directing all aspects of public life. For Fascism to succeed, the elements of image and performance required continual stress, so that the dictator's speeches and public appearances, ludicrous as these now seem in retrospect, dominated the media and as much reliance as possible was laid on news management, spin, rhetoric and spectacle.

As Italy accepted the dubious placebos and panaceas offered by a totalitarian regime, Venice was able to resume much of that atmosphere of glamorous hedonism which had characterized it during the immediate pre-war era. Giuseppe Volpi, influential as he already was as finance minister in Mussolini's government, now became a sort of doge in miniature, keeping an eye on the development of Porto Marghera and a portfolio of directorships that included the CIGA (Compagnia Italiana Grandi Alberghi) hotel chain and, from 1930 onwards, the Biennale. In the Giardini the exhibition space was substantially expanded and the whole event, with backing from the state, assumed the international profile it has never since forfeited. During this period further festivals devoted to theatre and contemporary music boosted the city's reputation as a European art capital, but it was the institution, in 1932, of an annual film festival which gained it the sort of worldwide media attention that Fascism most ardently courted.

A glittering epiphany on the Lido of Hollywood stars like Bette Davis and Katharine Hepburn was matched by the eclecticism of the annual programming, during which awards went not just to movie dramas but to cartoons and documentaries besides. Almost at once, the Venice Film Festival started drawing the kind of smart roster of foreign royalty and celebrities to the lagoon which could work towards enhancing Fascist prestige. At the same time the Lido's air of self-conscious elegance was given an additional fillip from the presence of a new casino, recalling the days of the Grand Tour when moneyed travellers had frittered their patrimony away in the Sala del Ridotto at San Moisè. Next to the gambling hall stood an eye-catching essay in hyper-modernism, the purpose-built Palazzo del Cinema by the architects Eugenio Miozzi and Luigi Quagliata. Amid a culture of such strenuous image-building, Venice, turning Fascism's handsomest features to the world, had nothing, apparently, to feel ashamed of.

Those, however, who felt like crossing the short stretch of water from the Lido to the historic centre might have had other ideas once they abandoned the tourist trail between the Piazza and the Rialto to plunge deeper into what remained, in many areas, a literally unreconstructed Venice. Ever since the 1890s a series of well-intentioned schemes for improving the city's poorer residential quarters had continued to emerge and, just as often, to be set aside. In 1935 public health

A 1930s poster fuses Venice's interwar roles as art city and seaside resort.

concerns prompted Venice's chief medical officer, Raffaele Vivante, to conduct a survey of inadequate or generally uninhabitable housing but this was shelved in favour of the Special Law, issued three years later, entitled 'Provisions for the Safeguard of the Lagoonar and Monumental Character of Venice'.

This document's terms of reference remained deliberately vague. Exactly whose responsibility was it to repair the housing stock or, if needed, to rebuild it altogether? The new legislation found it easier to be more precise when announcing a twenty-five-year tax exemption for whatever construction firms might be involved. Subsequent slum clearance measures basically reaffirmed proposals made in 1890 in rather more grandiloquent terms. The notion of thinning out various sections of the old urban centre rather than knocking them down altogether, it was reasoned, would better preserve the essential Venetianness of Venice, 'saving the lagoon city, the city of Rialto, from every contamination'. Architects were encouraged 'to emulate in new building, even in a modern form, Venice's vibrant and ebullient urban style, consisting of the free grouping of small details, bright colour, harmonies or contrasts, to which any geometric rigidity of line is foreign'. There was no suggestion, in any of these various decrees, plans or papers, that the state or the municipality should take an active role in clearance and reconstruction. The idea throughout seems to have been simply that of a nudge to private enterprise towards undertaking whatever operations it chose in return for financial rewards. Such hints were alas not readily taken and the Mussolinian imprint on Venice was generally slight, the contrast between smart and unsmart zones as marked as ever it had been in previous centuries.

Nothing of this dichotomy was to be revealed to the Duce's most important guest, arriving in Venice in 1934. Adolf Hitler, the German Führer, was making the first of his few visits to a foreign country. The two men were scarcely soulmates, whatever their need for an alliance, and each had been anxious to stress that it was the other who had made the earliest overtures leading to this supposedly momentous encounter. Mussolini, after more than a decade in his role, was naturally the more suave and easy-going of the two, neatly upstaging his guest by sporting a uniform, whereas the Führer, wearing an overcoat and a fedora hat, looked, in the Duce's words, 'like a plumber in a mackintosh'. There was an inspection of troops (Achille Starace, Fascist party secretary, had massed some 3,000 for display on this occasion) and the dictators then adjourned to the immense Villa Pisani at Stra for some hard talk about the future of Austria, as to which each of them had his own ideas.

Hitler appeared fretful and cross from the outset. A trip to the Biennale – hadn't the Führer, after all, shown talent as a painter before turning politician? – was decidedly not a success and art in any case bored the Duce. Neither a luncheon at the new golf club at Alberoni, on the Lido's southern tip, nor a grand reception at Villa Pisani seemed to thaw the atmosphere, the more so since most of the guests, male or female, were more interested in pushing their respective advantages with Mussolini than in trying to charm the German visitor. As for Austria's fate, Hitler had clearly settled this already. 'It is my will,' he told the Duce, 'and the indomitable will of the German people, that Austria should become an integral part of the Reich.' Since it suited Italy at this moment to sustain the independence of the forlorn remnant of that empire which had once dictated its fortunes, the encounter between the two leaders was distinctly inauspicious. What Hitler undoubtedly gained from his visit to Venice, as well as some hint of the Fascist regime's underlying weaknesses, was a renewed awareness, in watching Mussolini address a packed gathering in Piazza San Marco, of a seasoned orator's power in manipulating a crowd. Otherwise unsatisfied, the scowling Führer returned to Berlin resolved to make the Duce his client rather than his preceptor.

By 1936 such a reversal of roles had occurred in precisely the way Hitler anticipated. Wanting German support after his defiance of the League of Nations in pursuing his invasion of Abyssinia, Mussolini concluded a secret pact with the Führer which was soon followed by a further accord between both nations with Japan and Italy's formal withdrawal from the League. When in 1938 German troops entered Austria and the *Anschluss* absorbed the state into the Reich according to Hitler's wishes, the Duce refrained from protest. He had become, in the process, a creature as much as a partner of the other dictator. Just how much would now show itself in one particularly sinister aspect of the successive pacts being forged between them.

Italy's Jewish population at this period numbered almost 50,000. Jews had taken an important role in the later phases of the nineteenth-century movement towards Italian nationhood, eventually gaining the full citizenship and social emancipation denied them under the various sovereign rulers and becoming prominent figures in every area of public life. The support given by many of them to the Fascist regime was that of their fellow Italians grateful for stability and the return of commercial confidence following the riots and disorder marking the years immediately after the Great War. In Italy there was little manifestation, so far, of that menacing, pseudo-scientific antisemitism, rank with conspiracy theories, that had seeded itself so deeply in France and Germany during the early twentieth century. It would not be long, however, before the more toxic currents of German National Socialist propaganda began infecting the discourse of Fascism and in February 1938 a clear sign of this arrived with the announcement by the Italian Foreign Office that it intended to apply controls to immigration by foreign Jews. At this period most of these were in flight from the persecution already initiated by the Nazis in Germany and threatening the considerable Jewish population of an Austria poised for takeover by the Reich.

Strident canvassing by the Italian media of current racial theories was accompanied by talk of 'defending the race from pollution', while Fascist Party members were encouraged to read the widely circulated *Protocols of the Elders of Zion*, that classic horror scenario depicting a so-called international Jewish plot to infiltrate the workings of government in Western nations. During August 1938 the regime instituted a census of Jewish residents, 'regardless of whether these are observant Jews or profess no religion'. On this basis, developing the thesis of a 'Racial Manifesto' issued earlier which invoked the judgment of scientific experts in declaring that all true Italians were Aryan by ethnic inheritance, hence denying such authenticity to Jewish citizens, the first of a series of laws were signed off by the Duce in the autumn of 1938. These restricted the activities and civil rights of Jews under Italy's jurisdiction and expelled those who had recently sought refuge within the kingdom.

Venice's Jews, numbering around 1,700, were surprised and genuinely affronted by the abruptness and severity of the new legislation. They had demonstrated their generosity and patriotism in collecting funds for the war in Abyssinia, they had filled key roles in local government (health commissioner Raffaele Vivante, mentioned earlier, was one such example) and loyally backed the regime over the course of almost two decades. Now they found themselves ejected from every official or professional position, whether as lawyers, doctors, librarians or teachers in school and university. At Teatro La Fenice, meanwhile, a purge of the orchestra and the singers engaged for the winter season of 1938–9 resulted in a number of expulsions, at the Querini Stampalia cultural foundation all employees were required to submit a so-called 'race certificate' and the president of the august Istituto Veneto di Scienze, Lettere ed Arti strove in vain to prevent the dismissal of seven distinguished professors. Jewish children were now to be excluded from state schools and the whole venerable community was forced to turn in upon itself, mustering its own available resources, human or material, in order to survive.

The Racial Laws offered a foretaste of the international strife about to engulf the nation. Triumph in Abyssinia had seemed to strengthen Mussolini's hand, adding volume to the bellicose mood of the hour. Hitler's seizure of the Sudetenland from Czechoslovakia in March 1939 prompted the Duce to follow suit by invading and annexing the Kingdom of Albania. A so-called 'Pact of Steel', clinching the dictators' alliance still tighter, was rendered somewhat illusory by Mussolini's admission to Hitler that Italy was in no position to give adequate military support should Germany choose to go to war. As the Italian historian Giuliano Procacci observes, 'Italy's unpreparedness for the First World War was as nothing in comparison with her unpreparedness for the Second'. The Duce's attempted gamble in 1940 on a speedy German victory over England, at which point Italy might join in for the sake of a seasoning of glory and a seat at any ensuing peace conference, was ultimately doomed to fail, but in May of that year the nation, hurriedly abandoning an unwilling neutrality and apparently reckless as to a serious lack of raw materials for equipping its armed forces, hurtled jubilantly into battle.

As in the previous conflict, official propaganda encouraged chimerical notions of speedy victory, with the boys home triumphant by the end of the year. Venice was not, on this occasion, endangered by forming part of a front line. Germany now controlled the entire north-eastern Adriatic and it seemed, according to journalist and dramatist Gino Damerini, addressing the Ateneo Veneto, as if La Serenissima's glory days could easily be revived simply by standing shoulder to shoulder with the Reich so as to fulfil Fascism's 'Mediterranean and imperial destinies'. Life for Venice as an art city and a high-end seaside resort could go on pretty much as before, with concerts, exhibitions, fashion shows and open-air theatrical productions. The film festival went ahead in 1941, with another to follow next year, and the Biennale continued to loom large in Italy's cultural calendar. At La Fenice Magda Olivero and Beniamino Gigli dazzled in *Adriana Lecouvreur*, Maria Caniglia broke hearts in *La Traviata*, while in *Cavalleria Rusticana* the work's composer Pietro Mascagni, now seventy-eight, flustered the orchestra with his eccentric conducting style. Everything in Venice, smugly pronounced a journalist for the city's newspaper *Il Gazzettino*, was so much more enjoyable now that the English had cleared off.

'With the excuse that they had brought Byron, Browning and Ruskin to live in Venice they took us for incurable idiots and acted like the masters in our house.'

To those in control (including, of course, Giuseppe Volpi) an atmosphere of business as usual was vital to sustain. So too was devotion to the Duce. Conservative though Venetian society had often shown itself, reports noted that the city had never been a particular bulwark of Fascist Party activity and that its overall support for the ongoing war effort was lukewarm at best. By the end of 1942 Allied troops had landed in Algeria and began pushing eastwards against Axis forces. A signal British defeat inflicted on Erwin Rommel's German army at El Alamein severely weakened Italy's resolve, so that it needed only another few months before her total surrender in North Africa. At home a series of strikes by anti-Fascist workers in Turin and Milan were viewed with alarm by hard-line elements in the government as indicators of the war's growing unpopularity. On 17 July 1943, as Allied forces began landing in Sicily, Hitler journeyed in person to Feltre in the northern Veneto, where he subjected the Duce to a two-hour harangue on where the latter was falling short. On this subject the Italian army's high command had by now made its mind up and a week later the Fascist Grand Council demanded that Mussolini hand his resignation to King Victor Emmanuel.

A singular hiatus followed, a six-week period of political meltdown before Italy surrendered to the Allies on 2 September. This formed the prelude to a German military occupation of northern and central Italy, with most of the peninsula turned into a theatre of the most brutal and destructive warfare known in its history. Mussolini, spirited away from captivity with the help of a glider piloted by an Austrian Wehrmacht officer, now established a new Fascist administration, far more extreme in its methods and outlook, at the resort town of Salò on Lake Garda. This so-called Italian Social Republic took much of its style from the Duce's Nazi puppet-masters, whose vindictiveness and fanaticism in dealing with a people they saw as having effectively betrayed the Führer's sacred trust added a fresh species of bitterness to the Italian experience of the war.

Venice now fell directly within the sphere of Nazi–Fascist rule and felt its dire consequences. For the Salò republic there was almost no support among Venetians. As for the German presence as an occupying power across the Veneto, this was at best glumly endured, but here as elsewhere across Italy in the closing months of 1943 a serious resistance movement, its members known generically as *Partigiani*, Partisans, had sprung up, ready to work alongside the Allies but armed with its own toughness, ingenuity and determination. The anecdotal romance of the Second World War cherishes the French Resistance, which has fostered its own glamour and legends, but in truth the Italian Partisan movement was generally far better organized, more numerous in its membership and far more successful in its operations. 'By armed force,' wrote a British liaison officer to Allied headquarters in 1945, 'they helped to break the strength and morale of an enemy well superior to them in numbers. Without the partisans' victories there could not have been an Allied victory in Italy so fast, so complete and with such light casualties.'

By its very nature Venice was hardly the easiest place for partisan attacks to be carried out and a series of targeted killings of prominent officials and service personnel would be avenged by savage police reprisals. The most insolent gesture was made, somehow characteristically for Venice, inside a theatre, the former Teatro San Luca, where in 1818 the young Gaetano Donizetti had enjoyed his first operatic success with *Enrico di Borgogna*. Later styled Teatro Goldoni it became (and remains) the city's principal stage for the performance of what Italians call *prosa*, spoken drama, as opposed to *lirica*, referring to opera. On 11 March 1945, as the Allies moved steadily, albeit with strong German opposition, across the Veneto, the audience arrived for a performance of Luigi Pirandello's drama *Vestire gli ignudi*, 'Clothe the naked', a play whose theme, that of a woman committing suicide when her fraudulent identity is uncovered, was not altogether irrelevant, as one writer has observed, to Italy's current predicament. Towards the end of Act I the auditorium was convulsed by the sudden apparition on stage of twenty individuals wearing masks and carrying guns but clearly not connected with the production. Ten of these men and women were later identified as belonging to the Communist partisan unit known as Brigata Garibaldi. Loudly proclaiming the fall of the dictators as being likely to happen at any moment, they exhorted the terrified spectators to join them, showering the stalls with leaflets and warning that snipers were waiting outside, before slipping into the wings and out of the theatre unharmed. This exploit, known as *La Beffa del Teatro Goldoni*, quickly became part of modern Venice's folk memory.

For the Venetian Jews the Salò Republic and the German occupation spelt genuine catastrophe. Despite the limbo created for them by the Racial Laws, Mussolini had not seen fit, while still in power in Rome, to impose any kind of dire equivalent to Hitler's Final Solution on the community. Nazi propaganda minister Joseph Goebbels had

overleaf Jewish survivors gather in the Ghetto following Venice's liberation by British forces on 30 April 1945.